I0631807

Karen Leeder and Lyn Marven (Eds.)
Ulrike Draesner

Companions to Contemporary German Culture

Edited by
Michael Eskin · Karen Leeder · Christopher Young

Volume 9

Ulrike Draesner

A Companion

Edited by
Karen Leeder and Lyn Marven

DE GRUYTER

ISBN 978-3-11-047895-2
e-ISBN (PDF) 978-3-11-049594-2
e-ISBN (EPUB) 978-3-11-049338-2
ISSN 2193-9659

Library of Congress Control Number: 2022946199

Bibliographic information published by the Deutsche Nationalbibliothek
The Deutsche Nationalbibliothek lists this publication in the Deutsche Nationalbibliografie;
detailed bibliographic data are available on the internet at http://dnb.dnb.de.

© 2023 Walter de Gruyter GmbH, Berlin/Boston
Cover image: Ulrike Draesner, 2016 © Dominik Butzmann/laif.
Typesetting: Integra Software Services Pvt. Ltd.
Printing and binding: CPI books GmbH, Leck

www.degruyter.com

Acknowledgements

Above all the editors would like to acknowledge the support of Ulrike Draesner, who has been unfailingly generous with her time and energy during the preparation of this volume and kindly agreed to be interviewed and also to offer new work for publication in the volume. They are also grateful to the British Academy, the OUP John Fell Fund, University of Oxford, the Faculty of Medieval and Modern Languages, University of Oxford, the Oxford Research Centre for the Humanities (TORCH) and the Eugene Ludwig Fund, New College, Oxford and the Warden and Fellows of New College, who all supported Ulrike Draesner's stay in Oxford, and sponsored the international event at New College on which this volume is substantially based. They are also grateful for the assistance of the staff of the Deutsches Literaturarchiv in Marbach am Neckar and the Taylor Institution Library in Oxford. We are also especially grateful to Benjamin Schaper for assembling the Bibliography and for assisting with transcribing the interview; Sarah Stutt for translation; Tjeert Ulehake for assistance with indexing; Alexandra Lloyd for filming and photographs and Neil Leeder for the website. As usual the volume owes a great deal to Manuela Gerlof, Stella Diedrich and Myrto Aspioti from de Gruyter for their patience and careful advice.

The photograph on the cover is printed courtesy of Dominik Butzmann. The illustrations in the chapter by Noël Reumkens are reprinted by kind permission of the following: for Gerhard Richter, 'Ema-Akt auf Treppe', 1966: akg-images © gerhard.richter@netcologne.de; for Marcel Duchamp, 'Nu descendant un escalier', 1912: akg-images © The Estate of Marcel Duchamp / VG Bild-Kunst, Bonn, 2017; for 'Sonja mit Wasserglas' (1991) by Annelies Štrba: the artist and Galerie EIGEN + ART Leipzig/Berlin; for Helen Chadwick and David Notarius at work on *Piss Flowers* (1991) and Helen Chadwick, 'Piss Flowers' (1991–1992) sculpture © Estate of Helen Chadwick: Richard Saltoun Gallery; for Bruce Naumann, 'Anthro/Socio Rinde Spinnng' (1991–1992): © VG Bild-Kunst, Bonn, 2017. The illustration by Otto Czeschka in Ulrike Draesner, *Nibelungen. Heimsuchung* (Stuttgart: Reclam, 2016) in the chapter by Almut Suerbaum is © Reclam Verlag and the image from the manuscript from the 'Klage' at the end of the *Nibelungenlied* is reprinted with kind permission of the Manuscript archive, Karlsruhe, Badische Landesbibliothek, Cod. Donaueschingen 63, fol. 89r.

The photographs accompanying the interview with Ulrike Draesner are reprinted by kind permission of Alexandra Lloyd and Ulrike Draesner respectively. The image of the engraving is 'View of the College of Saint Mary de Winton, or New College, Oxford from the West 1907' by Edmund Hort. With permission of the Warden & Scholars of New College, Oxford.

https://doi.org/10.1515/9783110495942-202

The editors would like to acknowledge the kind permission of Luchterhand/ Penguin part of Random House in Munich to cite poems by Ulrike Draesner from *gedächtnisschleifen* (1998), *für die nach geheuerte zellen* (2001), *kugelblitz* (2005), *berührte orte* (2008), *subsong* (2014) © Penguin Random House.

The editors are also grateful for kind permission to cite the following original work: an excerpt from the Ulrike Draesner's novel *Schwitters* in German © Penguin Random House and in English © Ulrike Draesner and 'einem sommertag vergleichen, dich?' (Sonnet 18) © Ulrike Draesner; a selection of Draesner's poems translated by Iain Galbraith from Ulrike Draesner, *this porous fabric. Selected Poems*, trans. by Iain Galbraith, Shearsman Books, 2021 © Iain Galbraith; 'a summer day and you and recombine' © Tom Cheesman; an excerpt from T. S. Eliot, *The Waste Land*, reprinted by permission of Faber & Faber Ltd.

Preface

Ulrike Draesner is one of the most fêted contemporary writers in German: a prize-winning author of novels, short stories and poetry, she is also a translator and essayist whose works embody her intellectual curiosity in subjects of contemporary global significance and whose linguistic inventiveness evinces her particular affinity for the English language. Despite the many resonances her work has with Anglophone culture, Draesner has yet to find a substantial audience in English, something this volume seeks to address in a number of ways: it is the first-ever volume of essays in English on her oeuvre; quotations used throughout are translated into English, giving a flavour of her varied voices and the linguistic shifts and echoes across each of the texts examined here; and finally it presents not only an extensive interview with the author conducted originally in English but also a sample from her current bilingual project on the exiled German artist Kurt Schwitters, showcasing Draesner's practice of self-translation and her unique intervention in English as well as a selection of her poetry in English translation from a recent bilingual publication.

While this volume seeks to give a broad overview of Draesner's prose, poetry and essay publications, focusing on her major texts in each genre, it can only scratch the surface of her unusually versatile and varied output. Her first book-length publications in the early 1990s were academic works: the book of her thesis on medieval German poetry, Wolfram's *Parzival*, and a commented, edited collection of German-language novellas. Draesner has maintained a double perspective on writing as both practitioner and academic observer and analyst, as evinced by published volumes of literary-biographical analysis of other authors and poetological reflections. In 2007 she published a collection of essays on writing and reading key modern European (women) writers entitled *Schöne Frauen lesen*, which was followed in 2013 by a second collection, *Heimliche Helden*, focussing on the concept of heroism in male writers' lives and fictions. She has gathered further reflections on her own writing practice and on the nature of writing in general in the volumes *Zauber im Zoo* (2007), *Die fünfte Dimension* (2016) and most recently *Grammatik der Gespenster* (2018), which are based on her 'Poetikvorlesungen' (lectures on poetology) and talks in Bamberg, Munich and Frankfurt respectively. Her 2016 modern rewriting of the *Nibelungenlied* is another genre-crossing publication, encompassing poetry, script form and academic-reflective essays which respond to the medieval text as well as to the early twentieth-century illustrations of the *Nibelungenlied* by Carl Otto Czeschka which are reprinted in the volume. At the time of writing, Draesner had been appointed Professor of German Literature at the Deutsches Literaturinstitut Leipzig, with responsibility for Bachelors and Masters programmes in literary writing.

https://doi.org/10.1515/9783110495942-203

As an author, Draesner first came to prominence with her poetry, and she has published five major poetry collections: *gedächtnisschleifen* (1995), *für die nacht geheuerte zellen* (2001), *kugelblitz* (2005), *berührte orte* (2008), and *subsongs* (2014) along with the book-length poem *doggerland* (2021), and a Selected Poems, *hell & hörig* (2022), published for her sixtieth birthday. Her first novel, *Lichtpause*, came out in 1998, followed by *Mitgift* (2002), *Spiele* (2005) and *Vorliebe* (2010). Her substantial novel *Sieben Sprünge vom Rand der Welt* was published in 2014. It develops a multigenerational chorus of voices reporting the consequences of forced migration in Eastern Europe from 1939 up to the present day; this significant work is addressed by two chapters in this volume. Interspersed between these longer texts are three collections of short stories: the experimental *Reisen unter den Augenlidern* (1999), *Hot Dogs* (2004) and *Richtig liegen. Geschichten in Paaren* (2011), and a short novel *Kanalschwimmer* (2019) which appeared after the finalization of this collection.

More recently, Draesner has begun to explore creative non-fiction, branching out into the new terrain of travel writing in her hybrid memoir/essay *Mein Hiddensee* (2015), as well as writing a highly personal guidebook, *London. Lieblingsorte* (2016), to which she also contributed her own photographs. The latter is testament to Draesner's enduring fascination with the UK (and with the English language), which appears briefly as a setting or context in *Mitgift* and *Vorliebe* and more substantially in *Kanalschwimmer* about a man swimming the English Channel, as well as in the Kurt Schwitters project described below. At the same time, and reflecting the autobiographical aspects increasingly visible in her essays and on her own website as well as in her literary prose, she has also turned her writerly gaze on herself as subject in the double CD release, *Happy Aging. Ulrike Draesner erzählt ihre Wechseljahre* (2016), a project which in turn gave rise to a book-length memoir, *Eine Frau wird älter. Ein Aufbruch*, published in 2018.

Draesner is a translator of French (Michèle Métail, 2009) and Anglo-American poetry (Gertrude Stein, *The First Reader* 2001, Hilda Doolittle, *Heimliche Deutung / Hermetic Definition*, 2006, Louise Glück, *Averno* and *The Wild Iris*, 2007 and 2008), and also composes German versions of poems from Arabic, Romanian and Indonesian. In 2000 she also published 'Twin Spin', her 'radical translations' of Shakespeare's sonnets, in which the sonnets are also 'spun' to take in the modern world and genetic reproduction; these sonnets have in turn been translated back into English by Tom Cheesman. Draesner also works as an author of essays on media and cultural change and has a strong virtual presence in more contemporary formats and forums, such as her ongoing series of pieces for *Die Zeit*'s 'Freitext' section. For the publication of *Sieben Sprünge vom Rand der Welt*, she created the website www.der-siebte-sprung.de, which was conceived as the 'seventh leap' of the title; the site is multilingual with crowd-sourced contributions, and functions as an open-ended online extension of the novel's concerns. Draesner's multimedia collaborations further include a space poem for Hong Kong and Calcutta, radio soundscapes, poetic installations and an opera libretto – a version of Monteverdi and contemporary composer Katharina Schlünz – for the Schwetzingen festival in 2017.

The international scholars gathered here offer readings of Draesner's main texts to date in broadly chronological order. The volume builds on and extends the existing academic reception of her work which considers her representation of gender, relationships and the body, her engagement with science and her treatment of modern history, memory and migration. It also breaks new ground in examining her poetics and her depictions of animals and nature, and in addressing posthuman concerns; it foregrounds Draesner's engagement with the visual, and her reception of English literature and of medieval culture; and it positions her work not only in relation to issues of German culture and memory, but also in a wider context which is transnational, multilingual and European.

The volume is divided into five thematic sections, reflecting key concerns in Draesner's oeuvre and cumulatively casting light on all her major works either in chapters dedicated to those works themselves, or in references spanning a number of chapters, as is the case especially with the poetry. The opening section, History and the Text, addresses the ways in which Draesner, a medievalist by academic training, interrogates the past and its presence in the present. Erik Schilling analyses Draesner's engagement with history and historiography in her novels *Lichtpause*, *Spiele* and *Sieben Sprünge vom Rand der Welt*. Moving from micro- to macro-history, and utilising a range of narrative forms and structures, Draesner's fictional texts reflect on the relationship between present and past and demonstrate a shift towards metahistoriography. While *Spiele*, which focuses on the terrorist attack at the Munich Olympics in 1972, maintains clear boundaries between the fictional and historical or historiographical elements, the multiperspectival structure of *Sieben Sprünge* resists synthesis into a single understanding of history. Anke Biendarra reads *Sieben Sprünge* against the backdrop of a recent German-language 'memory boom', arguing that Draesner's use of multiple narrators from four generations and two families, one German and one Polish, sets her novel apart and places it instead in a broader transnational and specifically European context of migration and memory. Biendarra explores the intergenerational trauma affecting each of the characters in the novel as well as the novel's leap into a virtual space through its website, which provides a digital archive of heterogeneous but nonetheless shared memories. Finally, Almut Suerbaum explores how Draesner's *Nibelungen. Heimsuchung* re-voices the iconic medieval text through poetry, dialogue and academic commentary by way of the Art

Nouveau picture cycle also excerpted in the publication. Draesner's response reframes both text and image in a contemporary context, evincing affinities with the medieval epic while upholding and interrogating a sense of difference.

The second section, The Limits of the Human, focuses on the nature of humanity in the contemporary world and demonstrates Draesner's interest in current scientific discourses and the ethical and philosophical questions these raise. Emily Jeremiah analyses Draesner's engagement with posthumanism in the depiction of reproductive technologies and ethics in short stories from *Hot Dogs* and *Richtig liegen*. Drawing on Donna Haraway and Rosi Braidotti, Jeremiah considers how these texts negotiate issues of consent, marketization and maternity in contemporary sexual relationships and ultimately question the nature of the human self and agency. Thematizing scientific advances as well as interrogating corporeality and affect, Draesner's works stage an 'aesthetics of encounter' which extends to solidarity with other, non-human animals. Silke Horstkotte examines Draesner's use of imagery in poetry, and especially her treatment of photography in the novels *Mitgift* and *Vorliebe*. Draesner's work thematizes, and plays with, the two modes of visual perception and language which underpin human understanding of the world. The representation of photography and computer-generated images in *Mitgift* and *Vorliebe* explores the limits of the human, problematizing the connections between image and spectator, subject and object. Karen Leeder explores the reception of science in Draesner's poetry, placing her in the context of other modern poets who have taken up this challenge while also tracing the development of the theme in her work from *für die nacht geheuerte zellen* through her radical translations of Shakespeare to *subsongs*. Leeder follows an arc from poetry of the body to poetry exploring the makeup of our DNA and shows how Draesner's concern with science migrates to become part of the form of the poems themselves, along with her thoughts about the nature of language and what it is to be human.

The third section, Beyond Form(s), is concerned with Draesner's formal reflections and experimentation across a range of genres. Noël Reumkens' chapter on intermediality offers intensive close readings of poems which allude to visual art, examining the connection between image, language and the body. Reumkens describes Draesner's poetry as 'citation art', art which is self-aware and formally open. Her poems not only call into question the boundaries between subject and object and the dualism of the sexes, they also thematize and problematize the interpretative process itself. Lyn Marven continues by examining in detail Draesner's three volumes of short stories which showcase the author's experimentation with language and form. Their 'shortness' consists of a self-conscious focus on moments of intensity, both in the form of plot and on a structural or linguistic level. Together with the contemporary discourses which inform them, the texts attempt to reflect the fragmentary contemporary self in a form which has seen renewed interest since the 1990s.

The fourth section, 'Stoffwechsel', takes its title from a recurring metaphor in and for Draesner's work: the term means metabolic change, or more literally – and philosophically – the exchange of matter or changing of material. Chapters in this section analyse the way that Draesner's work incorporates other forms, media and languages, transforming these through her literary voice. Michael Braun's wide-ranging chapter sets Draesner's oeuvre – her poetry, translation, essays and prose fiction – in the context of a broad 'poetics of knowledge' which connects literature and scientific understanding, enacting the process of 'Stoffwechsel'. Metaphor and metamorphosis allow the writer to probe the unknowns of cultural knowledge. Braun concludes by examining two short stories from *Richtig liegen* that focus on self-representation through digital and televisual media, updating Kafka for the contemporary reader. Tobias Döring addresses the strikingly creative influence and presence of English language and literature in Draesner's poetry and prose, considering also to what extent one can describe Draesner as a 'German' writer. Döring reads Draesner's translations of Shakespeare as well as her own poetry in *subsong* as representing a 'polyglot poetics', a principle which grows in significance over the course of this volume. Just as in her poetological essays, Draesner's interest in language(s) converges on the contested term 'Heimat' (home or homeland); her linguistic inventiveness and appropriation serves to estrange and decentre German. Mary Cosgrove concludes by examining what she describes as an 'ode', the poetic travelogue and memoir *Mein Hiddensee*. Formally and stylistically varied, this text refracts autobiographical elements through a lyrical subject which is deeply embedded in the surrounding landscape and also develops a form of gendered 'body' language. The island's topography exemplifies Draesner's poetic principle of 'Stoffwechsel' and provokes reflection on the nature of embodiment and identity.

Together these chapters are intended to give new readers as well as those already familiar with Draesner's work a broad sense of the author's shifting concerns as well as her distinctive style; close readings draw attention to Draesner's use of language and form while broader thematic and theoretical analyses engage with the concerns that underpin her writing. By turns playful and poetic, erudite and explicit, Draesner's fiction combines intellectual discourses with thoughtful, occasionally outré plots, always with an awareness of language(s). Her poetry is experimental, visceral and visual, rooted in the real yet not afraid of intellectual ambition. Moreover, Draesner's texts draw on, and engage with, discourses from multiple fields of scientific and philosophical investigation from contemporary physics, bio-ethics and reproductive technology, through to photography, art and music, and medieval literature as well as twenti-eth-century European history, as expressed in and through multiple languages.

Draesner's multifaceted writing pushes the boundaries of form, while also in-vestigating the boundaries of the human – the posthuman as well as the relation-ship between human and animal – and the connectedness of the individual with the wider world both physically and ethically. The insistence on the embodiment of the subject in the world – the 'felt self', in Draesner's own words – runs through her fiction and non-fiction. This phrase provides the title of the final sec-tion, and was the inspiration for the interview in this volume in which Draesner took the editors on a walking tour of New College, Oxford, using natural and ar-chitectural landmarks as prompts for reflections on her own writing process. This section is concluded by a substantial extract from Draesner's novel *Schwitters* (2020), based on Kurt Schwitters, a multimedia poet who lived in exile in the UK from 1940 until his death in 1947, and made the switch from German to English in his own work. Fittingly, this new work draws on Draesner's own travels in the UK in the past years and sees the author herself writing simultaneously in German and in English.[1] At the time of writing, the English version of the novel has yet to find a publisher. Alongside this are new translations of poems from early collec-tions through to Draesner's most recent work by Iain Galbraith. These appeared in a new *Selected Poems* which was published while this volume was in press, at the beginning of 2022. The volume as a whole is rounded off with a substantial bibliography of Draesner's works and secondary work on her. As with all things, it cannot hope to be entirely up to date, nor entirely comprehensive, and is in any case geared primarily to the German-speaking audience for whom Draesner is already a fixed point in the literary landscape; but we hope that this volume more generally, and specifically the wider set of Draesner's writings and the broad critical reception of her work that the bibliography itemises, might also be helpful for the various English-speaking audiences yet to discover her. The vol-ume itself has been held up through illness and Covid-19 and can inevitably not keep pace with Draesner's own prolific creativity. Draesner continues to publish new work and explore new interests even as she celebrated her sixtieth birthday this year. However, the editors hope that this volume offers a snapshot of what has made her such a significant figure in the German literary landscape, and in-creasingly, in English, and that it will point the way for further research.

Oxford and Liverpool, 2022

---

1 Ulrike Draesner, *Schwitters* (Munich: Penguin, 2020).

Contents

History and the Text

The Limits of the Human

Beyond Form(s)

'Stoffwechsel'

The Felt Self

A Note on Translations

Quotations are generally given only in English, except where a particular linguistic or formal point is being made, or when a reader who has German might particularly benefit from having the original. In the case of quotations from Ulrike Draesner herself quotations are given in German and English. Contributors have, where appropriate, cited poems translated by Iain Galbraith and available online. Otherwise contributors have provided new translations where none exist, or in order to make a particular linguistic point. These follow the relevant German in square brackets and the primary aim is to provide an accessible working translation. Unless otherwise specified, all other translations are by the author of the chapter. Some poems including the sample at the end are taken from Ulrike Draesner, *this porous fabric. Selected Poems*, translated from the German by Iain Galbraith (Bristol: Shearsman Books, 2022).

To avoid unnecessary repetition, however, the titles of Ulrike Draesner's main works are given in the German only. The titles of individual essays and poems are given both in German and English throughout. For ease of reference a list of translations of these main works is included here, and a fuller Select Bibliography is given at the end of the volume.

Novels

Sieben Sprünge vom Rand der Welt (2014)
[Seven Leaps from the Edge of the World]
Vorliebe (2010)
[Preference]
Spiele (2005)
[Games]
Mitgift (2002)
[Legacy]
Lichtpause (1998)
[Light Interrupted]

Prose

Mein Hiddensee (2015)
[My Hiddensee]
Richtig liegen. Geschichten in Paaren (2011)
[Lying comfortably. Stories in Pairs]
Hot Dogs (2006)
[Hot Dogs]

https://doi.org/10.1515/9783110495942-205

Reisen unter den Augenlidern (1999)
[Travelling behind the Eyelids]

Poetry

Nibelungen. Heimsuchung (2016)
[Nibelungen. Haunting]
subsong (2014)
[subsong]
berührte orte (2008)
[touched places]
mittwinter (2006)
[midwinter]
kugelblitz (2005)
[ball lightning]
für die nacht geheuerte zellen (2001)
[cells hired for the night]
anis-o-trop. Sonettkranz (1997)
[anis-o-trop. sonnet cycle]
gedächtnisschleifen (1995, 2002, 2008)
[memory loops]

Essays

Die fünfte Dimension (2016)
[The fifth Dimension]
Heimliche Helden (2013)
[Secret Heroes]
Schöne Frauen Lesen (2007)
[Reading Beautiful Women]
Zauber im Zoo. Vier Reden von Herkunft und Literatur (2007)
[Magic in the Zoo. Four Talks about Origins and Literature]

Illustrations

Almut Suerbaum: Voices from the Past

Noël Reumkens: Intermediality in Ulrike Draesner's Poetry

Karen Leeder and Lyn Marven: The Indecipherable Stone

https://doi.org/10.1515/9783110495942-206

History and the Text

Erik Schilling
Narrating History. Ulrike Draesner's *Lichtpause, Spiele,* and *Sieben Sprünge vom Rand der Welt*

This chapter will address the intertwining of history and fictional story in three of Ulrike Draesner's novels: *Lichtpause* (1998), *Spiele* (2005) and *Sieben Sprünge vom Rand der Welt* (2014). Whereas Draesner's first novel focuses on the personal story of an eleven-year-old girl, her later texts show an increasingly significant interaction between micro- and macro-levels of history. This becomes especially important when multiple perspectives on past events result in competing versions of the same story. Different characters recount the same events in different ways; the border between history and fiction is blurred. Draesner's novels therefore pose a metahistorical question about how history may be reconstructed – and whether such history can be believed.

I follow Ansgar Nünning's typology that classifies historical novels on a spectrum ranging between 'fictionalized history' and 'metahistoriographic fiction'. Nünning distinguishes five forms of historical narratives with fluid boundaries between:[1] a historical narrative may be termed *documentary* if historical events and characters are at its centre. It may be called *realistic* if a fictional plot is integrated into a historical setting, which goes hand in hand with a chronological representation and a teleological implication. A historical narrative is *revisionist* if it manifests a critical stance towards the past, i.e. if it makes use of innovative forms of historical representation for critical purposes. The term *metahistorical* is used for a narrative that reflects on problems of historiography: cultural memory, the retrospective establishment of meaning and construction of a collective identity play an important role in this context. Finally, the term *metahistoriographic* denotes fiction in which problems of historiography are directly

---

1 Cf. Ansgar Nünning, *Von historischer Fiktion zu historiographischer Metafiktion*, vol. 1, *Theorie, Typologie und Poetik des historischen Romans* (Trier: WVT, 1995); Ansgar Nünning, 'Beyond the Great Story. Der postmoderne historische Roman als Medium revisionistischer Geschichtsdarstellung, kultureller Erinnerung und metahistoriographischer Reflexion', *Anglia*, 117 (1999), 15–48; Ansgar Nünning, 'Von der fiktionalisierten Historie zur metahistoriographischen Fiktion. Bausteine für eine narratologische und funktionsgeschichtliche Theorie, Typologie und Geschichte des postmodernen historischen Romans', in *Literatur und Geschichte. Ein Kompendium zu ihrem Verhältnis von der Aufklärung bis zur Gegenwart*, ed. by Daniel Fulda and Silvia Serena Tschopp (Berlin and New York: de Gruyter, 2002), pp. 541–569.

https://doi.org/10.1515/9783110495942-001

addressed. A discourse about the conditions of historical insight and an aware-ness of the distance between the historical event and its fictional representation are core aspects of this kind of narrative. This chapter will argue that *Lichtpause* is a realistic – and only partially historical – novel, whereas *Spiele* is metahistor-ical, and *Sieben Sprünge* explicitly deals with problems of historiography and can therefore be considered metahistoriographic.[2]

Individual and Family History in *Lichtpause*

Draesner's debut novel *Lichtpause* integrates historical events into a fictional text. However, the narrated events are not historical in a strict sense. Rather than mixing collective and individual events (as, to point forward for a mo-ment, *Spiele* does) or constructing history from different points of view (as in *Sieben Sprünge*), *Lichtpause* focuses on the biography of a single individual: an eleven-year-old girl named Hilde who dies after an accident. The novel starts with the accident itself, narrated from an external point of focalization. Then it switches to the girl's perspective (moving from 'sie' [she] via 'dich' [you] to 'ich' [I]), but split between an internal and external viewpoint. Hilde can feel what is happening to her, but at the same time she sees herself from outside as her body is lying on the street:

> Ich schließe die Augen wieder, der vertraute Geruch, ja –
> jetzt bin ich durch den Sack gekrochen. Stehe am Flieder, mehr als einen Meter über dem Asphalt.[3]

> [I close my eyes again, the familiar smell, yes –
> now I have crawled through the sack. Am standing by the lilac, more than a metre above the tarmac.]

The dual perspective is the starting point for an autodiegetic narration. The break between the two points of view is highlighted by the line break between 'ja –' and 'jetzt'. It marks the moment in which Hilde leaves her dying body to look at it from the outside, and the moment in which she starts to tell her story.

---

2 For a detailed analysis of realistic and metahistoriographic novels in the times of post-modernism, see Erik Schilling, *Der historische Roman seit der Postmoderne. Umberto Eco und die deutsche Literatur* (Heidelberg: Winter, 2012); Erik Schilling, 'Literarische Konzepte von Zeit nach dem Ende der Postmoderne', in *Poetiken der Gegenwart*, ed. by Silke Horstkotte and Leonhard Herrmann (Berlin and Boston: de Gruyter, 2013), pp. 173–187.
3 Ulrike Draesner, *Lichtpause* (Berlin: Volk & Welt, 1998), pp. 14–15.

Following this, the text presents events from Hilde's childhood, growing up in the suburban ambience of post-war West Germany. However, no recognizable historical events form part of the novel – in contrast to both *Spiele* and *Sieben Sprünge*. Whereas Draesner's more recent novels deal with historical facts and can be precisely dated to the years 1972 and 1945 respectively, *Lichtpause* simply evokes an atmosphere which is characteristic of many family narratives depicting life in the 1960s and 1970s. The text does not focus on the contrast between micro- and macro-history, but rather concentrates on the representative nature of a family that stands for many others of a certain time and place, for example with regards to communication within the family or their living situation.

As a consequence, the novel does not explicitly tackle the problem of historiographical subjectivity. The reader has to align with Hilde's point of view, just as s/he is asked to believe in Hilde's family as a typical West German family of the time. In this light the novel may be considered realistic in Nünning's terms. There are no implicit or explicit reflections concerning the reliability of narrated historical facts. The reliance on Hilde's narrative forces the reader to understand the whole novel as a work of fiction. It may include some autobiographical and historical facets (Draesner herself grew up in Planegg, a suburb of Munich similar to the one described in the novel), but there is no outside reference point with which to assess the quantity or quality of such material. The subjective perspective is established from the very beginning of the novel when Hilde leaves her dying body to recount the events that have led to the accident, and the point of view remains the same throughout the whole novel. There is neither a metahistorical questioning of memory (as Katja undergoes in *Spiele*) nor a metahistoriographic multi-perspectival review of historical and personal events as developed in *Sieben Sprünge*.

Micro- and Macro-history in *Spiele*

Spiele is divided into two longer parts (Olympia [Olympics] I and II) and two shorter ones (Reisen [Journeys] I and II) as well as a prologue and epilogue, both entitled 'Spirale' [Spirals]. The 'Reisen' passages deal with the personal memory processes of Katja, the main character, whereas the 'Olympia' parts mix elements of micro- and macro-history: 'Olympia I' recounts Katja's memories of her family's history and her first boyfriend Max, and sets both against the context of the Olympic Games in Munich 1972. Nonetheless, this part of the novel focuses on personal memories. It forms part of an explicitly 'communicative memory' and integrates history only where it is directly linked to Katja's life.[4] In 'Olympia II', however, Katja tries to reconstruct the collective memory concerning the terrorist attack which took place during the Olympic Games, the 'Munich massacre' where Palestinian terrorists took a group of Israeli team members hostage; all of the hostages were killed. For this purpose, she studies official records and talks to witnesses. The novel is no longer biographically oriented, but focuses on historical events.[5]

Katja's travels lead her from Munich, the centre of the novel, to different forms of periphery: 'Reisen I' shows Katja in India where she gets sick; while recovering, she develops her acute sensitivity towards the relationship between past and present. This leads her to attempt to come to terms with her own personal memories and to her historical research into macro-history in 'Olympia II'. 'Reisen II' concerns another illness: in both instances, Katja's recovery may be understood as an advancing process of insight. Brian, one of the witnesses whom Katja questions about Munich 1972, suggests, however, that Katja is mistaken in her belief that she has to reconstruct a version of collective history in order to understand her own personal story. Brian explains that there is neither historical nor personal truth. Although this sends Katja into crisis again, it finally leads to her reconciliation with history, her family, her love for Max and ultimately to a reconciliation with herself.

The two chapters entitled 'Spirale' illustrate the convergence of cultural and communicative memory. Together they narrate the continuation of a single sequence: the epilogue sees Katja leaving the hospital, buying a phone card and getting onto the underground. Then she calls Max. The prologue describes the phone call, interrupted by flashbacks, which refer to important aspects of the novel: the relationship with Max, the family history, and the 1972 Olympics. In addition, the prologue includes a phrase which already hints at the conclusion of the novel. Max tells Katja: 'Unsere Leben haben sich berührt und jetzt endgültig getrennt' [Our lives have touched one another and have now finally separated].[6] This sentence is directly linked to the so-called family motto: '[D]ie große und kleine Geschichte kümmern sich nicht umeinander, sie durchdringen sich bloß'

---

4 Cf. Jan Assmann, 'Kollektives Gedächtnis und kulturelle Identität', in *Kultur und Gedächtnis*, ed. by Jan Assmann and Tonio Hölscher (Frankfurt a. M.: Suhrkamp, 1988), pp. 9–19 (pp. 10–11).
5 Accordingly, the plotline is no longer chronological, but retrospective: 'The narrative processes of memory follow retrospectively, according to the chronology of past events, and lend perspective to the mediated nature of the memories', Michael Braun, 'Wem gehört die Geschichte? Erinnerungsverhandlungen in Ulrike Draesners Roman *Spiele*', in *Familien – Geschlechter – Macht. Beziehungen im Werk Ulrike Draesners*, ed. by Stephanie Catani and Friedhelm Marx (Göttingen: Wallstein, 2008), pp. 95–108 (p. 102).
6 Ulrike Draesner, *Spiele* (Munich: Luchterhand, 2005), p. 20. Further references to this text are made in the body of the essay.

(p. 20) [Big and small versions of history do not care about each other, they simply become intertwined]. The motto is central for the novel as a whole, suggesting in a paradoxical way the different possibilities of interaction between micro- and macro-history: individual and collective history may be separated, linked, or partially linked. For all of these, the novel offers examples.

The farewell with Max does not simply refer to the couple going their separate ways, as Katja and Max haven't met for more than 20 years. Instead, it indicates that Katja relegates her memories of Max to a past without a link to the present. The epilogue adds further layers to this: Katja is able to move beyond the idea that the Olympics and her family history share a common meaning. She gains a new perspective on her family history which becomes manifest when she tells the story of her grandfather's death with affection and love. Finally, Katja realizes that she does not have to link past events to present ones. She is finally able to overcome the past and live in the present. This is underlined in the novel's final scene: exiting the underground into the pouring rain, Katja throws off her clothes. Having arrived in her new, old hometown, she is able leave the past behind her and focus on the present, naked and free.

Notable within *Spiele* is the fact that different characters represent different ways of linking past and present (this anticipates the more formally differentiated perspectives in *Sieben Sprünge*).[7] Katja's grandfather Jozef uses a number of aphorisms to deal with history, for example: 'Geschichte ist alles, was man nicht versteht, fragen Sie ruhig' (p. 39) [History is everything you don't understand. Just ask]. The aphorisms provide him with a clear-cut framework when confronted with history and serve as a form of protection. Jozef's generation has lived through war and displacement; they want to forget but cannot. The rhetorical formulae allow Jozef to integrate single events such as his individual story into a wider context, which offers at least some handle on the way history intervenes in and subverts the individual life. Individual suffering loses part of its terror when it is part of a collective experience.

Katja, by contrast, defines her relation to the past differently. Her approach to history and memory is established bit by bit and changes over the course of the novel. Right from the beginning she sees connections between different times: 'Zeit lief in zwei Richtungen. Die Vergangenheit erzeugte Zukunft, die Zukunft Vergangenheit' (p. 68) [Time moved into two directions. The past generated a future, the future a past]. Despite noticing this connection, Katja remains reluctant to deal with the past. It is not until the second part of the novel that she chooses to reconstruct the events of the terrorist attack as a historian. In doing

---

7 Cf. Braun, 'Wem gehört die Geschichte?', pp. 100–101.

so, however, she immerses herself in the past in a way that begins to dominate her present. She relives the events of 1972 and loses the objectivity of the historiographer. Because of Katja's subjective involvement, her reconstruction may be called revisionist in Nünning's terms (the reconstruction is not objective, but led by a subjective idea), whereas the reflections on the intertwining of present and past are clearly metahistorical.

Moreover, tackling the past becomes part of finding the home Katja has lacked for many years. The new home is built on a surprising conclusion: 'Wo sie bleiben wollte, brauchte sie nicht mehr zu fragen. Vier Monate Recherche. Das Ergebnis knapp und klar. [. . .] Es hieß: Zuhause ist, wo dir auch die Katastrophen gehören' (p. 401) [She didn't have to wonder any more where she wanted to stay. Four months of research. The result was plain to see. [. . .] It was: home is where even the catastrophes are yours]. This new home is not a place to live, but a way of accepting one's past.

The ability to accept catastrophes is a central concern of *Spiele*. Most obvious is the example of the collective catastrophe: the terrorist attack carried out at Munich Olympics in 1972. Katja reconstructs it by tracing the historical events, and in doing so, she succeeds in accepting the catastrophe as part of her identity. The second catastrophe Katja deals with is her mother's death and the arrival of her father's new partner Susanne. Katja considers her father's new lover a rupture in her biography and connects her subjectively to the terrorist attack on the same day. Finally, however, she accepts the new family constellation. Katja's third catastrophe is the end of her relationship. In the last scene of the novel, Katja comes to terms with this aspect of her past, too.

While conducting her research, Katja also learns to see the past as a construction, depending on different perspectives. Her partner Paul stresses the relativity of every point of view when they both travel to Fürstenfeldbruck airport where the terrorist attack came to an end. Paul asks her:

> [W]o ist eigentlich deine Kamera? ich dachte, hierher nimmst du sie sicher mit. Nach einer Pause sagte Katja, die Hände tief in die Taschen ihres Mantels vergraben, ich übe aufzeichnen mit dem Hirn. Gehirnaufzeichnungen, rief Paul zweifelnd, und das nach allem, was ich dir gestern erzählt habe? Katja [. . .] sagte heiter, ja, genau deswegen, verschieblich und haltlos, höllisch ungenau, objektiv äußerst falsch und subjektiv exakt richtig. (p. 355)

> [Where is your camera, by the way? I expected you to take it with you. After a break, burying her hands deeply in her coat pockets, Katja said, I'm practising recording in my brain. Brain records, called Paul doubtfully. After all that I told you yesterday? Katja [. . .] said cheerfully, yes, that's precisely why, shifting and untenable, terribly unprecise, objectively completely wrong and subjectively exactly right.]

Katja thus emphasizes the constructed character of memory and perception. History is a mixture of 'Fakt und Fiktion, Mythos und Beweis, Deutung und Bild' (p. 454) [fact and fiction, myth and proof, interpretation and image]. If there is no reason to believe in historical truth, the personal story offers the chance to experience at least a subjective truth.

The perfect medium for this subjective truth is the historical novel: 'Fiktion kann haltbarer sein als Wirklichkeit' (p. 446) [Fiction may be more durable than reality]. A metahistorical novel demonstrates remembering and reconstructing as a complex process, being both objectively unreliable and subjectively true. *Spiele*, therefore, lets micro- and macro-history touch each other, retaining nonetheless a clear distinction between Katja's fictional biography and the events of 1972 that are recounted with a good deal of historical accuracy. This separation of spheres is important as this allows their mutual interference to become obvious. Being involved in macro-history imbues individual fate with importance.[8] Personal history, on the other side, allows collective memories to be projected onto individual experiences.

Spiele thus operates with a broad spectrum of historical narrative. It combines elements of a realistic historical novel with those of metahistoriographic fiction. The result is a mainly metahistorical novel. The relationship between past and present as well as the relationship between history and fiction create a discourse on remembrance. Katja does not turn to history for aesthetic pleasure, but for personal gain: she wants to reconstruct her past to achieve a sense of identity. The historical novel is the perfect medium to illustrate this process, as it offers the double link of past and present, and micro- and macro-history. In addition, it can reflect the freedom and limitations inherent in narrating history as well as constructing identity.

Different Perspectives on History in *Sieben Sprünge vom Rand der Welt*

Published in 2014, *Sieben Sprünge vom Rand der Welt* presents the connected stories of two families: the Grolmann family, consisting of grandfather Eustachius, mother Simone, daughter Esther, great-grandparents Lilly and Hannes,

---

8 Cf. Oliver Jahraus, 'Große und kleine Geschichte in München. Zum Olympia-Attentat in Ulrike Draesners Roman *Spiele*', in *München lesen. Beobachtungen einer erzählten Stadt*, ed. by Simone Hirmer and Marcel Schellong (Würzburg: Königshausen & Neumann, 2008), pp. 265–275 (p. 266).

and Eustachius's brother Emil who disappeared while fleeing from Silesia in 1945; and the Nienalt family, Boris who starts a love affair with Simone Grolmann, his mother Halka and his daughter Jennifer. The events, recounted from multiple perspectives, span the time from World War I to the present. All the narrators talk about fleeing from Silesia. While *Spiele* establishes a plurality of history refracted through Katja's point of view, *Sieben Sprünge* stresses its multiperspectival structure from the beginning. The reader gets to know various versions of the same story, which differ explicitly and implicitly.

As the perspectivity of the recounted events is highlighted at all times, the novel may be termed metahistoriographic. For example, Simone finds her father blending the memory of his flight from Silesia with similar incidents he has not himself witnessed. He mentions having been part of a journey undertaken by a group of refugees, but Simone finds out that no such group has taken his route.[9] She concludes that her father must have seen the images in a documentary and integrated them into his personal memory in retrospect. In addition, the multiperspective approach is a trait of the characters themselves. Many of them combine experiences of different countries and cultures. Boris, for example, describes himself as having four faces: 'schlesisch, polnisch, ukrainisch, deutsch' (p. 266) [Silesian, Polish, Ukrainian, German].

The characters differ in their approach to the past. Simone finds herself torn between a vivid interest in the past and the conviction of this being fruitless, dangerous even: 'Man konnte die Gegenwart durch die Vergangenheit nicht erklären, nur versäumen' (p. 17) [One could not explain the present through the past, one could only miss it]. But just like Katja she finds herself increasingly tackling the past in the hope of finding an explanation for her present situation. Her interest is piqued when her father declares the past a taboo zone. However, it is only with her relationship with Boris that Simone begins to investigate her father's youth. The final impulse is Boris's being a psychologist who deals professionally with the situation of refugees. From this point on, Simone sees the flight as a part of her family history, even as a legacy. Her husband Johnny reproaches her on this score, calling her a 'Fluchtparasitin' (p. 63) [parasite of flight]. According to Johnny, Simone does not confront the past for professional reasons, but for her own personal ends. He is proven right insofar as Simone develops a desire for flight of her own while doing research on her family history: she leaves her husband for Boris.

---

9 Cf. Ulrike Draesner, *Sieben Sprünge vom Rand der Welt* (Munich: Luchterhand, 2014), p. 46. Further references to this text are made in the body of the essay.

Boris serves as a contrast to Simone's scientific approach. As a psychologist, he adopts a qualitative focus. He does not look for objective explanations of historical processes but seeks the subjective experiences that go to make up history itself. In doing so, he reaches layers of memory and personality Simone and her father simply cannot access. Although Simone engages him as the therapist for her father, Boris soon becomes kind of a therapist for her, too.

Simone's father Eustachius, on the other hand, interprets the past in a physiological, not a psychological way. He aims to explore the relation between past and present as a 'neurologische[] Geschichte' (p. 37) [neurological history] reaching over generations. However, his insisting on empirical aspects of the past can be understood, on a psychological level, as a strategy of avoidance. He turns to the present in order not to be confronted with the past. He keeps the past locked within himself as a 'dumpfes, unausgesprochenes Leiden' (p. 57) [dull, unspoken suffering]. Yet there is a moment in which the past is conjured up, despite him. Vlak, one of the two apes nursed illegally by Eustachius at home, has run away and Eustachius sets off to find him. The scene evokes a vivid memory of his lost brother. 'Als er [Vlak] seinen Namen hörte, drehte er sich um und wartete auf mich. [. . .] Emil, hochgewachsener als noch vor einer Stunde, den Rücken durchgedrückt' (p. 168) [When he [Vlak] heard his name, he turned around and waited for me. [. . .] Emil, taller than one hour ago, his back stretched]. By mingling the present ape and the lost human, Eustachius reveals part of the motivation for his research. He is not only looking for the 'better human' in the ape, but also trying to succeed in the caring role he failed to fulfil when looking after his brother Emil. The ape that escapes nearly seventy years after he loses Emil evokes the trauma of the lost brother. But the adult Eustachius manages what the young one did not: exclaiming 'Mein Menschentier' (p. 177) [my human animal] he retrieves Vlak and embraces him.

Eustachius's hunt for the lost ape highlights the fact that his grasp on the present is becoming weaker. By telling his granddaughter Esther the story of Emil's disappearance, he finally gives in to the past. Yet by turning to the past, he also builds a future for her and himself. When Eustachius is about to die, Esther has the impression that her grandfather looks at her 'wie aus gespaltenen Augen [. . .], als sehe er in die Zukunft und die Vergangenheit zugleich' (p. 542) [as if through divided eyes [. . .], as if he saw future and past at the same time]. Thus, Eustachius accomplishes something many other characters do not: he reconciles the different phases of his life. Eustachius comes to terms with past, present and even future (manifest in his granddaughter) by productively working through his biography.

In contrast to Eustachius stands his mother Lilly. She represents what Boris identifies as a trait of all refugees: a loss of the present, which in turn makes memory the centre of her preoccupations. In Lilly's case, the reason for this is not only her displacement, but also the loss of Emil: 'Emil, dessen langsame Nähe mir / fehlte' (p. 197) [Emil whose slow closeness I / was missing]. A formal device is used to highlight Lilly's embeddedness in memories. While the novel has been typeset in justified text up to now, from this point on point line breaks begin to occur. The breaks become especially dominant where images of the past are conjured up. Thus, the processes of memory are connoted, and physically represented, as fragmentary. The constituent parts of memory are broken; only Lilly is able to put them together to form a coherent narrative. The line breaks emphasize this process-related aspect of remembering.

Lilly's husband Hannes partially adopts this fragmentary mode of remembrance. Primarily, however, he develops an approach to history characterized by a simultaneous presence of different layers of time: '[D]ie Zeit hat sich aufgerollt wie ein Farnwedel, ich weiß nicht, ob sie schrumpft oder wächst: Da steht Eustachius und ist noch nicht gezeugt' (p. 286) [Time has coiled up like a frond. I don't know if it is shrinking or growing: there stands Eustachius and is not yet conceived]. In Hannes's case, there is a functional reason for his losing his grip on time: his present perspective is interrupted by memories of World War I. To him, micro- and macro-history are inseparably linked, leading to speechlessness. Hannes has gone through experiences he cannot name: 'Die Kuhhaut ist klein, es geht nicht darauf. Sie schrumpft von Minute zu Minute, sie ist kleiner als gedacht. Sie ist gar nicht da. Das nennt sich Erinnerung. Erinnerung / ist, was er zu vergessen versucht' (p. 350) [The cowhide is small, too small. It shrinks from one minute to the next, it is smaller than expected. It is not there at all. This is called remembrance. Remembrance / is what he tries to forget]. Unlike his wife Lilly, Hannes does not want to preserve the past. He desperately tries to get rid of it, but does not succeed. Even the enforced confrontation with memory imposed on him by the occupying forces in the shape of a documentary film on the concentration camps does not change anything. Instead he turns to silence.

The two grandchildren in *Sieben Sprünge* – Jennifer, Boris's daughter, and Esther, Simone's daughter – embody two further ways of dealing with history. The difference between Jennifer and Boris is encapsulated in the contrast between plurality and teleology. While Jennifer sees her father trying to live within a clearly circumscribed radius, she finds herself in the midst of a plural society with multiple options. For both Jennifer and her grandparents, the material foundation of life is lost. Unlike her grandparents, however, Jennifer is faced with the ubiquitous availability of the digital world.

Esther too defines her relation to the past in this medium: 'Für unsere B.A.-Arbeiten hatten wir einen Antimigrations-Blog gegründet: Erzählungen aus

Paradiesen der Sesshaftigkeit, Berichte von Stubenhockern und Bewegungs-muffeln' (p. 491) [For our BA dissertations we had founded an anti-migration blog: stories from paradises of sedentariness, accounts of stay-at-homes and couch potatoes]. As a result of a nearly paradoxical twist, Esther – who has grown up without any national borders in Europe – develops a desire for boundaries, as those are the basis of home: '[Grenzen] konnten schwer erträglich sein. Seit ein paar Minuten spürte ich, dass es mindestens ebenso unerträglich war, wenn sie fehlten' (p. 495) [[Borders] could be difficult to bear. I had felt for a few minutes now that it was just as unbearable when there were none]. Her statement adds an aspect to the topic of home and flight as well as to the historiographical and fictional handling of history: by turning to the past without being existentially involved (as her grandfather and her mother are), Esther accepts the necessarily subjective element in historiography.

The story of Emil, Eustachius's lost brother, underlines the impossibility of an exact reconstruction of events. His disappearance during the flight of 1945 is narrated from different points of view without any of these gaining particular traction in the narrative. His mother Lilly, for example, notices that Emil is missing and that Eustachius follows shortly after. She does not discover what happens: 'Alles floss im großen Durcheinander dahin. Nach einer Viertelstunde, vielleicht auch früher, war Eustachius zurück, ohne Emil, er setzte sich zu unserem Gepäck' (p. 427) [Everything melted into a big chaos. After a quarter of an hour, maybe earlier, Eustachius had returned, without Emil, he sat down next to our luggage]. Lilly falls ill and does not regain consciousness until five days later. It remains unclear whether the missing days are caused by physical illness or are the result of a voluntary loss of memory. Some years later, Lilly insinuates that Eustachius may have killed his brother, but receives no response. Lilly will never know the truth.

Quite the opposite happens to her great-granddaughter Esther. She is told a brutally realist version of Emil's death by her grandfather: 'Ich habe meinen Bruder getötet. Damals, im kältesten Winter. Auf der Flucht. [. . .] Ich erschoss ihn' (p. 501) [I killed my brother. Back then, in the coldest of winters. During the flight. [. . .] I shot him]. Eustachius, however, does not explain or justify his actions. This causes Esther to react with scepticism: she tries in various ways to test the credibility of his assertion but does not come to any conclusion. Her grandfather's story may be the result of some mental disorder or the truth. Esther, too, will never know for sure what happened to Emil.

The reader of Draesner's novel seems to reach a deeper insight than the characters, with a short passage told from Emil's point of view. The uncertainty caused by multiple perspectives seems to come to an end, at least as far as Emil's disappearance is concerned. But there is no certainty, even for the reader. On the one hand, it is not clear whether Emil can be considered a reliable narrator. What is more, due to his disability, Emil inhabits an idiosyncratic world of his own making his narration even more difficult to interpret. In addition, the events surrounding Emil's disappearance are told fragmentarily. Just like some of the other characters, Emil blends present and past events. Fragments of childhood memories emerge to trouble the picture: the repeated humiliation because of his disability, for example, and the resulting desire to prove himself by joining the army. Emil's internal monologue also includes reflections on his brother and the family's future: 'es wird für dich [Eustachius] nicht leicht sein, nach Hause zu finden' (p. 554) [It won't be easy for you [Eustachius] to reach home], and finally to a farewell phrase: 'ich wünsche euch Glück' (p. 555) [I wish you luck]. What follows is a rather cryptic natural image. Then the novel comes to an end. Emil's situation remains uncertain. He may leave for the eastern front to finally become the soldier he has always wanted to be. He may carry the second revolver that has been mentioned before and commit suicide. Equally, the story Eustachius tells his granddaughter might be true: he has killed his brother.

Thus, the multiperspectival structure of the novel is not suspended in the final chapter; rather it is focused in a concrete example. It is a supremely metahistoriographic end: the reader will never know the truth about the story, just like the characters themselves. What remains are stories about history. In their plurality they offer an incomplete mosaic of the events in question. They do not lead to a 'true' grand narrative but may yet be more convincing in their diversity than a single narration could be.

Conclusion

Comparing Draesner's three historical novels, one can certainly trace a shift towards metahistoriographic fiction. Her first novel *Lichtpause* recounts a story that is realistic in most of its aspects (e.g. giving a linear account of events which – at least from the narrator's perspective – are not questioned in their authenticity). *Spiele* poses the metahistorical question of the reliability of historiography by illustrating Katja's subjective approach towards the events of the Munich Olympics in 1972. *Sieben Sprünge* reveals metahistoriographic aspects openly in form and content. The explicit reflections on historiography and memory along with subjective perspectives on history do not lead to a reliable account of the events in question. The overall effect is a pervasive understanding of the multiple ways in which history makes itself felt in the individual life at multiple levels ranging from broad tropes and events of (inter-)national significance to the epigenetic inheritances that are passed on silently through generations. As Draesner comments:

> Someone is dead and done but how do the dead live on in our genes, in our epigenetics, in our minds, in our behaviour, in our dreams and in nightmares and in bits of traumatic experience which have crossed generations.[10]

What is more, Draesner exploits the flexibility of the form of the novel along with its inherent self-reflexive qualities to suggest that fiction has a unique role in tracing and ultimately also in figuring history in all its aspects.

---

10 See the interview with Ulrike Draesner included in this volume.

Anke S. Biendarra
Regenerating Europe in *Sieben Sprünge vom Rand der Welt*

Ulrike Draesner's 2014 novel *Sieben Sprünge vom Rand der Welt* represents a key intervention within what critics have described as a 'memory boom' in literature and film. The popularity of historical (family) novels about the Second World War and its aftermath illustrates the continuing questioning of what it means to be German, even at a distance of more than seventy years from the Holocaust and the Second World War. Perhaps surprisingly, this also applies to the second and even third postwar generations of writers who have no personal memory of the events.

While Draesner has long demonstrated an interest in history, as shown for example in her 2005 novel *Spiele* that re-examines the attack on the Israeli team during the Olympic Games in Munich in 1972, *Sieben Sprünge vom Rand der Welt* is an even more ambitious project, since it spans over a century of both German and Central European history. At the centre of the novel are the experiences of flight and expulsion and the loss of a homeland. The novel intertwines the story of the German family Grolmann, expelled in 1945 from Silesia to Bavaria, with that of the members of the Polish family Nienaltowski, who in 1945 are forcibly removed from East Poland to Wrocław (formerly Breslau). Arranging her characters in a chiastic pattern, Draesner assigns a Polish equivalent to each one of the German characters who are grouped around Eustachius Grolmann, a famous primatologist and ethologist. As homodiegetic narrators, nine characters take turns telling their own stories that each illustrate the longevity of historical events. In the different narrative voices and respective chapters, *Geschichten* [individual life stories] and *Geschichte* [history] are shown to be inextricably linked.

The genre of the multigenerational family novel, to which *Sieben Sprünge vom Rand der Welt* belongs, runs the risk of naturalizing and thus normalizing German history by presenting collective history as an organic extension of family history.[1] Draesner's novel, however, turns this on its head by insisting that the lives of the protagonists are influenced by historical factors largely beyond their

---

1 Friederike Eigler makes this argument in her book *Heimat, Space, Narrative. Toward a Transnational Approach to Flight and Expulsion* (Rochester, NY: Camden House, 2014), pp. 130–31.

Note: This essay is dedicated to my father whose memories of his childhood and the flight from Eastern Prussia inspired and infused it in myriad ways. I wish he could have still read it, as well as Draesner's novel. I thank the editors for their comments on a previous version.

https://doi.org/10.1515/9783110495942-002

control, stressing time and again that events often exceed the characters' own understanding. In *Sieben Sprünge vom Rand der Welt* individual biographies are not portrayed as a microcosm of history, but are shown in all their randomness, as an effort to overcome the transgenerational effects of losing one's *Heimat* and attempting to establish a new home in the context of postwar west Germany and postwar Wrocław respectively. Furthermore, the novel utilizes the oft-discussed notion of 'generation'[2] without making it the dominant interpretative framework. Earlier novels in the same genre which have attracted substantial critical attention focus primarily on a single generation: Günter Grass's *Im Krebsgang* (2002) [*Crab Walk*] highlights with Paul Pokriefke a member of the second postwar generation, while the primary character of Tanja Dückers' *Himmelskörper* (2003) [*Heavenly Bodies*], Freia, is a member of the third. By contrast, Draesner's novel renders members of four distinct generations who are on equal footing as narrators and, in one way or another, are all affected by the traumatic past. In so doing, the novel challenges ideas about neatly separated and easily differentiated generational cohorts and in this way also challenges at least one longstanding paradigm of sociological research.[3]

The focus on the interlinked German/Polish experience also sets Draesner's project apart from the few narratives that have taken the perspective of individual histories of Germans and Poles, such as Olaf Müller's *Schlesisches Wetter* (2003) [*Silesian Weather*] and Sabrina Janesch's *Katzenberge* (2010) [*Cat Mountains*]. *Sieben Sprünge vom Rand der Welt* introduces a transnational European perspective on events that until recently had been discussed almost exclusively through a national lens.[4] The following reading thus focuses on the European dimension of the novel. My contention is that *Sieben Sprünge vom Rand der Welt* opens up both narrative and imaginative spaces within the transnational realm of European history. Draesner renders ideas of European identity and integration imaginatively through her German and Polish characters and their intertwined life stories in a complexly layered 555-page novel. Her main question

---

2 Sigrid Weigel, 'Generation, Genealogie, Geschlecht: Zur Geschichte des Generationskonzepts und seiner wissenschaftlichen Konzeptualisierung seit Ende des 18. Jahrhunderts', in *Kulturwissenschaften. Forschung – Praxis – Positionen*, ed. by Lutz Musner and Gotthard Wunberg (Vienna: WUV Universitätsverlag, 2002), pp. 161–90.
3 Cf. Heinz Bude, 'Zur Erinnerung der Generationen', in *Vergangenheitsbewältigung am Ende des zwanzigsten Jahrhunderts*, ed. by Helmut König and Andreas Wöll (Wiesbaden: Springer Fachmedien, 1998), pp. 69–85.
4 Eigler, *Heimat, Space, Narrative*, p. 9. There is a growing body of research on German-Polish issues in film and literature. Cf. chapter seven in Eigler, as well as *Germany, Poland, and Postmemorial Relations: In Search of a Livable Past*, ed. by Kristin Kopp and Joanna Niżyńska (New York: Palgrave Macmillan, 2012).

is how transgenerational trauma is processed individually and how the second and third postwar generations move beyond the traumatic legacy left to them. The novel suggests that only millennials are free enough of secondary trauma to reflect critically on the past *and* sustain strong, loving bonds with the family members involved in the war who might have been both believers in ideology and victims of expulsions. As a result, rifts become less frequent and healthier family relations develop that are unencumbered by the strife that characterized relations between earlier generations, such as the war generation and that of 1968. Members of this young cohort are thus also able to actualize the ideals of a united Europe, such as literacy of other cultures, openness to diversity, and multilingualism, while remaining cognizant of the historical specificities of their own countries.

European Memory Cultures

The larger questions that have informed my reading have been discussed intensively in a number of contexts, especially in the field of Transcultural Memory Studies.[5] At stake here is, among other things, the role that collective memory cultures are to play in the construction of a European memory and cultural identity. At the end of the Cold War and in the wake of German reunification, memory politics changed dramatically across the continent. Reflections about a shared approach to remembering and memorializing European history intensified. Inspired by the opening of previously inaccessible archives in Eastern Europe and the former Soviet Union and alarmed by the fact that ethnic cleansing was repeating itself in the wars in Yugoslavia in the 1990s, historians in particular began theorizing what the policies for encouraging transnational remembrance might look like in a European framework.[6] One implicit goal of this intensified discussion was to bridge the East-West divide through the project of a unified European memory. Identifying the Holocaust as the centre of European historical consciousness was a significant acknowledgement; it was, among other things, embodied both in the Stockholm Declaration on the Holocaust in 2000 and the European Day of Remembrance of the Liberation of Auschwitz on 27 January 1945,

---

5 Astrid Erll, 'Traumatic Pasts, Literary Afterlives, and Transcultural Memory: New Directions of Literary and Media Studies', *Journal of Aesthetics and Culture*, 3 (2011), without pagination.
6 Cf. *Conflicted Memories. Europeanizing Contemporary Histories*, ed. by Konrad H. Jarausch and Thomas Lindenberger, in collaboration with Annelie Ramsbrock (New York and Oxford: Berghahn Books, 2007).

as designated by the UN General Assembly in 2005. Yet despite these important achievements on the European level, it has become apparent that a shared memory must also include other dark elements of the European past, such as colonialism, ethnic cleansing and genocide, world wars, class struggle or totalitarian regimes, the omission of which led to the rejection of a proposed European Constitution by France and the Netherlands in 2005.[7]

In their book *Der Kampf um die europäische Erinnerung* (2011) [*The Battle for European Memory*] Claus Leggewie and Anne Lang have argued similarly that Europe can only construct a viable political identity that exceeds treaties, free trade and open borders if it acknowledges that trauma is at the heart of the European experience and establishes a shared memory about past conflicts that happened on the continent. In this context Leggewie and Lang identify six circles of memory that are concentrically entwined around the memory of the Holocaust, some mostly assimilated with it, others more distanced from it or indifferent towards it.[8] The discourse of flight and expulsion (which in their graphic is subsumed in the circle 'ethnic cleansings') has been quite separate from the discourse about the Holocaust, even though experiences of exclusion, removal and 'cleansing' of cities, provinces, states and societies were at the heart of both historical processes. Karl Schlögel's argument that writing and displaying a German national history that neglects experiences of flight and expulsion would be as untruthful and disingenuous as one that leaves out the Holocaust[9] thus signals the sea change with regard to the question of German victimhood that took place during the first decade of the millennium.[10]

---

7 Małgorzata Pakier and Bo Stråth, 'A European Memory?' in *A European Memory? Contested Histories and Politics of Remembrance*, ed. by Małgorzata Pakier and Bo Stråth (New York and Oxford: Berghahn Books, 2010), pp. 1–19 (pp. 1–3). Since that initial rejection, the Treaty of Lisbon (2009) has replaced the original draft of the European Constitution.

8 Leggewie and Lang specify these emanating circles, with the Holocaust at the centre: 'Ethnic Cleansings, Wars and Crises, Colonial Crimes, Migration History, and European Integration', in *Der Kampf um die europäische Erinnerung. Ein Schlachtfeld wird besichtigt* (Munich: C.H. Beck, 2011), p. 14.

9 Karl Schlögel, 'Nach der Rechthaberei. Umsiedlung und Vertreibung als europäisches Problem', in *Vertreibungen europäisch erinnern? Historische Erfahrung – Vergangenheitspolitik – Zukunftskonzeptionen*, ed. by Dieter Bingen, Włodzimierz Borodziej and Stefan Troebst (Wiesbaden: Harrassowitz, 2003), pp. 11–38 (pp. 31–32).

10 Winfried Georg Sebald's *Luftkrieg und Literatur* (1999) and Jörg Friedrich's *Der Brand: Deutschland im Bombenkrieg* (2002), both of which documented the devastation caused by the allied fire-bombings, are important texts that influenced public discussion.

Over the last fifteen or so years, a substantial number of literary texts have narrated the perspective of German victims of World War II.[11] Undoubtedly influenced by both a changing German self-understanding after unification, and large public media events,[12] the effects of the carpet-bombing of German cities and mass rapes of women at the end of the war became significant topics in the public discourse.[13] German-language authors of different generations have addressed memories of German suffering that had previously already been well established as a private and informal memory in many families. For example, Uwe Timm recalls in his 2003 book *Am Beispiel meines Bruders* [*In My Brother's Shadow: A Life and Death in the SS*, 2005] how his parents recounted events during the war almost ritualistically during his childhood:

> Noch Jahre nach dem Krieg, mich durch meine Kindheit begleitend, wurden diese Erlebnisse immer und immer wieder erzählt, was das ursprüngliche Entsetzen langsam abschliff, das Erlebte fassbar und schließlich unterhaltend machte [. . .] *Hamburg in Schutt und Asche. Die Stadt ein Flammenmeer. Der Feuersturm.*

> [Years after the war, accompanying me through my childhood, these experiences were retold again and again, which stripped them of their original horror and made what had happened comprehensible, and finally even entertaining [. . .] *Hamburg reduced to rubble. The city a sea of flames. The firestorm.*][14]

In contrast to these issues that were mostly relegated to the private realm, flight, expulsion and forced relocation were more prominent in the public discourse from the 1950s onwards.[15] The ongoing engagement of the *Bund der Vertriebenen*

---

11 For an overview see *Germans as Victims in the Literary Fiction of the Berlin Republic*, ed. by Stuart Taberner and Karina Berger (Rochester: Camden House, 2009).

12 Cf. the ARD production *Die Flucht* (2007) [*March of Millions*], a two-part film that was a parallel broadcast in the ARD and Arte and the most successful film of the decade for the ARD.

13 Cf. *Anonyma. Eine Frau in Berlin. Tagebuchaufzeichnungen vom 20. April bis 22. Juni 1945*. When the text was first published in 1959 in German (1954 in English), it received vicious criticism and was accused of 'shaming German women', which led its author Marta Hillers to prohibit any further publication of the autobiographical notes until after her death. When the book was republished in 2003, it became a popular success, so much so that it was subsequently made into a movie in 2008, directed by Max Färberböck.

14 Uwe Timm, *Am Beispiel meines Bruders* (Cologne: Kiepenheuer & Witsch, 2003), pp. 38–39; *In My Brother's Shadow: A Life and Death in the SS*, trans. by Anthea Bell (New York: Farrar, Straus and Giroux, 2005). All translations from the German in this essay are my own.

15 Historians such as Robert G. Moeller, in *War Stories* (Berkeley: University of California Press, 2001), Eva Hahn and Hans Henning Hahn, in *Mythos Vertreibung* (Hamburg: konkret, 2009), and Andrew Demshuk, in *The Lost German East* (New York: Cambridge University Press, 2012) have all argued against the notion that postwar West Germany was dominated by silence about the Nazi past and memories of flight and expulsion.

[League of Expellees] in particular ensured that the topic was memorialized in both public and political discourse, which had considerable impact in the Federal Republic and helped keep the loss of German lands in the East in the German consciousness. This was different from other contested memories, for example the role that the German Wehrmacht had played during World War Two, which only came under scrutiny in 1995 and 2001 with two traveling exhibitions prepared by the Hamburg Institute for Social Research that generated much controversy.[16] Other traumas were talked about only privately and remained obscured from the public view, often becoming family secrets. Friederike Eigler, Bill Niven and Karina Berger have all explored the long history of literary texts explicitly dealing with flight and expulsion but have not addressed Draesner's novel in their books.[17] Beyond these monographs however, *Sieben Sprünge vom Rand der Welt* has attracted significant scholarly attention[18] and stands as a genuine literary attempt to detail painful historical experiences that adds significantly to the textual corpus we already possess.

According to Aleida Assmann and others, literary texts are especially powerful as sites of memory (*Erinnerungsorte*), since they can render and conserve that which is gone: 'In order to last and be valid, a story must be told that substitutes and supplements the lost milieu. Sites of memory are blasted fragments of a lost and destroyed life continuum'.[19] The figurative and thematic expansion beyond simply German experiences in the novel signals its connection to the rest of Europe and makes the novel into a *lieu de mémoire* that aids in the construction of a collective European memory.

---

16 Cf. Christian Hartmann, Johannes Hürter and Ulrike Jureit, *Verbrechen der Wehrmacht. Bilanz einer Debatte* (Munich: C.H. Beck, 2005).

17 Eigler, *Heimat, Space, Narrative*, as above; Bill Niven, *Representations of Flight and Expulsion in East German Prose Works* (Rochester, NY: Camden House, 2014); Karina Berger, *Heimat, Loss and Identity: Flight and Expulsion in German Literature from the 1950s to the Present* (Frankfurt a. M.: Peter Lang, 2015).

18 See most recently Friederike Eigler's 'Post/Memories of Forced Migration at the End of the Second World War. Novels by Walter Kempowski and Ulrike Draesner', in *Migration: Changing Concepts, Critical Approaches*, ed. by Doris Bachmann-Medick and Jens Kugele (Berlin and Boston: De Gruyter, 2018), pp. 167–192; chapter 5 in Benjamin Schaper's *Poetik und Politik in der Lesbarkeit der deutschen Literatur* (Heidelberg: Universitätsverlag Winter, 2017), pp. 213–230; and Michael Dallapiazza's detailed analysis of formal aspects and aesthetics of the novel, 'Neueste deutschsprachige Literatur', *Jahrbuch für Internationale Germanistik*, XLVI.2 (2014), 263–278.

19 Aleida Assmann, *Erinnerungsräume. Formen und Wandlungen des kulturellen Gedächtnisses*, 5th edn (Munich: C.H. Beck, 2010), p. 309.

Coping with Transgenerational Trauma

The fragmented life context that determines the lives of all characters in *Sieben Sprünge vom Rand der Welt* is the experience of flight and expulsion and the loss of a homeland, a 'Heimat'. What is of particular interest in my reading is the creative and integrative writing of primary and secondary trauma. How does transgenerational trauma manifest in the different characters and how do especially the second and third postwar generation move beyond the traumatic heritage? Does the way they process trauma point the way forward, towards an integration of European memories? The legacy of trauma takes different forms; for the generation who experienced the war directly, it is the experience of remaining unmoored in their own lives. Echoing the novel's title, Ulrike Draesner expresses it in an interview on the German TV channel *3Sat* as an involuntary movement:

> Gezwungen zu werden, vom Rand der Welt zu springen, dessen, was bislang deine Welt war, die du kanntest, wo du zuhause bist. Man sprang also in ein Nichts. Und das Bild, das sich mir zusammensetzte, war, dass diese Menschen zwar physisch irgendwo angekommen waren, aber ein Teil von ihnen, ein Teil ihres Inneren oder ihrer Seele [. . .] eigentlich in dieser Luft hängen geblieben ist. Die waren weder dort noch da. Und die brachten quasi nie mehr im Leben beide Füße auf den Boden.

> [To be forced to jump off the edge of the world, a world that used to be yours, was known to you, was home. One jumped off into nothingness. And the image this conjured for me was that these people had arrived somewhere physically, but a part of them, of their insides or their soul [. . .] remained suspended in mid-air. They were neither here nor there. And over the course of their lives, they never managed to get both feet on the ground again.][20]

Marianne Hirsch has coined the term 'postmemory' for experiences of a traumatic past that are passed on to the following generation, defining this as a relational nexus, 'a *structure* of inter- and transgenerational return of traumatic knowledge and embodied experience'.[21] Members of postmemorial generations need to find their own stance towards the personal, collective and cultural trauma of their

---

20 'Buchmesse Leipzig: Ulrike Draesner', 14 March 2014 (https://www.3sat.de/kultur/buch/buchmesse-leipzig-ulrike-draesner-100.html).
21 Marianne Hirsch, *The Generation of Postmemory. Writing and Visual Culture After the Holocaust* (New York: Columbia University Press, 2012), p. 6.

predecessors. Even if trauma can only be 'remembered' in mediated ways, i.e. through 'imaginative investment', what emerges seems to constitute memories in their own right. Yet these might come at the price of evacuating one's own life stories, since inherited memories can be overwhelming and dominant.[22] Hirsch's key concept of the transgenerational transference of memories acknowledges and accepts the growing distance to key events of the twentieth century on the one hand, while it prioritizes imaginative investment and creation on the other. In her important study *Haunting Legacies* (2010), Gabriele Schwab similarly calls this delayed urge toward a recovery of memory 'the creative and integrative writing of trauma' and suggests that witnessing and working through traumatic historical events might only be accomplished by generations that follow the one who experienced them.[23] As we will see, the novel echoes the concepts referenced above in numerous ways; the literary utilization of theory, in this case trauma research and biological anthropology, constitutes a characteristic of Draesner's work in general.[24]

Since the postwar analyses by Hannah Arendt, the Frankfurt School, and Alexander and Margarete Mitscherlich appeared, the often incomprehensible coping mechanisms of the war generation have been the focus of countless books, oral history accounts and films, and they are the central conflict for the following generation as well. *Stunde Null* [Zero Hour], *Vergangenheitsbewältigung* [coming to terms with the past] and *1968* have become shorthand terms for the complex intergenerational conflicts that unfolded in postwar Germany. Draesner's novel presents these clashes as defining moments for both the German and the Polish characters of four generations.

The War Generation

The war generation, embodied in the novel by Hannes and Lilly on the German side, and Leszek and Grazyna on the Polish side, develops coping mechanisms that are primarily characterized by two key strategies: silence and avoidance. Individual behaviours range from denial of the new reality and withdrawal into

---

22 Hirsch, *The Generation of Postmemory*, p. 5.
23 Gabriele Schwab, *Haunting Legacies. Violent Histories and Transgenerational Trauma* (New York: Columbia University Press, 2010), p. 25.
24 Cf. Ulrike Draesner, 'Die drei Hälften der Torte. Von der Wissenschaft zum Schreiben', in *Familien – Geschlechter – Macht. Beziehungen im Werk Ulrike Draesners*, ed. by Stephanie Catani and Friedhelm Marx (Göttingen: Wallstein, 2008), pp. 13–22.

a fantasy world for the women through to reticence and retreating into work in Hannes and Leszek respectively. Talking about the experience of war, flight and expulsion is largely impossible even between family members, which leads to an ongoing intergenerational conflict between Hannes and Eustachius in particular. In the new and often hostile environment of West Germany (for which Munich stands in), no-one speaks publicly about the experience of expulsion, rather it is only shared with a clearly defined group of fellow expellees. Hannes and Lilly both perform extraordinary acts of mimicry in their attempts to adapt to their new environment, but both ultimately end up broken and depressed, as Hannes' summary makes amply clear:

> War der Föhn hart, ging die Geschichte so: Wir hatten ein Kind verloren, das Erbe verloren, alle Gräber, ein Stück unserer selbst, die Verbindung zu unserer Vergangenheit, die Verankerung in Besitz und Beständigkeit, das Vertrauen, da sein zu dürfen. Die Landschaft, in der wir lebten, taugte für Urlaub, blieb Kulisse. Die Menschen um uns sprachen die falsche Sprache, hatten die falsche Religion. Wir waren allein, jeder für sich, die Geschichte ließ sich nicht teilen. Ich musste nicht mehr in den Krieg ziehen, aber der Krieg hörte nicht auf.

> [When the warm foehn wind was blowing hard, the story went like this: We had lost a child, lost our inheritance, lost all the graves, a piece of ourselves, the link to our past, the grounding in our possessions and a sense of permanence, faith in our permission to exist. The landscape in which we lived was suitable for vacations, but remained scenery. The people around us spoke the wrong language, had the wrong religion. We were alone, by ourselves, history could not be shared. I would never need to go to war again, but the war had not ended.][25]

Even more traumatic than the experience of losing familiar places and a way of life is the loss of loved ones, embodied in the story of Emil that runs as a thread throughout the entire novel. The lost or dead child or sibling – a narrative staple both in oral history accounts, literary texts and theoretical works[26] – is the cardinal family trauma that underpins the entire novel. On the Polish side, it appears with the character Adam, a ten-year old German boy the family Nienaltowski takes in during the chaotic days in Wrocław after the end of the war. Halka's chapter begins and ends with Adam whom she loves like her own; a child who shows her the way around the destroyed city and helps her provide for the family, before his hand is cut off by Poles as vengeance for crimes committed by Germans during the war. After Adam is swallowed up by the recovering

---

25 Ulrike Draesner, *Sieben Sprünge vom Rand der Welt* (Munich: Luchterhand, 2014), p. 381.
26 Cf. Hanns-Josef Ortheil's autobiographical essay *Das Element des Elephanten* (1994), Hans-Ulrich Treichel's novel *Der Verlorene* (1998) or Gabriele Schwab's autobiographical account in *Haunting Legacies* (2010).

city and Halka's German lover Heinrich disappears west for the first time, she settles into 'eine Art Alltags-Lebensgefühl' [an attitude reminiscent of everyday life] in Wrocław,[27] yet retains a sense of life-long loss.

On the German side, the motif is taken up in the character of Emil, whose place in the text remains vacant, yet whose fate preoccupies all the characters until the very end of the novel. While Hannes is fighting on the frontlines, Eustachius, his mother Lilly and his older brother need to flee the Russian army in January of 1945. Emil, who suffers from a clubfoot and has some mental deficiencies as well, vanishes on their journey west in Sondershausen in Thuringia. The trauma his disappearance causes in all family members remains the enigmatic blind spot and family secret of the novel. While different characters offer various explanations,[28] the reader ultimately remains at a loss as to what really happened to Emil, which mirrors the experience of millions of families during and after the end of the war. According to the German Red Cross, the organization tasked by the German government with the search for missing persons, the fate of 1.3 million people remains unknown to this day, in part because the search excluded people who were looking for family members in the GDR and Eastern Europe.[29] Emil's disappearance becomes not only a symbol of the sustained irreversible loss of home and country, but also testament to his parents' inability to protect a son who was considered 'unwertes Leben' [worthless life] under the Nuremberg Laws. In both Lilly and Hannes, their grief for Emil manifests in a splitting of the homodiegetic narrator into 'Ich' [I] and 'Lilly' and 'Ich' [I] and 'Hannes, der Erinnerer' [Hannes the Rememberer] respectively, a process that Freud characterized in 'The Splitting of the Ego in the Process of Defence' (1938) as the result of inner conflict.[30]

The loss of Emil also appears as a form of penance the parents have to serve for their outward loyalty to the Nazi regime. Even though they attempt to comply with all regulations primarily to protect Emil, their *Mitläufertum* [status as fellow-travellers] also brings immediate economic benefits for their bakery.

---

27 Draesner, *Siebe Sprünge*, p. 479.

28 While Lilly claims to a distrustful Hannes that Emil died 'ein[en] rasch[en] Tod' [a quick death] of pneumonia (*Sieben Sprünge*, p. 45), she also reveals that she simply does not remember what happened due to being very sick with a high fever (p. 225). She had to rely on Stach's testimony.

29 Cf. https://www.drk-suchdienst.de/de/angebote/zweiter-weltkrieg/schwerpunkte/verschollene-des-zweiten-weltkriegs.

30 Nicole Sütterlin offers a detailed reading of this split narrator and illustrates the narrative techniques by which fragmented memories are integrated into the Lilly chapter in 'Trauma-Poetik: Ulrike Draesner's *Sieben Sprünge vom Rand der Welt* und die Körperpoetik der 1990er Jahre', *Gegenwartsliteratur: A German Studies Yearbook*, 15 (2016), 167–190 (176–178).

Especially for Hannes, his failure to protect his beloved son is linked closely to his shame of having been taking in if not by Nazi ideology, then at least by his 'Sehnsucht nach der irren Schönheit des Lebens im Krieg' [yearning for the bizarre beauty of life during war time], against his better judgment.[31] The war generation's trauma taints their remaining lives as refugees in the West. While they do not live in denial about the guilt they have amassed by participating in the war, they nevertheless feel that the losses they sustained are too high a price to pay.

Children of the War

The notion of transgenerational trauma has been widely discussed in Germany since the turn of the millennium. While qualitative research studies, especially in the fields of psychology, history and literary theory,[32] produced differentiated findings, the notion was promoted primarily through popular 'Sachbücher' [nonfiction books], particularly the work of journalist Sabine Bode.[33] All these publications have spurred the public discussion of transgenerational trauma and led to an acceptance of the differentiation into 'Kriegskinder' [children of the war], i.e. those born between approximately 1930 and 1945 who experienced National Socialism and the Second World War as children and young adults, and 'Kriegsenkel' [grandchildren of the war], i.e. those born between 1960 and 1975 as the children of the Kriegskinder, as well as their respective children who are considered 'Kriegsenkel' as well.

The story of Eustachius Grolmann is typical of many in the first postmemorial generation. Born in 1931 in Oels near Breslau, Eustachius, nicknamed 'Stach', is socialized into the Third Reich via the Hitler Youth and becomes an enthusiastic supporter of its ideology, 'aufgewachsen in einem ununterbrochenen Propagandafackelmarsch, manipuliert, eingeseift, auf Vaterland, Opfer,

---

31 Draesner, *Sieben Sprünge*, p. 392.
32 See the project 'Kriegskindheit' [Childhood at War] at Ludwig Maximilians University in Munich, which produced studies such as Christine Müller's *Kriegskinder – Wie haben sie ihre Kindheit verarbeitet? Kindheitsentwicklung im Nationalsozialismus, im Zweiten Weltkrieg und in der Nachkriegszeit* (Dissertation, LMU Munich, 2013); Angela Moré, 'Die unbewusste Weitergabe von Traumata und Schuldverstrickungen an nachfolgende Generationen', *Journal für Psychologie*, 21.2 (2013) (https://www.journal-fuer-psychologie.de/index.php/jfp/article/view/268/310#fn_N100BB).
33 Sabine Bode, *Die vergessene Generation. Die Kriegskinder brechen ihr Schweigen* (Stuttgart: Klett-Cotta, 2004) and *Kriegsenkel: Die Erben der vergessenen Generation* (Stuttgart: Klett-Cotta, 2009).

Kampf gedrillt, in eine enge Blut- und Rassewelt gesperrt' (p. 36) [having grown up in an unending propaganda march, manipulated, duped, indoctrinated into fatherland, sacrifice, battle, locked into a narrow world of blood and race].[34] Stach's postwar choice of profession as an ethologist working on animal behaviour is a direct response to his indoctrination, his 'déformation Nazi' (p. 139) as he calls it in conversation. More importantly, however, it is also a response to having grown up with a disabled brother. The text establishes the link via reference to Emil's insulting nickname 'Aff' [ape],[35] allowing the reader to draw connections between him and the apes on which the adult Eustachius later conducts his research.

An even more troubling association is the historically specific connection between disabled people and eugenic practices in the Third Reich that moved from testing on primates in the early twentieth century to experimenting on human beings like Emil.[36] While his parents manage to keep him safe from hospitalization and imminent murder during 'Aktion T4', the systematic killing of more than seventy thousand disabled people by the Nazi regime in the years 1940–45, Emil cannot escape a forced sterilization, which becomes the stipulation for allowing him to remain at home. Eustachius's postwar realization that people can be manipulated and brainwashed by political ideologues into killing their own species and committing unspeakable crimes leads to a deep-seated 'Menschenfurcht' (p. 379) [fear of human beings] that motivates him to work with primates rather than humans.

Throughout the novel various family members characterize Stach as both a luminary in his field and a workaholic. He is a distanced father to his two children, before and after his divorce from their mother Ines. Especially his relationship to his grown daughter Simone is complex, grounded in shared professional interests, yet emotionally fraught. Stach lacks the ability to relate to Simone on a personal level or to acknowledge that she might have problems of her own, 'Hatte ich Kummer, sagte er: "Wie gut es dir geht"' (p. 16) [When I was unhappy, he would say, 'You've got it so good']. The pain of the interlocutor can never quite match the psychological trauma of having been expelled from both ideology and homeland, leading the Kriegsenkel generation to the conclusion that their own problems ultimately have little validity and deserve no attention.

---

34 Draesner confirmed in conversation that the character of Eustachius is modelled on her father Hubertus Draesner and based on his biography and experiences.

35 'wie sollte ich mich fühlen / der Aff'/ hatte man uns auf der Straße hinterhergerufen, ihr / fürchtetet euch' [how was I supposed to feel / the ape / they called after us in the street, you / were afraid] (*Sieben Sprünge*, p. 553).

36 http://blogs.scientificamerican.com/primate-diaries/stalins-ape-man-superwarriors/.

Eustachius's coping strategy to come to terms with the trauma of flight and expulsion, as well as the violent act of killing the family dog, who could not be taken along, is to lock away his grief and suffering and become mute about it, to the point where even as children, his daughters cannot reach him: 'Zu spüren war es lange gewesen, ein dumpfes, unausgesprochenes Leiden, Vater schloss etwas in sich ein, hatte es fortgekapselt, tief und unerreichbar' (p. 57) [We had sensed it for a long time, a muted, unexpressed suffering, father shut something away in himself, he had encapsulated it, deeply and inaccessibly]. The psychoanalytic concept of the crypt, as developed by psychoanalysts Nicolaus Abraham and Maria Torok, entails the inability to grieve for a beloved person due to an inner conflict, instead hiding away and conserving the lost object in a hidden corner of the psyche, an intrapsychic crypt.[37] In reference to this idea Nicole Sütterlin has shown convincingly that Stach can be read as a 'Kryptenträger' [crypt carrier] who has encapsulated his grief for Emil in his subconscious, but passed on the silence emanating from the crypt intergenerationally to his daughter Simone.[38] Eustachius's outward coping strategy, however, is to favour discipline and a protestant work ethic that conceal any psychological impairment, paired with an 'auffällige Gefühlsstarre' [notable emotional numbness], i.e. the emotional detachment and inability to relate to others that the Mitscherlichs had seen at work in the psychosocial organism of postwar Germany.[39]

Yet in old age, the internalized memories of the flight from Silesia come back to haunt Stach. They manifest as depression and an inability to continue to repress the fate of his brother. Throughout his career, he had transferred the love he could never openly show his family to his research charges. In the bond between humans and primates, he experiences moments of happiness, giving credence to the realization that he loves his animals more than his family (p. 51). Long after his retirement he illegally raises two Bonobos in his house. In order to investigate the link between human and animal aggression Stach conducts behavioural experiments on them and himself. While he is trying to capture the escaped young Vlek in a nearby park, the smell of a mandarin triggers a memory of his brother 'mit dem schaukelnden, fast äffischen Gang' (pp. 168–9) [with his swaying, almost ape-like gait] and their last conversation. The Proustian experience eventually leads Stach to confess to his granddaughter Esther that he shot his brother when Emil wanted to join the much-admired SS: 'Großvater sagte:

---

37 Nicolas Abraham and Maria Torok, *Kryptonymie. Das Verbarium des Wolfsmanns* (Basel and Weil a.R.: Engeler, 2008).
38 Sütterlin, 'Trauma-Poetik', pp. 180–181.
39 Alexander and Margarete Mitscherlich, *Die Unfähigkeit zu trauern. Grundlagen kollektiven Verhaltens* (Munich: Piper, 2004), p. 38.

"Mit dem Zurückweichen und Verstummen aller vordringlichen Geräusche tritt das Untergegangene hervor und gerät vor die inneren Sinnesorgane. Ich habe meinen Bruder getötet. Damals, im kältesten Winter. Auf der Flucht [. . .] Ich erschoß ihn'" [Grandfather said, 'When urgent sounds recede and become muted, sunken things surface and come before the inner sensory organs. I killed my brother. Back then, during the coldest winter. During the flight [. . .] I shot him'].[40] Given Stach's ambivalent love-hate relationship with Emil, this is not entirely unlikely and is attested to by his fearful behaviour around guns later in life. Whether or not he killed him, Eustachius suffers from survivor's guilt that he cannot let go of – similar to the narrator in Hans-Ulrich Treichel's 1998 novel *Der Verlorene* [*Lost*, 2000]. Stach continues to think of Emil right up until his death. He dies reliving the one formative memory with which the novel also begins.

Grandchildren of the War

While the trauma of the postwar generation, as embodied in Eustachius, remains hidden and unprocessed, primarily manifesting in emotional detachment from their own family members and a reactivation of trauma in old age that results in depression, the so-called 'Kriegsenkel' [grandchildren of the war] in the novel have grown up with the understanding that other people's memories somehow have come to dominate their lives. This is in line with extensive trauma research, which shows that experiences such as war, or sexual or physical abuse leave wounds that can subconsciously be passed on to the next generation and lead to 'transgenerational haunting', a term coined by Lisa Appignanesi in her 1999 memoir *Losing the Dead*. The realization that the Kriegsenkel might be afflicted by past events just as their parents were – plagued by emotional turmoil, difficulties in building lasting relationships and addictive behaviours – has led both to a new social movement among the Kriegsenkel in Germany as well as scientific studies in the last few years.[41]

---

40 Ibid., p. 501. That Emil was conscripted by a member of the SS known to the family in the last, chaotic days of the *Volkssturm* [People's Storm; a militia set up by the Nazi Party] seems at least a possibility and is hinted at in Emil's chapter (*Sieben Sprünge*, p. 551).
41 Cf. www.kriegsenkel.de and the association *Kriegsenkel e.V.*, as well as the first academic conference about the topic in 2012, which led to the publication *Die Kinder der Kriegskinder und die späten Folgen des NS-Terrors*, ed. Heike Knoch et al. (Heidelberg: Mattes Verlag, 2012). See also *Vererbte Wunden. Transgenerationale Weitergabe traumatischer Erfahrungen*, ed. by Marianne Rauwald (Weinheim: Beltz, 2013).

In the novel it falls to Simone on the German side and Boris on the Polish side to take on the haunting legacy of their families' past and understand the psychological shortcomings of their emotionally distant parents and grandparents: 'sie übernahm die Geschichte, es musste jemanden geben, der das tat, in jeder Familie gab es jemanden, seit Eustachius ging es bei uns auf den Jüngsten, somit von ihm auf sie' (p. 384) [she took over the story; there had to be someone who did this, in every family there was someone; since Eustachius this fell to the youngest in ours, consequently it went from him to her]. Simone and Boris both grow up investigating the various family members' biographies in order to comprehend how their own paths are invariably shaped by their close relations' lives and choices. Simone characterizes this process as dreaming the nightmares of other people, 'eigenes Leben, umschlossen von Kopiertem' (p. 19) [my own life, enclosed by copies].

Working through the family legacy is less a conscious choice than an involuntary task and emotional burden. While both characters have developed different coping strategies, their choice of professions stands out as an obvious attempt to comprehend their parents. Simone has followed in Eustachius's footsteps as a primate researcher, and her work directly builds upon her father's fundamental research. Like him, she is interested in the quantitative differences between humans and apes and directs a research institute in succession of her father's university post. She also repeats patterns established by her father, such as privileging her work over her family, despite having resented his prolonged absences and inaccessibility as a child.

Simone's Polish counterpart Boris Nienalt, for whom she eventually leaves her husband, is the author of books such as *Geteiltes Gedächtnis* [*Divided Memory*] and a renowned psychologist throughout Germany and Eastern Europe. His primary research focus is on the German/Polish Kriegskinder generation born between 1920 and 1936. It has become his life project to assist them in processing their experiences and emotions about having grown up during the war, something which is directly linked to his own family history as the bilingual son of the Polish expellee Halka and German soldier 'Heinrich ohne Land' [Heinrich without Country]. Yet despite Boris's efforts to work through his complicated family history by lending therapeutic help to others, his hybrid, trans national identity still leaves him conflicted, unanchored and drained; when he makes Simone's acquaintance, he shows clear signs of alcohol dependency. One reason he is drawn to Simone is his realization that they share similar experiences and both need to process an inherited trauma, 'dass du das Gefühl kennst, in einer gespaltenen Welt zu leben, selbst falsch zu sein, vielleicht sogar schuld an allem' (p. 149) [that you are familiar with the feeling of living in a split world, of being somehow wrong, of maybe even being responsible for everything]. Sharing the task of *containing* the horrific experiences and *holding* their parents – both concepts of support advanced in psychoanalysis – allows Simone and Boris to recognize their similarities and bridge the specific experience of their German and Polish families; their relationship thus illustrates a dialogue between narratives of cultural memory.[42] In realizing that they are deeply marked by transgenerational haunting and finding new love in the process, Simone is able to accept Eustachius's neglect of her own needs as well as his flighty behaviour in old age and experiences a rapprochement with him. For Boris, Eustachius becomes a stand-in for the father figure he had been missing all his life. The couple's relationship thus becomes a metaphor for overcoming the boundaries erected by the troubled history shared by Germany and Poland, which has fundamentally structured the relationship between the two countries and is, maybe like no other in Europe, shaped by often negative images of the 'Other' that were preserved in the Cold War and continue to have a bearing on the present.[43]

Nevertheless, a generational conflict between the Kriegskinder and Kriegsenkel of the postwar generation remains, and the novel suggests that ultimately it cannot be overcome. The greater the rejection of memory and the larger the gaps in it, the more pressing the desire becomes to fill in the gaps after the fact, especially as the aging process progresses. Yet trauma does not only implode memories, it also severs communication between generations, as Aleida Assmann remarks.[44]

Interestingly, in the novel the opposite is true for the millennial generation of Kriegsenkel, a cohort represented by Simone's daughter Esther and Boris' daughter Jennifer. Whereas Simone and Boris and their relationship address primarily the similarities of the German-Polish experience, the characters of Esther and Jennifer stand for a postmemorial generation that is able to actualize the ideals of a united Europe. Both born in the 1990s, they are entirely removed from the experience of war and any existing trauma, but nevertheless still

---

42 Sofie Friederike Mevissen, 'Shared Memory: Transgenerational Transmission and Transcultural Junctions in Ulrike Draesner's *Sieben Sprünge vom Rand der Welt*', *Journal of Languages, Texts, and Society*, 3 (Spring 2019), 110–127 (122).
43 Oliver Schmidtke, 'Re-modelling the Boundaries in the New Europe. Historical Memories and Contemporary Identities', in *Collective Memory and European Identity. The Effects of Integration and Enlargement*, ed. by Klaus Eder and Willfried Spohn (Farnham: Ashgate, 2005), pp. 69–86 (p. 71).
44 Aleida Assmann, *Das Unbehagen an der Erinnerungskultur* (Munich: C.H. Beck, 2013), p. 42. Draesner has also confirmed in conversation that the events at the centre of the novel were not openly discussed in her own family, which made it all the more urgent for her to imagine and narrate them.

influenced by it in their own lives. Both gain access to the past via postmemories, that is, stories told by their grandparents and parents.

The novel shows a striking parallelism in the familial relationships of Esther and Jennifer, which further reinforces the chiastic arrangement of the German and Polish characters. In both cases, the bonds with their parents are frayed due to divorce and the fact that their respective home base 'hatte sich aufgelöst' (pp. 402, 490) [had dissolved]. Jennifer's former strong attachment to Boris turns into distance when she senses that she has to compete with Simone and Eustachius for her father's attention. Esther's relationship to her mother has always been emotionally distant, partly due to Simone's demanding work schedule and partly due to the strain of having to care for her increasingly frail grandfather largely by herself. The novel suggests here that behaviour patterns inherited by the Kriegskinder are passed on transgenerationally, albeit in mitigated ways.

Jennifer's and Esther's relationships to Halka and Eustachius, on the other hand, are portrayed as unreservedly positive. Growing up, the grandparents provide warmth, orientation and a sense of security that might otherwise have been missing from the girls' lives. Esther in particular, who is much more fleshed out as a character than Jennifer, represents an important perspective on Eustachius; in fact, she is the final voice in the book before Emil's letter and concludes it by recounting her grandfather's death. The chapter's underlying narrative thread is again the family secret, namely Eustachius's claim to have killed his brother, and Esther's attempt to gauge whether or not this murder really occurred. She clearly has an emotional investment in her grandfather's memory, but it does not engender a fundamental questioning of her love or sympathy for him. Since she never experienced anything but unconditional affection and support – different from the standoffishness he offered her mother – Esther has not been affected by postsecondary trauma and is thus able to approach the question from an interested, yet largely neutral standpoint. Even if Esther is realistic about her grandfather's capability of committing such an act, it would not change her positive view of him.

In the qualitative study *Opa war kein Nazi* (2002) [*Grandpa wasn't a Nazi*, 2005], the authors point out that within a family context, loyalties might prevent imagining heinous acts committed by a loved one, which is especially the case for grandparents and grandchildren.[45] The novel suggests that this important qualitative difference characterizes the relationship between the two generations

---

45 Harald Welzer, Sabine Moller and Karoline Tschuggnall, '*Opa war kein Nazi*'. *Nationalsozialismus und Holocaust im Familiengedächtnis*, 5th edn (Frankfurt a. M.: Fischer, 2005), p. 52.

in general. It also points to an underlying belief set out in the novel that is crucially important: the only viable way to construct a shared memory for the postmemorial generations is through the principle of love and compassion for the Other, if one understands love as an ethical responsibility of the kind that Emmanuel Levinas developed in *Totality and Infinity* (1961). Levinas states that by opening a space for the Other, man can become free of his past and guilt, as well as the postmemories of others. Nicole Sütterlin has suggested in this context that all nine narratives are an appeal to a counterpart – and, I would add, the reader – to listen empathically, creating what she calls a 'Zeugengemeinschaft' [witness community] that shares in the ethical work that war trauma and memory have imposed on the nation.[46]

Esther and Jennifer stand for the perspective of young people in contemporary Europe, widely travelled, conversant in various languages, and open to cultural diversity. Their globalized existence is grounded and bolstered by a close-knit group of both ethnic and non-ethnic German friends; it is also problematized in the thematization of youth culture and traditional as well as social media. Examples are rendered in Jennifer's escapist use of video games and the wide network of her pan-European Facebook contacts as well as Esther's B.A. dissertation, which she conducts with her best friend Pawani. They construct an 'Antimigrations-Blog' (p. 494) [an anti-migration blog] that seeks to collect stories of people who deny their own life stories of movement, immigration or relocation. Since migration has shaped both Esther's and Pawani's personal lives and is one of today's defining experiences, their blog is a personal attempt both to establish a counter-narrative to their families' histories and to construct a digital repository reflecting the plurality of the human experience of migration in the twentieth and twenty-first century. With these characters of the millennial Enkelgeneration [generation of grandchildren], the narrative perspective takes contemporary realities as a departure point for exploring historical and personal events and illustrates how they shape the imagined and real geographies of Europe.[47]

In addition to the specific historical perspectives expressed through the characters, a professionally built website extends the literary text further into the transnational realm. On www.der-siebte-sprung.de, Draesner gives testimony about her motivation for the project and documents both her material sources and the research process she underwent. The site thus serves as an important paratext, adding photographs, poetological essays, translations of select material into Polish, and a 'Lexikon der reisenden Wörter' [dictionary of travelling words].

---

46 Sütterlin, 'Trauma-Poetik', p. 180.
47 Eigler, *Heimat, Space, Narrative*, p. 155. This constellation is similar to the one in Sabrina Janesch's 2010 novel *Katzenberge*.

This digital archive thus actualizes the text further for the reader. It assembles and curates both the heterogeneous pasts and memories of Germans and Poles while at the same time illustrating via different media the shared European memory these experiences have created. Even in the 'post-digital age' this two-pronged approach is still unusual; it allows us to understand the intellectual trajectory of both novel and website as pedagogical, taking memory building and historical education to the next level.[48]

Apart from being an extensive interpretation of transgenerational trauma, *Sieben Sprünge vom Rand der Welt* is also a commentary on the European project. It makes visible a *Kulturraum* [cultural space] that, while destroyed, has left traces in human bodies and environments. It exposes the dividing lines and binary thinking contained in the historical and present categories of 'East' and 'West'. Absolving the notion of identity from its formulaic abstractness, *Sieben Sprünge* reveals interconnections in the European cultural tradition that might assist and propel us in our current state where many migrate for work or love or undergo existential migration. In its approach to working through European trauma via its multigenerational and multifaceted characters, the novel formulates a literary project for regenerating Europe.

48 The project has been supported by Europäische Ost-West-Akademie e.V. für Kultur und Medien, a non-profit organization that funds interdisciplinary and cross-national projects in arts and cultures, with the goal to build knowledge and bridges between Eastern and Western Europe (https://eowa.de).

Almut Suerbaum

Voices from the Past? Poetic Presence of Medieval References

Writing from the margins, as the only non-modernist in this collection on an established contemporary poet, is a challenge – not least because it reveals one of the tacit assumptions of scholarly traditions. Medieval scholarship embraced Barthes and the 'death of the author' early and enthusiastically, because his theory offered a way out of a methodological dilemma: many medieval texts are anonymous, and even where the name of an author has been transmitted, we mostly have to rely on statements from within the texts. Moreover, there is an awareness that such statements may often be conscious self-stylizations which we cannot check against independent external evidence.[1] Barthes there-fore was a way of turning a lack into an asset, and as a result, the focus of re-cent medieval scholarship has been on texts, or more specifically, textuality. Its fluidity entails that texts change in transmission and may be shaped by readers and scribes more than by a single author.[2] What had been a defect in editorial endeavour inspired by classical philology could suddenly be turned into a posi-tive – the insight that texts are shaped by readers as much as their authors, that textual culture, or reading and writing, are reciprocal if not always sym-metrical activities, often, especially in the case of medieval religious writing, undercutting neat hierarchies between the poet and the reader.[3]

Discussing qualities of poetic voice in Ulrike Draesner's oeuvre thus poses a two-fold challenge: looking at contemporary writing from the perspective of a different discipline, but also assessing an author who is herself an accom-plished medievalist and whose first prize-winning book publication was a

---

1 Alastair Minnis, *Medieval Theories of Authorship. Scholastic Literary Attitudes in the Later Middle Ages*, 2nd edn (Aldershot: Gower Books, 1988).
2 See Almut Suerbaum, '*Es kommt ein Schiff, geladen*. Mouvance in mystischen Liedern aus Straßburg', in *Schreiben und Lesen in der Stadt. Literaturbetrieb im spätmittelalterlichen Straß-burg*, ed. by Stephen Mossman, Felix Heinzer and Nigel Palmer (Berlin: de Gruyter, 2012), pp. 99–116.
3 Almut Suerbaum, 'Tauler reception in religious lyric. The (pseudo)-Tauler cantilenae', *Ons Geestelijk Erf*, 84 (2013), 41–54.

Note: I am grateful to Ulrike Draesner for allowing me to see the manuscript of her *Nibelungen* project as it progressed, and for lively discussions.

https://doi.org/10.1515/9783110495942-003

monograph on narrative coherence in Wolfram.[4] Yet that perhaps is precisely the kind of border-crossing which Draesner herself so eloquently advocates. For her, turning away from academic medievalism has never, it seems, been a rejection of medieval literature. From early on there have been occasional allusions to medieval literature in her poetry, especially to Gottfried's *Tristan* (one could comment on the significance of names – but that is another story); the essay collection *Heimliche Helden* opens with reflections on the *Nibelungenlied*, and her website gives a first glimpse of one of her recent projects – a poetic reworking of the *Nibelungenlied* around an early twentieth-century cycle of illustrations by Otto Czeschka. This appeared in autumn 2016; and it was a great privilege to see a little of the process of composition at first hand during Draesner's stay in Oxford.[5] Having an opportunity to discuss plans, intentions, revisions with the author, seeing a text take shape and change, has been excitingly different from the way in which medievalists usually work. Yet being allowed to watch a little of this process has also highlighted to me that there are similarities – not between the poet of the *Nibelungenlied* and the modern poet Ulrike Draesner, but rather between the poetic voice of the early thirteenth century and the twenty-first-century response or resonance.

What is Draesner's subject matter? We know next to nothing about the poet of the *Nibelungenlied* beyond a plausible hypothesis that there was such a poet, and that he may have been associated with Passau – it is likely, from internal as well as external evidence, that Wolfger of Erla, Bishop of Passau and later patron of Aquileia, commissioned the work.[6] One hypothesis is that the commission was part of a calculated attempt to raise donations for a major building project, or to raise the profile of the diocese generally by highlighting its illustrious past. This suggests an intriguing structural parallel, because part of the interest of Ulrike Draesner's *Nibelungen* project lies in the way in which it navigates similar constraints: the publisher's commission, the need to interact with the pre-existing illustrations by Carl Otto Czeschka, the response to a well-known if not well-read literary source. As in the medieval *Nibelungenlied*, these

---

4 Ulrike Draesner, *Wege durch erzählte Welten. Intertextuelle Verweise als Mittel der Bedeutungskonstitution in Wolframs 'Parzival'* (Frankfurt a. M.: Peter Lang, 1993).
5 Ulrike Draesner, *Heimliche Helden* (Munich: Luchterhand, 2012); Ulrike Draesner, *Nibelungen. Heimsuchung* (Stuttgart: Reclam, 2016), hereafter cited in the text.
6 *Das Nibelungenlied und Die Klage. Nach der Handschrift 857 der Stiftsbibliothek St. Gallen*, ed. and trans. by Joachim Heinzle (Frankfurt a. M.: Deutscher Klassiker Verlag, 2015), pp. 998–1004. English translations are my own; cf. *Das Nibelungenlied. The Lay of the Nibelungs*, trans. by Cyril Edwards (Oxford: OUP, 2010), p. 1007.

constraints are not, it seems, limitations, but rather a creative challenge which allows an instantly recognizable poetic voice to emerge.

Aspects of this poetic voice are what this contribution sets out to explore – not, as in other chapters of this volume, predominantly in relation to Ulrike Draesner's oeuvre, but in its interaction with the medieval text and its specific voice, though the resonances with many aspects of the rest of her work are striking. In musical terms, her *Nibelungen* project is a three-part invention, creating polyphonic tensions and resolutions between the medieval narrative, the Art Nouveau reading of this narrative in the image sequence, and the modern work. The following chapter will concentrate on the interplay between the medieval and the modern text; nevertheless, it will touch on aspects of the visual, but only in so far as they relate to 'textualized' images. Ulrike Draesner's *Nibelungen* project is a creative adaptation, or, as I would like to call it, a re-voicing, and, like much of her work, it is both musical and strongly visual.[7] This process of re-voicing can be defined by a set of five coordinates, which the following essay will explore.

Epic and Lyric

One of the characteristics of Ulrike Draesner's work is the way in which it challenges traditional distinctions between fiction and non-fiction, but also between narrative and lyric voice.[8] Her *Nibelungen* project is no exception in this sense, in that it adapts the medieval narrative as shaped through Czeschka's picture cycle, and does so by replacing or erasing the prose paraphrase included in the early twentieth-century edition with a series of lyric monologues by the four main figures, Kriemhilt, Sîvrit, Brünhilt, Hagen.[9] These monologues are interspersed by a chorus of crows (burgkrähen) whose songs combine Greek tragedy with the language of computer games, and are rounded off by a prose coda which reflects and comments on the different ways of reading the *Nibelungenlied* – as a narrative

---

7 On the significance of voicing rather than voice in lyric, see Jonathan Culler, *A Theory of the Lyric* (Cambridge, MA: Harvard University Press, 2015), p. 35.

8 Karen Leeder, '"Eine Grammatik der Liebe". Ulrike Draesners Lyrik', in *Familien – Geschlechter – Macht. Beziehungen im Werk Ulrike Draesners*, ed. by Stephanie Catani and Friedhelm Marx (Göttingen: Wallstein, 2008), pp. 37–60; Lyn Marven, 'Ulrike Draesner, '*Mitgift*: On Bodies and Beauty', in *Emerging German-Language Novelists of the Twenty-First Century*, ed. by Lyn Marven and Stuart Taberner (Rochester: Camden House, 2011), pp. 17–31.

9 Names for figures from the *Nibelungenlied* differ widely; this paper will use the forms preferred by Draesner, though with capital letters.

of intrigues, as a love story, political thriller, a narrative about a treasure, about water, a shocker about child murder, an erotic farce of thwarted male sexuality (the Nagelroman), or as a story of migration (Migrationsroman). The final section of this prose commentary is entitled 'Immer wieder vergesse ich' (p. 105) ['I keep forgetting']. It refers to the discontinuities in the narration and their effect on the modern reader, using the term 'springen', which echoes the titles of Draesner's 2015 *Sieben Sprünge* project. The word may mean 'to leap', but also carries connotations of 'rupture' and can be read as a response to the inherent 'otherness' of a medieval narrative which mostly shows actions but not causal motivation, the movement 'by leaps and bounds' rather than orderly psychological development, but also an evocation of the fragility and the ruptures.[10]

Draesner's comments in *Heimliche Helden*, but also in her prose commentary on the *Nibelungenlied*, highlight the essential difference between medieval culture and its sense of collective identity and narration from the outside, and modern, psychological exploration of how it feels to say 'I'.[11] Yet its postmodern rejection of stable, rigid identities, and its interest in fluid boundaries, meets with its medieval subject matter in very interesting ways. Draesner's oscillation between poetry and prose turns into a peculiarly apt way of capturing something of the poetic greatness, but also the difficulty, of the *Nibelungenlied*. It is commonly pigeonholed in literary histories as 'heroic epic'. My argument will return to the concern with heroes and heroism in the next section; here, I would like to focus on the concept of epic. The *Nibelungenlied* is undoubtedly epic in scale, since it tells the story of the wholesale destruction of a powerful empire, that of the Burgundians who are also referred to as the Nibelungs. It is also apocalyptic, culminating in an image of destruction which so radically confounds any hope of solution or salvation that medieval Christian readers found its bleakness unpalatable and joined it with a poem of elegiac lament, the so-called *Klage* [*Lament*].[12] From its rediscovery in the eighteenth century, the *Nibelungenlied* has often been claimed as Germany's answer to Virgil, giving Germany a much-desired national epos. That is not, of course, entirely without foundation – it is clear that the poet of the *Nibelungenlied* knew Heinrich von Veldeke's adaptation of Virgil (c. 1175), and the intellectual climate of the Passau episcopal court means it is at least not implausible to assume familiarity

---

10 Medieval scholarship refers to the notable breaks in narrative coherence within the *Nibelungenlied*, notably the disrupted chronologies and the lack of causal motivation; cf. Jan-Dirk Müller, *Rules for the End-Game. The World of the Nibelungenlied*, trans. by William T. Whobrey (Baltimore: The Johns Hopkins University Press, 2007), esp. pp. 426–445.

11 Draesner, *Heimliche Helden*, pp. 49–83.

12 Heinzle, *Nibelungenlied und Klage*, pp. 997–998.

with Virgil as well.[13] Like Virgil, it tells the story of an entire civilization; unlike Virgil, however, it does so in a mode which is the closest the Christian Middle Ages get to tragedy proper. Like most medieval epic narratives, the *Nibelungenlied* is anonymous, foregrounding collective memory. This is sometimes seen as the result of medieval orality, a sort of primitive feature of a pre-literate, pre-individual society. That is a widespread, but perhaps also a slightly misleading picture: Virgil's *Aeneid* is the most striking example of a work which preserves epic anonymity, yet is the product of an individual poet. It may be more appropriate to see the *Nibelungenlied* as a prominent example of fictional orality – the deliberate, conscious evocation of an oral voice within a medium that is itself firmly rooted within a book culture of written sources, Latinate devices of structuring book-learning as well as narrative, and a self-awareness of the act of narration.[14] The *Nibelungenlied* is fascinating as a literary work precisely because it so patently struggles with the task of adapting from one culture into another, and it marks that struggle by means of its mixed aesthetic – epic in scale, yet often lyric in tone. In this sense, Draesner's transposition into lyric monologues highlights the differences in form, yet also the affinities.

Visuality and Voice

The second aspect of the *Nibelungenlied* to which Draesner's form, i.e. a series of monologues framed by prose commentary, responds is the choice of poetic language. Unlike other twelfth-century narratives, the *Nibelungenlied* uses the long lines familiar from Germanic staved poetry, evoking the by then old-fashioned heroic subject matter, yet framing these lines into rhymed strophes almost certainly designed for sung rather than recited performance. This use of strophic form for extended narrative is both innovative, inspiring a whole range of experiments by later authors, and backward-looking, since the strophic form is that of the courtly love lyric of a generation before the *Nibelungenlied*, from the 1160s and 1170s.[15] Its characteristic is an overlong fourth line, emphasizing metrically the closure of the strophic form and often used for the ominous instances of foreshadowing in which the narrator anticipates the catastrophic ending. This is evident from the beginning; in the less well-known but

---

13 Ibid., pp. 1007–1013.
14 Dennis Green, 'Fictive Orality. A Restriction on the use of the Concept', in *Blütezeit. Festschrift für L. Peter Johnson zum 70. Geburtstag*, ed. by Mark Chinca, Joachim Heinzle and Christopher Young (Tübingen: Niemeyer, 2000), pp. 161–174.
15 Heinzle, *Nibelungenlied und Klage*, pp. 1016–1021.

perhaps older version of the *Nibelungenlied* in manuscript B, the song opens with a strophe which illustrates the use of such foreshadowing in the final line:

> Ez wuohs in Burgonden ein vil edel magedîn,
> daz in allen landen niht schoeners mohte sîn,
> Kriemhilt geheizen, si wart ein schoene wîp.
> das umbe muosen degene vil verliesen den lîp. (*NL* 1, 1–4)

> [A noble young lady grew up in Burgundy. No one anywhere could be more beautiful than she. Kriemhilt was her name. She was a beautiful woman. Many fighters would lose their life for her sake.]

The strophe illustrates the complexity of a seemingly simple narrative: it locates the action in the past, more specifically, the realm of the Burgundians; it introduces the fairytale beautiful princess who will shortly meet her prince and fall in love, yet simultaneously undercuts the 'once upon a time' of the timeless fairytale past by culture-specific vocabulary – the princess is a medieval aristocratic lady who is both noble ('edel') and beautiful ('schoen'), terms which in the neo-Platonic conception of medieval aesthetic serve as a reminder that there is a strong link between ethics and aesthetics: what we might see as surface or external elements is, in this model, intrinsically linked to inner values. In a sudden turn away from such ideals, the final line undercuts any expectation of a happy ending: love in this story leads to catastrophe. At the same time, the final line subtly positions the narrator, despite the fact that he does not overtly step outside the narrated world: he, like his readers, knows and articulates that Kriemhilt is also Helen, 'the face which launched a thousand ships'. Draesner's text equally gives the first words to Kriemhilt.

> fiederung dunkler fluff – tüpfel
> sehe schuss siena gebrannt um flügel
> karmin karneol spüre herzschlag siena
> flirres gespan klöppel der schwinge
> luftwärts gebannt unter eines körpers
> flitsch (p. 5)

> [plumage dark fluff – spots / see a shot of burnt sienna around wings / carmine carnelian feel heartbeat sienna / jittering shard, clapper of pinion-tongue / forced airwards under a body's / swish]

On one level, this is a response to Czeschka's image (Fig. 1), which shows Kriemhilt reclining on her Art Nouveau-style decorated couch under an embroidered cover. Yet this opening is also a condensing of poetic strategies on a number of levels. Like the *Nibelungenlied*, the opening lines offer more than a representation of the female protagonist in creating a *mise en abyme*, because in dreaming of a falcon

Fig. 1: Kriemhild on a couch, by Otto Czeschka in Ulrike Draesner, *Nibelungen. Heimsuchung* (Stuttgart: Reclam, 2016) © Reclam Verlag.

torn to pieces by two eagles, Kriemhilt in the *Nibelungenlied* anticipates her own story – Sîvrit her lover represented as the falcon, killed by Gunther and Hagen. When the medieval text refers to textiles, this is often interpreted within the cultural context of visual representation, where costly fabrics signal aristocratic status. In contrast, the textile metaphors in Draesner's poem introduce a complex trail of references to the fabric of the story: Hagen persuades Kriemhilt to mark the one spot where Sîvrit's skin, bathed in dragon's blood, had remained vulnerable, by a cross stitched onto his cloak, and therefore knows where to aim his spear. At the same time, Draesner evokes the oldest literary metaphor of all, the making of a text, though in this case, the fabric is not woven, but embroidered, stitch by painful stitch.[16] What we hear in Draesner's opening monologue is a woman struggling to articulate what 'I' might mean, and as a result, the voice of her Kriemhilt also evokes echoes of a long poetic tradition in which raising such questions in a female voice has particular poignancy:

---

16 Draesner's original here plays with the ambiguity of the noun 'Stich', which refers to the embroidery stitch, but can also mean 'a stab with a knife or sharp instrument'.

die frauen sitzen auf bildern
und träumen das nichts (p. 12)

[the women brood on images / dream-weaving nothingness].

Heroes and Heroines

Draesner's poetic condensing of the epic narrative into a quartet of voices responds to a narrative principle of the *Nibelungenlied* which structures the fictional world through repetitions and symmetries. It hinges on the uneasy and ambiguous elective affinities of the four main players: Kriemhilt and Sîvrit, the prince and princess of the fairytale so obviously designed for each other; Brünhilt who, in an older version of the story which the poet of the *Nibelungenlied* appears to know yet suppress, had been liberated by Sîvrit; and Hagen who kills not just Sîvrit but eventually also Kriemhilt. Two beautiful women, two virile men – two heroes, two victims. Or perhaps it is not quite as simple.

Draesner's commentary highlights the ambivalence of a love story in which the loving husband can nevertheless get away with beating his wife:

> Minne kommt nur für Sîvrit und Krimhilt ins Spiel, zumindest in der ersten Phase der maere in Worms. Sie wird als Verhaltenscode aus dem höfischen Minnediskurs zitiert. Sîvrits langes Werben um Krimhilt, der ihrer Familie zu leistende Dienst. Aber dieses (typische) Minnemuster ist im *Nibelungenlied* durchschossen von Elementen einer älteren, heldischen Kampfordnung – und wird vergessen, als Krimhilt und Sîvrit zehn Jahre später Worms ein zweites Mal besuchen. Minne und Ehe, zwei Paar Stiefel: Sîvrit verprügelt Krimhilt dafür, dass sie die Wahrheit zu Brünhilt sprach. Eine Wahrheit, die er seiner Frau beibrachte. Das maere erzählt von diesen Schlägen nebenbei. Usus, offensichtlich, im Verhältnis zwischen Mann und Frau. Auch für eine Königin. (p. 115)

> [Courtly love plays a role only for Sîvrit and Krimhilt, at least during the first phase of the story, in Worms. It is introduced as a code of conduct, part of a courtly discourse on love: Sîvrit's long drawn-out wooing of Kriemhilt; the service owed to her family. Yet this (typical) pattern of courtly love is undercut with elements of an older, heroic order – and is forgotten by the time Sîvrit and Kriemhilt visit Worms a second time ten years later. Love and marriage – two completely separate things: Sîvrit beats Kriemhilt for having spoken the truth to Brünhilt. A truth that he himself had taught his wife. The story tells of this beating in passing. Common practice, quite clearly, between husband and wife. Even if she is a queen.]

As is evident from Draesner's comment, the way in which the *Nibelungenlied* poet takes marital violence for granted scandalizes modern readers – yet it may have disturbed medieval audiences as much, since contemporary texts repeatedly problematize violence against women, whether intended or unintentional.[17] The *Nibelungen* poet does not comment; our only guide to understanding the situation is the figure of Kriemhilt, whose love for Sîvrit is unwavering, who never questions any of his actions. Yet the scene raises the question: what makes a victim, and how does one become a victim? Conversely, how does one become a hero? Does one entail the need for the other – no heroes without victims?

Often, answers to these questions are constructed along gender lines: women are defined through their constraints, condemned to passivity, victims of male aggression, and the passage from the *Nibelungenlied* to which Draesner refers supports such readings. Kriemhilt herself in the *Nibelungenlied* articulates the constraints – she is keenly aware of the injustice committed by Hagen, but also of the fact that only her brothers could take action on her behalf, which they refuse. Yet the Kriemhilt of the *Nibelungenlied* is not only self-aware, but also active: in marrying Etzel, the powerful king of Hungary, she acquires precisely the power base for revenge which her brothers, who are cowardly complicit in Hagen's murder, had denied her. Appropriating masculine forms of behaviour, she uses her husband to gain influence, buys the loyalty of his fighters, and tricks both Etzel and her brothers into believing that the invitation to Hungary is an attempt at reconciliation. Thus, the Kriemhilt of the *Nibelungenlied* is a politician who finds her match only in Hagen. Neither Sîvrit, her first husband, nor Etzel, the second, have any understanding of what is going on, and both are portrayed as naive, or worse, wilfully blind. In Etzel's case, this blindness is motivated by his obvious love for Kriemhilt – to the point where he is described as effeminate in his indecision and gullibility. By contrast, Kriemhilt, like Hagen, understands and exploits the unspoken codes, using her ability to second-guess how others behave in order to further her own game. Some interpretations see this as a critique of courtly deception, yet the medieval narrative is much more ambivalent than such readings of the text as Christian parable suggest.[18] It creates a world in which political actions may require different standards of conduct, and highlights that the ability to anticipate one's opponent is a necessary step for political survival.[19]

---

17 Müller, *Endgame*, pp. 272–279.

18 Edward R. Haymes, 'Heroic, Chivalric, and Aristocratic Ethos in the *Nibelungenlied*', in *A Companion to the Nibelungenlied*, ed. by Winder McConnell (Woodbridge: Camden House, 1998), pp. 94–104; Müller, *Endgame*, pp. 377–425.

19 See Brian Murdoch, 'Politics in the *Nibelungenlied*', in *A Companion to the Nibelungenlied*, ed. by McConnell, pp. 229–250.

The *Nibelungenlied* therefore exposes a tension between two very different medieval conceptions of heroism: ideal masculinity in the 'old' world of Germanic heroic epic, as we know it from the ninth-century *Hildebrandslied* or from *Beowulf*, is defined by virility, physical strength and the determination to face fate. In this world, heroes almost without exception demonstrate their greatness not in glorious victory, but in a great death.[20] Hagen in the second part of the *Nibelungenlied* is such a hero – yet he is denied the great death, since he falls at the hands of a woman. Arguably, however, Kriemhilt, the woman, shares many of Hagen's characteristics – all she lacks is physical strength, and in the end, she musters even that when, with her own hand, she kills both Gunther her brother, and Hagen. Conversely, neither Gunther nor Etzel is at any stage willing to stand up for their political views, relying on substitutes – deemed effeminate and deficient in the world of the heroes.

Within twelfth-century literature, such models began to appear old-fashioned, and the *Nibelungenlied* openly displays the resulting ambivalence towards models of the heroic. In the first part, in particular, the new world of Christian knighthood is shown as superior – Gunther presides over a model court, in which celebration, representation and dialogue have replaced the wordless single combat, and in which, significantly, ideals of masculinity rely both on a relationship with God and on the love of an ideal woman.[21] A perfect knight is the one who can win the hand of an equally perfect woman, and one whom God as the defender of justice supports. Despite its presentation of a modern, courtly ideal at Worms, however, the *Nibelungenlied* refuses a black-and-white story of progress, and as a result, the figure of Sîvrit, like that of Kriemhilt, embodies the rift between the two views of the world: Sîvrit is introduced as the perfect courtly knight, having been educated in Xanten by his parents, falling in love with Kriemhilt, and winning her hand. Yet he is also what he always had been – the heroic dragon-slayer, whose back-story the listeners know as well as Hagen, the ultimate heroic warrior.[22]

This tension between two very different sets of values and conceptions of masculinity has repercussions which touch on what Draesner identifies as the central 'otherness' of the medieval world: its lack of what we call 'individuality', and its reliance on a collective sense of identity. In Draesner's words:

---

20 Brian Murdoch, *The Germanic Hero. Politics and Pragmatism in Early Medieval Poetry* (London: Hambledon Press, 1994).

21 Müller, *Endgame*, pp. 330–376.

22 Ursula Schulze, *Das Nibelungenlied* (Stuttgart: Reclam, 1997), pp. 142–183.

Mittelalterliche Erzählwelten kennen Gefühle, aber bieten sie im Modus der Rüstung, des Panzers, des Gewandes und seines Glanzes dar. Befremdlich, doch besser zu begreifen, wenn man nachvollzieht, wie es zur Entstehungszeit der Epen um 1200 bestellt gewesen sein mag um das für uns so zentrale Ich. Es gibt das Wort im Mittelhochdeutschen, gewiss, als grammatisches Pronomen. Was es nicht gibt: die Vorstellung davon, neutral, friedlich, gar positiv oder harmlos "eine(r)" zu sein. "Eine sein" bedeutet "allein sein". Allein sein bedeutet Gefahr. Held ist, wer es wagt, ohne die anderen auszureisen. Vor der Burg: der Wald. Die Ungeheuer. Das Neue. (p. 109)

[Medieval narrative worlds are not devoid of emotions, but they present them as armour, defence, cloak, radiance. Strange, yet easier to comprehend if we try to imagine how that 'I' which is so central to us may have been constituted around 1200 when these narratives were composed. True enough, the word 'I' exists in Middle High German – as a grammatical pronoun. What does not exist is the concept of being 'someone' (eine(r)). The phrase 'eine sein' means 'to be alone'. To be alone signals danger. A hero is someone who has the courage to venture out alone. Outside the castle: the forest; the monsters; the unheard-of.]

In other words: heroes are the ones who are willing to face danger on their own. In this sense, Kriemhilt, isolated from her family and friends, is as much a heroine as Hagen is a hero. What separates Hagen and Kriemhilt is the way in which masculine heroes embody the collective. Draesner captures this difference poetically in a passage from *Heimliche Helden*, which sets this out in a series of declaratives:

Held: wer im Glanz des Wir erscheint.
Held: wer abweicht, einer Obsession folgt, einem Traum.
Held: ein innerer Widerspruch.

[Hero: the one appearing in the radiance of a We.
Hero: the one taking a different path, following an obsession, or a dream.
Hero: an inner contradiction.][23]

Erasures and Fissures

The concluding prose section of Draesner's *Nibelungen* text is entitled 'Immer wieder vergesse ich' ['I keep forgetting', pp. 107–28]. With this caption, Draesner comments on her reading experience of the *Nibelungenlied* – the fact that, while central images are very vivid, it is difficult to recall the plot, the sequence

---

23 Draesner, *Heimliche Helden*, p. 58.

of what happens. She refers to it as a narrative of erasure ('ein Epos der Löschungen', p. 107). It is not easy to capture Draesner's term 'Löschung' in English – it refers to erasure, the act of deleting something that had once been there, an act which is both deliberate and conceived of as deception. Yet it also alludes to the world of computer games – the setting in which the echoes of the medieval world perhaps survive most prominently today.[24] Furthermore, it could be argued that it also evokes Derrida's concept of the 'palimpsest' – the manuscript from which an earlier writing has been erased, yet which still carries the traces of that erased text.[25] Finally, 'Löschung', in referencing the act of extinguishing, may thereby evoke one of the central images of the *Nibelungenlied*, the fire in the Great Hall which cannot be extinguished.

Draesner's term thus ingeniously characterizes one of the fascinations of the *Nibelungenlied*, since its refusal to tell a straightforwardly coherent story is at least in part the result of its attempt to re-frame an older story for a different culture. The narrative is bi-partite: a first section set in Worms and Iceland, culminating in the double marriage and subsequent murder; the second, taking place thirteen years later in Hungary, with the Burgundians travelling to Etzel's court and their destruction. Yet the bi-partite action is more than a filmic fast-forward, because it reveals a fundamental difficulty in reading the *Nibelungenlied*, which lacks causal and psychological coherence.[26] In particular, the two central figures, Hagen and Kriemhilt, do not conform to modern notions of psychological coherence: Hagen in the first part is the ruthless murderer. Draesner, in a running marginal note, reads the figure of Hagen against the psychological profile of a homicidal maniac running amok, picking up on the way in which the narrator of the *Nibelungenlied*, in one of the rare extradiegetic comments, accuses Hagen of treachery ('untriuwe', *NL* 876,2; ed. Heinzle, p. 280). What such a reading underplays is the switch in the second part of the narrative, in which Hagen is the positively-connoted hero. This Hagen of the second part was the preferred figure of nineteenth- and twentieth-century readings: the hero who is willing to ride into certain death. By contrast, Draesner sees Hagen in the second part as a terrorist, a figure whose conception means that he does

---

24 Bent Gebert, 'Mittelalter-Mogelpackung? Kulturen des Heroischen im mittelalterlichen Heldenepos *Rolandslied* und dem modernen Online-Rollenspiel *World of Warcraft* im Vergleich', *Praxis Deutsch*, 230 (2011), 52–58.

25 Sarah Dillon, *The Palimpsest. Literature, Criticism, Theory* (London: Bloomsbury, 2007).

26 Müller, *Endgame*, pp. 221–226; on 'personality as surface', cf. Almut Suerbaum, '*weinen si began*. Male and female tears in the *Nibelungenlied*', in '*Vir ingenio mirandus*'. Studies presented to John L. Flood, ed. by William J. Jones, William A. Kelly and Frank Shaw (Göppingen: Kümmerle, 2003), pp. 23–37.

not experience inner conflict and acts with increasing recklessness and self-destructiveness.[27]

Conversely, Kriemhilt in the first part of the *Nibelungenlied* is the model of idealized medieval femininity: beautiful, noble, in love. In the second part, however, the narrative plots her transgression against all rules of human behaviour: she appears monstrous as a woman who deceives her second husband as well as her family, sacrifices her child, and finally kills Hagen with her own hand. Modern tabloid news coverage underlines how strongly the child-killing mother is seen as the extreme of deviation – infinitely worse than a male killer, because the act is seen as transgressing against what is often understood as the essence of femininity, motherhood.[28] Kriemhilt, in the words of Dietrich of Bern – though notably not those of the narrator – is the 'vâlandinne', a she-devil.

Medieval audiences may not have had the same expectation of psychological coherence as modern readers, but the manuscript transmission of the *Nibelungenlied* nevertheless reveals something of the unease which such split figures clearly caused. This is most obvious in a comparison between the different versions of the poem: whereas the B version, represented by the St Gall manuscript dating from c. 1230, narrates the change from princess to monster but refrains from comment, the C version (in the Donaueschingen manuscript now in Karlsruhe) reworks the figure of Kriemhilt by motivating her actions as an act of loyalty. Her actions at the end are thus no longer incomprehensible acts of transgression, but can be seen as the flip-side of her absolute love for Sîvrit. The C version thus presents her actions as a response to a loss, where the enormity of her response mirrors the absoluteness of her love. In this reading, what is terrifying is not the figure so much as the emotion – a love which is at once ideal and utterly destructive.[29]

Medieval scholarship connects the emergence of this all-encompassing, French-inspired 'amour fou' with twelfth-century reception of Ovid's psychologically nuanced pathology of love, but also the 'birth of the individual'. A love which takes hold of those whom it afflicts like a disease sets them apart, isolates them, yet also forces them to articulate that sense of isolation – Gottfried's Tristan and Isolde are the most prominent example of the inherently anti social nature of such love.[30] Seen in the context of such conceptions of

---

27 Draesner, *Heimliche Helden*, pp. 57–58.
28 Otfried Ehrismann, '"ze stücken was gehouwen dô daz edele wîp". The Reception of Kriemhilt', in *A Companion to the Nibelungenlied*, ed. by McConnell, pp. 18–41.
29 Müller, *Endgame*, pp. 192–198.
30 Stephen Jaeger, *Ennobling Love. In search of a lost Sensibility* (Philadelphia: University of Philadelphia Press, 1999).

love, Kriemhilt is one of the most obviously 'modern' figures: heroic, in that she is willing to stand alone and fight her corner; yet also closest to a modern conception of individuality in which the narrative allows us to see what a figure feels and thinks as well as what she does. The poet of the *Nibelungenlied* is sparing with such interior perspective, so it is telling that Kriemhilt is one of only two figures to whom he gives monologues, the classic dramatic means by which we are allowed to see a figure's thoughts. Even when the narrator does not directly comment, he creates situations in which Kriemhilt's body is legible for others – it expresses what courtesy does not allow her to say, for example when Rüedeger conveys Etzel's offer of marriage. Kriemhilt's words welcome him and give him permission to speak – yet that is not what she feels, and this is obvious to those who know her:

> die andern dô wol hôrten ir unwilligen muot (*NL* 1230,4; ed. Heinzle p. 392)

> [the others heard only too well that she was unwilling]

The *Nibelungen* poet goes even further, in that he establishes a distinction between those observing her closely at court and us as readers, on the one hand, and her family on the other: her brothers as well as Ute urge her to accept the offer, which would allow her to erase the past and, in their words, offer the prospect of a new life and new happiness. She rejects the offer and changes her mind only when Rüedeger, in private conversation ('heimliche'), promises that he and his men will fight her cause against anyone who has harmed her. Here, the poet inserts an internal monologue:

> So gedachte die getriuwe 'Sit ich vriunde han
> also vil gewunnen, so sol ich rede lan
> die liute, swaz sie wellen, ich jamerhaftez wîp.
> was ob noch wirt errochen des minen lieben mannes lîp.' (*NL* 1259,1–4; ed. Heinzle, p. 400)

> [She, the loyal [widow of Sîvrit] thought: Since I have made / so many friends, I will let people say / whatever they wish, poor miserable woman that I am. / What if my beloved husband were to be avenged after all?]

We as audience are allowed to see what neither Rüedeger, Etzel nor indeed her family understand: paradoxically, Kriemhilt agrees to marry Etzel not in order to forget and erase the past, but because it will keep the past alive – both the injustice done to her, which Rüedeger's offer will allow her to avenge, and the love for Sîvrit, because she will demonstrate that she is loyal to him ('getriuwe'). Deception as the result of certain figures being unable, or unwilling, to see the truth is a frequent concern in the *Nibelungenlied*. This passage is, however, unusual, because the *Nibelungenlied* poet allows us to see the dissembling of emotions. As readers, we witness what is hidden from all other figures in the narrative: in her monologue, we hear a Kriemhilt whose sense of self depends not on her family, her social standing, or that of her husband, but on her love. Against all entreaties towards pragmatism, Kriemhilt insists on the fact that it is this love which makes her who she is and sets her apart from all others, and she retains that sense of self precisely because it is kept hidden. While the switch from ideal princess to she-devil remains inexplicable in psychological terms, the narrator thus suggests that the core of her figure, her love for Sîvrit, is unchanged and unchangeable. In this view, Kriemhilt's internal distancing from family, friends and the status conveyed by a royal marriage, can be seen as acts of erasure: her outward conformity the way to allow internal consistency.

Finally, we should briefly consider an act of poetic erasure which concerns the other truly modern figure, one whom Draesner omits from her *Nibelungen* project: Rüedeger of Bechlarn. In the framework of the *Nibelungenlied,* he, like Hagen, is a heroic warrior: when one of the men taunts him for his passivity, he takes heroic action and slays the detractor with a single stroke; action, not re-flection is what makes a hero.[31] Yet Rüedeger is also the only figure except Kriemhilt who is given an interior monologue. In this monologue, he not only faces, but also articulates an irresolvable conflict of loyalties: the Burgundians have been his guests; he has exchanged gifts with them when they stayed at his castle; and he has promised his daughter to the youngest of the Burgundian brothers, Giselher. They have thus become family – by marriage, not by blood, but related in such a way that fighting them is not acceptable. Etzel, however, is his feudal lord, and Rüedeger has moreover given Kriemhilt the fateful prom-ise to defend her rights – so when both demand he defend the cause of the Huns, he has no choice but to attack the Burgundians. He fights Gernot, the middle brother, and they kill each other (2221,4). Thus Rüedeger, like Kriemhilt and Sîvrit, and unlike Hagen, is a split figure: he is the archetypal heroic war-rior, yet he is also the one character in the *Nibelungenlied* whose Christianity functions not just as a social code: he has what in twelfth-century philosophical terms is a modern concept – he has a conscience. When Rüedeger realizes that he will have to obey Etzel's command, he is troubled ultimately not by the breach of social code protecting guests and relatives, nor by the certainty of his own death – but the fact that he will endanger his soul by killing others. The narrator

---

31 The *Nibelungenlied* tells of Rüedeger's heroism in characteristically heroic terms, by re-counting the actions and bodily signs rather than psychological processes: he 'sees' red – 'des muotes er retobete' (2206,2) – and wields his sword.

confirms that curtly: 'nu liez er an die wage sele unde lip' (2166,1) [Thus, he risked soul as well as body]. This is as bleak as it gets: no offer of divine forgiveness, no reminder of a God who atones for what humans consider unforgivable, no hope.

The modernity of the figure has led some to argue that the *Nibelungenlied* as a whole should be read as a rejection of pagan heroism, or, alternatively, a critique of the worldliness represented by courtly culture, reinforcing 'true' Christian values *ex negativo*. Neither view is very persuasive – for a Christian morality tale, it would be very odd indeed to condemn the one unambiguously and self-aware Christian not just to death, but to eternal death. Indeed, the presence of this one Christian figure throws into relief how thoroughly un-Christian the *Nibelungenlied* is – what pervades it is a sense of inevitable fatality rather than divine providence.

The unease at a world without any promise of redemption is manifest in the *Klage*, a kind of sequel to the *Nibelungenlied* which is almost always transmitted together with it. Aesthetically, it appears to modern readers as a very different work, in that its bland couplet-verse narrative of elegiac lament re-interprets the world of the *Nibelungenlied* in unambiguously Christian terms.[32] As a result, Kriemhilt becomes the epitome of loyalty and fidelity, no matter the consequences, focussing on the need for Christian lament and remembrance, and shifting to meta-poetic levels by telling the story of how the *Nibelungenlied*, the account of unimaginable events, came into being. The manuscripts attempt to obscure the difference to the point where end-rhymed couplet verse is made to look just like the strophic song of the *Nibelungenlied*.[33] (Fig. 2)

In Ulrike Draesner's revoicing, such conflict between an introspective Christianity and the unease at its absence play no part. Hence, it is plausible that the figure of Rüedeger has become obsolete in her version; what she reflects instead is the unending nature of the story. Poetologically, her version can thus be seen as the modern analogue of the *Klage*, re-framing and perhaps perpetuating the momentum of the *Nibelungenlied*, while shifting it to a different culture. Aesthetically, however, her voice responds very closely to the challenge of the *Nibelungenlied* and its self-conscious movement between different worlds. She offers a response very much of her own time, in which Christianity and Christian values are no longer an issue. Acts of erasure, on the other hand, matter as an aesthetic

---

32 On the manuscript transmission of *Nibelungenlied* and *Klage,* see Michael Curschmann, 'Nibelungenlied und Nibelungenklage. Über Mündlichkeit und Schriftlichkeit im Prozeß der Episierung', in *Deutsche Literatur im Mittelalter. Kontakte und Perspektiven. Hugo Kuhn zum Gedenken*, ed. by Christoph Cormeau (Stuttgart: Metzler, 1979), pp. 85–119.

33 The beginning of 'Klage' from the end of the *Nibelungenlied*, with kind permission of the Manuscript Archive, Karlsruhe, Badische Landesbibliothek, Cod. Donaueschingen 63, fol. 89r.

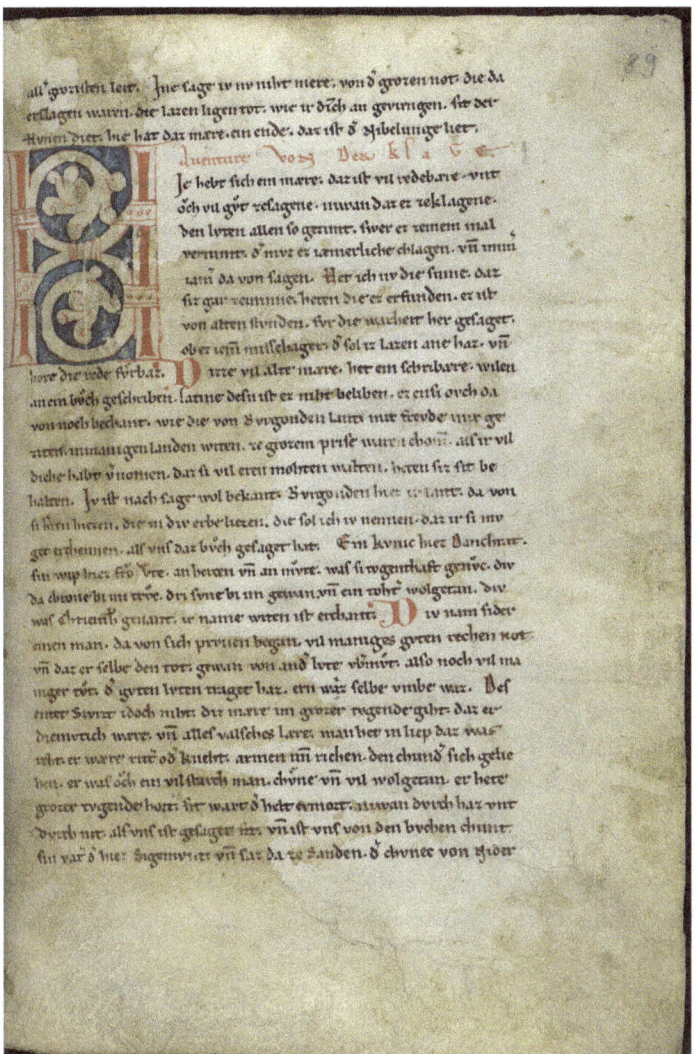

Fig. 2: Strophic song of the *Nibelungenlied*, Cod. Donaueschingen 63, (Nibelungenlied C) and beginning of the *Klage* fol. 89r, BLB Karlsruhe.

strategy, because they lay open the traces which remain legible across time and shifts in values – as is evident in the voices of the concluding computer-game dialogue between Kriemhilt's sons:

> O: Wer bist du?
> G: Das fragt der Richtige. Du schleichst mir doch hinterher. [. . .]
> O: Alles hier sieht komisch aus.
> G: Drück shift-s! S bringt dich nach hinten.
> O: S wie Sîvrit, klar. (p. 100)

> [O: Who are you?
> G: You are a fine one to ask. Creeping up on me like that. [. . .]
> O: Everything here looks funny.
> G: Press shift-s! S will take you back.
> O: S for Sîvrit – of course.]

The Sense of an Ending

The *Nibelungenlied* is a text which offers no answers – it shows the ruptures and the wounds, and tells of the bloodshed. There is no moral to its story – however much interpretations, whether Christian, romantic, national socialist or feminist, have attempted to bend it to a single cause. In a world shaped by neo-Platonic views on the correlation between ethics and aesthetics, it is extraordinarily pessimistic about human nature – not because the world it presents is primitive, but because even the most sophisticated of its inhabitants are powerless against a force which ends in destruction, no matter what human beings intend or plan. And yet, what remains is the poetic form to which Draesner responds – the strophic song which leads a world into catastrophe while itself remaining legible, across a distance of 800 years.

Perhaps the most telling aspect of this is the language, in particular Draesner's skill in allowing echoes of Middle High German to resonate through her own word-play, thus manifesting another form of the bilingualism that plays such a significant role in her poetic oeuvre.[34] These traces are never historicizing

---

34 This is most evident in her use of English, especially in the recent collection *subsong: Gedichte* (Munich: Luchterhand, 2014), and William Shakespeare, Ulrike Draesner, Tom Cheesman and Olive Ond, *THYMINE. 17 Sonnets x 4*, Boiled String Poetry Chapbooks #7 (Swansea: Hafan Books, 2013), no pagination, reproduced also in *Twin Spin. 17 Shakespeare Sonnets* (Oxford: Taylor Institution Library, 2016), but bilingual wordplay is a recurrent feature in most of her other works as well; cf. Marven, 'Mitgift', p. 30, n. 7, and see in particular the chapter by Tobias Döring in this volume.

accessory. Indeed, wherever they are introduced, they are self-consciously flagged as exotic, different, in need of explanation – precisely where they appear to be self-evident: MHG 'eine' is not, Draesner highlights, the same as a modern German sense of identity.[35]

The crows sum this up at the end of Brünhilt's monologue:

> heros ist eine eintönigkeit
> die summend umhüllt. das gebiet
> in dem handlung aus männern beendet
> werden konnte liegt jenseits. (p. 73)

> [heroism is a monotony / which, humming, envelops. the space / in which actions consisting of men / could be brought to an end lies beyond].

The passage demonstrates that there are significant differences of voice between the medieval work and Draesner's poetic adaptation. The language of the *Nibelungenlied* is not mimetic, and unlike the modern work with its layers of discourse, from lyric to computer game, figures in the medieval work do not have differentiated voices. There are differences also in melodic or musical terms, in that the *Nibelungenlied*, unlike the mystical writers of a generation later, does not translate a crisis of human experience into a crisis of language or a fragmentation of voice. On the contrary, it contains the catastrophic and cataclysmic end of the world it had created within the confines of tightly controlled strophes, quite unlike the characteristic staccato of Draesner's poetic voice.

Nevertheless, this rejection of monophonic simplicity in favour of hidden polyphony constitutes, as I hope to have shown, both the poetic strength of Draesner's voice and its affinity with the *Nibelungenlied*. Draesner's coda cautiously and hypothetically explores ways of rescuing some aspect of humanity from the apocalypse: at the end of her version, the two sons G and O meet in the computer game. Their dialogue exposes the rift between their worlds, and yet the very fact that the game offers a space for an encounter is closer to the world of the *Klage*, insisting on the enduring power of the poetic word to transcend, and to bridge gaps – for those who are prepared to listen closely.

---

35 Draesner, *Heimliche Helden*, p. 54–55.

The Limits of the Human

Emily Jeremiah
Just Hanging in There. Reproduction, Humanity and Ethics in the Work of Ulrike Draesner

Following the 'ethical turn' of recent years, questions of morality are the subject of ongoing discussion and debate within critical and literary theory.[1] Equally pressing is the matter of (post)humanism: what defines the human subject? And – a linked question – what are the status and purpose of the humanities today? Given advances in medicine and technology, and especially reproductive technologies, and given also the emerging and diversifying fields of animal rights and animal studies, these concerns are complex and urgent.[2] Three short stories by Ulrike Draesner – 'Anna selbzwei' ['Anna Binary'] and 'Gina Regina' in the collection *Hot Dogs* (2004), and 'Süße Kaverne' ['Sweet Cavern'] in *Richtig liegen* (2011) – offer compelling insights here. The stories are concerned with human reproduction, which emerges as a key site of ethical complexity and difficulty, in ways that resonate with and extend theoretical treatments of the issue. The texts – and Draesner's oeuvre more broadly – point up the potential of literature to explore what it means to be human, and what it means to be ethical.

As an affective, relational practice, reading is arguably a quintessentially human activity. Yet it also permits recognition of humanity's connectedness to non-human life: itself an ethical gesture. In their posthumanism, Draesner's texts recall the work of Donna Haraway. For Haraway, humanity represents a cumulative, layered state, at once 'natural' and 'cultural'. As she puts it in her famous 1985 essay 'A Manifesto for Cyborgs', we (that is to say, humans) are 'theorized and fabricated hybrids of machine and organism'.[3] Haraway notes elsewhere that being members of a biological species, *Homo sapiens*, 'puts us solidly inside science, history, and nature, right at the heart of things'.[4] The

---

1 Emily Jeremiah and Frauke Matthes, 'Introduction: Ethical Approaches in Contemporary German-Language Literature and Culture', in *Ethical Approaches in Contemporary German-Language Literature and Culture*, ed. by Emily Jeremiah and Frauke Matthes, *Edinburgh German Yearbook*, 7 (2013), 1–11 (p. 3).
2 See, for example, Paul Waldau, *Animal Studies. An Introduction* (Oxford: Oxford University Press, 2013).
3 Donna Haraway, 'A Manifesto for Cyborgs', in *The Haraway Reader* (New York and London: Routledge, 2004), pp. 7–45 (p. 8).
4 Donna Haraway, 'Introduction: A Kinship of Feminist Figurations', in *The Haraway Reader*, pp. 1–6 (p. 2).

https://doi.org/10.1515/9783110495942-004

question of humanity, and the importance of science and technology in redefining the category, emerges in and through developing reproductive technologies, an area in which 'collective preoccupations and national politics are played out'.[5] Draesner thematizes such preoccupations and their political and ethical implications in three short stories in particular. 'Anna selbzwei' involves a heterosexual couple's struggle to conceive, and the identification of a possible solution in sperm donation and artificial insemination. The stories 'Gina Regina' and 'Süße Kaverne' both feature protagonists called Gina, and in both cases sperm is taken from a sleeping male, in one case for money – it will be sold via the internet to couples or individuals seeking donor sperm – in the other, in the interests of scientific advancement, for use in a bizarre experiment. Gina in the first story is a student of French and International Relations. In 'Süße Kaverne', Regina ('genannt Gina' [who goes by the name of Gina]), is a scientist.[6]

These texts present a posthuman, postmodernist view of reproductive ethics and of corporeality, grounding this view in ethical questions concerning autonomy, choice, consent and control. Refusing sentimental, nostalgic longings for a lost golden age before scientific advancements and before global capitalism, Draesner nonetheless forces us to question the implications of, in 'Anna selbzwei' and 'Gina Regina', the commercialization and commodification of gametes and, in 'Süße Kaverne', the relativization and modification of the human body. As becomes clear, reproduction and the related matter of the status of the human have profound ethical implications. As well as the work of Haraway, the stories bring to mind, at points, the Deleuzian notion of 'becoming-animal', which involves an attempt to rethink ideas of human mastery and control, to stress our enmeshment with and our responsibility to the non-human or 'earth other'.[7] Rosi Braidotti spells out the ethical importance of this gesture: she argues that the assertion of the earth other is urgent given the 'cannibalization' of nature by the global market, a process

---

5 Natalia Gerodetti and Véronique Mottier, 'Feminism(s) and the Politics of Reproduction', in *Feminist Theory* (Special Issue: *Feminist Politics of Reproduction*), 10.2 (2009), 147–52 (147).

6 Ulrike Draesner, 'Süße Kaverne', in *Richtig liegen* (Munich: Luchterhand, 2011), pp. 139–51 (p. 139). Draesner explained that she plans to insert a story featuring a character called Gina into four short-story collections in total, meaning two more 'Gina' stories are set to be published – this during a discussion at 'Leaping from the Edge of the World: A Symposium on the Work of Ulrike Draesner', April 2016.

7 Gilles Deleuze and Félix Guattari, *A Thousand Plateaus. Capitalism and Schizophrenia*, trans. Brian Massumi (London: Continuum, 2004), pp. 256–341. The term 'earth other' is taken from Val Plumwood, *Feminism and the Mastery of Nature* (London: Routledge, 1993), p. 137.

that is legitimized by the 'categorical and self-congratulatory' distinction between human and non-human in Western thought.[8]

Like Haraway, Draesner ultimately advocates *'pleasure* in the confusion of boundaries' as well as *'responsibility* in their construction',[9] an argument to which I will return. I discuss the stories separately, in the first two cases drawing on debates concerning the marketization of the human body, in the third, focussing on posthumanist ideas of the subject. Draesner complicates ideas of morality and agency to suggest a view of subjectivity as embodied, posthuman and relational. Her works thus chime with materialist-feminist studies of ethics in ways I will expand on further in conclusion.

Markets in Babies?

Michele Bratcher Goodwin, the editor of a collection of essays concerning money and 'the creation of families', refers to 'the deeply contested and complicated nature of becoming a parent', and points to the role wealth and status play in the matters of reproduction and adoption.[10] At least since Elisabeth Landes and Richard Posner's 1978 discussion of the marketization of adoption, the idea of a market in babies has been controversial. Numerous voices in the US have challenged the idea of a market in babies or gametes, as Martha Ertman notes: from those who argue that transactions in this sphere corrupt the value of life, to conservative commentators who fear the decline of the 'traditional' family or contend that 'personhood' is at risk.[11] In the German context, the writer Sibylle Lewitscharoff recently attacked artificial insemination and surrogate motherhood, controversially terming the offspring resulting from these procedures 'Halbwesen' [semihuman].[12]

---

8 Rosi Braidotti, *Transpositions: On Nomadic Ethics* (Cambridge: Polity Press, 2006), p. 47. See also Emily Jeremiah, 'Creature Comforts. Economadism in the Poetry of Dorothea Grünzweig', in *Nomadic Ethics in Contemporary Women's Writing in German: Strange Subjects* (Rochester, NY: Camden House, 2012), pp. 63–97.

9 Haraway, 'Manifesto', p. 8.

10 Michele Bratcher Goodwin, 'Introduction', in *Baby Markets. Money and the New Politics of Creating Families*, ed. by Michele Bratcher Goodwin (Cambridge: Cambridge University Press, 2010), pp. xix–xxi (p. xxi).

11 Martha Ertman, 'The Upside of Baby Markets', in *Baby Markets*, ed. by Goodwin, pp. 23–40 (pp. 26–27).

12 See this response as an example of the criticism her speech prompted: Jo Lendle, 'Ich ertrage es nicht', *Zeit Online*, 7 March 2014 (http://www.zeit.de/kultur/literatur/2014-03/Lewit scharoff-Jo-Lendle-Brief).

Ertman's view is that 'market mechanisms provide unique opportunities for law and culture to recognize that people form families in different ways'. Instead of privileging 'tradition and divine or biological mandates', contemporary societies have here an opportunity to prioritize instead liberty and innovation. Drawing on Millian liberalism, and the values of consent, equality and freedom of action, Ertman argues that '[t]he ideal of freedom of contract imports these norms'.[13] Marketization, she notes, takes various forms, and it need not involve objectification.[14] For this commentator, the marketizing of sperm – compared with the marketizing of eggs, which she does concede might be difficult, especially given the very different processes involved – is unproblematic since a person is not greatly harmed by knowing that her mother paid for the sperm to conceive her and since medical care and childcare are both already marketized relatively uncontroversially.[15] The fact of being alive is a good thing, she suggests, so benefit has come about.

Yet there are risks with marketization. On the matter of women versus men as donors, Ertman concedes that women are more likely than men to be coerced or objectified 'because their status as full citizens and legal subjects is relatively recent'.[16] But what of the men in Draesner's 'Gina Regina' and 'Süße Kaverne', whose sperm is taken from them without their knowledge or consent, or the male partner of Anna in 'Anna selbzwei', to whom the protagonist does not divulge her plan to use another man's sperm to conceive? In the first two stories especially, the men are objectified: by the Ginas as well as by the marketplace and its mechanisms, and by scientific institutions and practices. Draesner negotiates such problems in instructive ways.

'Anna selbzwei'

In 'Anna selbzwei', Anna and her partner Kai are trying unsuccessfully for a baby: 'Ach, die Verneblungen und Vernablungen, das Dickicht des Wünschens, sie hätten gern ein Kind, aber bekommen es nicht' [Oh, the rambling and roaming, the thicket of longing; they would gladly have a child, but one won't come].[17] Agency,

---

13 Ertman, 'The Upside of Baby Markets', p. 23.
14 Ibid., p. 25.
15 Ibid., p. 27.
16 Ibid., p. 32.
17 Ulrike Draesner, 'Anna selbzwei', in *Hot Dogs* (Munich: Random House, 2006), pp. 35–49 (p. 37). Further references given in the body of the chapter.

here, is not a simple matter; will is thwarted by biology. This goes for another story in the collection, 'Der Jodler' ['The Yodler'], in which Jana and her partner Matze have tried unsuccessfully to conceive for two years.[18] In 'Anna selbzwei', it emerges that the problem lies with Kai. In a challenge to the more familiar cautionary tale of the 'selfish' career woman delaying motherhood and then regretting her childlessness, he reflects mournfully on the fact that he should have tried sooner to have a child (p. 44). Anna's friend Marina whispers the solution to the couple's dilemma to her in a cafe; a jaunty rhyme spells out her suggestion shortly afterwards: 'Auf daß aus der Passionsfrucht noch was werde, geht rank und schlank Anna morgen zur Samenbank' (p. 40) [In order for the passion fruit [her womb] to grow, off to the sperm bank Anna will go]. This jocular tone is continued when the narrator jokes: '*befruchten ohne wuchten*, arbeiteten wir in der Werbung, wäre das unser Spruch!' (p. 41) [*insemination without perspiration* – if we worked in advertising, that would be our motto!]. This tone makes for an uncertain ethical stance, at once suggesting ironic distance from the narrative and at the same time discouraging po-faced moralizing, an effect also to be discerned in the other texts looked at here. The citational language – the references to advertising slogans, the effects redolent of fairy tales or folk wisdom – gives rise to a complex form of intertextuality that means the tone is not easily pinned down. Here, for example, psychological states are briskly and rhymingly evoked: 'Anna-kuchen in Anna rein, auch Kai wird erleichtert sein' (p. 47) [Anna-bun into Anna-oven goes, Kai'll be relieved, I suppose].

As in 'Gina Regina', discussed shortly, we find here a female protagonist duping a man, and so a view of men as oblivious and manipulable emerges: a view that is arguably subversive, but also uncomfortable. Anna sources sperm from elsewhere,[19] checking out a 'young white male aus Amsterdam' (p. 47) [young white male from Amsterdam]. This description reflects the international market in gametes. Weighing up whether or not she should tell her partner, Anna reflects that it is probably better for the child if Kai does not know, thereby appealing to the as-yet unborn baby as justification for her failure to tell the truth. The evasiveness that characterizes her reflections is made clear when she further muses, without conviction: 'Und später kann sie es ihm ja immer noch sagen' (p. 42) [And she can always tell him later on]. The narrator also reflects with typical breeziness: 'nur was man weiß, macht einen heiß' (p. 47) [what you don't know can't give you aggro] – but as elsewhere, this flippancy paradoxically heightens the ethical drama being staged here. The murky

---

18 Ulrike Draesner, 'Der Jodler', in *Hot Dogs*, pp. 97–118 (p. 99).
19 In 'Der Jodler', incidentally, Jana has sex with another man (p. 106).

morality of Anna's activities also emerges in this reflection: 'Das ist nicht illegal
[. . .] nicht ganz legal, aber möglich, nicht ungerecht' (p. 46) [That's not illegal
[. . .] not quite legal, but possible, not unjust], with the terms 'not illegal' and
'not quite legal' signalling a slippery form of self-justification, and a problematic slippage between concepts of legality and rightness.

Anna has another doubt, one that raises the questions of affect and authenticity. She asks herself: 'Wär's im eigenen Bett nicht nett?' (p. 47) [Wouldn't it
be nicer in your own bed?] That is, the 'artificial' environment of the clinic is
less authentic, or at any rate less pleasant, than the experience of sex with a
partner in private. The fertility clinic as setting also appears in 'Der Jodler' and
is problematized in a comparable way. Jana goes to the clinic with Matze in an
unsuccessful attempt to conceive via artificial insemination. There she imagines the souls of babies yet to be born, a vision reminiscent of Hieronymous
Bosch, and she later reflects:

> Im nachhinein kamen ihr Zweifel, ob dieses Fertility Centre eine gute Idee gewesen war.
> Wer wußte, was sie da in den Labors wirklich taten. Spitze Finger, Pipetten, und dann?
> Saubere Bilder kamen in jedem Fall heraus. Der Mensch als Gast, selbstgemacht. Fragen
> meldeten sich, seltsam begleitet von einem diffusen Wort, das Jana noch nie verstanden
> hatte: Moral. Ein Wort, das es sich zu einfach machte, ein Wort wie Fett, einem in die
> Kehle gedrückt, um die Neugier aufs Leben zu beschneiden, hatte sie bislang gedacht.
> Und jetzt?

> [In retrospect, she had doubts about whether this Fertility Centre had been a good idea.
> Who knew what they really got up to in the labs? Expert manipulations, pipettes, and
> then? Clean pictures came out of it, in any case. The human as guest, self-made. Questions announced themselves, accompanied, strangely, by a diffuse word Jana had never
> understood: morality. A word that made things too simple for itself, a word like fat,
> shoved down your throat to cut off curiosity about life – or so she had thought until now.
> And now?][20]

Reproduction here acquires a suspect quality. It is haunted by a formless yet
urgent set of questions pertaining to morality. Questions also present themselves to Anna. When a pregnancy is established, the narrator reflects on the
ontological status of the foetus, which nonetheless is asserted as living: 'Ohne
die Wand in Anna wäre er tot, aber lebte er zuvor? Komische Frage, jetzt jedenfalls ist der Fötus da, stimmt, er sitzt an der Wand und pocht' (p. 47) [Without
the wall inside Anna it would be dead, but was it alive before? Funny question.
In any case, now the foetus is there, yes, it sits at the wall, throbbing]. Reproduction is figured here, notably, as involving a multiplication of Anna's self, as

---

20 Draesner, 'Der Jodler', p. 113.

the title of the story also implies, something that produces a sinister and un-canny effect and implies narcissism (pp. 47, 49).

As it happens, Anna's friend Marina does tell Kai what is going on at the clinic, and so a kind of double deception takes place (47–48). Questions of fer-tility and reproduction are thus interwoven with issues of trust, truth and loy-alty, in an arch reflection on the complexity of relationships and bodies. The narrator at one point makes an interjection – 'soweit sich das unterscheiden läßt: das Gehirn und sein Stoff' (p. 40) [as far as those things can be differenti-ated: the brain and its matter] – that constitutes a typically Draesnerian com-ment on materiality and consciousness as interwoven, a concern that also appears elsewhere, and especially in the monumental *Sieben Sprünge vom Rand der Welt*.[21] The story thus emphasizes matter, at the same time exploring constructedness, most notably as manifested in reproductive technology, and it introduces ethical and ontological dilemmas, deploying literary means to com-plicate discussions about agency and morality.

'Gina Regina'

'Gina Regina' is similarly concerned with matter and mind, with 'nature' and 'culture', terms that are unstable and shifting. In the first paragraph, we learn that Gina is afflicted by hay fever: 'Ein Cocktail auf der Haut, ein Extraschuß von Mutter-Droge-Natur' [A cocktail on the skin, an extra shot of mother-drug-nature].[22] The term 'mother nature' is disrupted here; instead of signalling an inert, benevolently figured entity, it is an active force, here irksome to the human. For Draesner, as for Haraway – as is even clearer in 'Süße Kaverne' – nature is not merely a serviceable and convenient other. Elsewhere, however, there is a reference to 'Größenwahnsinns-Mutter-Natur' (p. 12) [Mother-Nature-With-Her-Delusions-of-Grandeur], though this is playfully ironic, and so, like much of Draesner's arch and slippery narration, not necessarily to be taken at face value.

Nonetheless, nature here is relativized, subject to manipulation and styliza-tion. Gina occupies a world in which the body is adorned according to the latest fads and fashions, and is interpellated by these trends: 'Lackierte Brustwarzen waren der neueste Hit, frisch aus Japan importiert' (p. 7) [Varnished nipples were

---

21 Ulrike Draesner, *Sieben Sprünge vom Rand der Welt* (Munich: Luchterhand, 2014).
22 Ulrike Draesner, 'Gina Regina', in *Hot Dogs*, pp. 7–20 (p. 7). Further references given in the body of the chapter.

the latest thing, fresh out of Japan]. It is notable, in light of ideas of agency and consumer choice, that '[m]an lackierte nicht selbst, sondern ließ lackieren' (p. 7) [you didn't do the varnishing yourself, you got it done]. On the one hand this formulation implies the sovereignty of the subject-as-consumer – the service is contracted out – on the other, it suggests the passivity of the interpellated self in the context of neoliberalism, with the masculine and/or universal 'man' acting as the actual agent here. Gina's job as a collector of sperm is explained in terms of her financial motivation; it funds her studies in 'Romanistik mit Nebenfach International Relations' (p. 8) [French with International Relations]. The playful narration informs us that Gina's varnished nipples aid international relations – her job even more so (p. 8; compare p. 15). The intertwining of technology and consumerism becomes clear: 'Sperma auffangen, dachte Gina-Regina, immer im outlook express, immer auf der Suche nach dem schnellen Geld, und kramte im Gucciplastik nach dem Röhrchen' (p. 11) [Gather sperm, thought Gina-Regina, always in outlook express, always on the hunt for a quick buck, and she rummaged in Gucci plastic for the test tube]. Occupying as she does a globalized, technologized, commodified world, Gina recalls Camilla Grigger's 1997 description of woman as 'an abstract-machine concretely produced by late-twentieth-century technologies and capital' whose forms of expression are determined by 'optical and electronic media, psychopharmacology, the war machine, the chemical industry, plastics technology, bioscience'.[23]

Gina's activities are in a sense justified by her and the narrative, or at any rate contextualized, when the narrator tells us of the many men Gina knows afflicted by 'Bindungsangst' (p. 9) [fear of commitment] and by 'alter Freudscher Panik' (p. 9) [old Freudian panic]. This panic resides in men like a swarm of bees in a hollow trunk, who suck at nectar then flee; 'Mutter-Droge-Natur machte es vor' (p. 9) [Mother-Drug-Nature showed them how]. The social enactments of heterosexuality – here intertwining with technologization and globalization – are shown as complex performances founded on accumulated histories, *pace* Haraway, for whom we are 'congeries' formed of such legacies.[24] While this panic should be 'überholt' (p. 9) [outdated], it persists, and it grants Gina an enjoyable business opportunity. Gina is opportunistic, then: an agent who is simply turning circumstances to her advantage. She rationalizes her actions and, as with Anna, ethical wrangling and evasion occur. The narrator reports her thoughts to the effect that she is not, strictly speaking, committing theft (p. 10); although she will

---

23 Camilla Griggers, *Becoming-Woman* (Minneapolis: University of Minnesota Press, 1997), p. ix.
24 Haraway, 'Introduction', p. 2.

not return his 'property' to him, her partner will never miss it. She compares her job favourably with prostitution: for a start, she earns better; second, she chooses her sexual partners; third, no one watches over her; and fourth, it is illegal, which gives her a kick (pp. 11–12). This arch set of reflections again discourages moralism, but also, by means of satire, encourages scrutiny of sexual mores and morality.

As with Anna, matters of the heart complicate things. Gina's relationship to her lover, Gordian – the Gordian knot is alluded to, significantly, implying an intractable dilemma (pp. 8, 14) – is one of possessive tenderness; other women are potential rivals for the affection of 'ihr Pferdchen, ihr Herzchen' (p. 7) [her little horse, her little heart]. The motif of the heart is prominent in the story and signals the persistence of affect in this world of brands and surface (pp. 8, 11). For while love is one of the 'Retrovalues' (p. 12) [retro-values] that Gina – 'wie alle anderen' [like everyone else] – rejects, it does still signify. Yet the heart is here lurid and associated with branding: 'Gina [. . .] sah ein rot schlagendes Herzchen vor sich, wie aus einer Piemontkirsche geformt, getaucht zu Mon Chéri!' (p. 12) [Gina [. . .] saw a little heart beating red before her, as if formed from a Piedmont cherry and dipped to make Mon Chéri!]. Stephen Brockmann notes that this description 'sums up Gina's problem: she cannot conceive of romantic love as anything other than a cliché or a consumer advertisement'.[25]

The story raises the question of the nature and status of the human self. For example, there is a reference to '[d]as Sperma von Ferdi, der sich in dem Leben, das er als seines kannte, nur Gordian nennen ließ' (p. 10) [sperm belonging to Ferdi, who in the life he knew as his called himself Gordian]. Life, then, is not a matter of ownership or control. The slipperiness pertaining to names here also implies an unstable, ungraspable self: Gina is referred to as 'Gina Regina' in the title, and elsewhere as 'Gina-la-Minna', 'Ginna-la-Minna', 'Regina', 'Ginaregina', 'Gina-Benigna', 'Rinchen-Geninchen', 'Ginnina' and 'Reginni' (pp. 8, 14, 13, 13, 15, 16, 16, 17). The questions of humanity and selfhood, matter and being, are complex:

> Lag hier der Inhalt, schwappte im Röhrchen die Form? Dort der Genotyp, hier der Phänotyp, und dazwischen die schlaue Abbildungsregel der Reproduktion? Wie im *Tractatus*, als Lucki Ludwig die Sprachteilchen und Wirklichkeitsteilchen ganz klein wurden, atomar, subatomar, lunar! Gen- und Menschenteilchen heutzutage. Unklar blieb nur, wer bestimmte, wie sie zueinander gehörten. (p. 11)

---

25 Stephen Brockmann, 'Berlin as the Literary Capital of German Unification', in *Contemporary German Fiction. Writing in the Berlin Republic*, ed. by Stuart Taberner (Cambridge: Cambridge University Press, 2007), pp. 39–55 (p. 52).

[Was the content here? Was form itself sloshing about in the test tube? Here the genotype, there the phenotype, and in between the cunning rules of resemblance dictated by reproduction? Like in the *Tractatus*, when Lucki Ludwig got to the bottom of all the particles of language and reality: atomic, subatomic, lunar! Particles of gene and human being nowadays. The only thing that remained unclear was who decided how they all fitted together.]

Gordian, who studies mechanical engineering, muses on what it would take to construct a human being artificially (p. 14). The notion of the heart as central to humanity recurs: Gordian is 'eine Person' (p. 16) [a person], Gina establishes, even though he claims not to know his heart. But still, feelings do not reside in the heart – 'die Biologen wußten es längst, nur die Sprache war nicht auf der Höhe der Zeit' (p. 18) [the biologists had known it for a long time; it was just language that wasn't keeping up] – and so models of selfhood emerge as shifting and contingent upon context.

The end of the story is especially rich and slyly suggestive. Gina is in her flat anticipating her next client. She decides not to sell Gordian's sperm – '[i]hr ganz spezielles Geschenk an Gordian' (p. 19) [her very special gift to Gordian] – and:

> Für einen Augenblick, eine Nanosekunde, kam Gina sich vor wie ein Rättlein in einer riesigen Falle. Doch was sollten diese Schübe von Nostalgie, von Glauben an eine Ordnung, die sie steuerte. In den Zeiten vor dot.com hätte man bei solch einem Satz gerätselt, ob 'sie' Subjekt oder Objekt war, und immer falsch geraten. Gina lächelte, als sie sich, bevor sie ging, die Brustwarzen im Spiegel noch einmal genau ansah. Der Lack war unverletzt. (p. 20)

> [For a moment, a nano-second, Gina seemed to herself like a rat in a giant cage. But what were these bouts of nostalgia all about, this belief in an order directing her / directed by her [*die sie steuerte*]? In the times before dot.com you would have to guess who or what was doing the directing and you would invariably get it wrong. Gina smiled as, before leaving, she looked closely at her nipples in the mirror. The varnish was intact.]

The tripping-up of the reader – is *sie* the subject or the object of the *Ordnung* being steered? – leaves open the question of agency. Is Gina merely a guinea-pig in the new order of things? But nostalgia is no answer, according to the narrative. The final image, of the intact varnish, suggests the triumph of the artificial; there is no going back to pre-dot-com times.

'Süße Kaverne'

For Haraway, as already implied, nature is 'not "the other" who offers origin, replenishment, and service'. Rather, nature is 'a co-construction among humans and non-humans'.[26] 'Süße Kaverne' can be aligned with such posthumanist views, as is signalled in its first line: 'Sie hatte gelernt, sich vorsichtig zu bewegen [. . .] so dass kein Tier erschrak, auch das Menschentier Mann nicht' [She had learnt to move carefully [. . .] so as to avoid startling any animal, even human-animals, men].[27] As in 'Gina Regina', the sleeping male is here subjected to the female gaze in an inversion of the traditional power relation. Observing the man's penis, which is '[f]reihängend' (p. 139) [free-hanging], the protagonist Gina reflects: 'Kam nur bei Säugetieren vor' [Only mammals have that]; and the relativization of humanity continues with the reference to Gina's awareness of 'die Zerbrechlichkeit der Säugetierzelle' (p. 140) [the fragility of the mammalian cell]. The ethical force of such gestures is heightened by the reference to humanity's destructiveness, which recalls Braidotti, in the allusion to the destruction of bats' natural habitats which means they are endangered (p. 143). Braidotti argues against exploitative anthropocentrism, affirming 'trans-species solidarity', a move also suggested by this story.[28]

This Gina is termed a 'redevelopper of female life' [sic.] (p. 139), and – amusingly, since it undercuts any possible self-importance on the scientist's part – 'Deutschlands profilierteste Teichfledermausforscherin' (p. 140) [Germany's highest-profile pond bat researcher]. Like the other Gina, she is playfully defined and redefined, and she is indeed herself 'Königin der Wechsel, Regina der innovativen Biologie' (p. 141) [queen of transformation, regina of innovative biology]. Draesner's interest in scientific knowledge and discourse emerges here as in other works, and it involves a complex form of dialogue between the arts, the humanities and (in *Vorliebe* notably) theology. Here, Gina's partner, an English specialist, is working on Milton's *Paradise Lost*, a significant detail in light of ideas concerning knowledge as opposed to innocence, and questions of origin, creation and humanity (p. 142).

While Gina in the earlier story is in thrall to consumerism and individualism, Gina here is concerned with making the world 'praktischer' (p. 140) [more practical]. Her agency is stressed here, but as we shall see, it is later problematized by matters of the heart and by ethical concerns. At the start, though, Gina is a sovereign subject, with dominion over her surroundings: 'Die Stadt [. . .] gehörte Gina allein' (p. 141) [The town [. . .] belonged to Gina alone]. The narrator indeed protests in a tellingly defensive fashion: 'Tags durfte eine Forscherin [. . .] sich frei durch ein eigenes Leben bewegen' (p. 141) [Surely a researcher [. . .] had the

---

26 Donna Haraway, 'The Promises of Monsters. A Regenerative Politics for Inappropriate/d Others', in *The Haraway Reader*, pp. 63–124 (pp. 65, 66).

27 Draesner, 'Süße Kaverne', p. 139. Further references given in the body of the chapter.

28 Braidotti, *Transpositions*, 99.

right to move freely through her own life], stressing her claim to autonomy and freedom. As for her scientific endeavours, we learn that Gina has recently had an operation, and the background to it: with her team, she had tried to observe the movement of sperm in female bats, but the experiment failed, leading Gina to an alternative solution (p. 141). Gina, we are informed, was ready to donate her body to biology – this in contrast to the timidity of German law-makers, who would prohibit such an experiment as Gina now undertakes (p. 143).[29] Gina's project of simulating within her own body a bat's reproductive organs arises from this willingness and may, she hopes, lead to significant advances in artificial insemination in humans (p. 145). Her motivation thus becomes explicit; and as with the earlier Gina, monetary concerns feature here too, though they are not central: 'Die Sache stank nach Geld' (p. 146) [The thing stank of money].

Again as in 'Gina Regina', we find here too a relativization of humanity and of scientific endeavours. Gina is fascinated by the reproductive capacity of the bat, whose reproductive organs constitute '[e]ine Wunderkammer der Zeugung, besser als das höchstentwickelte Labor' (p. 143) [a procreative cabinet of wonders, better than the highest-spec laboratory]. After a description of the bats' mating process comes the exclamation 'Mutter Natur!' (p. 145) [Mother Nature!], which is at once admiring and ironic. Once again, Draesner insists on a view of the human subject as both natural and cultural, in line with Haraway. There is a reference here too to the stylization of the female body, which points up the manipulability of matter and the power of cultural norms, which are here violently coercive; Torge tells Gina that in China, beauty contests are held for those with and those without leg extensions, describing a painful process whereby legs are artificially made longer in girls (p. 147).[30]

As with the earlier story, too, there is an implicit contrast between the ambitions of the protagonist and her feelings for her male partner (pp. 146, 147). Torge's sperm is too sluggish for her purposes, hence her use of other men's sperm, which might be seen as constituting infidelity (p. 148). When Torge rings her, and she cries, without knowing why, there is a hint of the feelings she habitually represses; she is forced at this moment to recognize: 'Sie fühlte also doch etwas' (p. 150; compare 147) [So she did feel something]. By the end

---

29 A detail that raises interestingly the question of a specifically German attitude towards genetic research and scientific experimentation, in view of the legacy of National Socialism: matters touched on in *Sieben Sprünge*.

30 In the earlier novel *Mitgift* (2002), the gendered body is subjected to medical manipulation. This novel features an intersex protagonist, Anita, who is assigned femaleness at birth but transitions to maleness in the course of the novel. Ulrike Draesner, *Mitgift* (Munich: Luchterhand, 2002).

of the story, she is 'Gina, Idiotin, Närrin' (p. 150) [Gina, idiot, fool]: no longer, then, a queen or owner of the town. The ending of the text is, as with 'Gina Regina', richly suggestive and inconclusive:

> Gina [. . .] spürte die Leere im Bauch, den Tag im Gehirn, das Gerenne, das ihr Leben war. Sie vermisste Torge, rief ihn aber nicht an, rief niemanden an. Als es dämmerte, ging sie ohne Ziel aus dem Haus. Das Fahrrad, treu angekettet, ließ sie am Laternenpfahl stehen. (pp. 150–1)
>
> [Gina [. . .] felt an emptiness in her stomach, the day in her brain, the toing and froing that constituted her life. She missed Torge, but didn't ring him – she didn't ring anyone. As dusk fell she walked out of the building, no particular destination in mind. She left her bike loyally chained to a lamppost.]

There is a sense, then, of emptiness behind the hectic facade; Gina wishes for human contact but fails to reach out for it. She is 'ohne Ziel' [lit. without an aim]; her experiment will not be continued today. There is no easy or obvious answer, then, to the questions the text poses: what is the human cost, potentially, of scientific experimentation? What do we owe others, especially intimates? What defines humanity, and 'life'? On this last term: Gina is baffled by the fact that Torge, who just reads old books all day, seems 'lebendiger als sie' (p. 148) [livelier than her]. The humanities, then – or, more broadly, affect, imagination – render one living. This reflection recalls the references to the heart in 'Gina Regina'. It also forms an important plea in an era defined by homogenizing and instrumentalizing approaches to humanity and culture.[31]

Corporeality, Family and Genealogy in Draesner

The works are characteristic of Draesner's oeuvre in their engagement with medical and scientific debates and practices, and with the questions of subjectivity and agency. In the earlier novel *Mitgift* (2002), for example, the gendered body is subjected to medical manipulation. This novel features an intersex protagonist and as Lyn Marven suggests 'sets out and distils the thematic interests that recur in subsequent texts; namely, bodies, relationships, gender, sex, and reproduction'.[32] Anita

---

31 Compare Martha C. Nussbaum, *Not for Profit. Why Democracy Needs the Humanities* (Princeton: Princeton University Press, 2010).
32 Lyn Marven, 'Ulrike Draesner, *Mitgift*. On Bodies and Beauty', in *Emerging German-Language Novelists of the Twenty-First Century*, ed. by Lyn Marven and Stuart Taberner (Rochester, NY: Camden House, 2011), pp. 17–31 (p. 17).

is assigned femaleness at birth, but uncomfortable in this state, she transitions to maleness, assuming the name Axel. The questions of family and inheritance are given complex treatment. Aloe, Anita's sister, eventually becomes parent to Anita's son, Stefan, and so non-biological parenthood features, as the reference to Kleist's *Das Erdbeben in Chili* [*The Earthquake in Chile*] highlights.[33] Aloe's inability to conceive represents another instance of the trope of infertility and associated lack of agency already identified in Draesner, and the references to family background, and legacies of trauma, anticipate the later *Sieben Sprünge von Rand der Welt* and further complicate the novel's exploration of identity.

In the 2010 novel *Vorliebe*, Harriet, a physicist, is reunited with her first love, a pastor, by chance. This incident is the trigger for a revaluation of Harriet's life and a reassessment of her relationship with her partner Ash, who she realizes prioritizes himself, his work and his son Ben over her.[34] Step-parenting is positively valued here, nonetheless: Harriet 'mochte ihren Ash-Sohn; waren sie zu drei unterwegs, hielt man sie stets für eine Familie' [liked her Ash-son. When they were all out together, the three of them, people always took them for a family].[35] The transitoriness of human life – Harriet's lover dies – and the power of affect come into play in this text, which as mentioned involves a dialogue between science and theology that illustrates Draesner's aesthetics of encounter and of dialogue.[36] The exploration of subtly shifting human relations sits alongside these intellectual concerns, so that heart and mind, affect and intellect, are, once again, intertwined.

Draesner's posthumanism is developed in her 2014 novel *Sieben Sprünge vom Rand der Welt*, which also deals with memory, generationality, inheritance and humanity in a complex and bravura fashion. Its investigation into intergenerational trauma – in particular the trauma caused by the flight and expulsion of ethnic Germans after World War II – is bound up with its exploration of human identity as opposed to – or as involved with – animality, specifically primates. Its concern with neurology involves an elaboration on Draesner's earlier interests in matters relating to cognition, will and agency.[37] These ideas are not only explicitly investigated and discussed by characters, they are also worked out in and

---

33 See here Marven, 'Ulrike Draesner, *Mitgift*', pp. 20–21.
34 Ulrike Draesner, *Vorliebe* (Munich: Luchterhand, 2010), p. 29.
35 Draesner, *Vorliebe*, p. 70.
36 Karen Leeder termed Draesner's 'an aesthetics of encounter' during 'Leaping from the Edge of the World', and the term 'aesthetics of dialogue' arose during a discussion during that symposium.
37 See e.g. Draesner, *Sieben Sprünge*, p. 36, p. 37.

through their relationships, and what emerges is a compelling study of family and its relationship to forces of historical, cultural and scientific change.[38]

Conclusion

Reproduction and maternity; materialism and corporeality; and ethical, affective self-other relations have long been concerns of feminist theory, as they are for Draesner.[39] Draesner's posthumanist texts stress female subjectivity and agency and emphasize embodiment, affect and relationality.[40] In Draesner, the questions of family and inheritance are additionally given complex treatment. The exploration of subtly shifting human relations sits in her texts alongside intellectual concerns, so that heart and mind, affect and intellect, are intertwined. Her work combines an acknowledgement of emotionality, family and relationality with an awareness of genetics, neurology, reproductive technology, socio-biology and so on. Draesner's aesthetics of encounter or dialogue indeed involves frequent citation of concepts and terms from diverse fields. The work invokes literary, philosophical, psychoanalytic and theological discourses, among others.

It is this distinctive aesthetic that makes her work poised to respond with particular nimbleness and fruitfulness to Haraway's call for a new figuration of humanity. Haraway asserts: 'Feminist humanity must, somehow, both resist representation, resist literal figuration, and still erupt in powerful new tropes, new figures of speech, new turns of historical possibility'.[41] Draesner's stories constitute such eruption; with their taut and surprising style, their lyricism and their trickery, they involve new ways of speaking, imply new 'turns of possibility'. Draesner has expressed her interest in '[d]ie Einmischung der Materialität des Körpers in Sprache' [the interference of bodily materiality in language],

---

38 See e.g. Draesner, *Sieben Sprünge*, p. 53.

39 See also Gerodetti and Mottier, 'Feminism(s) and the Politics of Reproduction'; Emily Jeremiah, *Troubling Maternity. Mothering, Agency, and Ethics in Women's Writing in German of the 1970s and 1980s* (Leeds: Maney/MHRA, 2003); Emily Jeremiah, 'Introduction: Developing a Nomadic Ethics', in *Nomadic Ethics*, pp. 1–28.

40 On the importance of relationality in Draesner, see Stephanie Catani and Friedhelm Marx, 'Vorwort', in *Familien – Geschlechter – Macht. Beziehungen im Werk Ulrike Draesners*, ed. by Stephanie Catani and Friedhelm Marx (Göttingen: Wallstein, 2008), pp. 7–11 (p. 8).

41 Donna Haraway, 'Ecce Homo, Ain't (Ar'n't) I a woman, and Inappropriate/d Others: The Human in a Post-Human Landscape', in *The Haraway Reader*, pp. 47–61 (p. 47).

observing how powerful are the senses in comparison with language.[42] Draesner's prose, at once intellectual and sensual, invites both theoretical reflections and affective responses, contributing to an ongoing feminist redefinition of humanity and humaneness.

The work itself constitutes a form of (re)production and (re)generation, involving what Braidotti terms 'transposition': 'an intertextual, cross-boundary or transversal transfer, in the sense of a leap from one code, field or axis into another'.[43] Thus it demonstrates the potential of literature and of literary studies – and of the humanities more broadly – to probe, and also make us feel, what it is that may define humanity, such as the capacity to develop ethical systems and inventive artworks as well as medical and scientific technologies. Exploring the links between poetry and science, Karen Leeder notes that poetry has the capacity to express scientific ideas and 'anchor[] them within the broader cultural and historical context'. Poetry can test out, and flesh out, scientific discoveries and debates; as Leeder argues, it thereby becomes 'an instrument of investigation': 'not one that seeks to eliminate ambiguities, rather one that comes into its own where those ambiguities begin, and [that] can offer a different and perhaps greater truth'.[44] In particular, I suggest, literary discourse is well placed to introduce and explore questions of ethics, as Draesner's work illustrates strikingly and importantly.[45]

Stephanie Catani and Friedhelm Marx observe that Draesner's prose, poetry and essays thematize medical and scientific progress, as well as the social change that this gives rise to, and that literature itself participates in such social shifts.[46] Indeed, Draesner's work enters productively into dialogue with the culture at large, addressing urgent questions relating to humanity and ethics. It forces us to confront and to seek to articulate what remains of our humanity, advocating '*pleasure* in the confusion of boundaries' as well as '*responsibility* in their construction', as we have seen. At the end of her book *Metamorphoses*, Braidotti describes a bungee performance she witnesses, noting 'the triumph of the technobody' and going

---

42 Ulrike Draesner, 'Wie das Deutsche sein Wesen treibt. Esel und Seele auf der Brücke der Sprache', in *Literatur im Fluss: Brücken zwischen Poesie und Religion*, ed. by Erich Garhammer (Regensburg: Pustet, 2015), pp. 51–59 (p. 57).

43 Braidotti, *Transpositions*, p. 5.

44 Karen Leeder, 'Durs Grünbein and the Poetry of Science', in *Durs Grünbein. A Companion*, ed. by Michael Eskin, Karen Leeder and Christopher Young (Berlin and New York: de Gruyter, 2013), pp. 67–93 (pp. 74, 92).

45 See also Jeremiah and Matthes, 'Introduction', pp. 4–6.

46 Catani and Marx, 'Vorwort', p. 7.

on to reflect: 'I was watching a collective metamorphosis. Those in it were no float-ing signifiers, but rather fleeting reminders of a humanity that has half-gone, and yet still endures: just hanging in there. Aren't we all?'[47] Draesner's work too offers us fleeting reminders of our half-gone humanity, indicating its enduring traces and asking us if we are indeed 'just hanging in there'.

---

47 Rosi Braidotti, *Metamorphosis. Towards a Materialist Theory of Becoming* (Cambridge: Pol-ity Press, 2002), pp. 269–270.

Silke Horstkotte
Photography and the Posthuman in Ulrike Draesner's *Mitgift* and *Vorliebe*

Between Language and Images

To be human is to have language. In his preface to the Psalms, Martin Luther cites the ability to speak as the decisive criterion that separates humans from non-human animals.[1] Medieval anthropology knew of several specific differences between human and non-human animals; besides language, these also included walking upright and the ability to write. Luther, however, insists exclusively on the exceptionality of human language. Following in his wake, and radicalizing Luther's thought, Johann Gottfried Herder concludes 250 years later that 'even as an animal, man has language'.[2] For Herder, humans are linguistic beings through and through. Language is not a higher faculty that separates us from non-human animals because we have reason and they do not; language permeates us so much that even our animal nature includes the use of language. As Arnold Gehlen remarks, Herder's sentence anticipates modern anthropology in its entirety.[3] As a rational and linguistic being, humans are part of nature but at the same time we are something different, all the way through our anatomy and physiology. To be human is to be, uniquely, both animal and not-animal.

To be human is to have images. Before we speak, images order our world and shape our experience. Painted and graven images constitute some of the oldest archaeological evidence of human cultural activity – predating records of human speech and writing by tens of thousands of years. Set against an exclusive emphasis on man as a linguistic being, an understanding which has dominated philosophical anthropology since Luther's time, art historians and Visual Studies scholars have recently focused on image-making and image-viewing as crucial activities that make us human. For the art historian Gottfried Boehm,

---

1 Martin Luther, *Luthers Werke. Kritische Gesamtausgabe; Die Deutsche Bibel*, 12 vols (Weimar: Böhlau, 1912–1961), vol. 10.1, p. 100. Compare Albrecht Beutel, *Protestantische Konkretionen: Studien zur Kirchengeschichte* (Tübingen: Mohr Siebeck, 1998), p. 112.
2 Johann Gottfried Herder, 'Abhandlung über den Ursprung der Sprache', in *Werke in zehn Bänden*, vol. 1: *Frühe Schriften*, ed. by Ulrich Gaier (Frankfurt a. M.: Deutscher Klassiker-Verlag, 1985), pp. 695–810.
3 Arnold Gehlen, *Der Mensch. Seine Natur und seine Stellung in der Welt*, 14th edn, (Wiebelsheim: Aula, 2004), p. 84.

https://doi.org/10.1515/9783110495942-005

man is first and foremost a *homo pictor*, a maker of images.[4] Hans Belting's *Anthropology of Images* describes the practice of image-making as closely interwoven with the archaic cult of the dead and as a fundamental human cultural technique: images come into being as alternative embodiments of the dead and are therefore dependent on a distinct carrier medium. While the image is embodied in this medium, the medium also regulates the bodily experiences of contemporary spectators. For this reason, the history of images forms part of a history of the human body, and refers both to the cultural history of bodily constructs, and the history of sense perception as a physical activity.[5]

The two designations of humans as linguistic beings, on the one hand, and as makers and spectators of images, on the other, make strange contact in Ulrike Draesner's poem 'formation fontanelle' ['fontanelle formation'].[6] The poem reflects a conversation between an I, most likely a woman, and her former lover, most likely a man. Although the two interlocutors are not explicitly gendered, the majority of Draesner's poems speak from a female perspective and articulate female bodily experience and knowledge. More specifically, such a gender distribution seems probable because of the positions that are ascribed to both speakers, positions that concern the two conflicting anthropological theses sketched out above. The poem 'formation fontanelle' consists of a patchwork of quotations from a conversation between the two figures, and reflections made during that conversation, partly by the speaker and partly by the lover. The overall perspective of the poem, however, is a retrospective one, in which the speaker remembers fragments of what her lover said – winter being over, a flight of geese 'in wechselnder, stets / wachsender [. . .] formation' [in shifting, ever / growing formation], and wonders whether the two will ever get back together: 'ob wir noch mal / zusammen kommen' [whether we will ever / come together again].

Interwoven with these unmarked fragments of speech is a second type of utterances which reflect on and develop the lover's remarks into trains of images. Thus, the formation of geese first becomes 'ein halber tulpenkelch' [half a tulip calyx], then 'das späte alphabet' [the late alphabet] – 'ein v ein z ein w' [a 'v' a 'z' a 'w'] – finally trickling into the (speaker's?) fontanelle, 'wo / wir aus bildern sind' [where / we are made of images]. The second strophe, while clarifying that

---

4 *Homo Pictor*, ed. by Gottfried Boehm (Munich and Leipzig: K. G. Saur, 2001).
5 Hans Belting, *An Anthropology of Images. Picture, Medium, Body* (Princeton, NJ: Princeton University Press, 2011).
6 Ulrike Draesner, *kugelblitz* (Munich: Luchterhand, 2005), pp. 26–27. Translations are my own unless otherwise stated.

the alphabet remark originates with the man – 'sagtest du' [you said] – leaves it open whether that remark was made in reference to the 'härtester Winter' [harshest winter] or to the formation of geese. The strophe also further complicates the relation between what is being seen, what is being said, and the metaphoric expressions in the poem that emerge from both, by introducing the enigmatic image of a ray of light that confuses itself, leaps away, and finally becomes a small three-legged black dog 'wie ein känguruh wie / unruh see und himmelsformation' [like a kangaroo like / unrest sea and sky formation]. The third strophe rearranges and varies the motifs of birds, flowers, dog and sky once more, again referring to the 'fontanellen wo wir bildern' [fontanelles where we [make] images] before closing the poem with a final one-word 'fort' [away].

The poetic technique of rearranging and varying a limited number of sentences, images and motifs has an ancestor in Clemens Brentano's 'Der Spinnerin Nachtlied' ['The Night Song of the Girl Spinning'].[7] The pious 'Gott wolle uns vereinen' [please God to unite us] of the Brentano here becomes the more mundane question 'ob wir noch mal / zusammen kommen'. Like its famous precursor, 'formation fontanelle' is both a love poem and a poetological poem. But where Brentano's poem draws explicit parallels between spinning and singing, drawing both together in the person of the spinning girl, Draesner's poem leaves open where its reflections and metaphoric transformations originate. Do they all come from the poem's speaker, are some of them also contributed by the lover, or are they situated in a sphere beyond the individual figures of speaker and lover? A second difference between pretext and intertext concerns the means by which connections are made and variations are held together. Brentano uses a musical pattern of rhyme, sound, and tone, uniting the one-line clauses that make up 'Der Spinnerin Nachtlied' through an alternating pattern of 'a'- and 'ei'-rhymes (Jahren / waren, Nachtigall / Schall; weinen / scheinen, allein / rein). Draesner relies on what may be described as a visual equivalent of this sound pattern, as the v of the bird formation finds a counterpart in the image of the tulip calyx or chalice, while the formation inside the fontanelle is mirrored in the second strophe's 'himmelsformation' [sky formation]: microcosm rhyming (metaphorically speaking) with macrocosm. The lovers themselves become a flock ('schwarm'). Thus, rather than finding rhymes, 'formation fontanelle' uses images to evoke a train of thought and to create coherence. However, because these are metaphoric images they are situated ambivalently between visual imagination and linguistic expression.

---

7 Clemens Brentano, *Sämtliche Werke und Briefe. Historisch-kritische Ausgabe*, ed. by Jürgen Behrens, Wolfgang Frühwald and Detlev Lüders (Stuttgart: Kohlhammer, 1975–), Frankfurter Brentano-Ausgabe, vol. 19, pp. 96–97.

At the heart of this chain of metaphorical equivalences sits the idea of a 'fontanellenloch (wo / wir aus bildern sind)' [fontanelle gap (where / we are made of images)] which also lends the poem its title. In this complex image, the two anthropological conceptions of the human as a linguistic and as a pictorial being come together in uneasy tension – a tension which also underlies the plotting and characterization in some of Draesner's prose fiction, especially in the novels *Mitgift* and *Vorliebe*. I see this tension as key to Draesner's ongoing literary engagement with what it means to be human in a posthuman age, and with biopolitics more generally. The poem 'formation fontanelle' evokes two different modes of perception, one that sees the world in terms of language and of discrete signs ('ein v ein z ein w'), while the other turns the same shape into the integral form of the tulip, which then becomes an independent visual metaphor that can drip into the (speaker's?) fontanelle 'where we are made of images'. Thus, the poem implies that our brains – inside our skulls – are the place where what we have visually perceived makes us into what we are: beings who are put together by the images we receive.

This anthropological thesis mirrors a phenomenological concept of the image which emphasizes the activity of the image in the process of being perceived. Since Ulrike Draesner is a widely-read author whose texts are, at least partly, shaped by a poetics of knowledge, it is well worth pursuing the phenomenological line of thinking which underlies the implicit poetics of the image in Draesner's texts, but from which Draesner also diverges in some ways. For Jean-Luc Nancy, the image effectuates an intimate force that moves us; activity in this process is wholly on the side of the image.[8] Bernhard Waldenfels describes every perception as a reciprocal action of 'pathos' (that which comes toward me) and 'response' (my answer to this other).[9] Like Nancy, Waldenfels proceeds from Husserl's theory of the image act, according to which the image is only that which appears or presents itself to me, not its material shape.[10] For a phenomenological theory of the image, the image is 'not an object that we see additionally, as another thing, but a medium of seeing which is itself involved in seeing and of which we become aware as a medium'.[11] The term 'medium', in

---

8 Jean-Luc Nancy, *The Ground of the Image*, trans. by Jeff Fort (New York: Fordham University Press, 2005).

9 Bernhard Waldenfels, *Sinne und Künste im Wechselspiel. Modi ästhetischer Erfahrung* (Berlin: Suhrkamp, 2010).

10 Edmund Husserl, *Phantasy and Image Consciousness [1904/1905]. Phantasy, Image Consciousness, and Memory (1898–1925)*, trans. by John B. Brough (Dordrecht: Springer, 2005), pp. 1–206.

11 Waldenfels, *Sinne und Künste*, p. 43.

this context, refers to any kind of in-between, in the broadest sense. Jean-Luc Nancy goes even further when he identifies the image itself with the process of its being seen, a process in which I become entangled in the image even as the material ground of the image disappears.

It is tempting to associate this kind of phenomenological understanding of the image (that Draesner seems to evoke in 'formation fontanelle') with the putatively female perspective of the poem's speaker. After all, the alphabet reading, against which the tulip image is pitched, seems to be contributed by the male lover. While the alphabet reading implies a disembodied deciphering of signs and a clear distinction between object and subject of perception, the tulip image only becomes realized when it appears to the viewer, who then takes it up into her body, thus negating a subject-object distinction. Both the passivity of this reception and the lack of a clear subject-object distinction appear suggestive of a female gender stereotype. At the same time, however, it is important not to overstate the opposition between an active male deciphering and a passive female absorption of images in 'formation fontanelle'. It should be noted that the poem's speaker does not receive the tulip image through her eyes but through the fontanelle, which is ossified in adults. The 'formation fontanelle' produced in this process cannot be a simple reception of an outside image, but needs to be understood as a complex formation process in which linguistic and cognitive faculties as well as the poetic imagination take an active part. The halved tulip calyx dripping into the fontanelle, after all, is a metaphor invented by the speaker, and it is only through this metaphor that we reach the place 'where we are made of images'. The poem itself, then, proves to be a 'formation fontanelle', because it is here that images and language are joined together so closely that the alternative between the human as a linguistic and as a pictorial being becomes meaningless. According to this first reading of Draesner's work, then, humans are both linguistic and pictorial beings, and they realize the potential for both as men and as women.

Digital Image Culture and Posthumanism

Ulrike Draesner develops this phenomenologically-affected anthropology in greater detail in her novels *Mitgift* and *Vorliebe*.[12] She does so from a decisively contemporary standpoint by evoking a situation in which images are

---

12 Ulrike Draesner, *Mitgift* (Munich: Luchterhand, 2002); *Vorliebe* (Munich: Luchterhand, 2010).

omnipresent, but in which their representational potential has become, nevertheless, extremely problematic. Never before in the history of humankind have as many pictures been produced as today – most of them digital photographs which are staged, edited and adapted to the fantasy of their photographers to a previously unthinkable extent. In the words of photography critic Fred Ritchin,

> photography in the digital environment involves the reconfiguration of the image into a mosaic of millions of changeable pixels, not a continuous tone imprint of visible reality. Rather than a quote from appearances, it serves as an initial recording, a preliminary script, which may precede a quick and easy reshuffling.[13]

The photograph, which many critics until recently took to be a mechanical trace and inscription of the real, without an intervening human subjectivity, has become almost indistinguishable from imaging techniques such as 3D-ultrasound images or the pictures produced by the Hubble telescope, which look like photographs but are in fact visualizations of non-visual data or combinations of optical camera images, spectrographies and thermal images.

On the one hand, these technologically produced images realize the fantasy of a non-subjective perspective. On the other, however, they do not picture a reality we could have seen in any other way than through these images – thereby undermining the entire idea of an objective 'real'. Moreover, these images coexist, sometimes even overlap with, digital photographs which are extremely subjective (because highly edited according to the subjective preferences of their photographers). These images, too, although they have been adapted to their photographers' visual preferences, do not express a way of seeing the world that has any basis outside of the images themselves. They are much more radically divorced from a sense of objectivity, and of realism, than analogue photographs, which also show an image of reality that diverges in important ways from the image given to us through our senses. What a photograph – even an analogue one – shows us is not an image of the real but a model of seeing, based on a culturally specific way of constructing pictures (through monocular central perspective), that in turn shapes our idea of visual sense perception.[14]

Into the abyss opening up between images and things that are not quite images – into this evacuation of the image from itself – Ulrike Draesner's novels introduce the following two-fold question: what happens to the image if it is not an expression of the human body, and radically divorced from sense perception? And

---

13 Fred Ritchin, *After Photography* (New York: Norton, 2009), p. 18.
14 Joel Snyder, 'Picturing Vision', in *The Language of Images*, ed. by W. J. T. Mitchell (Chicago: University of Chicago Press, 1980), pp. 219–246.

what happens to man as a *homo pictor* in the digital visual culture in which these non/images have their place? How – to draw both questions together – does the idea of the human as a pictorial being change if the images with which men and women have to deal do not assure them of their humanity, but represent a posthuman view of the world? With these questions, Draesner's novels lead us into current debates about the posthuman, and about a bioaesthetics which reflects the philosophical discourse of biopolitics through artistic means.

As Rosi Braidotti explains, posthuman theory reacts to the double challenge to the concept of the human posed by present-day scientific advances (in, for instance, reproductive medicine, stem cell research or cosmetic surgery), and by global economic concerns.[15] The resulting posthuman condition introduces a 'qualitative shift in our thinking about what exactly is the basic unit of common reference for our species, our polity and our relationship to the other inhabitants of this planet'.[16] In the biogenetic age known as the 'anthropocene', the 'historical moment when the Human has become a geological force capable of affecting all life on this planet', Braidotti calls for a 'new ecological posthumanism [that] raises issues of power and entitlement in the age of globalization and calls for self-reflexivity on the part of the subjects who occupy the former humanist centre, but also those who dwell in one of the many scattered centres of power of advanced post-modernity'.[17] Defined within an 'eco-philosophy of multiple belongings', the posthuman subject is 'a relational subject constituted in and by multiplicity, that is to say a subject that works across differences and is also internally differentiated, but still grounded and accountable', 'embodied and embedded'.[18]

The changing conception of the image, and the accompanying changes to the status of individual images, may appear less threatening to our ideas of the human than the changes associated with a globalizing neoliberalism, or with genetic engineering. But the posthumanity of digital images, too, has its part in the discourse of the anthropocene. In this context, images and imaging practices are beset with fears of dehumanizing representation, but also with utopian hopes for a better posthuman future. Critics like Elizabeth Grosz and Boris Groys, who consider the role of visual art within the radically shifting biopolitics of the anthropocene, argue that art has the potential to overcome the containment of the present by elaborating on futures yet to come. For Grosz, art has an intensely political function because it is a bioaesthetics charged with

---

15 Rosi Braidotti, *The Posthuman* (Cambridge: Polity, 2013). On the posthuman see also the chapter by Emily Jeremiah in this volume.
16 Ibid., p. 2.
17 Ibid., p. 5, p. 49.
18 Ibid., p. 49.

the creation of new worlds and forms of life.[19] Boris Groys sees life and art as infused with technology in a biopolitical age. Just as images of the real turn into simulacra of imaging technologies, life can be artificially altered or enhanced until natural and artificial life become undistinguishable. Groys compares the tendency of art galleries no longer to show original artwork in favour instead of documenting happenings or installations to the substitution of artificial simulations for real life in cloning, which to him emblematizes the biopolitical age.[20]

Ulrike Draesner is a knowledgeable author, always up to speed on developments in cultural theory. Her novels *Mitgift* and *Vorliebe* constitute carefully constructed interventions in the discussions of which I have sketched out only a few strands. Indeed, a number of early contributors to these debates are named explicitly in *Mitgift*, including such classics as Judith Butler and Michel Foucault. Both novels also engage with new scientific advances that throw into doubt long-held convictions about what it means to be human. Lukas, one of the central characters of *Mitgift*, is an astrophysicist, as is Harriet, the protagonist in *Vorliebe*. The research programs of these two characters challenge an anthropocentric world view, while the intersex character Anita subverts the splitting of the human into male and female. Both *Mitgift* and *Vorliebe* can therefore be read as repositories for a poetics of knowledge of the present, a poetics of knowledge that is centrally concerned with biopolitics or maybe anthropopolitics, a policing of the human.[21]

But that poetics of knowledge needs to be understood through the lens of the photographic images through which biopolitical issues are introduced and addressed in both novels. More than anything else, *Mitgift* and *Vorliebe* are important literary contributions to the study of contemporary visual culture. Both engage with visual culture theory to address the contested question of human nature as linguistic or as pictorial, but also as counting, measuring and calculating, and to the simultaneous interweaving and growing problematization of these assignations in the present. In his post-photographic theory, Fred Ritchin argues that 'at very fundamental levels our media, in the digital environment, will profoundly and permanently change us – our worldview, our concept of soul and art, our sense of possibility'.[22] In *Mitgift*, and to a lesser extent also in

---

19 Elizabeth Grosz, *Chaos, Territory, Art. Deleuze and the Framing of the Earth* (New York: Columbia University Press, 2008).
20 Boris Groys, 'Art in the Age of Biopolitics. From Artwork to Art Documentation', in *Katalog*, ed. by documenta11 (Ostfildern: Hatje Canz, 2002), pp. 108–114.
21 On a 'Poetics of Knowledge' see also the chapter by Michael Braun in this volume.
22 Ritchin, *After Photography*, p. 10.

Vorliebe, Draesner illustrates some of these changes through her carefully crafted plots and characters. However, she goes beyond a mechanistic view, in which the image works on us, by outlining a phenomenological understanding of the image in which image and spectator are not fully separated from each other. In *Mitgift*, photography constitutes a central focus through which all other discourses which Draesner introduces into the novel – such as scientific criticism, biopolitical and gender theory, and the postmodern deconstruction of the subject – are viewed. In *Vorliebe*, photographs are somewhat less conspicuous, but here too the ways of being in the world that are embodied in the four protagonists cannot be detached from their respective engagement with images. The second half of this chapter concentrates on describing this poetics of the image in *Mitgift* and draws on *Vorliebe* to support that argument.

Mitgift and Memory Mania

Mitgift tells the story of the two sisters Aloe and Anita. Anita was born with an enlarged clitoris which was adjusted to a heteronormative female anatomy during a long series of invasive operations. Her family, however, have kept stubbornly silent about Anita's intersexuality. Only in her mother's rare outbursts and later also those of her sister Aloe is she called a 'Zwitter' [hermaphrodite]. Yet Anita's deviant sexual identity finds indirect expression through all other characters: the uptight mother begins an affair with her childhood sweetheart, the US soldier Gary; Aloe denies her sexuality by becoming anorexic; Aloe's boyfriend Lukas seeks pleasure in a luxury brothel. The novel's title *Mitgift* calls up the complex of familial inheritance, so prevalent in German literature at the time of the novel's publication (2002). But the family secrets in *Mitgift* relate less to the historical inheritance of the Nazi era than to biological heredity and reproduction. In the two sisters Aloe and Anita, Draesner draws the signature of an era in which hygiene has been replaced by stress-management, sex by genetic engineering, and reproduction by replication, as the Oxford postgraduate Patrizia remarks in the novel (*Mitgift*, pp. 26–27). The photographic images in *Mitgift*, too, gain their meaning within this biopolitically charged context.

Compared with other novels which describe or include photographs, the wealth and breadth of photographic discourses and practices evoked in *Mitgift* is remarkable. In 2002, when *Mitgift* came out, the key author whose use of photographs dominated the literary scene and the study of photography in fiction was W.G. Sebald, whose novel *Austerlitz* had been published the previous year. With

Schwindel. Gefühle [*Vertigo*], *Die Ausgewanderten* [*The Emigrants*] and *Die Ringe des Saturn* [*The Rings of Saturn*], Sebald had already published three previous prose works interspersing printed texts with reproductions of photographs, maps, charts and other images to great acclaim. Monika Maron's *Pawels Briefe* [*Pavel's Letters*] had come out in 1999 and Marcel Beyer's *Spione* [*Spies*] in 2000. In 2003, Stefan Wackwitz's *Ein unsichtbares Land* [*An Invisible Country*] would be published alongside a re-edition of Peter Henisch's *Die kleine Figur meines Vaters* [*The small Figure of my Father*]. Alongside these books, which include photographic reproductions, stands Ulla Hahn's novel *Unscharfe Bilder* (2003) [*Blurred Images*], which describes photographs but does not reproduce them.

The 2000s were the decade of a memory boom, or even 'memory mania', when a large number of generational or new family novels reconsidered German history through the lens of family memories.[23] The photographs in these books – often family snapshots, but also publicly known documentary photographs – explored an ambivalent relation between documentation, imagination and memory. Often directly or indirectly influenced by theories of photography from Walter Benjamin to Roland Barthes, they exposed photographic objectivity as a myth; Sebald in particular went to great lengths to show how the photograph is always subject to interpretation, if not outright manipulation and distortion, and is also deeply dependent on contextual information external to the image.[24]

This is the context in which Ulrike Draesner's *Mitgift* has to be considered, since these books – especially Sebald's work – have been studied extensively and have been extremely influential in directing critical thinking about photography in fiction.[25] It is a context with which *Mitgift* shares some connections, but in which it also stands out. One of the common concerns highlighted by the use of photographs within the new family novel is the role of family and the structuring of history through the pattern of generations. *Mitgift* tells the story of the Böhm family, Holger and Ingrid Böhm and their daughters Aloe and Anita. Numerous motifs and structures serve to highlight the theme of inheritance. There is the grandmother Katja with her amber necklace, for example; the motif of the family

---

23 See Friederike Eigler, *Gedächtnis und Geschichte in Generationenromanen seit der Wende* (Berlin: Erich Schmidt, 2005); *Generational Shifts in Contemporary German Culture*, ed. by Laurel Cohen-Pfister and Susanne Vees-Gulani (Rochester, NY: Camden House, 2010).
24 *Searching for Sebald. Photography after W. G. Sebald*, ed. by Lise Patt and Christel Dillbohner (Los Angeles: The Institute of Cultural Inquiry, 2007); Silke Horstkotte, *Nachbilder: Fotografie und Gedächtnis in der deutschen Gegenwartsliteratur* (Cologne, Weimar, Vienna: Böhlau, 2009).
25 *Photography in Fiction*, ed. by Silke Horstkotte and Nancy Pedri, special issue, *Poetics Today*, 29.1 (2008).

heirloom and the theme of inheritance is further underscored by the title, *Mitgift* (literally, dowry, but more evocative of giving or passing on than the English term). There is the ambivalent, if not hostile, relationship between Aloe, the protagonist, and her sister Anita, who was born with indeterminate sexual organs but whose intersexuality has been hushed up in the family. There are other family secrets too, especially Ingrid's clandestine relationship with the American soldier Gary, and this secret in particular goes back to the early post-war years, to Germany's Allied occupation, and thus broadly speaking to the Nazi theme which is at the heart of the vast majority of family novels from the early 2000s. This connection to history through family, family secrets and family heirlooms aligns Draesner's novel with family novels such as Tanja Dückers' *Himmelskörper* (2003) [*Celestial Bodies*].

In *Mitgift*, however, this entire thematic complex remains in the background, forming the backdrop to the unfolding love story between Aloe and her boyfriend Lukas, and to the story of Aloe's complicated relationship with her sister Anita. Both stories are told in retrospect: each of the novel's five chapters is introduced by an episode set in the present where we encounter Aloe raising Anita's son Stefan. On each of these three narrative layers, photographic practices and the consumption of photographs serve to regulate the characters' relationships with one another, and with their environment. Different ways of using and of looking at photographic images also connect the three narrative layers with one another. The generational pattern on the third, chronologically most distant, layer (Aloe and Anita) situates photographs in relation to the human body. On the second layer, however, that relation is radically questioned by Aloe's and Lukas's thinking about photography, since both privilege a posthuman photography that cuts ties with the human body. This view is paralleled in *Vorliebe*, where Harriet also engages with the images from the Hubble telescope that fascinate Lukas in *Mitgift*. The third temporal layer of *Mitgift* extends the posthuman discourse of photography, but it also modifies Aloe's attitude towards photography by showing how photographs can express a human subjectivity even in a digital anthropocene.

Surface and Distance

The story of Aloe and Lukas, the most important of the three narrative layers in *Mitgift*, begins with a visit that Aloe pays to Lukas at Oxford. Both met at Oxford as undergraduates; now Aloe has moved back to Germany in order to complete a doctorate in art history, while Lukas stays on at Oxford. As Aloe walks out of the customs area at Heathrow, the first sight that greets her is an advertising hoarding with a fashion spread: 'Werbung für den Sommer: eine junge Frau unter Wasser, oder Werbung für Taucherbrillen, denn was die Frau trug, war gelb und grün und riesengroß' (p. 14) [an advertisement for summer: a young woman under water, or an ad for diving goggles, since the thing the woman wore was yellow and green and huge]. Everything about this placard reminds Aloe of her intersex sister Anita, whose hormonal treatments have given her a highly desirable feminine physique, while retaining a more masculine muscula-ture. Anita is the walking image of 1990s fitness culture, and a sought-after fashion model. A few pages before the Heathrow episode, the topic of fashion photography is introduced through a recurring daydream of Aloe's in which she sees a woman just like the one on the hoarding – under water, with yellow and green goggles – who smiles lovingly at Aloe. In the dream, Aloe has an in-tense physical reaction to the woman's smile: 'und immer pocht Aloes Herz an dieser Stelle so sehr' (p.10) [and at this point Aloe's heart always beats so hard]. But when she encounters the hoarding at Heathrow, Aloe rejects the closeness which the photo seems to promise by turning away, refusing to be reminded of Anita. Of course, the connection offered by the poster is a superficial one. The image does not reveal anything about Anita or about their relationship. It is not even a photo of Anita, just reminiscent of the types of photos that Aloe associ-ates with Anita. Moreover, it is not a private family photograph but a public image calling for fast consumption which is available to everyone. But whether the image really shows Anita herself or not is not the point, as the woman on the poster has stopped being a human subject and become a consumer commodity. The hoarding itself is placed in an environment – the arrivals area at an airport – where the viewer is bombarded with images that are endlessly repeated as he or she stumbles, stiff and dehydrated, out of the sensory deprivation of the plane. Unlike the family photographs in the novels by Sebald, Maron or Beyer, the ad-vertisement does not point to the past but illustrates a contemporary global media culture in which the same anonymous images circulate everywhere we go.

While Aloe shoots a parting glance at the poster that does not permit the connection she both seeks and avoids, her boyfriend Lukas is interested in a distanced or elevated perspective on the universe, which does not aim at seeing details but at grasping the big picture, and for which digital screens are better suited than photography. Lukas's fascination with a cosmos that cannot be per-ceived by human means finds a continuation in the mathematician Harriet in *Vorliebe*. In a key scene of the latter novel, a series of satellite images of the galaxy published in the magazine *Geo* are confronted with the reproduction of a Ruysdael painting that Harriet has put up in her kitchen. The Ruysdael is said to remind Harriet of her childhood feeling that the world does not end where it stops (*Vorliebe*, p. 32). Ruysdael evokes this border metonymically (by implying that the world continues behind the horizon), but the satellite images pretend to actually show what lies behind the perceivable world. In *Vorliebe* this pretence is exposed as a fiction: the *Geo* images do not show the cosmos as it has been recorded by the satellite. The images had to be edited by Harriet to conform to the human idea of the starry sky. The unedited images would not be legible for uninstructed spectators. What the cosmos really looks like, according to recorded data, is unbearable:

> Die nicht gesäuberten Computerzeichnungen hatten etwas Schreckliches. Als sehe man, für Sekunden, durch die Maske eines viel größeren, mehrdimensionalen Wesens. Es war mechanisch, überlegen, unendlich kalt. (*Vorliebe*, p. 48)

> [Before they were cleaned up, the computer graphs had something terrifying about them. As if one were seeing, for seconds, through the mask of a far larger, multidimensional being. It was mechanical, superior, infinitely cold.]

A genuinely posthuman vision of things that do not conform to our perception, and that exist outside of any relation with human measure, is unbearable for human spectators. Harriet gets out of this conundrum by using numbers to produce patterns and create connections even if these do not necessarily mean anything.

Besides the satellite images, Lukas, in *Mitgift*, is also associated with a second type of image. When he visits Aloe in her Oxford college room for the first time, Lukas leaves behind a stack of pornographic postcards:

> Eine gut trainierte, stark geschminkte Frau, Oberkörper in einem roten Lederbody, schwarze Weichgummistiefel bis übers Knie, Brustwarzen frei, blickte in die Kamera, als ginge es sie nichts an. Sie erledigte ihre Aufgabe, kalt, geschäftstüchtig, mit der Präzision eines Insektes, das einem anderen den Hinterleib in Stücke säbelt. (*Mitgift*, p. 36)

> [A muscular woman wearing a lot of make-up, her upper body trussed in red leather, soft black rubber over-the-knee boots, nipples uncovered, looking into the camera as if all this were of no concern to her. She carried out her duty coldly, efficiently, with the precision of an insect slicing another insect's abdomen into pieces.]

With their obviously staged, unemotional depiction, the postcards seem at first to invite a cold, distanced gaze; Aloe takes them to be a present from Lukas, promising her a secure life by his side, a functional relationship based on give or take without emotional involvement ('geben und nehmen, ohne sich auszusetzen', ibid.). In the course of the novel, Lukas does indeed prove to be unable to see Aloe as a person in her own right, rather than as an object of his needs and his desires. The pornographic cards are just as symptomatic of this inability as the satellite images which Lukas examines after his first date with Aloe.

As Lukas stares at the images of blue or red stars gleaming on his computer screen, he soon forgets Aloe again. The reader, meanwhile, is led to understand that the main function of celestial images in *Mitgift* is not in fact to reference outer space, but rather to indicate the personality of Lukas who looks at them. The meaning and importance of photographic images in Draesner's novels does not lie in their content – what the images show – but in the way(s) in which they are seen and experienced. Particularly in *Mitgift*, photographic discourses do not centre on the photographic image itself, its technology or its reference, but on the relation between images and their spectators, on the ways in which spectators arrive at their interpretation of photographic images, and on the underlying statement these make about the subjectivity of the spectator. Thus, even the Hubble telescope images, which were not shot by a human photographer and do not correspond to a human gaze, and may therefore be rightfully called an example of posthuman photography, remain bound to a human horizon.

Mitgift offers us a phenomenological idea of the photographic image: a photograph is not so much about what it shows as about how that is seen and experienced by the viewer. That experience emerges out of a collusion between the subject, the photographic surface and the objects that it depicts. Thus, the photographic image opens up a space of potentiality in which subject and object may encounter each other. In this way, photographs make or unmake relations. Theorists of photography such as Ariella Azouley, Susie Linfield or Margaret Olin have recently argued that photography makes connections with people, that photographs build community, create affect and foster engagement with others, even altruism.[26] Draesner's novels seem to arrive at a more sceptical conclusion. When Aloe later takes pictures of Lukas, this does not provide her with knowledge of who he is; indeed, her picture-taking seems more a form of estrangement than a method for fostering affect and empathy.

Abstraction

In the opening episode of chapter 2, Aloe is a moderately successful photo artist discussing photography with her new partner, Frank. Asked by Frank how long

---

26 Ariella Azoulay, *The Civil Contract of Photography* (New York: Zone Books, 2008); Susie Linfield, *The Cruel Radiance. Photography and Political Violence* (Chicago: University of Chicago Press, 2010); Margaret Olin, *Touching Photographs* (Chicago: University of Chicago Press, 2012).

she has been taking pictures, Aloe replies not with a date but with her justification for photography as an art form:

> Weil du lernst, etwas zweimal zu sehen. Und wenn du es zweimal sehen kannst, dann auch hundertmal. Auf einem guten Foto durchschaust du einen Körper als all die Körper, die er einmal gewesen ist und die er noch werden kann. (*Mitgift*, p. 61)

> [Because you learn to see something twice. And if you can see it twice you can see it a hundred times. In a good photo you see through a body, recognizing in it all those bodies it has been and it can still become.]

Photography, for Aloe, is intimately connected with the body; at the same time, she finds in photography a tool for distancing the body from its human subjectivity. A body is all bodies, past and future, nothing individual. The artist who for Aloe most embodies this dehumanization and desubjectivation is Spencer Tunick, who photographs large crowds of naked people. Aloe, who has written her doctoral dissertation on photography of the masses, admires the abstraction in these photos, which turn individual bodies into dehumanized ornaments. As Aloe remarks to Frank, their nakedness means that the bodies in Tunick's photographs are all alike, rendering them less individual. But this does not foster a sense of connection between the participants. Indeed, any communication within these photos seems directed at a spectator from the future, rather than taking place between the participants within the image. In this sense, Tunick's photos, even though they are full of people, point towards the posthuman, which according to Rosi Braidotti marks a shift in the construction of subjectivity from a unified self, endowed with a determining will, to a multilayered, multimodal subjectivity constructed through mediated and digital relations to organic and inorganic (technological) others. Braidotti argues that the posthuman helps us make sense of our flexible and multiple identities, and although Tunick's photographs do not foster community, photography does become therapeutic for Aloe.

In the present of the framing episodes, Aloe draws on photography to ward off affect, but she also uses photographs as tools for embodied viewing and knowledge production. Her photographs of malformed beetles from the perimeter of nuclear power plants make visible the effects of radiation, but when she retouches and assembles only the images on the beetles' scutella (part of the carapace) into ornaments, she creates an uneasy tension between documentation and abstraction. This photographic practice can be seen as a contribution to the concept of posthuman photography also envisaged in Reinhard Jirgl's *Die Stille* (2009) [*The Silence*], where the character Dorothea takes pictures of landscapes that have been ruined through strip mining and been made unsuitable for human habitation.[27] However, Aloe's photographs appear less pessimistic: her malformed insects are beautiful; in fact the ornaments are then used as textile patterns. The novel that tells of her photography also ends hopefully when Aloe and Stefan go to the airport to pick up Lukas.

Aura

The terms I have used to capture some of the image practices and photographic discourses in *Mitgift* and *Vorliebe* – surface, distance and abstraction – have been bywords of photography criticism since the 1920s. For instance, Walter Benjamin's 'A Short History of Photography' (1931), which became highly influential in photography studies from the 1980s onwards, disputed photographic realism by arguing that photographs only ever show us the surface appearance of things and places. The tension between surface and an underlying, possibly withheld, depth also concerns Benjamin in his remarks about the aura. According to the better-known definition in 'The Work of Art in the Age of Technological Reproducibility' (1936), the aura is bound to a presence in the here and now: 'there is no facsimile of the aura'.[28] Critics often take this to mean that 'the authenticity of the aura cannot be reproduced', and associate the aura with original artwork rather than the mechanical images of photography.[29] But when Benjamin first introduced the aura concept in his essay 'A Short History of Photography', he described early portrait photographs as intensely auratic, concluding that 'the most precise technology [could] give its products a magical value, such as a painted picture can never again have for us'.[30] Thus, as Douglas Crimp points out, 'the aura is not an ontological category as employed by Benjamin but rather a historical one. It is not something a handmade work has that a mechanically made work does not have'.[31] Even further, Diarmuid Costello argues that the aura, for Benjamin, does not pertain to objects of perception

---

27 Reinhard Jirgl, *Die Stille* (Munich: Hanser, 2009).
28 Walter Benjamin, *The Work of Art in the Age of its Technological Reproducibility, and Other Writings on Media*, ed. by Michael W. Jennings et al. (Cambridge, MA: Belknap Press, 2008), p. 31.
29 Marita Sturken and Lisa Cartwright, *Practices of Looking. An Introduction to Visual Culture*, 2nd edn (Oxford and New York: Oxford University Press, 2009), p. 196.
30 Benjamin, *The Work of Art*, p. 276.
31 Douglas Crimp, *On the Museum's Ruins* (Cambridge, MA: MIT Press, 1993), p. 112.

(works of art, photographs or other things) at all, but to the structure of perception itself.[32]

Aura, in Costello's reading, describes a way of seeing the world to which photographic as well as non-photographic images invite us. A similar point could be made regarding Siegfried Kracauer's understanding of abstraction, which he develops in the 1927 essay 'The Mass Ornament'.[33] The ornament is an empty form of modern rationality, but its abstraction also grants the spectator an indirect way of perceiving otherwise hidden social and political structures. For both authors, the dehumanizing aspects of modern visual culture contain within them the dialectical possibility of a humane vision that counteracts the dehumanization of modernity, although the connection of such a counter-gaze with the humanity of its agent is much stronger in Benjamin than in Kracauer. The logic of the photograph that Ulrike Draesner explores in *Mitgift* seems to arrive at a similarly dialectical conception of the photographic image. The critical attitude towards photography as distancing, dehumanizing and commodifying that is associated with the young Aloe's perspective has to be modified in light of the more mature experience of Aloe in the present. In a digital anthropocene, humans can still understand and fashion their world as *homines pictores*. Aloe's life is proof of this capacity. Neither a postmodern rejection of the image nor a technologically minded glorification of the posthuman offer viable alternatives to the close connection between humans and their images.

---

32 Diarmuid Costello, 'Aura, Face, Photography. Re-Reading Benjamin Today', in *Walter Benjamin and Art*, ed. by Andrew Benjamin (New York and London: Continuum, 2005), pp. 164–184.
33 Siegfried Kracauer, *The Mass Ornament. Weimar Essays*, ed. and trans. Thomas Y. Levin (Cambridge, MA: Harvard University Press, 1995).

Karen Leeder
'Twin Spin'. Ulrike Draesner's Poetry of Science

Ulrike Draesner is one of several German poets who have used their work to explore contemporary science over the last three decades or so. In many ways it is not surprising. With what the British poet Lavinia Greenlaw has called the widespread 'domestication of technology' during the twentieth century,[1] it is almost inevitable that science should become an integrated part of cultural expression and challenge the notion of the 'two cultures'. Writing about science might thus even be thought of as a necessary mark of one's engagement in the present day: 'a way of writing for the moment' as the Austrian poet Raoul Schrott put it, writing about his own interest in the subject.[2] Indeed, Peter Geist went so far as to call the 'paradigm shift from a historical interrogation of reality to one drawing on the natural sciences' one of the defining characteristics of German poetry in the 1990s.[3] Hermann Korte, too, saw the rapprochement between the two spheres of knowledge (poetry and science) as one of the key developments of that decade.[4]

In fact, the interest in science among literary practitioners has sometimes been understood as part of the modern renaissance of the ancient trope of the *poeta doctus* or 'learned poet' along with the concern with classical tropes.[5] This has also been taken up in recent research; for example, the project based in Lorraine, in conjunction with the Deutsches Literatuarchiv, and led by Sylvie Grimm-Hamen, on the 'poeta doctus' / 'écrivain savant', including study of

---

1 Lavinia Greenlaw, 'Unstable regions: poetry and science', in *Cultural Babbage. Technology, Time and Invention*, ed. by Francis Spufford and Jenny Uglow (London: Faber and Faber, 1996), pp. 215–226 (p. 224).
2 Raoul Schrott, '"Die Wahlverwandschaften": Raoul Schrott im Gespräch', *heureka!*, 3 (1999), 17–18, p. 17.
3 Peter Geist, '"die ganz großen themen fühlen sich gut an". Die Wiederkehr des Politischen in der jüngeren Lyrik', in *Junge Lyrik*, ed. by Heinz Ludwig Arnold (Munich: Text + Kritik, 2006), pp. 98–117 (p. 102).
4 See also: Hermann Korte, *Deutschsprachige Lyrik seit 1945*, 2nd rev. edn (Stuttgart: Metzler, 2004), p. 280.
5 Karen Leeder: 'The "poeta doctus" and the new German literature', *Germanic Review*, 77.1 (2002), 51–67. Wilfried Barner, 'Poeta Doctus. Über die Renaissance eines Dichterideals in der deutschen Literatur des 20. Jahrhunderts', in *Literaturwissenschaft und Geistesgeschichte. Festschrift für Richard Brinkmann*, ed. by Jürgen Brummack et al. (Tübingen: de Gruyter, 1981), pp. 725–752.

https://doi.org/10.1515/9783110495942-006

Schrott.[6] It is striking that Draesner is not generally discussed in these terms at all – something that undoubtedly has to do with perceptions of gender and learning.[7]

The new interest has also been seen as contributing to a 'scientific turn', a 'cognitive turn' in modern writing engaged in a 'poetics of understanding'. Friedrich W. Block, exploring 'experience as experiment' in twentieth-century German poetry, was one of one of a number of prominent writers to explore this area.[8] Today 'cognitive poetics' is a mainstay of research and this kind of approach chimes with Draesner's own interests.[9]

It is worth identifying the broad mode of such poetry in order also then to distinguish Draesner's approach. First, the 'aesthetic of coldness', addressed by Helmut Lethen in his *Verhaltenslehren der Kälte* [*Behaviour Theories of Coldness*] of 1994, has been taken up by several commentators to identify a dominant tone in contemporary writing.[10] The cool, cerebral, ironically detached view of the observing outsider that characterised German poet Gottfried Benn's diction arguably became a hallmark of one strand of poetry of the 1990s onwards. Poetry has even been classed by Durs Grünbein as one of the 'kalte Medien' [cold media] in a phrase taken from one of his early sequences of 'MonoLogische Gedichte' ['Mono-Logical Poems'], themselves a tribute to Benn.[11] Benn's influence extends not

---

6 Compare: http://cegil.univ-lorraine.fr/content/lecrivain-savant-defis-et-enjeux-dune-pos ture-dans-la-culture-allemande-du-xxeme-siecle.

7 A notable exception is Anna Alissa Ertel's book *Körper, Gehirne, Gene: Lyrik und Naturwissenschaft bei Ulrike Draesner und Durs Grünbein* (Berlin and New York: de Gruyter, 2011). The Nancy project also looks at female authors although not (yet) at Draesner. Compare also: Aura Heydenreich und Klaus Mecke, 'Auf der Suche nach Sprache: Ulrike Draesner im Dialog zu *Mitgift* und *Vorliebe*', in *Physik und Poetik: Produktionsästhetik und Werkgenese. Autorinnen und Autoren im Dialog*, ed. by Aura Heydenreich and Klaus Mecke (Berlin and Boston: de Gruyter, 2015), pp. 23–49.

8 The term 'scientific turn' comes from Swantje Lichtenstein, *Das lyrische Projekt. Rhetorik, Räumlichkeit und Wissenschaft* (Munich: Iudicium, 2004), p. 15; 'the cognitive turn' based on 'a poetics of understanding' is explored by Friedrich W. Block, '"Erfahrung als Experiment". Poetik im Zeitalter naturwissenschaftlicher Erkenntnistheorien', in *Lyrik des 20. Jahrhunderts. Text + Kritik Sonderband*, ed. by Hans Ludwig Arnold (Munich: Text + Kritik, 1999), pp. 248–264.

9 Peter Stockwell, *Texture: A Cognitive Aesthetics of Reading* (Edinburgh: Edinburgh University Press, 2009) and Peter Stockwell, *Cognitive Poetics: An Introduction* (London and New York, NY: Routledge, 2019, 2nd rev. edn 2020) offer a useful introduction.

10 Helmut Lethen, *Verhaltenslehren der Kälte* (Frankfurt a. M.: Suhrkamp, 1994). See, for example, Erk Grimm: 'Mediamania? Contemporary German poetry in the age of new media information technologies: Thomas Kling and Durs Grünbein', *Studies in Twentieth-Century Literature*, 21.1 (1997), 275–301.

11 Durs Grünbein, *Grauzone morgens* (Frankfurt a. M.: Suhrkamp, 1988), p. 81.

only to the use of medical imagery and anatomical vocabulary, however, but also to an understanding of the place of the poet at work:

> It [the modern lyric subject] enters its laboratory for words, and it is here that it models, and produces words, opens them, explodes them, destroys them, in order to load them with tension, which will in its essence perhaps last several decades.[12]

This approach situates the concern with science then as part of an engagement in the historical moment, but also as a withdrawal from a conventional understanding of the lyric as the province of feeling, towards something akin much more to observation and experiment. Finally, it foregrounds as integral to that approach (as here in Benn) the importance of the mode of expression available to the lyric.

Grünbein, for example, points to the influence of Zbigniew Herbert as one of those poets who had cultivated both the coolness of precisely observed reality, but also a vocabulary of science, both as a nod to the modern but also as a way of refreshing poetic diction. Alongside the concentration 'on the immediate', 'the focus on things: buttons, stools, tables, inanimate objects' comes a language which moves away from the everyday. Grünbein's example is instructive:

> 'While the head of the sperm sinks into the oocyte, the tail beats vigorously, so that the egg shifts in a slight rotation and the tail of the sperm slips completely into the perivitelline space. The force of the flagellum then suddenly abates.' This little gem comes from a standard medical work, a pocket atlas of embryology. A pictorial, powerful language, don't you find? Pure poetics; and there is a sense of drama there, too. Everything is so clear that one feels one is directly involved in the sacred process of fertilization.[13]

He continues focussing in on the phrase *'perivitelline space'*:

> Pure technical jargon that repels most who hear it. Nevertheless, it is this that is used to describe the origin of the human life. And now the question: what speaks against refreshing the repertoire of language from time to time, if that helps to open new perspectives? Tell me, Brother Herbert, whom I never met?

---

12 Gottfried Benn, *Sämtliche Werke*, ed. by Gerhard Schuster and Holger Hof (Stuttgart: Akademie 1986–2003), 7 vols, vol. I, p. 544.
13 Durs Grünbein, 'Brief an Zbigniew Herbert, Dankesrede', Warsaw, 15 September 2020. This speech, written for the award of the Zbigniew Herbert prize, was published as Durs Grünbein, 'Bei lebendiger Dichtung verschwinden: An und über Zbigniew Herbert', *Frankfurter Allgemeine Zeitung*, 29.11.2020, and can be accessed in my English: https://fundacjaherberta.com/en/the-herbert-prize/the-ceremony-of-presenting-the-zbigniew-herbert-prize/the-zbigniew-herbert-award-ceremony-2020/.

For Grünbein the language of science and the formulae of poetry are discourses that are profoundly intertwined: 'these two things belong together and depend on one another'.[14]

Both can be seen as allied ways of apprehending the world. Others have also supported this view. Raoul Schrott points to what he calls the 'elective affinities' between poetry and science in interviews and in his numerous essays on poetry and physics.[15] The Nobel Laureate and immunologist Miroslav Holub too posits a profound complementarity between the disciplines.[16] To quote Greenlaw again: 'There is a relation between poetry and science. It is shaped by culture and history, by affinities of subject and motivation, and the influence of paradigm and epistemology on perception and response. Inspiration, discovery and connection are integral to both disciplines. As are tedious hours spent learning a craft and practising technique.'[17]

The two discourses can thus be said to share an economy based on perception and articulation, whether in the form of conceit or hypothesis, metaphor or proof. What is more, poetry can be used to express scientific ideas in a manner that takes them beyond the narrow realm of scientific discourse and anchors them within the broader cultural and historical context.[18] This focus on a shared and often reciprocal use of metaphor has been a key driving force for several writers in their interest in science and language. In his *Handbuch der Wolkenputzerei* (2005) Schrott cites this kind of analogy – the 'Aha-Erlebnis' [light-bulb moment] of metaphor as 'the most elementary form of creating meaning that we have. The new only becomes comprehensible through the familiar, because we always explain things through comparison with other fields'.[19] It has also been the starting point for critics who have addressed the links between them and tried to develop a 'poetics of science'.[20] The best of the poems written in recent years, however,

---

14 Ibid.
15 Schrott, '"Die Wahlverwandschaften"': Raoul Schrott im Gespräch', p. 17. See also Raoul Schrott, *Die Erde ist blau wie eine Orange. Polemisches, Poetisches, Privates* (Munich: Hanser, 1999).
16 Miroslav Holub, 'Poetry and science: the poetry of science / the science of poetry', in Holub, *The Dimension of the Present Moment and Other Essay* (London: Faber, 1990), pp. 122–146.
17 Greenlaw, 'Unstable Regions', p. 226.
18 Holub, 'Poetry and science', p. 135.
19 Raoul Schrott, *Handbuch der Wolkenputzerei: Gesammelte Essays* (Munich: Hanser, 2005), p. 114.
20 I go into this in greater detail in Karen Leeder, 'Durs Grünbein and the Poetry of Science', in *Durs Grünbein: A Companion*, ed. by Michael Eskin, Karen Leeder and Christopher Young (Berlin and New York: de Gruyter, 2013), pp. 67–94.

go further to incorporate scientific principles into the very fabric of the poetry – raising questions about the role and position of the observer, the nature of metaphor, and the possibilities of poetic language.

Ulrike Draesner is one of the poets who navigate this fraught territory most successfully. In this next section I would like to explore how it is treated in her poetry, in the light of these reflections. But also, by focussing on examples from several collections, to show how this theme, and her engagement with it, develops over the course of her work to become a structuring principle of her thinking and her writing. Science is never merely a backdrop for her poetry, nor the lyric subject, nor a casual raid on an exotic range of vocabulary. Rather, from the beginning, her poetry claims an interest in science as a mode of apprehending and articulating the place of the subject in the world, which is fundamental to its project.

Draesner treats scientific themes in many of her works (fiction, poetry and essay). Striking in her presentation, right from the off, is the humanness of the interest. Science is not treated as a thing apart, not an attempt to grapple with the sublime as in her Austrian contemporary Raoul Schrott, for example. Nor is it characterized by a sarcastic laying bare of the stuff of the human in the anatomic flaying of another contemporary, Durs Grünbein's early poetry. It is altogether more human and more intimate. Draesner's interest is first and foremost bodily: starting with the realm of medicine and then branching into more theoretical reflections on epigenetics, brain research, and reproduction. This is unsurprising in a way since the scientific advances in genetics have had, and will continue to have, some of the most profound and immediately palpable effects on day-to-day life. But this is far from the 'cold media' adumbrated above, despite Draesner's documented interest in Benn.[21] Nor does she take recourse to the laboratory of words; rather the dilemmas are played out within the intimate sphere of the body itself, in the business of everyday life, in the encounter with an intimate other and in the processes of reproduction (essential in a human sense but also of course for a writer).[22]

A second related point should be made straight away. Perhaps because for Draesner science is so much part of human life, biological or bodily themes go hand in hand with reflections on zoology, the climate crisis, flora and fauna, language, subjectivity, etc. That is: science is not seen as a thing apart, in any sense, but part and parcel of the business of living, knowing and of writing

---

21 Ulrike Draesner, 'Kleines Gespenst. Gedanken zum lyrischen Ich', in *Ich bin nicht innerlich. Annäherungen an Gottfried Benn*, ed. by Jan Bürger (Stuttgart: Klett-Cotta, 2003), pp. 9–30.
22 See also Emily Jeremiah's contribution in this volume.

and, in line with this, her engagement develops and shifts in the course of her work. This might in other hands seem instinctive or naïve, precisely unscientific. In fact, the opposite is the case. Draesner is concerned, beyond the business of scientific knowledge itself, with the poetic and ethical implications of this knowledge, that is a second order of knowledge:

> the knowledge of how to know, or how to acquire knowledge and how to judge that knowledge. This last might be the most important and is influenced by emotion, by personal states, by memories, by your whole life-history.[23]

Vital here is that science, and knowing more generally, is not limited to the rational but is bound up with intimate life. What is more: this implies important things about how we speak about this knowledge. Draesner again:

> Since my childhood I've always felt that all these realms of life are intrinsically connected. Language to me seems to penetrate all areas of what we now call science. All forms of science rely on signs and concepts that are phrased in language. There is no mathematics without a special language, for example, scientists must think in language too. And these languages rely on metaphors. A striking one, which has been used for a while now, is that of the genetic code, the genetic alphabet; but that, for example, implies all kinds of interesting questions about syntax, letters or rules. Also, as we know, metaphors tend to be helpful and illuminating, on the one hand, but they are good at hiding things as well. I feel there might be a specific competence that can be added by linguists and people who deal with languages in a real dialogue with science.[24]

Draesner and the Body

I'd like to turn to some examples from her work, which make some of these observations concrete and demonstrate how such thinking is not merely about a particular vocabulary but also about a structure of being, and of writing.

Draesner's early poems have often been discussed in terms of their relation to the body.[25] Anna Alissa Ertel, for example, begins her chapter on Draesner's

---

23 See Karen Leeder and Lyn Marven, 'The indecipherable Stone. Interview with Ulrike Draesner on the Processes of Literature', in this volume. In English in the original.
24 Ibid.
25 Jörg Magenau, 'Der Körper als Schnittfläche. Bemerkungen zur Literatur der neuesten Neuen Innerlichkeit: Texte von Reto Hänny, Ulrike Kolb, Ulrike Draesner, Durs Grünbein, Thomas Hettche, Marcel Beyer und Michael Kleeberg', in *Baustelle Gegenwartsliteratur*, ed. by Andreas Erb (Opladen: Westdeutscher Verlag, 1998), pp. 107–21; Anne-Rose Meyer, 'Physiologie und Poesie. Zu Körperdarstellungen in der Lyrik von Ulrike Draesner, Durs Grünbein und Thomas Kling', *Gegenwartsliteratur. A German Studies Yearbook*, 1 (2002), 107–33; Michael Eskin, 'Body Language. Durs Grünbein's Aesthetics', *arcadia*, 37.1 (2002), 42–66; Ruth Owen,

poetry and the body with a quotation from the writer herself: 'Was sich durch mein Werk zieht, ist die Frage nach Körperlichkeit' [what runs through my work is the question of corporeality].[26] Ertel describes the approach of her writing, rightly I think, as 'not psychological, but rather quasi physiological'.[27] Indeed, essays throughout Draesner's writing life return to this most fundamental precondition and obsessive centre of her work.[28] As an essay from 1999 puts it, 'Das heißt nicht: nach innen vordringen, ins Seelenleben, Numinose. Sondern in den Körper. Die Sprache des Körpers destillieren/abziehen. Als Rhythmus, Bild und Wort ist das Gedicht der Extrakt eines körperlichen Zustandes.' [That does not mean: penetrating inside, into the life of the soul, the numinous. But into the body. To distil/extract the language of the body. As rhythm, image and word, the poem is the extract of a bodily condition].[29]

More precisely, her early poems often reflect the body as the object of medical intervention, and the work is driven by medical metaphors.[30] Poems chart the concrete effects of medical intervention and research on the body, especially in relation to reproductive technology. But this is always also seen in the context of the individual's struggle for identity and subjectivity in a time in which organ transplantation, artificial means of prolonging life, illness, and the possibilities of surgical intervention make the boundaries of subjecthood more permeable than ever before. But the work also pays attention to the way these things make themselves manifest in language: 'den Konnex von Sprache und Körper' [the connection between body and language].[31] Draesner's debut volume *gedächtnisschleifen* (1995), for example, boasts an array of body parts, often seen through the lens of medical procedures. Take as an example the poem 'sekret' ['secretion']:[32]

'Bodies in Contemporary German Poetry', in *Schaltstelle: Neue deutsche Lyrik im Dialog, German Monitor* 69, ed. by Karen Leeder (Amsterdam: Rodopi, 2007), pp. 269–291.

26 '"Jenseits der Norm". Ulrike Draesner im Spiegel-Interview', in *Der Spiegel*, 13/2002, p. 207.

27 Ertel, *Körper, Gehirne, Gene*, p. 85.

28 For example: Ulrike Draesner, 'Atem, Puls und Bahn. Das Denken des Körpers im Zustand der Sprache', in *Lettre International*, 44 (Spring 1999), 62–67, which sets out key ideas, right through to Ulrike Draesner, *Die fünfte Dimension: Münchner Reden zur Poesie*, ed. by Holger Pils and Frieder von Ammon (Munich: Lyrik Kabinett, 2016).

29 Draesner, 'Atem, Puls und Bahn', p. 68.

30 Meyer, 'Physiologie und Poesie', p. 110.

31 Draesner, 'Atem Puls und Bahn', p. 64.

32 Ulrike Draesner, *gedächtnisschleifen* (Munich: Luchterhand, 1995), p. 19. Translation by Iain Galbraith, from Draesner, *this porous fabric*, p. 25.

Heimlich lohender hinter schwarzen Ästen
Wintermorgen klebte an doppelten Scheiben
völlig keimfrei die Ärzte sagten ›Drüsen‹
betasteten nacheinander den Stoffwechsel
kein Grund zur Sorge ein Salzeinlauf löst
die Verklemmung ich kam auf die Schüssel
im Gesicht wiederholte sich Schließmuskelglätte
mein stockendes Sprechen – da habe ich plötzlich
auf dem Pythiastuhl habe kein Wort mehr heraus-
bringen, plötzlich den Mund nicht mehr bewegen können,
mir war, ich würde nie mehr, solche Kehlenangst
schnürte mir den Speichel, darunter meine zuckenden,
rasenden Muskeln, jemand sagte: vielleicht
Drüsenpressen, unerklärlicher Eiweißausfluß, alle
Instrumente kreiseln ja, da hob ich mich schon
nicht mehr ab von dem Wintermorgen, dem Weiß,
dem Grau, hob mich nicht mehr vor dem Hintergrund
als Eigenfigur heraus, kleine Rauchwölkchen,
Körper geheime Sekrete schwebten mir aus allen
Schädelöffnungen, dampften zu den Ohren,
Nasenlöchern, Augen, den, ja, wieder geöffneten
Fontanellen heraus – betäubende Buchstabentiere,

       vergleiche Holzschnitt, um 1450,
       über Hautgrund abgebildetes Entweichen,
       sogenanntes schönes Durcheinander-
       kriechen, von Seelen.

[secretly blazing behind black branches
a winter's morning clung to double panes
wholly aseptic the doctors said "glands"
in succession palpating my metabolism
no cause for worry a saline enema will
undo the deadlock i was put on the pan
levelling of the facial sphincter recurred
my speech faltered – and then suddenly
on the seat of pythia could not speak
not a word could not move my mouth
felt i'd never again, such pharyngeal anxiety
choking my saliva, below which my twitching
raging muscles, someone said: possibly
glandular pressure, inexplicable protein discharge
all the dials were spinning, by now i no longer
stood out from the winter's morning white
and grey no longer stuck out as a separate
figure against the background tiny smoke-
clouds secret secretions fumed from my

>every cranial orifice wafted from ears
>nostrils eyes my, yes, reopened
>fontanelles – numbing animal letters
>>compare woodcut ca. 1450
>>depicted on a skin background the escape
>>the so-called beautiful inter-
>>seething of souls]

This is a good example of the kind of poem that worries at the bodily periphery and sets medical definitions against a humorous discourse of myth. The self is identified as a suffering I in the poem; the doctors (they) define the problem with medical language and reassure that the issue can be put right. And yet even here we see the blurring of the sense of self as it becomes lost against the background and lost to speech. There is also the indicative 'betäubende Buchstabentiere' (numbing letter animals) at the end that suggest, along with the reference to an oracle, that we are also thinking about the creation of the self and more to the point, the self in poetry.

By the 2001 volume *für die nacht geheuerte zellen*, the focus on medical procedures which also provoke questions about on the nature of the self are well established. Here though they are more drastic and are also framed in terms of their scientific context: anatomy, anthropology, physiology, medical technology, neuroscience and genetics.[33] Again this is unsurprising, as these represent key advances in the science of the late twentieth and early twenty-first century which have impacted on society as central interpretative paradigms. Major poems like the 'autopilot I–IV' sequence from *gedächtnisschleifen* (pp. 101–105) and the 'bläuliche sphinx (metal)' cycle from the next collection, *für die nacht geheuerte zellen* (35–49) have been interpreted in detail.[34] Both challenge the limits of the human body; both depict the human body as the subject of medical

---

33 Ulrike Draesner, *für die nacht geheuerte zellen* (Munich: Luchterhand, 2001). See also 'falkisches, völk' (pp. 24–25), 'luna matutina' (p. 30), 'pissblumen' (p. 33), 'a, b, photon c' (pp. 72–73), 'oxygen' (pp. 76–77), 'zoom ins moor' (p. 115), 'post dolly' (p. 117), 'nackt ist die wahrheit' (p. 123), 'stoffen' (pp. 124–125).

34 On 'autopilot I–IV' see, for example, Bettina von Jagow, Florian Steger, 'Bilder des Menschen zwischen Selbstbestimmung und Fremdsteuerung: Ulrike Draesners autopilot Gedichte', in *Repräsentationen. Medizin und Ethik in Literatur und Kunst der Moderne*, ed. by von Jagow and Steger (Heidelberg: Universitätsverlag Winter, 2004), pp. 51–65; Ertel, *Körper, Gehirne, Gene*, pp. 116–139; Michael Braun, 'Gedichte wollen gedacht sein: Ulrike Draesners autopilot-Zyklus', in *Gedichte von Ulrike Draesner: Interpretationen,* ed. by Christoph Jürgensen, Erik Schilling, Rüdiger Zymner (Leiden and Boston: Brill, 2020), pp. 39–48. On 'bläuliche sphinx', see Sonja Klimek, '"fehlt das kind im bauch": Ulrike Draesners Zyklus "bläuliche sphinx (metal)"', in *Gedichte von Ulrike Draesner: Interpretationen,* pp. 67–82.

interventions (organ transplantation and a so-called 'missed abortion', a miscarriage, respectively). Both move beyond the medical to explore the scientific background behind the experience of medical technology, also touching on many different areas along the way. Both are strikingly marked by emotion and very far from any sense of the coldness discussed earlier. Jörg Magenau discussing 'autopilot IV', for example, comments:

> Draesner thematises feeling. She does not move the body away from her as a thing like in Benn, she does not make the body a dead object. On the contrary, her body-nurseries remain very much alive, and marked by affect, she even cries at the grave of the dead subject (her own). In her verses there is no place for self-assurance any longer, and at the same time they are a challenge to the over- engineered dream of the reproducibility and technical feasibility of the body.[35]

But Magenau's comment also highlights a further important aspect at play in both poems. They both deal centrally with the creation and potential obliteration of self both in bodily terms but also as a voice in the poem. One might even feel that the seedbed of the poem is about giving birth to a voice for poetry. Galbraith, reading 'autopilot', sums up the role of science in these poems well:

> It is true that the sciences of the body – organ transplantation, reproductive medicine, genetics and cloning, neurobiology, psychology and other disciplines have haunted Ulrike Draesner's poems from the start, but it is equally the case that the presence of such matter, [. . .] is not intended to further our STEM-field education.[36]

Instead, the poetry becomes 'Bewegung in Sprache' [movement in language], a 'form of research' into human 'mentality', a form of highly self-conscious language-work that attempts to investigate the 'human tissue' of our 'feelings, thoughts and actions' or, as she also describes it, 'the way we are put together' within contemporary reality and all the discourses available to us.[37]

By 2005, in an important interview Draesner describes in detail how the poem comes into being as a result of physiological processes and diverse external stimuli in the course of the writing process, revealing physiological rhythms, the heart, the pulse, as the foundation of her creations.[38] By now it is clear that this poetry

---

35 Magenau, 'Der Körper als Schnittfläche', p. 112.

36 Iain Galbraith, 'from possible closeness: a translator's preface', in Ulrike Draesner, *this porous fabric*, trans. by Iain Galbraith (Bristol: Shearsman, 2022), pp. 9–18 (p. 16).

37 Ulrike Draesner, 'Bewegung in Sprache. Ulrike Draesner im Gespräch mit Rolf Bernhard Essig', *neue deutsche literatur* 51.6 (2003), pp. 42–61, (p. 52).

38 'Ulrike Draesner im Gespräch mit Christian Schlösser', *Deutsche Bücher. Forum für Literatur* 35.4 (2005), pp. 269–271. Galbraith, 'from possible closeness', p. 14.

is not simply focussed on a scientific, anatomical examination of the body *per se*, but uses it as a stepping-stone to generate a poetic programme of sorts.

Reading the Genetic Code

Draesner's sequence of 'radical translations' of Shakespeare's sonnets, published in the volume *:to change the subject* of 2002 takes this further. The cycle moves inside the body to interrogate genetic manipulation, and read the genetic code, again in the context of an explicitly literary concern.[39] The translations are accompanied by an essay 'Dolly und Will' ['Dolly and Will'] in which what Draesner calls her 'wilful misunderstanding' of Shakespeare is brought to bear on the revolutionary cloning of Dolly the sheep.[40] Draesner explains in her essay that she chanced on the *Sonnets* on her shelf after news of the successful cloning, and realised with a kind of epiphany that the semantic structure of the poems could be reproduced in the same way: '[d]ie Gedichte [. . .] sprachen von Klonen' [the poems [. . .] were speaking about cloning].[41] Her choice of the seventeen sonnets for translation is already indicative, in that she chooses those that deal with reproduction, which she then shifts into the present of gene technology. Sonnets 1–17 are known as the 'Procreation Sonnets'; or as Don Paterson, in his commentary on the Shakespeare puts it, 'Multiplication. That's the name of the game'.[42] This chimes with Draesner's reading entirely: '"zeugen, zeugen, sich selbt reproduzieren" – nur das flüstert ihr obsessiver Traum' [procreation, procreation, reproducing themselves, – that's all their obsessive dream whispers].[43] Five of the so-called procreation sonnets are included in Draesner's selection. Manfred Pfister concludes: 'Shakespeare's neo-platonic discourse of idea and image, original and copy, love and

39 Ulrike Draesner, 'Twin Spin', in Peter Waterhouse, Ulrike Draesner, Barbara Köhler, *:to change the subject* (Göttingen: Wallstein, 2000), pp. 11–29 and the accompanying essay 'Dolly und Will', pp. 30–33. A couple of earlier poems also make this leap: compare 'post Dolly' and 'kaspar hausers unterhose', in *für de nacht geheuerte zellen*, p. 17 and p. 96.

40 I deal with Draesner's poems in terms of their response to Shakespeare in Karen Leeder, '"A second Life": Shakespeare-Übersetzungen in der Gegenwartsliteratur', in *From the Enlightenment to Modernism: Three Centuries of German Literature. Essays for Ritchie Robertson*, ed. by Carolin Duttlinger, Kevin Hilliard and Charlie Louth (Cambridge: Legenda, 2021), pp. 348–362.

41 'Dolly und Will', p. 30.

42 Robert Crosman, 'Making Love Out of Nothing At All: The Issue of Story in Shakespeare's Procreation Sonnets', *Shakespeare Quarterly*, 41.4 (Winter 1990), 470–488; Don Paterson, *Reading Shakespeare's Sonnets: A New Commentary* (London: Faber, 2010), p. 7.

43 Draesner, 'Dolly und Will', p. 31.

procreation is translated into the current lingo of informatics and bio-technology, proclaiming Love in the Age of Mechanical Reproduction'.[44] However, one can be more precise; this is in fact rather a kind of 'Fear in the Age of Bio-technical-Reproduction'. Shakespeare's sonnets are dogged by the obsessive desire for continuity, reproduction and self-reproduction in the flesh and in words: 'Träume des Überlebens' [dreams of survival]. But Draesner's view is ambivalent: 'Traum und Alptraum ist der Klon, dessen Erscheinen das Subjekt grundlegend, fundamental, in allem, wie wir es je verstanden haben, ändert – indem es sich gleichen läßt.' [The clone is at once dream and nightmare. Its appearance changes the subject essentially, fundamentally in all that we have ever understood – in that it allows itself to be copied.][45]

Draesner is centrally concerned here with the nature of the self and how it can be expressed in poetry but also changed.

> Das Ich-Subjekt der Rede wechselt ständig, ohne jemals das Thema zu wechseln (wie krieg ich dich und wie überleben wir, was ein Teil dessen ist, wie ich dich kriege). Als Spirale gesagt: in der Unwechselbarkeit des Themas wird das Subjekt dann allerdings seinerseits unverwechselbar und somit zu einem Subjekt, das sich nicht unterwirft, indem es sich dem Rondo der Rollen stets unterwirft, um am Ende dadurch, daß es nicht mehr wechselt, sondern sich als Wechselndes fixiert, dem Thema eine weitere Spiraldrehung zuzufügen im Bäumchen-wechsel-dich-Spiel der Rede.[46]

> [The I subject of the speech changes constantly without ever changing the subject (how do I win you and how do we survive, which is part of how I win you). To put it as a spiral: in the unchangeability of the theme, however, the subject then becomes unmistakable in turn and thus a subject who does not submit, by dint of constantly submitting itself to the rondo of roles, only, in the end, to add another spiral rotation to the theme, by no longer changing, rather fixing itself as something changeable in the game of tag [swapping] that is speech.]

Here Draesner is talking about the 'ich' of Shakespeare's sonnets and the way she reads it as a presentiment of cloning (hence the reference to the DNA helix). More important, the radical translations at once reconfigure and reconceptualise the Shakespeare, containing a temporal horizon of the present and the diverse technologies that it brings with it, but also an interpretation, which allows for local misunderstandings and misinterpretations.[47] Several of the

---

44 Pfister, 'Made in Germany: Shakespeare's Sonnets', *ANGERMION: Yearbook for Anglo-German Literary Criticism, Intellectual History and Cultural Transfers*, 5.1 (2012), 29–57 (p. 42).
45 Draesner, 'Dolly und Will', p. 33.
46 Draesner, 'Dolly und Will', p. 32.
47 Draesner, 'Dolly und Will', p. 31.

Shakespeare texts are deliberately reproduced with errors and thus changed. What is more, Draesner has 'triangulated' existing translations of the sonnets (including some of the most radical by Stefan George and Paul Celan), creating a kind of echo-chamber in which issues of authorship, originally and reproduction intertwine.[48] But on top of this, in her own 'wilful misunderstandings', Draesner also follows obscure etymologies, combs Shakespearian polysemes for non-canonical interpretations, lifting words up by their roots and transplanting them, works with homophony, homonymy, or shifts into other languages, to create new meanings – a process that Tobias Döring has dubbed a 'polyglot poetics'.[49] Her radical translation, with the conscious inclusion of typographical errors, misunderstandings, mis-translations, mis-fits and linguistic games, all work to make legible what for Draesner is the basic fluidity of all texts. But, of course, this has particular significance when considering the genetic code, the misreading of which allows variability in the populations and evolution. Replication is never perfect; instead, DNA recombines to create new meaning and new forms. For Draesner, this is not just a theme – it is translated into her linguistic approach. Almost any poem from the sequence could stand as an example of the way in which language is stretched or split to produce surprising metaphors or sequences which run along lines of sound or association alone, or borrow from the English, or in which myth and modernity, slang and the archaic, the poetic and the scientific are set off against one another.[50] As an example: Sonnet 18.

> Shall I compare thee to a summer's day?
> Thou art more lovely and more temperate:
> Rough winds do change the darling buds of May,
> And summer's lease hath all too short a date:
> Sometime too hot the eye of heaven shines,
> And often is his gold complexion dimm'd;
> And every fair from fair sometimes declines,
> By chance, or nature's changing course, untrimm'd;
> But thy eternal summer shall not fade,
> Nor lose possession of that fair thou owest;
> Nor shall Death brag thou wander'st in his shade,
> When in eternal lines to time thou growest;
> So long as men can breathe, or eyes can see,
> So long lives this, and this gives life to thee.

---

48 Personal conversation with Ulrike Draesner.
49 See Tobias Döring's contribution in this volume.
50 Draesner, 'Twin Spin', p. 18.

einem sommertag vergleichen, dich?
gesünder bist du, besser temperiert:
stickstoffwinde nagen die teuren maiknospen an,
geleaste sommerzeit fault dattelbraun, zu schnell:
zu viel UV strahlt durchs ozonloch ab und brennt,
oft ist der sonne teint von smog verhängt;
alles helle beugt periodisch helles in den fall,
chaotisch ist zufall, genetisch unser roulette;
doch in deinem zeitimmunen sommer tanzt keine zelle den fado,
keine verliert, dem du dich verdankst, ihr DNA-eldorado;
noch wird der tod prahlen, in seinem schatten wandre deine pracht,
wenn als buchstabenhelix du der zeit entwächst;
    solange einer atmen kann, solange augen sehn,
    solange lohnt auch dies und klont dir leben ein.

A radical re-translation is offered by Tom Cheesman:[51]

a summer day and you and recombine?
you're better for you, quality controlled:
rough nitrous gusts aggress the precious may-buds,
and summers time-share option's all too short-date:
too much uv glows through the ozone hole and burns,
and sol's complexion's tanned by frequent smog;
periodically, in the case of brightness bright declines,
chance-entrammelled chaos is our gene roulette;
time-immunized, your summer cells, though, dance no fado,
none loses its, what you owe you to, el-dna-dorado;
nor'll loud-mouth death proclaim your glory straggles in his gloom
when as double-stranded letter-vines you outclimb time;
    so long as breath is drawn as eyes have sight
    so long this loan replays its own and clones you life.

In Draesner's version the nature that in Shakespeare becomes a benign, if fleeting, comparison for the beloved, is a nature blighted by choking winds, UV rays, smog, and a hole in the ozone layer. The Shakespearian sense of inevitable decline in nature is picked up by Draesner and dramatized as ecological catastrophe. But the poem pivots on 'Zerfall' [decline], 'fall' [fall or case] and 'Zufall' [chance] to shift from external change to internal

---

51 Tom Cheesman, 'Shall I Compare, Vergleichen, Recombine? Reversioning Ulrike Draesner's "Twin Spin"', *In Other Words*, 30 (2007), 6–15 (p. 10). See also: *Twin Spin: 17 Shakespeare Sonnets radically translated by Ulrike Draesner and radically back-translated by Tom Cheesman; with an Exhibition Catalogue for 'Shall I Compare thee: Shakespeare in Translation'* (Oxford: Taylor Institution Library, 2016).

alles helle beugt periodisch helles in den fall,
chaotisch ist zufall, genetisch unser roulette;

[Literally:
all bright/fair things are bent by brightness into fall
chaotic is chance, genetically our roulette.]

The focus now is inside on the processes of cellular change; the cloned Dolly is 'immune to time', since the cells do not enter upon a process of recombination with all its attendant flaws and opportunities – boldly caught in the image of the dance, the fado. We move now into the realm of the 'DNA-eldorado' leading to the key line 12: 'wenn als buchstabenhelix du der zeit entwächst' [when you grow out of time as a letter-helix]. Reduced to the letters of the DNA-molecules of the genetic code, the creature leaves time behind and becomes what Shakespeare's own sonnets always aspire to: immortal. But it is a curious immortality, of the self-same and self-sufficient, with codes that will be handed down with no exposure to the random nature of difference. And, in the reference to the 'letter helix', Draesner is playing at once on the metaphor of letters in our conventional alphabet, but also that which governs genetic science with is powerful abbreviations, A, T, C and G, for the textual building blocks of DNA. Indeed, the poem works throughout by running the metaphor of reading DNA and reading literature alongside one another, leading to the ambiguity of the final couplet. Here it is left unspecified what the 'dies' [this] refers to: the process of cloning and genetic manipulation or the business of poetry writing? Both, it seems, can offer a new life.[52] But, of course, precisely the form and project of the work answer the question, in that it precisely does not pass down the self-same, the achieved, but opens it to a radical polyvalency born of the encounter of the original text with Draesner's response in a specific historical moment.

The essay coins the term 'Anklangsgedicht' [re-sound poem or hark back poem] to describe its processes.

Im Sonett als klassisches Anklangsgedicht klingt heute der Reim selbst nurmehr an bzw. wird in (Teil-)Anagramme aufgelöst: in der Welt der reproduzierbaren und damit gesteigerten Einzelheit reimt sich nichts mehr. Es besteht nur mehr aus den gleichen Buchstaben (wie für die Genetiker, wir).[53]

[In the sonnet as a classic Anklanggedicht today, rhyme is only suggested or dissolves in (part-)anagrams. In the world of reproducible and hence heightened singularity, nothing

---

52 See Ertel, *Körper, Gehirne, Gene*, pp. 271–283.
53 Draesner, 'Dolly und Will', p. 32. That the letters A, C, G und T represent the 'four-letter word' [das vier-buchstaben-wort] (Sonnet 65, 'Twin Spin', p. 27) of genetics is a constant theme in Draesner's cycle.

rhymes any more [or nothing makes sense anymore]. The poem consists of nothing but the same letters (as do we for geneticists).

In fact, despite its characteristic shifts – the translation of 'date' in a temporal sense with 'dattel' [date – the fruit] and the multiple games with 'hell' as bright, fair and genetically favoured – the poem is remarkably true to Shakespeare's original. And rhymes (and makes sense) more than one might originally think. It is an attempt in the very process of creation to playfully misconstrue meaning, recombine letters and thus to mimic genetic translation/transcription errors. That is to enact the playful discontinuity in continuity of genetic reproduction in the very form of the poem.

Twin Spin: Science as Form

In her essay 'Dolly und Will', Draesner makes it clear that 'Twin Spin' turns on the anxiety that the human subjecthood, the language-making mind in all its complexity and self-dividedness, that dreams of survival in the sonnets, might make itself extinct by letting replication take the place of recombination. The quotation from Shakespeare's 15th sonnet – 'And, all in war with Time, for love of you, / As he takes from you, I engraft you new' – appears in Draesner's version as: 'und, ganz und gar überworfen mit zeit aus liebe zu dir, / während sie an dir frißt, dreh ich dich neu, die retorte von mir' [literally: 'and totally at war with time for love of you, / as it feeds off you i spin you, retort/ text tube mine, anew].[54] The word 'retorte' is a noteworthy mutant intervention which operates on a number of levels. At one level it plays on the English 'retort'; and, as in the Shakespeare, a response is being offered in the face of time and its destruction of the beloved other. However, it also encompasses the sense of a 'turning back to its originator': the German version of the sonnet is turned back to the English writer and the English text. It is noteworthy in this context that Draesner 'turns' the English so that the 'you' – in the original indicating the lover – also becomes the verse. Poetry is turned and re-turned, as a response to time. The English is also reinvented in the German version ('dreh ich dich neu' [turn/spin you anew]) to take account of the interventions which have occurred since Shakespeare's time. However, the word 'retorte' also gestures to the realm of science as 'test tube'. Of course, the original English itself ('engraft') is already oddly suggestive to an ear alive to the processes of genetic manipulation. But Draesner shines the

---

54 'Twin Spin', p. 17.

light of her polyglot poetics on the word so as to refract several new aspects. We see quite clearly the familiar image of test tubes being spun in a centrifuge, as part of the chemical process. But in the word 'drehen' [turn] there are two further references. At one level there is the spiral form of the genome referred to earlier in the accompanying essay, which draws Draesner back to the question of gene manipulation. But, from the beginning, of Draesner has conjured a 'twin spin' (her title, after all); and it is here that the other level is made explicit. The turn/spin is also that of the poem. This is made clear in a short poetic essay 'Dreh Gedanken zum Gedicht' ['Turn thoughts about the poem'] published by Draesner on the web in 2003.[55] This essay begins:

> Vielleicht ist alles in der Welt gedreht? Atome, Moleküle, Kristalle, ebenso wie Schneckenhäuser oder Zweige in ihrem Ansatz am Baum. In Spiralen wickeln sich die aus den Wirbeln kommenden Nerven zu Arm und Bein. Das Spermium dreht sich durch den Eileiter, von Augenblick der Zeugung wachsen wir in Symmetrien und Spins. Planeten, Sterne und Galaxien: sie drehen. Die Stimme: Luft wird eingesogen, ausgestoßen, dringt in den Raum, baut Wellen, dreht sich an Luftschwaden hinauf, herab, nach vorn. Schraubt sich in den Raum, ins Ohr.

> [Maybe everything in the world is turned? Atoms, molecules, crystals, as well as snail shells or branches in their attachment to the tree. In spirals, the nerves coming out of the vertebrae curl to form the arm and leg. The sperm rotates through the fallopian tube, from the moment of conception we grow in symmetries and spins. Planets, stars and galaxies: they rotate. The voice: air is sucked in, expelled, moves out into space, creates waves, turns on air currents, up, down, forward. Spirals its way into the room, into the ear.]

Draesner points out that everything turns, from spinal nerves to sperm, planets and galaxies. The recognition that patterns are repeated on the micro- and macro-levels is an insight familiar from contemporary science and from a body of early twentieth-century poetry that founded an aesthetic upon such correspondences. And indeed, Draesner follows suit: 'Wenn die lebendige Welt Gedrehtes ist, dann wird, was später "Gedicht" sein will, draus übersetzt' [if the living world is created of turning, that which later desires to become a 'poem' is translated from it]. The transformation or translation is here accomplished by what Draesner calls an 'algorithm', in line with her argument. But tellingly she also uses a number of other phrases: 'Er ist die kleine Maschine des Gedichts' [The algorithm is the little machine of the poem]; or finally:

---

55 See Draesner, 'Dreh Gedanken zum Gedicht: Eine Poetik', on *Metroprolet Blog* (http://www.metroprolet.net/wordpress/index.php).

> Bei Gedichten: erscheint er als Dreh (oder Spin) des sinnlichen Verarbeitungsapparates in den Sprachapparat. Er 'geht über' und informiert das Gedicht; drückt es in seine Form, die zugleich eine Nachricht ist.

> [In poems it appears as the turn or spin of the sensual mechanism of processing into the process of language. It 'goes across' and informs the poem; expresses it in its form, which is also a message.]

The poem functions as a retort in all senses; that is, it works at the interface between I and you, experience and time, and operates its own spin. It is at once a process and an experimental instrument: 'Maschine' [machine], 'Verarbeitungsapparat' [processing mechanism] or, as Nico Bleutge terms it in a review, 'Erkenntniswerkzeuge' [the tools of knowledge].[56] This understanding of the aesthetic processes of poetry brings Draesner into line with other poets working through the knowledge of modern science, like Durs Grünbein or Raoul Schrott, for whom: 'das Gedicht [ist] die präziseste erkenntnistheoretische Maschine, die es überhaupt gibt' [the poem is the most precise epistemological machine that exists].[57] But it is Draesner's verbs that are particularly interesting: 'übersetzt' [translates, lit. carries over, 'geht über' [crosses over]. Draesner has returned to a notion of translation between realms, correspondence in its broadest sense, the 'Stoffwechsel' [exchange of material; metabolism] mentioned before that makes of the poem a body, a living thing.

The final example comes from her most recent collection of poetry to date *subsong* (2014) and demonstrates that twin spin at work in the body of the poem.[58] The volume takes its cue from research on bird song and the notion of subsong, which is understood as a kind of practising of vocabulary, a kind of training, without regard to territory or mating, akin ultimately, Draesner implies, to poetry. Beyond this broad scientific backdrop, this collection is in a sense furthest from the core scientific material that marks earlier work, although essays from around the same time and since indicate that scientific preoccupations (especially with reproduction and genetics) continue.[59] What is striking about this volume, however, is that these preoccupations are not treated as themes simply; they are taken up into the very forms of the poems: whether those poems that themselves attempt to transliterate the sounds of bird song, for

---

56 Nico Bleutge, 'Sinnverschiebungen in Versen "kugelblitz": Gedichte von Ulrike Draesner', *Neue Zürcher Zeitung*, 28 July 2005; see: http://www.lyrikkritik.de/bleutge-draesner.html.
57 Raoul Schrott, 'Die Mitte zurückgewinnen', p. 151.
58 Ulrike Draesner, *subsong* (Munich: Luchterhand, 2014).
59 Ulrike Draesner, *Grammatik der Gespenster. Frankfurter Vorlesungen* (Stuttgart: Reclam, 2018).

example, the concrete poems in the shape of trees, or those that transliterate the auditory slippages of listening to Beatles records. One poem also picks up the 'theme' of spin and embodies it in the form of the poem 'taumel der trennung' ['separation spin'].[60]

morgens vor dem spiegel **ich**
träumend denk und **dreh**
um dich **da** wird die kehle
mir **noch** eng denn du sagst
durch welches öhr willst du
dass ich schlüpf um dich **da**
rauszudrehen sage **ich** hat
mir gerade **noch** gefehlt
dass **durch** zu vieler spiegel
dreh ich dich nirgends mehr
versteh der an der gläser **dreh**
glaubt er säh wie **ich** mir uns
als wir gedacht **da**rin ein du das
drückt und **noch** mit schaum
durch die zähne zu mir spricht
was musst du wütend sein **da**bei
obwohl, welch blitz, du **durch** den
spiegel lachst als **dreh**te mich
um dich **noch** immer munter
ich und schaute nie an dir
vorbei

[in the morning at the mirror **i'm**
in dreams thinking and **going**
breathless twirling a**round**
you whisper **the** spell you think will
bend my ear to tell which needle's
eye to pass to get **round** me
to winkle me out **the** hell with
that light **bend**s and i
can see **i'm** only flailing
going nowhere just a blur
a spiral where you see **the**
face as mine at every **bend**
at every whirl think **i'm** a
you that's **going** to hurt and
spin a**round** to spit your rage
through the mirror i **round**

60 Draesner, *subsong*, p. 13.

> on this laughing you **i'm** sure
> thought i was **going** to blithely
> orbit like **the** circling moon
> and **bend** to please not turn
> away][61]

This is a difficult poem to interpret, indeed read, partly because of the density of the word play and partly because the form, with its lack of punctuation, encourages sematic instability and multiple possible readings. It feels unaccountably claustrophobic, always turning in on itself. Indeed, the word 'Taumel' invokes turning, spinning and potentially dizziness. At first glance the poem seems to stage the painful end of a relationship ('Trennung' [separation]) between an I and an intimate you [du] projected into the bathroom mirror. One could be forgiven for reading it as a mini-drama of sorts: one can discern a kind of setting, stage directions ('da wird die kehle /mir nocheng' [then my throat constricts]) and a sequence of dialogue that implies tetchy or bitter reproach: 'du sagst / durch welches öhr willst du/ dass ich schlüpf' [you say / which needle's eye do you want / me to pass through]; 'sage ich hat / mir gerade noch gefehlt [I say that's the last thing I need]; 'was musst du wütend sein' [how angry you must be]. The poem seems to end with the potential of escape in seeing past: 'und schaute nie an dir vorbei' [and never looked past you]). Though even this is uncertain and could be read in different ways.

However, the fact that this is staged in front of a mirror also implies that we might here be dealing with multiple versions of self, either as a straightforward reflection or even one of those winged mirrors that offer multiple reflections. Even the 'er' [he] that appears could, at a pinch, reflect the fact that mirror ('der Spiegel') is masculine in German. This makes of the poem a struggle in a sense to find a way out of an uncomfortable matrix of versions of self, that issue eventually into a speculative seeing past the you. That the poem riffs on, and makes manifest, the turn, the 'spin' of the poem is evidenced in two things: the word 'dreh' [turn, spin, bend] appears five times in the German as a kind of spine to the poem; but it is also refracted through a variety of idioms that use the word 'drehen', which culminate in the phrase 'ich drehe durch', roughly equivalent to 'I'm going round the bend'. These appear in a kind of spiral through the poem, caught brilliantly in Iain Galbraith's translation. One starts, then, by reading this as a poem about a painful altercation conducted in the mirror,

---

61 Translation by Iain Galbraith from *this porous fabric*, p. 183. The translation follows the spirit of the poem to catch the spin; in the following discussion I shall refer to the literal meaning of individual lines.

during the habitual bathroom routines. It then offers itself as an internal dialogue of sorts with I and you as figures in the mirror testing out battling versions of self. In any case, it is a meditation on the identities that I, you and we play out in a rondo of roles: 'glaubt er säh wie ich mir uns' [believes he looks like I me us]. In this sense it is like many of Draesner's 'mirror' poems that highlight the possibilities of speaking likenesses to alter our sense of self.[62]

The twist of the poem, however, comes in the 'Dreh' [the knack, the spin, the turn]. This ties in with Draesner's comments on the turn of poetry and links back to the title of her Shakespeare translations which give their title to this chapter too. But more important, of course, is the fact that the poem makes visible through the vagaries of shifting identity that can be read, misread and read anew, the helix shape that runs through it, demonstrating how we and it are constructed. The phrase is constantly reconstituted, shifting its meaning as it turns and recombines, through the poem. The integrity of the subject and poetry is interrogated at the same time – even constituted before our eyes. Its twin spin seeks to change the poetry but also to change the subject.

---

62 I discuss this aspect of Draesner's work in '"Übungen der Zugewandtheit": Ulrike Draesner's Poetics of Correspondence', in *Schaltstelle*, ed. by Leeder, pp. 231–262.

Beyond Form(s)

Noël Reumkens

The Connection between Body, Language and Image. Intermediality in Ulrike Draesner's Poetry

Ulrike Draesner's oeuvre is a prime resource for intermedial research in many respects. Among other things, the author has frequently collaborated with visual artists; these collaborations include more traditional projects, like the 1997 volume *anis-o-trop* (published two years after her debut collection), where fifteen of Draesner's sonnets are combined with four works by the relatively unknown artist Joachim Jung. Owing to its (typo)graphical format, the small, ostensibly minimalist volume stands in stark contrast to other multimedia collaborations the poet has been involved in. These other projects reveal Draesner's preference for new media; she has often produced her texts for installations which combine different media forms, for example *Fähren* (2001) [*Ferries*] for the Basel Rhine Ferry service, which she performed together with the composer Annette Schlünz, and the audio-visual installation *space poem (walk-in-poem)* (2002), created in collaboration with visual artist Andreas Schmid for the Goethe Institutes of Calcutta and Hong Kong. In addition to these, Draesner has also written texts to accompany works by (audio)-visual artists which are not collaborations but act rather as accompanying texts. A prime example of this is her text 'Mit/Schrift' ['Trans/Script'], which she wrote to accompany three short films by Hannes Schüpbach, *Portrait Marriage*, *Spin* and *Toccata*.

Alongside these multimedia projects the often unconventional and playful typographical style of Draesner's poetry should not be overlooked. The occasionally unorthodox typography, reminiscent of Modernist experiments, is an important feature of her work. The absence of upper-case letters is perhaps the most obvious typographical feature of the early collections, even if this is not yet consistent throughout *gedächtnisschleifen*. But this is not the only distinctive facet. Draesner's poems often have a deeply fragmented visual aspect which disregards the conventional layout of the poem. The formal appearance of her texts is perhaps most arresting in her debut volume *gedächtnisschleifen* and in her third collection *kugelblitz*. In *kugelblitz*, for example, there are striking visual-poetic details: a lightning symbol hovers above one of the poems and gives it its title; and in the poem 'frauen in der produktion' ['women in pro-

https://doi.org/10.1515/9783110495942-007

duction'] a jagged shape created by what looks like a lightning arrow appears to be biting its own tail.[1]

In this chapter I shall discuss poems whose linguistic content alludes to visual works of art, or whose meaning is at least partly based on visual works of art. It is worth saying straightaway that, in her poems, Draesner never presents the simple description of an image; visual art is always intertwined with the everyday or anecdotal. To begin with I shall discuss a text which typifies Draesner's interaction with pictures.

'Leben im Blick'

Draesner's poetological text 'Zeugen' ['Begetting' or 'Witness'] sets the scene: 'Wir haben einen Zoo. Andere schauen wir darin an. Doch auch selbst leben wir im Blick' [We have a zoo. We look at others in it. But we too are being watched].[2] Seeing and optical perspectives are a recurring theme in Draesner's poetry, repeatedly associated with language and the human body. The following excerpt from the untitled introductory passage in *kugelblitz* is particularly eye-catching:

> als ob es nicht das erste aber einzige
> mal wäre dass zungengelenke eingescannt wurden
> zu direkt mit dem körper verbundenen wörtern.[3]

> [as if it were not the first but the only
> time that tongue joints were scanned
> into words directly connected with the body.]

The organ responsible for language, the tongue, is 'scanned' here, that is, optically fixed; words still emerge from it, however, and these words are linked to the body. This piece of text exemplifies the relation between body, language and image as it frequently appears in Draesner's poetry.

In this context, I would like to draw attention to a text which illustrates the topos of 'Leben im Blick' particularly well; not a poem but a prose text Draesner wrote for the anthology *Muscheln und Blumen* [*Mussels and Flowers*], published

---

1 Ulrike Draesner, *kugelblitz* (Munich: Luchterhand, 2005), p. 39. Draesner herself describes this symbol as 'ein narbenähnliches Zeichen' [a scar-like symbol] in Ulrike Draesner, *Zauber im Zoo. Vier Reden von Herkunft und Literatur* (Göttingen: Wallstein, 2007), p. 35; 'frauen in der produktion', *kugelblitz*, p. 69.

2 Draesner, 'Zeugen', *Zauber im Zoo*, p 5.

3 Draesner, *kugelblitz*, p. 6.

by Aargauer Kunsthaus in 2003. The volume includes texts by a selection of authors on works of visual art on display in the Swiss museum.

Draesner's text refers to the photograph 'Sonja mit Wasserglas' (1991 ['Sonja with a Glass of Water'] (Fig. 1) by Annelies Štrba. Draesner multiplies the description of the image by writing not one but two related texts in response to it. Unusual is the fact that the names she uses in her titles are different to the name in the title of the photograph: '1 (Rosa)' and '2 (Maria)'. These two texts symbolize an unconventional approach to describing an image: on the one hand, both texts systematically describe, even offer an inventory of, what can be seen in the photograph: a young woman sitting in a kitchen. On the other hand, Draesner at the same time implicitly and explicitly questions what she describes:

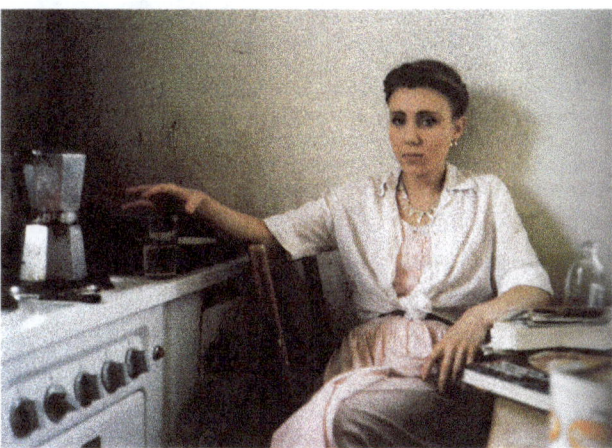

Fig. 1: 'Sonja mit Wasserglas' ['Sonja with a glass of Water'] (1991/2018) by Annelies Štrba. Photography, behind glass. 50 × 76 cm.

In der Küche einen Kaffee trinken, sie hat ihn schon getrunken, wird ihn noch trinken, die Espressomaschine steht auf dem Herd.[4]

[Drinking a coffee in the kitchen, she has already drunk it, is going to drink it, the espresso machine is on the cooker.]

In the first part of the sentence Draesner provides an interpretation of what can be seen in the picture: coffee is being drunk in a kitchen. In both the subsidiary clauses she suggests different possible moments within the course of that action:

---

4 *Muscheln und Blumen. Literarische Texte zu Werken der Kunst*, ed. by Beat Wismer, Stephan Kunz and Sibylle Omlin (Zurich: Ammann, 2003), p. 383.

either the woman has already drunk the coffee or she is about to drink it. In the last clause she gives the reason for the need to interpret the coffee-drinking: there is an espresso machine on the cooker.

What we think we see is in fact made up of suppositions: it is nothing more than a potential meaning expressed in language, a hypothesis. In 'Zeugen' Draesner writes:

> Wir sprechen über bildgebende Verfahren.
> Wir sprechen von Möglichkeiten.
> Wir sprechen von Literatur.
>
> [We talk about imaging processes.
> We talk about possibilities.
> We talk about literature.][5]

Literature *creates* pictures and presents the reader with possibilities. The multiplication of her thoughts on the image in '1 (Rosa)' and '2 (Maria)', and the fact that there are two texts, reinforces this idea succinctly: the picture does not exist until it is presented in literature, in language. In this way literature demonstrates that the photograph does not convey or contain any inherently concrete or straightforward truth. Instead we are presented with two possible worlds, whose potentialities are questioned once again even within the text. Suppositions are presented here as part of the fictive reality.

This theory underpins the statement 'und man sieht, was man nicht sieht' [and you see what you don't see] in the first of the two texts.[6] Everything is illusory, even though one might believe that the camera produces an objective record of reality. After a short description of the young lady in the photograph, this assertion is made again more decisively: 'zu sehen ist das nicht' [it cannot be seen].[7] The description of the picture undermines itself and in doing so, demonstrates that the photograph is not a two-dimensional surface, but a vessel that can be filled with meaning.[8] In keeping with this idea, the lyrical voice of the first text asks: 'Erinnerst du dich, oder kannst es dir vorstellen, wie es ist, in einem Gefäß zu sein, etwa einem Foto?' [Do you remember, or can you imagine

---

5 Draesner, *Zauber im Zoo*, p. 8.
6 *Muscheln und Blumen*, p. 383.
7 Ibid.
8 This is similar to the motif of the screen in Draesner's poetry, where screens are repeatedly dived into and therefore represent a three-dimensional space, e.g. in the poems 'megasex' in Ulrike Draesner, *für die nacht geheuerte zellen* (Munich: Luchterhand, 2001), p. 23; and 'feed me, eat me', *kugelblitz*, pp. 17–18.

what it's like to be in a vessel, a photo, perhaps?].[9] The connection to the human body comes to the fore again in this question: the picture is a three-dimensional space in which the human finds him/herself. In the text *anis-o-trop* which Draesner created together with the artist Joachim Jung, she writes:

> aber in wirklichkeit ist es zu spät, um zu wissen, ob man
> draußen oder drinnen gefangen ins ende des bildes ist.[10]

> [but, in reality, it is too late to know whether you
> are trapped inside or outside into the end of the image.]

The question as to whether one is outside or inside is obsolete, for 'unser körper glimmt im netz / der sprache' [our body glows in the net of language], according to the poem 'post-dolly' in the collection *für die nacht geheuerte zellen*.[11] Or to put it another way: our body is always 'im Zustand der Sprache' [in a state of language];[12] it cannot be released from the net of language, it is forever in what Draesner calls the 'Signifikantenstrom' [tide of signifiers].[13] In any case, language is irrevocably tied to images, for according to Draesner the world essentially appears to us 'in Riten und Gesten, Bildern und Sprache' [in rites and gestures, images and language].[14]

In both texts '1 (Rosa)' and '2 (Maria)' the blurring of boundaries between the subject – in this case the object being observed – and its environment, is also conspicuous. At one point in the first text '1 (Rosa)' Draesner writes 'die anfransenden Ränder, die Mauern – fort. Wie gegangen oder geblieben wird?' [the fraying edges, the walls – gone. How going or staying happens?].[15] This makes apparent the openness of what is being observed. Since the young woman only exists as a possible feature of the picture, that is, a product of language used to describe it, even she is not a fixed, closed entity, but is instead open to interpretation. Throughout the text this openness to the other, the strange and the unlimited nature of the object in question is clearly reinforced. For example, the gender of the figure in the picture is brought into question when Draesner describes how the person holding the glass 'wie ein Mann von oben darüber [greift]'

---

9 *Muscheln und Blumen*, p. 383.
10 Ulrike Draesner, *anis-o-trop* (Hamburg: Rospo, 1997), p. xi.
11 Draesner, *für die nacht geheuerte zellen*, pp. 116–117.
12 Ulrike Draesner, 'Atem, Puls, Bahn' ['Breath, Pulse and Track'], in *Minima Poetica. Für eine Poetik des zeitgenössischen Gedichts*, ed. by Joachim Sartorius, 2nd edn (Berlin: Suhrkamp, 2003), pp. 48–63 (p. 48).
13 Ibid., p. 48.
14 Draesner, *Zauber im Zoo*, p. 8.
15 *Muscheln und Blumen*, p. 385.

[goes to grasp it from above it like a man] and a bit later, we read that the person in the picture is 'fast ohne Geschlecht' [almost without gender].[16]

The name Sonja in the title of the painting is quite simply one of many possibilities, something explicitly marked by the use of the other names Rosa and Maria. Neither the title of the work of art, then, nor the name can offer a real clue: 'Sie hat einen Namen, kannst du dir vorstellen, das Bild heißt Sonja mit Wasserglas. Und wie heißt sie? Hieß sie so, oder blieb es sich gleich?' [She has a name, you can imagine, the picture is called 'Sonja with a Glass of Water'. And what is her name? Was she called that or does it not matter?].[17] As far as the names are concerned, they are simply there to provide a label. This labelling, the allocation of names, draws our attention to the subject of discussion, so to speak, and gives the deceptive impression of an identity. In reality, though, everything remains vague, uncertain and complex. In the first text '(1 (Rosa)' Draesner writes:

> Die Geräte, die Hauswaren. Ihr Gesicht, Fenster und Wand. Wo unterscheiden sie sich? Wer zieht einen Strich, trennt, wer weiß?[18]

> [The utensils, the household goods. Her face, window and wall. What makes them distinct from each other? Who draws the line, separates, who knows?]

It is not easy to differentiate between subject and environment; everything runs together: utensils, household goods, face, window and wall. Perhaps more to the point: in the second text, which thematizes the system of digital photography as a picture-generating process, Draesner observes:

> Die Wand, weiß, grobporig, beschmattert wie Quark. Von nahem besteht das Gesicht nur aus Pünktchen, dass es lauter Pixel sind, ihr Gesicht. Blaugrüngelborangerot. Ohrring vor der Wand. Die Wand, die Kamera, die Wand, die Kamera, jetzt haben sie sich gefunden, jetzt.[19]

> [The wall, white, grainy, splodgy like quark. Close-up, the face is made up solely of small dots, so her face is simply pixels. Bluegreenyelloworangered. Earring in front of the wall. The wall, the camera, the wall, the camera, now they have found each other, now.]

In this passage, the processes of digital photography are pursued as a metaphor for experiencing reality. When you focus, try to get nearer to something, everything becomes unclear, you only see the pixels. Everything appears pixelated or as if 'von pixeln durchwuchert' [overrun with pixels], as the poem 'er sagt,

---

16 Ibid., p. 384.
17 Ibid.
18 Ibid., p. 384.
19 Ibid., p. 385.

dass wir in einer röhre gehen' ['he says we're walking in a tube'] has it.[20] In this way the intrinsic connection between image and language, as foregrounded in Draesner's poetry, remains intact. In the second text, Draesner expands on this: 'Nein, kein Wort hat hier Platz. Alle Wörter in Büchern sind unscharf geworden' [No, there is no room for a single word here. All words in books have gone out of focus].[21] Towards the end of the second text the indivisible connection between word and image is emphasized again in the synaesthetic combination 'Sie schaut die Kamera an, schaut das Wort an, das durch den Raum ging [. . .]' [She looks at the camera, looks at the word that went through the room].[22]

Just as in these texts, Draesner frequently deconstructs boundaries between subject and its surroundings, or between subject and object in her poetry. Each and every boundary is exposed as a fictional construct. This is also the case for those poems that allude explicitly to visual works of art. These are always simultaneously associated with the everyday and also with other works of art, meaning that they never form a closed unit. For this reason, there is no classical ekphrasis in Draesner's oeuvre, but only ever references, which generate possible interpretations for the rest of what is said in the text. In the following section I shall discuss several poems which demonstrate this link and the connection between body, language and image.

'Beuystafel'

Just like her contemporaries Thomas Kling and Durs Grünbein, Ulrike Draesner has written a poem which can be understood as a tribute to the artist Joseph Beuys. The poem 'Beuystafel' ['Beuys Tableau'] was published in Draesner's debut collection *gedächtnisschleifen* in 1995.

Beuystafel

Sie sagen, aus gewaltsam Getöteten steigen,
Augenblick des Todes, Sekrete auf, kleine
unregelmäßige Wölkchen, keiner weiß woher
und kaum zu sehen, du, jetzt, wo du bist,
wir haben uns nicht mehr gesehen, seit
vielen Wochen uns nicht mehr
angeblickt, du wolltest diese Reise,
jetzt, denke ich, bist du in der Luft,

---

20 Draesner, *für die nacht geheuerte zellen*, p. 99.
21 *Muscheln und Blumen*, p. 385.
22 Ibid.

wehende Stiefmütterchen, blaßlila, dazwischen
postgelb, du schließt die Augen,
schläfst schon ein, ich stehe
vor diesem 300fach heißen Flimmern
über der Aschebahn, über den weißen
Kerzen in roten Haltern halte ich den Atem
an, vor diesem eisernen Bett, verhalte mich
an dieser Opferstatt bis zur Auflösung,
sie sagen, den Verlassenen heile die Zeit,
wie von selbst, aber wir haben uns nicht
wirklich angesehen, haben uns nicht mehr
nachgesehen, nichts, keinen Abschied
genommen, die flackernden Teelichter,
300 brennende Augen, möchte ich austrinken,
in das schwimmende weiß tauchen möchte ich,
mit dem Georgsspeer das weiße, das erstarrte
Fleisch meiner Hand schneiden, du bist
schon in den Wolken, du ißt schon
von einer anderen, schwimmendes Wachs

ich berufe, was eilig war, wer tötet
endlich den Drachen, der uns auseinander treibt
das Flackern der Flammen aus meiner, der Haut,
aus meinen Augen dieses Hervorschießen von
über der langen Trage, 300 Kerzen, sie sagen,
die Erinnerung bleibt, 300 brennende Kerzen,
die Ausbreitung der eigenen Gedankentrauer,
wie das Rot sickert, wie die Stumpen
flackern, dieses irre, mein züngelndes
Schmerzensgelichter, als ich da stehe
als ich da in meine Sonne zoome.[23]

[They say, from those killed violently / in the moment of death, secretions / rise up, small irregular clouds, no-one knows where from / and hardly visible, you, now, where you are, / we haven't seen each other not glimpsed each other for weeks, / you wanted this journey, / now, I think, are you in the air, / swaying pansies, pale violet, post-office / yellow in amongst them, you close your eyes fall asleep already, I'm standing / in front of this 300x hot flickering / above the cinder track, above the white / candles in red holders I hold my breath, / before this iron bed, behave / at this sacrificial altar / until dissolution, / they say, time heals the one is left behind, / as if by itself, but we haven't really / looked at each other, haven't looked out for / each other, nothing, haven't said / goodbye, the flickering tea-lights, / 300 burning eyes I'd like to drink up / I'd like to dive into the swimming white, / cut the frozen white flesh of my hand / with St George's lance you are / already in the clouds, you're already eating / another, swimming wax. I appoint, in

23 Ulrike Draesner, *gedächtnisschleifen*, 2nd edn (Munich: Luchterhand 2008), pp. 19–20.

a hurry, whoever finally / kills the dragon, the one that drives us apart, / the flickering of the flames out of my, the skin, / out of my eyes, this shooting from / above the long stretcher, 300 candles, they say, / the memory remains, 300 burning candles, / the spreading out of one's own grief / how the red seeps, as the pillar candles / flare, this mad, my flickering / painful rabble, as I stand there, / as I zoom into my sun.]

This poem sketches a relatively intimate scene in a church. A lyrical 'I' is grieving over the loss of a 'you'. Boundaries blur between well-meaning platitudes intended as comfort ('Sie sagen' [They say]) and allusions to the official hagiography of St George. The same is true in a way of Joseph Beuys' oeuvre, described as a 'dialectic of superstition' and a 'draft of a theodicy' by Friedhelm Mennekes.[24] The comforting words are presented as a kind of consolation, intended to ease the pain of losing a loved one.

The first part of the poem ends with the notion of dissolution [Auflösung]. This idea can of course be construed in terms of the decay of the body of the lyric 'you' after its death; it can also be read as the 'Bildauflösung' [image resolution] in light of optical perspective which is repeatedly emphasized in the poem: 'nicht mehr gesehen' [haven't seen each other]; 'angeblickt' [glimpsed]; 'angesehen' [looked at]; 'nachgesehen' [looked out for]. The subject remains 'an dieser Opferstatt bis zur Auflösung' [at this sacrificial altar / until dissolution]. The verb 'verhalten' in the same line (to react, behave, comport one's self, also to contain one's self, among many other meanings) turns into something visibly active: the subject behaves in such a way as to itself become an image. First it 'sees' ('kaum zu sehen, du, jetzt, wo du bist' [hardly visible, you, now, where you are]), and is then itself seen. Whilst images normally burn themselves onto the retina, it is the eyes here that burn. In this way, the passive eye becomes active.

In contrast to the white candle wax which is portrayed as something flowing or 'swimming', the skin of the lyric subject, the 'flesh of [its] hand', is 'erstarrt' [frozen]. The subject wants to cut into his/her hand with 'St George's lance'. This is a particularly direct reference to the work of Joseph Beuys, where wounds play an important role as they can help overcome extreme physical and psychological situations.[25] This last element also features in Draesner's poem. Boundaries are opened between the 'I' and the 'you', and similarly between the 'I' and its surroundings. The many references to warmth in the poem are therefore to be considered as

---

24 Friedhelm Mennekes, *Joseph Beuys. Christus Denken* (Stuttgart: Katholisches Bibelwerk, 1996), p. 5.
25 Doris Leutgelb, 'Blut', in *Beuysnobiscum*, ed. by Harald Szeemann, 2nd edn (Hamburg: Philo Fine Arts, 2008), pp. 61–64 (p. 61).

a play on Beuys' concept of 'warmth-plastic', in which the alienation between people, symbolized through 'cold-plastic', is eradicated.[26]

The skin of the lyric subject represents a boundary between itself and the lyric you; it drives them apart. It is opened when the 'I' injures itself. Four lines from the end of the poem, when red 'seeps', this could be both the melting 'red holders', whose melted substance drips into the white candle wax, and the blood that drips from the skin as a result of the lyric subject's self-mutilation. Here too there are allusions to Beuys' interest in blood and wounds.[27] In addition to this there are also parallels between the whole scene and the well-known Beuysian 'Christ impulse'. In this context cutting into one's flesh could be compared to the idea of Christian stigmata. Beuys considered Christ to be an 'energetic impulse, effectively present as a spark in every human being'.[28] The poem 'Beuystafel' can be interpreted in terms of this impulse, even if this is not the only allusion.

Moreover, there is a noticeable abundance of sibilants, especially in the last four lines. They amplify the semantic aspect of fire, wax and blood in the poem by conveying the strong acoustic impression of gushing substances, or secretions. This underscores the theme of opening of physical and psychological boundaries between subject and object and similarly between the subject and its environment. The end of the poem is also interesting in this respect, where the subject 'zooms into his sun', for Beuys equates Christ with a symbol of the sun.[29] Thus we have here another parallel with the conceptual apparatus of Beuys' whole oeuvre.

In this poem Draesner's own idea of an art space is paired with the concept of the Beuysian 'social plastic' (sometimes also translated as social sculpture). Beuys's dictum 'every man an artist' is evident here. You don't need a work of art to create a 'social plastic' or 'warmth-plastic' yourself. The ecclesiastical background of the poem is pertinent too. The term 'Tafel' in the title (generally, in an artistic context, meaning panel or tableau) can be placed in a religious context, linked to the most famous tablets of the Judeo-Christian tradition: Moses' commandments. The tablet is thus to be read as a form of artistic commandment, initiated by Beuys. The call to a 'social plastic' and the idea, that within this social order every person can become an artist, can thus be seen as the underlying idea of Draesner's poem. What we have here therefore, is not a direct reference to a specific work of art but rather to a whole conceptual apparatus.

---

26 Compare in this context Noël Reumkens, *Kunst, Künstler, Konzept und Konzept. Intermediale und andersartige Bezugnahmen auf Visuell-Künstlerisches in der Lyrik Mayröckers, Klings, Grünbeins und Draesners* (Würzburg: Königshausen and Neumann, 2013), p. 272.
27 Mennekes, *Joseph Beuys. Christus Denken*, p. 57.
28 Doris Leutgelb, 'Christus(impuls)', in *Beuysnobiscum*, pp. 65–70 (p. 65).
29 Ibid., p. 67.

'akt, die treppe hinab'

The poem 'akt, die treppe hinab' ['nude, down the stairs'] which also appeared in Draesner's debut collection *gedächtnisschleifen*, contains an implicit and highly complex intermedial reference. There is no traditional description of an image here either. Instead, the poem skilfully demonstrates how the meaning of a work of art or a body of art arises out of an open dialogue with other works of art and the world outside of the work itself.

> akt, die treppe hinab
>
> I
> die treppe hinab, dieser
> Akt, wie wir uns umsprangen,
> sturz des gelächters
> durch stiegen und nacht
> das haus auf-abpolterten,
> segelhemden im laken
> umeinander der geschlechter
> als wir halsten, sagten
> die eltern es spuke
> treppauf treppab
> wo wir, bruder, einander
> lehrten: *dies* heißt tag,
>
> II
> heißt gelächter,
> überm mittagsmahl redete
> vaterfleisch uns umeinander
> bis wir, hart die stiege,
> fragten das leinen
> spannten von bann zu spuk
> am abendhals einander, bruder,
> unter hunderten dieser eine,
> und *dies* hieß: jede nacht, diese
> heiß
>
> III
> hieß bis zum klingensprung bruder
> um schwester trieb man uns aus,
> dies, die füße voran, mußten
> die sprache wir wechseln, wo
> *dies* heißt fort und fortan:

würfeln wer stirbt, er sie es
sterbend daran.[30]

[nude, down the stairs

I
down the stairs, this / act, how we jumped round each other, / crash of laughter / through staircases and night / clattered up, down the house / sailing shirts in the sheet / the sexes around each other / as we embraced / the parents said, it's haunted / upstairs downstairs / where we, brother, taught / one another: *this* is called day,

II
is called laughter, / over lunch father-flesh / spoke to us around each other / until we, the staircase hard, / asked stretched the linen / from spell to spectre / around the neck of evening each other, brother, / this one from hundreds, / and *this* was called: every night, this / hot

III
was called right until the swipe of the blade brother / and sister we were driven away / *this*, feet first, we had / to change language, where / *this* is called carrying on and from now on: / let's throw the dice to see who dies, he she it / dying from it.]

The poem evokes an intimate scene, where the subject revives memories from his/her youth. It is clearly the sister's voice speaking in the poem, for in the first strophe we have: 'wo wir, bruder, einander / lehrten' [where we, brother, taught / one another]. There is a clear development in the relationship between the siblings in the poem and in the relationship with the parents. This begins in a jovial mood ('gelächter' [laughter]) and ends in the death of the brother or sister ('würfelnd wer stirbt, er sie es / sterbend daran' [let's throw the dice to see who dies, he she it / dying from it]).

The title of this poem is an explicit reference to both Marcel Duchamp's 1912 'Nude descending a Staircase, No. 2' (in German: 'Akt eine Treppe herabsteigend') (Fig. 2) and one of the most well-known intericonic citations of the twentieth century: Gerhard Richter's 1966 allusion to Duchamp, 'Ema (Akt auf einer Treppe)' ['Ema (Nude on a Staircase)'] (Fig. 3). The reference to this painting, which itself explicitly refers to another work of art, places the poem in a constellation of affiliations with visual art. Also in terms of semantics, the memories of the childhood home allude to Duchamp and Richter, and the style of both paintings. In the first part of the poem the speaker remembers that the parents said it was haunted, and equally in the second part there is talk of a spectre. These references acknowledge the diffuse, ghostly character of both paintings. They are

---

30 Draesner, *gedächtnisschleifen*, p. 23.

Fig. 2: 'Nu descendant un escalier, No. 2' ['Nude descending a Staircase, No. 2'] (1912) by Marcel Duchamp 1912.

Fig. 3: 'Ema (Akt auf einer Treppe)' ['Ema (Nude on a Staircase)'] (1966) by Gerhard Richter.

in large part defined by a lack of material definition, which corresponds to the elusiveness of the siblings.

The question now arises as to how these allusions to Richter's 'Nude' and Duchamp's iconic template correlate with the text of Draesner's poem. With this in mind, it is worth examining the paratextual framework of the volume *gedächtnisschleifen*. Draesner explains in the volume what she means by *gedächtnisschleifen*, namely criss-cross, mixed references to texts, and she allows the reader to gain insight into the way references are woven into the fabric of her poetry.[31] It is here she mentions that the poem 'akt, die treppe hinab' also refers to (texts by) Ingeborg Bachmann.

In her 2007 volume *Schöne Frauen Lesen* Draesner dedicates the chapter entitled 'Frau Bachmann und der Schwindel im Erzählen' ['Frau Bachmann and the Vertigo/Swindle of Narration'] to the author Ingeborg Bachmann.[32] Draesner expresses a particular interest in Bachman's short story 'Drei Wege zum See' ['Three Paths to the Lake'] taken from the 1972 collection *Simultan* [*Simultaneous*]. The poem 'akt, die treppe hinab' alludes to this same short story. The Bachmann story shares with the Richter painting the notion that it should be understood as a continuation, in this case of the 1938 novel *Die Kapuzinergruft* [*The Emperor's Tomb*, 1984] by Joseph Roth. The phrase 'fort und fortan' [carrying on and from now on] at the end of Draesner's text alludes to this concept of continuing to write, or paint from where the originals left off.

A further point of connection for the interpretation of Draesner's poem in Bachmann's story is the relationship between Elisabeth Matrei and her brother, which was intense to the point of incest. The poem 'akt, die treppe hinab' contains implicit indications that suggest actual or suspected incest in the brother and sister relationship outlined in the text. For example, there is talk of 'umeinander der geschlechter' [the sexes around each other], which has potentially sexual connotations, but this could also refer to the playful 'umspringen' [jumping round each other] or 'Herumtollen' [romping around] of the siblings. The most explicit intertextually inspired suggestion of incest is created by the location of the scene on the stairs. In Freud's dream theory, the erotic significance of staircases, steps and ladders is thematized in different instances. The fact that Draesner's poem expressly includes the word 'stiege' [staircase] sets up a direct reference to Freud's 'Stiegentraum' ['A Staircase Dream'].[33] The poem thus can

---

31 Ibid., p. 106.
32 Ulrike Draesner, *Schöne Frauen Lesen. Über Ingeborg Bachmann, Annette von Droste-Hülshoff, Friederike Mayröcker, Virginia Woolf* (Munich: Luchterhand, 2007), pp. 133–155.
33 The term 'treppauf, treppab' [upstairs and downstairs] in Draesner's poem correlates with this excerpt from Freud's *The Interpretation of Dreams*: 'Staircases, ladders, steps, climbing up

be seen to thematize the infringement of the Lacanian Symbolic Order upon the lives of the children.[34] Tellingly, only the father is mentioned directly, not the mother. The Symbolic Order is the law of the father. The father is responsible for the 'bann' [spell; also banishment] in the second section: he attempts to eradicate the 'spuk' [spectre] of incest, but in doing so breaks the unity between brother and sister; paradoxically, by describing the children as brother and sister, he drives a wedge between them, and they from then on regard each other as 'others'.

With this interpretative constellation in mind, it is particularly interesting to see a significant change in the relationship between Duchamp's and Richter's paintings. Duchamp's nude, like many other of the artist's works, is often presented in specialist literature as an artistic exploration of the incestuous relationship with his sister.[35] Richter's 'Ema', on the other hand, portrays the artist's wife of the time. Tellingly, the theme of incest, visible in the relationship between the two works of art (the sister becomes wife), is symbolic; it is imposed upon the artwork through language; it is not inherent within it, or rather, it cannot be extracted from it. The poem perpetuates this theme by showing how the language between brother and sister changes.

These reflections demonstrate that the term 'Akt' in the poem's title is ambiguous. In the first instance, in its allusion to the Duchamp-Richter affiliation, it points to the artistic portrayal of a naked body. Secondly, the term can be read in relation to incest as a sex-act, and thirdly there is the possibility of interpreting the act as a form of ceremony. In this last case, the 'Akt' denotes the ritual expulsion from carefree childhood, which can also be conceived as banishment.

The poem 'akt, die treppe hinab' illustrates that an image, like a word, is never static, it oscillates all the time, just like the female figures in the paintings of Duchamp and Richter. The pictures are moving, open. Whilst Richter's 'Ema' can be considered the epitome of a 'work of art as quotation', Bachmann's text

---

as well as down them, are symbolic representations of the sex-act', Sigmund Freud, *Die Traum-deutung. Studienausgabe*, Vol II. ed. by Alexander Mitscherlich et al. (Frankfurt a. M.: Fischer, 2000). p. 349. Also on the theme of stairs in dreams see 'Ein Stiegentraum', ibid., p. 361.

34 'The socialization experiences of the protagonists in all genres of Draesner texts are harnessed, on the one hand, within the Freudian coordinates of the "super-ego" (also extended by Lacan in his literary theory) with the formative genetic and psychological pressure of the parents; but on the other hand, a certain scepticism towards a biologically determined sexual identity established prediscursively is also thematized', Volker Wehdeking, *Generationenwechsel. Intermedialität in der deutschen Gegenwartsliteratur* (Berlin: Erich Schmidt, 2007), p. 197.

35 For further reading on the incestuous relationship between Duchamp and his sister Suzanne see Lieven Jonckheere, *Het seksuele fantasme voorbij. Zeven psychoanalytische gevalsstudies* (Leuven: ACCO, 2003), pp. 64–65.

'Drei Wege zum See' is an explicit continuation of Roth's literary cosmos. Draesner's poem 'akt, die treppe hinab' takes up the threads of these artistic kinships and pairs them with the difference between the sexes and its hypothetical character. The poem positions the intericonic and the intertextual side by side and thus creates a work of art which posits a plurimedial experience of reality in which image, language and body are intertwined.

'pissblumen'

Draesner has regularly collaborated on multimedia works of art in the last fifteen years. Her strong interest in multimedia is also evident in her poetry, a good example of which is her poem 'pissblumen' ['piss flowers'].

> pissblumen
>
> pflanzbare namen, die zunge der schiffer geknetet ins netz.
> hündisches. einsam verspritzender sand.
> flutlöchter. nadel ertastet gesteine gehirn. tastbare.
> knopfdruck in flügelartiges: zwillings
>
> haft. aufgespreizt. gebahrte gebrüstete flocken. lichtsaft. sie
> lüster gewesen sich tief in den schnee.
> knisternder tritt es aus dem körper: bei ihm eine scheibe, bei ihr:
> stangentief, gesprenkeltes hält sich an
>
> der hand. gelber phallus aus eis, erstarrt, an ihr lutscht er, sie an
> ihm, jeder das andre geschlecht. kommt zur
> gleichen zeit, einem fernen ort, heiß, er die straße herab, sie,
> die begebenheit voll vertiefungen,
>
> leer, gedankenversunken, und sie, die nicht spricht, langsam
> schwappend
> in wässrigen feldern, im reißenden,
> haut. mikrophonetisches knistern, es könnte auch weinendes
> sein. körper. eben. die hunde geben den kopf.
>
> diese schmelzenden flächen sind wir. schön sind wir auch.
> morgen lassen wir uns vergessen.
> pissblumen gewesen. namen, geschissen zu schnee.[36]

---

36 Draesner, *für die nacht geheuerte zellen*, p. 33.

[plantable names, the boatmen's tongue kneaded into the net / doggish. lonely squirting sand. / flood holes. needle tests boulder brain. palpable ones. / push of a button in wing-like: twin- / like. spread open. laid-out breasted flakes. light-juice. they / were chandeliers deep in the snow. / crackling even more it flowed out of the body: a disc in his case, in / her case: stalk-deep, speckles stick to her hand. yellow phallus made from ice, frozen, he sucks her, she / him, each the other sex. comes at the / same time, a far-away place, hot, he down the street, she / the occasion full of dips, empty, lost in thought, and she, who doesn't speak, slowly / wading / in watery fields, in the tearing, / skin. microphonetic crackling, it could also be crying. / body. [even.] the dogs lift their heads. / we are these melting surfaces. we are beautiful too. / tomorrow we will let ourselves forget. / were piss-flowers. names, shitted to snow.]

Acknowledging that the allusion to *Piss Flowers* is not self-evident for every reader, Draesner supplies the following information in a paratextual, indexical annotation to the poem at the end of the volume:

pissblumen: Der Titel dieses, nach Silbenzählung und Strophenform archilochischen Ge-dichtes, bezieht sich auf Helen Chadwicks Kunsthappening *pissflowers* [sic!]. Chadwick ließ einen Mann und Frau in gefrorenen Schnee urinieren und grub aus, was sich ergab. Bei dem Mann eine kreisförmige, eher flache Scheibe, bei der Frau ein tief nach unten reichender, schmaler Zapfen. Diese schmelzenden *pissflowers* leuchteten im Licht wie weißgelbe Lüster. Auf-fallend war, dass Mann und Frau jeweils Formen produzierten, die an das andere Geschlecht erinnerten.[37]

['pissblumen': the title of this poem, whose syllabic count and strophe-form are archelochean, refers to Helen Chadwick's art happening *pissflowers* (sic!). After asking a man and woman to urinate in the snow, Chadwick dug out what they had left behind. The man produced a circu-lar, flattish disc, the woman a deep, narrow cone which reached down into the snow. These melting *pissflowers* glowed in the light like white-yellow chandeliers. What was striking was that the man and woman each produced forms that resembled the other sex.] (Fig. 4)

In fact, this poem is not any more codified than many of the other texts in the volume *für die nacht geheuerte zellen*, for which there are no explanatory annotations. However, Draesner offers the reader background information about the production aesthetic of Chadwick's *Piss Flowers*, which enables valuable inferences to be drawn for the interpretation of the poem. One can only conclude that Draesner's poem refers to the happening in the Canadian snow and not the ensuing bronze, white-enamelled sculptures later cast from the snow forms (Fig. 5). This is sug-gested by the fact that Draesner writes in the second strophe of 'lichtsaft. sie / lüs-ter gewesen sich tief in den schnee' [light-juice. they / were chandeliers deep in the snow] and in the third of a 'gelbe[n] phallus aus eis' [yellow phallus made from ice]. The urine moulds were like chandeliers at first, not only because of their

---

37 Ibid., p. 128.

Fig. 4: Helen Chadwick and David Notarius at work on *Piss Flowers* (1991).

Fig. 5: 'Piss Flowers' (1991–1992) sculpture by Helen Chadwick.

crystalline transparency but also because they were 'hanging' in the snow. But after they had been removed from the snow they stood upright, like a 'phallus'.

The fact that each sex produced forms reminiscent of the sexual organs of the other sex is the cue for the poem. The poem fluctuates between opposites. The male-female dichotomy therefore, as so often in Draesner's writing, lies at the crux of the poem. At a certain point in the poem the background changes: the landscape is suddenly tropical or sub-tropical. The ice-sculptures, the 'piss flowers' melt, and watery fields appear. The lines 'im reißenden, / haut' [in the tearing, / skin] are linked to the differences between the sexes. Deconstructive forces come into play at this point in the poem. The piss flowers melt, the skin 'tears'. This 'mikrophonetische[] knistern' [microphonetic crackling] awakens the 'fire' that appears in brackets as part of the title of the sequence in which this poem appears: 'soma-ma-tische träume (feuer)' ['soma-ma-tic dreams (fire)']. This notion of the 'microphonetic crackling' also, however, refers to the formal play on sound in the poem itself. It 'crackles', as it were, in the assonantal pairs ('könnte-körper', 'weinendes-sein', 'eben-heben') and the strings of alliteration ('knistern-könnte-körper-kopf', 'hunde-heben').

The differences between the sexes here are becoming more fluid, expressed through sound. In addition, the word 'eben' [even] 'dances' out of line of type; it hovers, printed higher than the other words. In this way Draesner establishes a contrast between its high position and its more 'horizontal' meaning. This last point is relevant in relation to the inverse horizontal and vertical shapes of the 'piss flowers'. At the end of the poem the sense of erotic intimacy introduced in the poem is consummated; we are introduced to a 'wir' or we. The boundaries between 'I' and 'you' have been removed, as the piss flowers have melted and we are left only with melting surfaces. The difference is now ironically denounced: it came about through 'names', which are now pejoratively 'geschissen zu schnee' [shitted to snow]. Thus, the physical and linguistic are explicitly bound together.

In this way, the theme of this text is similar to the poem 'Beuystafel' discussed in the previous section. The poem focuses on linguistically constructed differences between the sexes which are unravelled through the microphonetic crackles of the poem. Chadwick's open, conceptual work of art is not simply described in Draesner's poem but is intricately bound in poetic language.

'feed me, eat me'

Draesner has produced two poems in which she openly quotes works by the American artist Bruce Nauman. In the poem 'rückkehr, doch amphibisch, die augen im flugzeug, gewalt' ['return, still amphibian, eyes on the plane, violence'] in the collection *für die nacht geheuerte zellen* she quotes the title of Nauman's 1967 photograph 'Eating My Words'. The poem 'feed me, eat me' in the volume *kugelblitz* takes its title from verbal features of Nauman's video-installation 'Feed me Anthro/ Socio. Rinde Spinning' (Fig. 6) and also mentions the artist between parentheses:

Fig. 6: 'Feed me Anthro/Socio. Rinde Spinning' (1991–1992), by Bruce Naumann, video-installation with video projectors and monitors.

> feed me,
>   eat me
>   (Bruce Nauman, Hamburg)
>
> dieses auseinander &
> aufeinander & auseinander
> meine braille-finger tasten
> deine wirbel ab. du schläfst
> mit dem rücken zu mir. knorpel
> halten köpfe & pfannen
> in position. im inneren becken
> aber zappt er munter, dein roter
> roter, der eine andere küsst. du
> schläfst, ich. mundartig
> wölben sich ufer & grund.
> ineinander verbissen »schwärme«
> scham. *need me, cheat me*

kommst du zurück? wir tauchen
in kochende monitore
die schreienden köpfe, sie
heißen gesicht. wir langen
zu nichts. *feed me*
eat me. container weiß grün
säumen den weg. *you cheated*
you joked, deine sprünge
in meinem ich *you fed*
me i

    .ate you
träumen
den weg

[this apart & / on top of one another & apart / my braille fingers feel / along your spine. you sleep. / with your back to me. cartilage / holds heads & pans / in position. but in the inner pelvis / it zaps happily, your red / red that kisses another. you / sleep, I. like a mouth / bank & ground curve. / bitten into each other 'swarms' / shame. *need me, cheat me* / are you coming back? we dive / into boiling monitors / the screaming heads, they / are called face. we amount to / nothing. *feed me* / *eat me*. white green containers / line the way. *you cheated* / *you joked*, your jumps / in my I *you fed* / *me i* / *.ate you* / dream / the way.][38]

The poem 'feed me, eat me' focuses on the act of experiencing of Bruce Nauman's work of art: a video installation with various monitors featuring the large-scale head of opera singer Rinde Eckert chanting loudly in a loop. There is a reason why the poet mentions where the artwork was exhibited in brackets: Hamburg. An image of the North German port is summoned later in the poem in the lines 'container weiß grün / säumen den Weg' [white green containers / line the way]. The work of art writes its way into the poem in the form of quotations in italics.

The Nauman extracts appear not only true to the original, that is, cited word for word; occasionally they are incorporated into the poem having undergone minor changes. In addition, Draesner creates her own variations, such as 'you cheated / you joked', which do not feature as chants in the video-installation. It is interesting that these linguistic elements in particular, taken from the multimedia constellation of the artwork, activate the extra-artistic, external reality as an experiential space in a way which emulates Nauman's video-installation. In this sense 'feed me, eat me' bears similarities to the poem 'Beuystafel' discussed earlier in the chapter.

---

38 Draesner, *kugelblitz*, p. 17.

The lines quoted from the choral speech section are in keeping with the scene evoked in the poem. In the poem, there is a recognizable 'I' and a 'you', lying in bed. The speaker touches the back of the sleeping 'you' and describes first the external, calm nature of this body and then its internal state, the turbulence invisible to the eye. Body and language are interconnected: the backbone can be read like a braille text. The human body is thus a 'Textum' [weaving or network] of encoded tissue. It is silent tissue, which knows no sound, and consequently exists in contrast to the 'schreienden köpfe[n]' [screaming heads] of the video-installation. At the same time the altered lines of the chant accompany the mute dialogue between 'I' and 'you', which briefly becomes 'wir' in the second half of the poem, until it becomes clear that 'wir [zu nichts] langen' [we amount to nothing].

The physical turbulence in the poem 'feed me, eat me' is linked to the relationship problems between the 'I' and the 'you'. There is a sense of betrayal on the part of the 'you', even if the 'I' is perhaps only betrayed in a dream. Especially the line 'dein roter / roter, der eine andere küsst' [your red / red that kisses another] alludes expressly to a betrayal of some kind. The lines '*need me, cheat me*', and equally '*you cheated / you joked*' can be read as variations of the words repeated incantations 'Anthro / Socio' 'Feed me / eat me' and 'Help me / hurt me' that appear in the video installation. Draesner herself only uses the line 'Feed me / eat me', but the reader interested in art also involuntarily adopts the pairings in Nauman's title, and the lines 'Help me / hurt me', which correlate with the theme of the poem.

The duality of the opposing pairs in Nauman's installation is taken further by Draesner in her poem 'feed me, eat me'. It is striking how frequently Draesner uses the ampersand in the lines 'dieses auseinander & / aufeinander & auseinander', 'halten köpfe & pfannen in position' and 'mundartig wölben sich ufer & grund', for example. More than a simple 'and', the ampersand articulates a close connection, a smooth transition from one to the other. This concept occurs time and again in Draesner's poems: emphasizing the interwovenness of different elements and the accompanying blurring of boundaries. It is telling that Draesner does not incorporate the slash of Nauman's title into her opposing pairs. She uses the ampersand, commas ('*need me, eat me*') or enjambment ('*feed me / eat me*', '*you cheated / you joked*') to adjoin the components of the pairs.

In this way, a gradual dissolution of the division of both elements takes place. The first half of the poem is characterized by the use of ampersands; in the middle (line 13) a comma appears; and in the lines 18–19 and lines 20–21 lines, enjambment is used to separate without punctuation. In lines 22–24 the duality is unravelled typographically when Draesner spreads both the micro-sentences 'you fed me' and 'I ate you' over three lines so that the indirect object 'me' of the first sentence appears to be paired with the subject 'I' of the second sentence. The borders between 'I' and 'you' are eliminated or shifted.

It is not by chance that Draesner writes of 'deine sprünge / in meinem ich' [your jumps / in my I], which have potential sexual connotations and, at the same time, could be perceived as a shift of physical boundaries. The antithetical structure of Nauman's 'Feed me / eat me', which itself harbours sexual undertones, breaks down in Draesner's poem, for whilst Nauman uses the 'I' twice as the object, in the line *'you fed / me i / .ate you'* Draesner reverses the 'I' and 'you'. The full stop, which appears unexpectedly at the beginning of the line, albeit after a small indentation before 'ate', illustrates the suspension of the interpersonal boundary. This full stop could also be understood as an ellipsis, for there is no visible space between it and the word 'ate'. In this way, the poem takes on more ambivalent connotations, for 'I / .ate you' could be understood as 'I hate you'.

There are recurrent, explicit references to the medial otherness of video installation in this poem through the mention of elements such as 'kochende monitore' [boiling monitors] and 'schreiende[]köpfe' [screaming heads]. These are intermedial references whereby particular features and the medial dynamic of installation are described using verbs such as 'zappen' [to zap or channel hop] and 'schreien' [to scream]. In this way a bridge is constructed in the poem between a problematic, domestic bed-scene with sexual undercurrents and the work of art by Bruce Nauman. The medial format of the installation, its dynamic, the continuous repetition of the self-same chant 'feed me / eat me / sociology – help me / hurt me / anthropology' are of great importance for the poem too. The quotations appear in the poem as if they were the result of a perpetual channel-hopping, exactly as they appear in the installation. Similarly, the lines 'dieses auseinander & / aufeinander & auseinander' [this apart & / on top of one another & apart] and 'wir langen / zu nichts' [we amount to / nothing] point to a rhythmical form of repetition. The semantic element of the repetition is also evoked through the reference to the 'container weiß grün', which allude to the shipping company Evergreen's white and green containers in ports all over the world. This name is also used to denote a popular song played time and again, despite its age, on the radio. In such a way, the poem evokes the sense of something hackneyed or clichéd but also unavoidable. In other words: it's always the same song.[39]

---

39 Compare *Zauber im Zoo*, p. 5: 'während wir weiter um den Weltkreis im Kreis laufen, alle mit den gleichen Maschinen in den Taschen, *ähnlichen Songs im Ohr*, der Modeuniform am Leib' [whilst we keep on running in circles around the earth, all with the same machines in our pockets, *similar songs in our ears* (my emphasis, NR), wearing the same fashionable uniform].

The sexual turmoil of the sleeping 'you', as intuited or interpreted by the 'I', is linked to the 'zappen' [to zap or channel hop] of the images. The sensual experience of the installation is thus experienced anew in this scene and joined to the present experience of the 'I' and his/her thoughts about the 'you'. Moreover, the chanting in the art-installation thematizes the relationship between subject and object, between one person and another, between 'I' and 'you', in a laconic fashion. In the repeated chants of Nauman's work there are pleas articulating rudimentary human requirements (food, help of others); but they also tend towards one's own annihilation ('eat me') or the destruction of the relationship between 'I' and 'you' ('hurt me'). This almost sadomasochistic idiosyncrasy of the relationship between 'I' and 'you' is thematized in the poem and relies on the (partial) citation of the installation title and the word groups related to along with Draesner's variations of this demand. This is how a poem is created in which the trivial, the everyday and the artistic are combined.

Conclusion

Ulrike Draesner's poetry is true citation art, characterized by the bringing together and linking of disparate elements, which, however, almost never go to create a single, unified image. The poems are patchworks, the forms and themes of which mirror the complexity and relentless dynamic of reality. In this way, the poem always shows that the image it conjures represents only one of many possibilities; that reality is not fixed, even if it perhaps seems that way in everyday life. According to Draesner, truth is 'voller Bezüge und Auslassungen' [full of references and omissions] and lies 'schräg im Menschen und in der Welt' [at an angle in people and in the world] because it includes things which differ from itself.[40] Consequently, Draesner's poetry is to be understood as forever 'in between', in a constant back and forth between new and old, inside and out.

A consequence of this is that there is no ekphrasis in the traditional sense in Draesner's oeuvre. Instead, those of Draesner's poems which refer to visual art show the reader that works of art, even when they perhaps appear so closed and simple are intertwined in many ways with the reality around them. The work of art is open and allows insights into scenes and anecdotes which cannot

---

40 Ulrike Draesner, 'Möblierte Mädchen', in *Einsam sind alle Brücken. Autoren schreiben über Ingeborg Bachmann*, ed. by Reinhard Baumgart and Thomas Tebbe (Munich: Piper, 2001), pp. 124–137 (p. 134).

be perceived by superficially observing them. Draesner's poetry on the other hand, brings them into sharp focus.

It is not only the spatial, situative context which is activated by Draesner but also the (para)medial context of certain works. In this way works of art are thematized in different poems, in the process of which it becomes difficult to separate this context and the work itself. In the poem 'pissblumen', for example, Draesner confidently positions her own text within the multimedial, conceptual project *Piss Flowers* by Helen Chadwick. A similar thing happens in the poem 'Beuystafel'. In this case Draesner makes the art-space of her poetry into a part of the Beuysian cosmos of images and ideas known as 'social plastic'. The poem 'akt, die treppe hinab' relies on the connections *between* works of art, between paintings by Duchamp and Richter and literary texts by Roth and Bachmann respectively.

Whilst the four poems discussed in this chapter manifest their openness by alluding to works of art employing alternative media-forms, at the same time they attempt to reveal the openness of the work of art they are referring to. The material works of art themselves are largely side-lined (for example, where the title of the work of art concerned only appears in the poem title), and are simply allotted a role in the network of Draesner's text.

Lyn Marven
Ulrike Draesner's Short Stories. The Intensity of Form

Ulrike Draesner has published three collections of short stories to date, returning to the form at different points in her writing career: *Reisen unter den Augenlidern* (1999), *Hot Dogs* (2004) and *Richtig liegen* (2011),[1] in addition to further, so far un-collected short fictional texts such as Berlin-based 'Atmer' (1999) ['Breather'] or the extended monologue 'Kanalschwimmer' (2013) ['Channel Swimmer'] in a themed multi-author anthology.[2] She has furthermore published a wide range of short prose in other contexts, ranging from the gaming scenario meta-story 'Der Wolf' (2014) ['The Wolf'],[3] through more autobiographical, essayistic but also poetic, re-flections such as 'Das Kind mit den nichtgrünen Augen' (2016) ['The Child whose Eyes are Not Green'][4] and occasional standalone publications on her website such as the 2017 meditation 'Morgenmuffel'[5] ['Morning Grump'], to her wide-ranging newspaper columns for *Die Zeit*'s Freitext series, as well as the short texts in *Mein Hiddensee* (2015) or *London. Lieblingsorte* (2016), which blur the boundaries be-tween the literary-fictional form of the short story, prose poetry, and the autobio-graphical or reflective essay mode.

While short stories are a recurring feature of Draesner's output, they are not as prominent in criticism of Draesner's work. Very little has been written on her short stories in relation to form or to the collections as structural entities: Su-sanna Brogi addresses the theme of 'sexualization of the world of work and com-modification of the world of relationships' which runs through the collection

---

1 Ulrike Draesner, *Reisen unter den Augenliedern* (Klagenfurt: Ritter, 1999); *Hot Dogs. Erzäh-lungen* (Munich: Luchterhand, 2004); *Richtig liegen. Geschichten in Paaren* (Munich: Luchter-hand, 2011). References to all three texts will be given in the body of the essay; references to *Hot Dogs* are from the paperback version (Munich: btb, 2006).
2 Ulrike Draesner, 'Atmer', *Park: Zeitschrift für neue Literatur*, 51/52 (1998), 28–32; 'Kanal-schwimmer', in *Ein extraherrlicher Meersommerabend*, ed. by Jan Christophersen (Hamburg: mare, 2013), pp. 259–275. Reworked material from the latter is incorporated into the short novel *Kanalschwimmer* (Hamburg: mare, 2019), published after the writing of this chapter.
3 Ulrike Draesner, 'Der Wolf', in *New Level. Computerspiele und Literatur*, ed. by Thomas Böhme (Berlin: Metrolit, 2014), pp. 80–83.
4 Ulrike Draesner, 'Das Kind mit den nichtgrünen Augen', in *Wie wir leben wollen: Texte für Solidarität und Freiheit*, ed. by Matthias Jügler (Berlin: Suhrkamp, 2016), pp. 9–19.
5 Ulrike Draesner, 'Morgenmuffel' (2017), no longer available online.

https://doi.org/10.1515/9783110495942-008

Richtig liegen.[6] Otherwise a small number of articles treat thematic concerns in individual stories: Andrea Stopfer examines anorexia in 'Magern' ['Thinning'] from *Reisen unter den Augenlidern*;[7] Stephen Brockmann considers the depiction of contemporary Berlin in 'Gina Regina' and Friedhelm Marx analyses incest in 'Zucken und Zwinkern' ['Twitching and Winking'], both from *Hot Dogs*;[8] Michael Braun examines intertextuality and Kafka in 'Rosa Käfer' ['Rose Beetle'] and 'Das Denkmal der Läuferin' ['The Monument to the (female) Runner'], both in *Richtig liegen*;[9] and Ulrike Vedder examines dementia in an earlier version of 'Ichs Heimweg macht alles allein' ['I's Way Home makes Everything alone'].[10] As shown in this volume by Emily Jeremiah amongst others, broader themes such as relationships and reproduction, and attendant concerns with ethics and the law, depictions of bodies and gender, especially sexuality and also eating, and an interest in science and modern technology further link the stories to each other and to Draesner's other prose writings. These same themes echo and in turn update the developments that Draesner herself suggests characterized the modern German-language novella's renewed engagement with the nature of the subject, its autonomy and bodily experience, after the French Revolution.[11]

---

6 Susanna Brogi, '"Kein richtiges Liegen im falschen". Die Sexualisierung der Arbeitswelt und die Ökonomisierung der Beziehungswelt in den Erzählungen Ulrike Draesners', in *Ulrike Draesner*, ed. by Susanna Brogi, Anna Ertel and Evi Zemanek (Munich: Text + Kritik, 2014), pp. 48–56.

7 Andrea Stopfer, 'Die Darstellungen von Magersucht in "Magern" und *Mitgift* von Ulrike Draesner im Vergleich', in *Transitträume. Beiträge zur deutschsprachigen Gegenwartsliteratur*, ed. by Andrea Bartl (Augsburg: Wißner, 2009), pp. 349–359.

8 Stephen Brockmann, 'Berlin as the Literary Capital of German Unification', in *Contemporary German Fiction. Writing in the Berlin Republic*, ed. by Stuart Taberner (Cambridge: Cambridge University Press, 2007), pp. 39–55; Friedhelm Marx, 'Inzest. Grenze und Grenzüberschreitungen bei Ulrike Draesner und Thomas Mann', in *Familien – Geschlechter – Macht. Beziehungen im Werk Ulrike Draesners*, ed. by Stephanie Catani and Friedhelm Marx (Göttingen: Wallstein, 2008), pp. 61–73.

9 Michael Braun, 'Intertextueller Zauber im Zoo. Ulrike Draesners Poetik der Verwandlung', in *Ulrike Draesner*, ed. by Brogi, Ertel and Zemanek, pp. 37–47; see also his chapter in this volume.

10 Ulrike Vedder, 'Erzählen vom Zerfall. Demenz und Alzheimer in der Gegenwartsliteratur', *Zeitschrift für Germanistik*, Neue Folge, 22.2 (2012), 274–289. N.B. that this article references the version published with the slightly different spelling 'Ichs Heimweg macht alles alleine' in *Es schneit in meinem Kopf: Erzählungen über Alzheimer und Demenz*, ed. by Klara Obermüller (Munich and Vienna: Nagel and Kimche, 2006), pp. 59–81, which differs quite substantially in form from the later version in *Richtig liegen*.

11 Ulrike Draesner, 'Nachwort', in *Verführung. Deutschsprachige Novellen von Goethe bis Musil*, ed. by Ulrike Draesner (Munich: Goldmann, 1994), pp. 273–349 (see especially pp. 273–275).

Draesner's collections must also be viewed against the backdrop of a boom in short story writing since the mid-1990s, beginning with Judith Hermann's celebrated *Sommerhaus später* (1999) [*Summerhouse, Later*]; short stories continue to be a prominent feature in twenty-first-century German-language literature. It is a commonplace of literary criticism of the short story that it thrives best in a fragmented society: the post-reunification growth in short forms is in some ways reminiscent of the turn by Böll, Borchert et al. to short prose after 1945, but in recent years in particular it has been further inflected by technological advances which open out a new set of short forms for literary use, such as Twitter stories and micro-fiction, 'Sprachfotos' [language-photos] and blogs,[12] or the return of the epistolary form for the age of email. Interestingly though, Draesner's most experimental short prose is in her earliest collection – contemporaneous with Hermann's debut – whereas her most recent one turns back to classic short story forms reminiscent of the older novella.

While Draesner's short stories share many themes with her novels, my interest is in what the short story format can do that the longer texts cannot, '*as a result of*, rather than in spite of, its brevity'.[13] Such a quality of 'shortness' (short story writer Elizabeth Bowen's term) manifests in the way that Draesner works with the intensities and ellipses of the narrative structure, and particularly in the way that the texts employ wordplay and intrusive narrative voices to a degree which would be difficult to sustain – and to read – over the course of a novel.[14] The brevity and intensity of the short story format also lends itself to a concentration of symbolic or poetic imagery, perhaps paradoxically given the tendency of contemporary short stories to focus predominately on the everyday; the overlaying of reality with overt symbolism in *Hot Dogs* in particular adds to the deliberate artifice of this collection. Such aspects are not necessarily different in nature to the stylistic form of Draesner's wider prose; rather, the shortness of the texts allows these aspects to be exaggerated, intensified and isolated in a manner and to an extent which nonetheless distinguishes her shorter prose from her longer fictional work.[15]

---

12 Larissa Boehning's term for short prose sketches, published on her blog (https://abschied vondenillusionen.wordpress.com/).
13 Adrian Hunter, *The Cambridge Introduction to the Short Story in English* (Cambridge: Cambridge University Press, 2007), p. 2. For an overview of recent German as well as Anglophone approaches to short stories and short story theory, see amongst others Anne-Rose Meyer, *Die deutschsprachige Kurzgeschichte. Eine Einführung* (Berlin: Erich Schmidt, 2014), especially pp. 18–28.
14 Bowen cited by Hunter, *The Cambridge Introduction to the Short Story in English*, p. 1.
15 Short story theory has shifted towards describing tendencies (rather than essential qualities) of short stories, placing emphasis on difference of degree rather than difference in kind:

The three collections put different emphases on these various aspects of narrative and form: the ten stories in *Reisen hinter den Augenliedern*, for example, are more overtly experimental and visual, with plot as such at a minimum or only glimpsed through a veil of wordplay and linguistic patterning. The cryptic titles, foregrounding of language and voice, and the decontextualization and ambiguity of the majority of these texts leaves these texts closest to prose poems or even dramatic performances, as many constitute monologues. *Hot Dogs*, with twelve stories, is characterized largely by the use of a prominent narrative voice keeping the reader at an often ironic distance, and schematic plots often revolving around a rather dramatic event, which is, however, rarely depicted directly; this collection also supplies a range of resonant poetic images, often related to animals.

The more recent collection *Richtig liegen* is less overtly poetic in voice and style or in its use of imagery, and is perhaps the most similar of Draesner's collections to the American-influenced, laconic mode of contemporary German-language short story writing spearheaded by Hermann and Ingo Schulze. The collection's subtitle 'Geschichten in Paaren' [Stories in Pairs], is a deliberate pun on relationships, which are a key theme in the collection, but also a playful wink to the reader: there are an uneven number of stories (seventeen). Further self-consciousness about the context, form and mode of narration is evident: for example, in the pair of stories 'Sei versichert' ['Be assured'] and 'Weiche Wände' ['Soft Walls'], which explicitly set up story-telling situations reminiscent of the Decameron's framework narrative, as well as the intertextuality of the pair which deliberately echo texts by Kafka.[16] Time rather than imagery seems to be the structuring principle of this collection, as many texts utilize multiple levels of narrative and plot loops; texts in this collection also offer memorable snapshots anchoring the texts to a moment of intensity without the poetic symbolism which characterizes *Hot Dogs*. Here the narrative voice recedes into the background relatively speaking compared to the earlier collections, focalizing less intrusively through protagonists. However, the broad sweep of these stories also takes in a variety of forms and perspectives including narratives in the first person, especially in the more experimental texts such as the two which depict dementia and which hark back to the monologues in *Reisen unter den Augenlidern*.

---

see Per Winther in the 'Introduction' to the special issue of *Narrative* journal on short stories: Per Winther, Michael Trussler, Michael Toolan, Charles E. May, Susan Lohafer, 'Introduction', *Narrative*, 20.2 (2012), 135–170 (pp. 140–142).

16 See Braun, 'Intertextueller Zauber im Zoo', p. 41.

Together with the wide range of short prose that she has published elsewhere in anthologies, online or in book-length publications such as *Mein Hiddensee*, Draesner's short stories demonstrate the range and variety of short fiction as a set of interlinked types and genres. Different as they are from each other, *Reisen unter den Augenlidern*, *Hot Dogs* and *Richtig liegen* all evince a particular interest in form and narrative (structure and storytelling) over and above content (action or characterization) that locates these somewhere between the experiment and wordplay of her poetry and her more extensive novels; the shortness of these texts becomes a positive invitation to showcase language as style.

Structure

Earlier short story theories tend to focus on structure or plot (as opposed to content, mood or symbolism) as a key defining element of the story; writer David Constantine suggests that 'In every short story, there should be something at stake. Start at the crux, end at the crisis'.[17] This is perhaps most clearly seen in Draesner's 'Rosakäfer' in *Richtig liegen*, a modern, gender-reversed rewrite of Franz Kafka's *Die Verwandlung* [*Metamorphosis*].[18] This follows Kafka's structure (reminiscent of a three-act drama as well as the more formal novella with its turning point), beginning with the transformation of Rosa into a beetle and ending, like *Die Verwandlung*, with her death and an ironically happy familial coda, here with an outing in a helicopter rather than an excursion in a tram. Constantine's motto evokes the open-ended or end-loaded form of many short stories: the crisis does not represent closure, but rather an ending that also implies a beginning of something else, whether positive or negative. Thus this apparently simple structure does not imply a linear progression or plot, but makes use of the brevity of the story to open out onto other unspoken narratives: 'With a short story, the meaning of the ending is projected in both directions, backwards (illuminating an unseen plot or a misread character) as well as forwards, into the surviving future'.[19]

---

17 Galen O'Hanlon, 'David Constantine Interview: Invasions of the Past', *The Skinny*, 8 October 2015 (http://www.theskinny.co.uk/books/features/david-constantine-interview).
18 See also the chapter by Michael Braun in this volume.
19 Ra Page, 'Introduction', in *Morphologies: Short Story Writers on Short Story Writers*, ed. by Ra Page (Manchester: Comma Press, 2013), pp. v–xix (p. xiii).

Texts in *Reisen unter den Augenlidern* tend to eschew plot or action in favour of extended associative thoughts and reflections; nine out of the ten stories are written in the present tense, limiting the perspective to the decontextualized, ongoing moment of narration. The story 'An' ['On'], for example, alludes to time passing and an ostensible linear development by including the time signature of the video which the (unnamed) characters have made and one is watching. However, the act of watching the film is superimposed with memories or flashbacks of acting for the video camera, while the characters' real life is entirely subsumed by staging it for the camera. The patterning of repeated phrases, 'Ein Verbrechen ist es doch nicht' (p. 12 and passim) [But it's not a crime] and 'klopft, hämmert, pocht' (p. 19 and in different configurations elsewhere) [beats, hammers, thuds], sets up denial and physical intensity as the overarching modes of experience in which the characters are stuck. 'Magern' is also structured initially by numbered exercises (sit-ups for example), and then by a series of 'paradoxes', but this semblance of control falls away as Helena's anorexia takes hold; language too loses its structure as the story progresses.

A number of texts in *Hot Dogs* and *Richtig liegen* use dual-level chronology, with flashbacks or memories embedded in a present-day or framework narrative; texts work towards revelations or climaxes that may be explicit or implicit, and either simultaneous or staggered throughout the text. In 'Büßerschnee' ['Nieves Penitentes'], in *Hot Dogs*, the revelation and climax converge. Gerard, climbing a mountain in the Andes apparently to rescue another climber, himself collapses and needs to be rescued from a field of nieves penitentes: snow formations reminiscent of praying penitents, particular to high altitudes. His confused thinking at high altitude (indicated visually with colons interrupting sentences) returns to memories of his younger brother Nick drowning on holiday as a child. The coincidence of these two levels of the text suggests Gerard's inability to overcome the death of his brother, as well as his inability to deal with his elder brother's confession that Nick had clung to him in the water, but he 'ihn abgeschüttelt hatte, um nicht mit unterzugehen, in Todesangst' (p. 149) [had shaken him off, so as not to be dragged under with him, in fear of his life]. This confession, rather than the death, coincides with Gerard blacking out and being found on the sandy ground – the high Andean desert recalling the beach in the childhood holiday, with the snow formations standing as a striking symbolic reminder of penance and guilt; unlike his younger brother, he is rescued and revived.

The structure of the texts often circles back on itself, beginning not with the crux but a hint of the crisis which is then only fully revealed towards the end; as John C. Gerlach states, 'the short story is that genre in which anticipation of the ending is always present'.[20] This mode of anticipation verges in places on horror, especially in the eponymous 'Hot Dogs' which refers from the start to 'diesem gräßlichen Samstag' (p. 23) [this terrible Saturday], on which, it is finally revealed, a whole litter of illegally-bred puppies died. In 'Sei versichert' in *Richtig liegen*, about three insurance salespeople trying to manipulate holiday-goers into signing up for costly insurance schemes, the opening paragraph sets up a portentous scene: one of the salesmen is suddenly standing in the sea on a beach, which the text later reveals has a dangerous current: 'seit einer Minute stand er fünf Meter vom Strand entfernt, höchstens sechs, er winkte nicht, sondern schrie, seit einer Minute war es zu spät' (p. 73) [A minute ago he was standing five metres away from the shore, six at most, he was not waving but shouting, a minute ago it was too late]. The rest of the story loops back to this same moment of crisis in an enactment of traumatic repetition, before continuing briefly with the aftermath of Pider's drowning and a police interrogation narrated in the present tense; the displaced ending is by no means the end of the story. Notably in the initial description the crisis has already happened a minute ago, it is already too late, so the moment itself virtually precedes the narrative as well as being its end point. The shortness of the story means that it focuses entirely on this one event, conforming to what one of the first theorists of the short story, Brander Matthews, describes as the 'unity of impression', or Edgar Allan Poe's 'single effect': everything preceding the drowning is in fact leading up to it, everything afterwards is determined by it.[21]

Similarly, 'Harmonische Methode' ['Harmonic Method'] in *Richtig liegen* opens in the middle of a court case, before going back to the events leading up to the criminal act of arson. This doubling of narrative levels is overtly signalled in 'Zarte Ration' ['Tender Portion'], also in *Richtig liegen*, where the narrating instance frequently draws attention to what hasn't yet happened in the story as it is being told (the *récit* in Genette's terminology), but which has already happened in the narrative 'reality' (the *histoire*), with frequent time markers of 'Damals' [back then], 'Noch' [Still / not yet], 'Später' [later] emphasizing that fact. The apparent turning point of this story – the memorable image of what appears to be a couple caught in flagrante – isn't one, while the actual turning point of morbidly obese Ed's collapse from uncertain causes is all but elided in a switch into the pluperfect tense, so it has always already happened. This tale ends with an ironic narratorial comment – 'denn nun wussten sie, warum

---

20 John C. Gerlach, *Toward the End: Closure and Structure in the American Short Story* (Tuscaloosa: University of Alabama Press, 1985), p. 160.
21 See Per Winther, in Winther, Trussler, Toolan, May, Lohafer, 'Introduction', p. 137.

Buddha fett ist' (p. 28) [for now they knew why Buddha is fat] – which offers an almost parodic closure as former couple Birte and Tonja reunite in silence.

'Wackelkontakt' ['Loose Connection'] in *Hot Dogs* combines external revelations with internal realizations, James Joyce's celebrated 'epiphany', which according to him, characterizes the modernist short story.[22] These are narrated in an order which diminishes the force of the external revelations both for characters and reader: they are doubly retrospective, coming at the end of the tale and making sense of earlier puzzles, as well as coming (too) late for the characters. The focalizer of the tale is schoolgirl Sonja, invited to visit a nuclear bunker maintained by her friend Ruth's divorced father; during the visit, there is a power cut and Ruth takes Sonja's hand in the complete darkness, leading Sonja – 'ohne es beschlossen zu haben' (p. 58) [without having decided to do it] – to kiss Ruth. This brief interlude is narrated in the present tense, interrupting the preterite of the rest of the narrative. Sonja's confusion and attraction is met by a sudden change in Ruth, who appears after the weekend wearing lipstick and flirting loudly with a boy; 'Sonja war erleichtert' (p. 61) [Sonja was relieved]. The turning point or epiphany here is ambiguous: it certainly changes Ruth's behaviour, but it is unclear the extent to which it provokes any internal reassessment or moment of clarity within Sonja, who nonetheless builds a 'Ruth-Abschieds-Schrein aus 30 Hanutas' (p. 61) [Farewell-Ruth-shrine made of 30 Hanutas] after the next revelations.

After the visit, Sonja naively ponders the fact that there are three camp beds in the bunker, apparently for Ruth, her father and the woman who lives in the bungalow next to the bunker: but Ruth lives some distance away, and '[e]in Bunker nützt ja nur, wenn man direkt neben ihm wohnt. [. . .] Die dritte Pritsche ist Unsinn, dachte Sonja' (p. 60) [A bunker is only useful if you live right next to it. [. . .] The third camp bed doesn't make sense, Sonja thought]. This realization – that Ruth would not in fact be safe in a nuclear attack – both sets up and undermines the inevitable revelation in the final paragraph that Ruth's father has a child with the woman in the bungalow, something only revealed when Ruth's father dies unexpectedly of a heart attack. Ruth is bundled off to her mother, leaving the school.

Prompted by the mutual embarrassment when the girls are dropped off after the bunker visit, or perhaps only anticipating the return of her own father, Sonja also casually reveals the affair that her father is having with the girls' physics teacher, which is hinted at in the first page of the text: 'Frau Ihle machte ein

---

22 See especially Dominic Head, *The Modernist Short Story. A Study in Theory and Practice* (Cambridge: Cambridge University Press, 2010), particularly chapter 1.

schnelles Zeichen am Fenster, das nur Sonja sah' (p. 50) [Frau Ihle made a hasty sign at the window, which only Sonja noticed]. Presumably the sign is in fact intended for the father; the misdirection of 'nur' [only] reveals the remark to reflect Sonja's perspective rather than being a narratorial observation. Like the other revelation, this too is undermined, this time by the admission that Sonja has known about it all along. It is – if anything – a revelation for the reader's benefit only, and not a revelation for the character, playing with the conventions of the revelatory plot.

In 'Der grüne Koffer' ['The green Suitcase'], also in *Hot Dogs*, the narrator self-consciously and deliberately reveals the identity of 'Hund' [Dog] only on the final page: 'Hund, der kleine grüne Koffer meiner Mutter – bestimmt vergaß ich, das zu erwähnen –, steht neben mir' (p. 170) [Dog, my mother's small green suitcase – no doubt I forgot to mention that – is standing next to me]. Intended to make the reader (or here: the listener, as the first-person narration is addressed to an unnamed, second person familiar 'du') reassess the whole text, this revelation is reminiscent of the bathetic revelation about Rosebud in *Citizen Kane*. The self-awareness of the aside 'bestimmt vergaß ich' [no doubt I forgot] signals the deliberate withholding of information and thus serves to lessen the impact of the revelation, which more importantly only repeats the same information given in an exchange on the second page:

> Hund war, glaube ich, ein Geschenk meiner Mutter:
> – Dieser kleine grüne Koffer wird dir gute Dienste leisten (p. 165)

> [Dog was, I think, a present from my mother: – This little green suitcase will serve you well].

Far from casting new light on the object or the story being told, this apparent revelation in fact only reveals the narrator's attempts to control the narrative and her failure to do so. Despite appearing in the title, the green suitcase is largely absent in the text, hidden by its incongruous and misleading nickname.

Draesner plays with form not only on the level of individual stories, but also in the wider structures of the collections: the entire collection of *Reisen unter den Augenlidern*, for example, is, as Draesner herself suggests, a 'Frauenbogen' (women's trajectory), albeit not in chronological order, from pre-conception through childhood and motherhood to very old age and senility.[23] *Richtig liegen* consists

---

23 Ulrike Draesner quoted in Katrin Hillgruber, 'Reise unter den Augenlidern', *Deutschlandfunk*, 30 August 1999 (http://www.deutschlandfunk.de/reise-unter-den-augenlidern.700.de.html?dram:article_id=79250).

of 'paired' stories; Brogi and Braun suggest ways of pairing the seventeen stories according to themes or relationship constellations.[24] What is more, the connections go beyond individual collections: the theme of anorexia in 'Magern' in *Reisen unter den Augenlidern*, resurfaces in *Richtig liegen* in two stories about disordered eating: 'Zarte Ration' and 'Das Lächeln der Ehefrau' ['The Wife's Smile'], but also forms a key strand of the narrative of *Mitgift*.[25] Likewise the obsessive running which can be a symptom of the illness also links 'Magern' and *Mitgift* further to runners in both *Hot Dogs* ('Der Läufer wird im Winter gemacht' ['A Runner is made in Winter']) and *Richtig liegen* ('Das Denkmal der Läuferin'). The eponymous story in *Hot Dogs* plays with the image of puppies and an oven, along with trauma, which emerges in reconfigured form in *Sieben Sprünge vom Rand der Welt*;[26] memorable images of dogs occur also in 'Der Jodler' ['The Yodler'] (*Hot Dogs*) and 'Canis Canens' (*Richtig liegen*). Bats link 'Süße Kaverne' ['Sweet Cavern'] and 'Gold aus Mäusen' ['Gold from Mice'], both in *Richtig liegen*, with the latter in turn recalling the title 'Unter der Rattenwelt liegt die Mauswelt' ['Under the World of Rats lies the World of Mice'] in *Reisen unter den Augenlidern*.

Moreover, the two later collections are linked through individual characters: Gina Regina in *Hot Dogs* is evoked by a second Gina – 'Regina, genannt Gina' (p. 139) [Regina, who goes by the name of Gina] – in 'Süße Kaverne'; Draesner herself has said that a further two Gina stories are planned for future publication. 'Süße Kaverne' was published previously in a different version in a themed collection (about animals, a common motif in *Hot Dogs*), where the connection between the two Gina stories is made explicit as the first Gina is mentioned in the text; the later text effectively writes beyond the ending of the earlier story:

> Vier Ginas in der Klasse! Regina wollte keine sich rufen lassen, also rief man die Nummern. Nummer Eins hatte zum letzten Klassentreffen lackierte Brustwarzen und High Heels mit einem Absatz vorgeführt, den man nicht sah. Der Schuh war sogar in der

---

24 See Brogi, 'Kein richtiges Liegen im falschen', and Braun, 'Intertextueller Zauber im Zoo'.

25 'Magern' was intended to be chapter from a planned novel 'Lück' (a pun on the English luck, 'Glück' [happiness], and 'Lücke' [gap]); the excerpt from what became *Mitgift* that Draesner entered for the Bachmann Preis in 2000 also refers to this title. See the entry on Ulrike Draesner on *ORF*, 'Tage der deutschsprachigen Literatur 2000'(http://archiv.bachmannpreis.orf.at/bp_2000/autoren/fs_autoren.html) and Ulrike Draesner, 'Auszug aus Lück', in *Ortstermine. Wolfenbütteler Lehrstücke zum zweiten Buch*, ed. by Hugo Dittberner, Linda Anne Engelhardt and Andrea Ehlert (Göttingen: Wallstein, 2004), pp. 24–33.

26 Cf. here also Mary Louise Pratt's description of the 'asymmetry' of the relationship between the novel and the short story, with the latter dependent on the former: Mary Louise Pratt, 'The Short Story: The Long and the Short of It', *Poetics*, 10.2/3 (June 1981), pp. 175–194 (p. 180).

Zeitung besprochen worden, 3900 €, eine rein mentale Konstruktion. Nummer Eins hatte nach ein paar Schnäpsen etwas von e-commerce, Kommilitonen und Spermien gemurmelt; rosedotcom.[27]

[Four Ginas in the class! None of them wanted to be called Regina, so they were called by their numbers. At the last reunion Number One had been sporting varnished nipples and high heels with a heel you couldn't see. The shoes had even featured in newspaper columns, 3900 Euros, purely mental constructions. After a few shots Number One had mumbled something about e-commerce, fellow students and sperm; rosedotcom.]

The varnished nipples and the website URL are taken directly from 'Gina Regina'; the further detail of the high heels with the invisible heel is new, but of a piece with the original Gina's consumerist interests – the earlier text namedrops her Gucci handbag – and implies furthermore that she earned good money from the sperm she collected in the earlier text. In the version of 'Süße Kaverne' in *Richtig liegen* this passage has been omitted, but the two Ginas remain linked through a love of designer footwear (Marimekko rubber boots for Gina Two, as she is called in the earlier version of the text), the repeated refrain of 'Mutter Natur' [mother nature] in both texts, and the echo of 'lackierte Zehen' (*Richtig liegen*, p. 150) [varnished toes], as well as more widely through shared thematic concerns with reproduction and technology that echo throughout Draesner's oeuvre.[28]

Imagery and Moments

The condensation and compression of the short story, as well as its use of suggestion, means imagery can gain in prominence as a way of structuring the story and pointing to further layers of meaning. A striking image is central to Eileen Baldeshwiler's lyric short story type, and is also reminiscent of a key element of the older Novelle form, the 'Falke' [falcon] in Heyse's novella theory.[29] Imagery is particularly noticeable in *Hot Dogs*, which draws on evocative images of animals and nature: the basenji dog and the raven (immediately calling to mind Edgar Allan Poe) in 'Der Jodler', a singing dog further echoed in 'Canis

---

27 Ulrike Draesner, 'Süße Kaverne', in *Kein Hügel für die wilden Pferde. Ein Tierbuch*, ed. by Anke Bastrop and Katja Thomas (Leipzig: Connewitzer Verlagsbuchhandlung, 2010), pp. 56–68 (p. 58).
28 See the chapter by Emily Jeremiah in this volume.
29 Eileen Baldeshwiler, 'The Lyric Short Story: The Sketch of a History', *Studies in Short Fiction*, 6 (1969), 443–453.

Canens' in *Richtig liegen*; the restaurant cat in 'Scham' ['Shame'] whose presence seems to be a distraction both for the characters and on the level of the narrative, as well as the multiple imaginary cats in 'Europa' ['Europe']; the poetic frozen lake cracking across a reflected face in 'Der Läufer wird im Winter gemacht'; and particularly the unruly hedge in 'Zucken und Zwinkern'.

'Zucken und Zwinkern' is about two siblings who finally act on their suppressed desire for each other and at the end of the story leave to start a life together; their incestuous liaison is symbolized in the text rather blatantly by the recurring image of sun and moon and solar eclipse, and slightly less overtly in the references to the double slit experiment, which proves that light is both wave and particle.[30] Such deliberately overloaded symbolism[31] overtly intertwines and overlays mythical overtones as well as references to particle physics onto the real, but contrived, situation of the text. The text also contains a more subtle and lasting image in the hedge, which fits writer David Constantine's description of such motifs as 'not symbols, they are not there as mere instruments, pointing to something beyond themselves. They are moments, real concrete details around which the story's developing sense accrues, precipitates'.[32] The hedge grows in the garden in the siblings' parents' house; Franz is the only one who tends it and chops it back, but neglects it once he has a girlfriend and leaves the house. It has grown there 'so lange sie hier wohnten' (p. 79) [as long as they have lived here] and the passing of time is measured in part by the height of the hedge: 'Die Hecke stand damals bereits ziemlich hoch' (p. 85) [The hedge was already quite high back then]. The hedge is obliquely linked to the other symbols in two ways: it blocks the sunlight in the parents' living room and it also leads to an encounter between Fritzi and a student of Physics who appears at the door one day offering to cut it back, 'das mache er gerne, wenn er ihr helfen könne, daß er einmal auf eine Leiter steige und eine Hecke schneide, sozusagen im Realversuch' (p. 88) [He'd be happy to do it, if

---

30 The same experiment is mentioned by the uncanny twins L. and L. (Lara and Laura) in 'L x L', in *Reisen unter den Augenlidern*, who are described as 'zwei Körper wie einer, Welle oder Teil' (37) [two bodies like one, wave or particle]. There are further references to the experiment in *Vorliebe*, and it also underlies *Mitgift* as a metaphor for the dualism that is not one in hermaphroditism; see also Draesner's comments in interview with Aura Heydenreich and Klaus Mecke, 'Auf der Suche nach Sprache: Ulrike Draesner im Dialog zu *Mitgift* und *Vorliebe*', in *Physik und Poetik: Produktionsästhetik und Werkgenese. Autorinnen und Autoren im Dialog*, ed. by Aura Heydenreich and Klaus Mecke (Berlin: de Gruyter, 2015), pp. 23–49 (p. 39).

31 In his review of the collection Michael Braun describes the tale as 'overburdened with symbolic objects': Michael Braun, 'Zucken, Zwinkern', *Frankfurter Rundschau*, 24 March 2004 (http://www.fr.de/kultur/literatur/michael-braun-zucken-zwinkern-a-1199753).

32 David Constantine, 'D. H. Lawrence', in *Morphologies*, ed. by Page, pp. 117–136 (p. 122).

he could help by climbing a ladder and cutting a hedge, a real life experiment as it were]. The day after the siblings consummate their relationship, Fritzi sprinkles the hedge with an unnamed substance from a pharmacy, and the hedge slowly dies: 'Die Hecke wuchs weiter, den Sommer hindurch. Mehrfach zogen Mond und Sonne darüber hinweg. Dann starb sie langsam, ächzend, mit Widerwillen' (p. 95) [The hedge carried on growing, all summer long. The sun and moon passed over it many times. Then it died, slowly, groaning, reluctantly]. The sunlight triumphs, and the siblings (sun and moon) have disappeared together.

The last text in *Hot Dogs*, 'Europa', portrays a family visit to Yugoslavia, thirty years before the narrative present. The narrator's memories of the holiday are interspersed with accounts of the end of the Second World War in East Berlin, which focus on the narrator's father's pet cat, which is supposed to have met its death in a number of almost comically horrific ways (the uncertainty here is evocative of Schrödinger's famous cat, of course). Despite its association with wartime violence, the image refuses easy interpretation by remaining fluid in its detail, instead becoming a symbol merely of the act of storytelling itself: the father's last version of the tale merges contemporary historical reality with a fairy tale ending:

> Wenn ich es recht bedenke, ja, jetzt ist es mir eingefallen, unser Hausmädchen von früher, ihr wißt schon, hat den Kater mitgenommen, sie lebt in Ostberlin, besuchen kann man sie dort nicht, aber den Kater hat sie immer sehr gemocht, und wenn er nicht gestorben ist, dann lebt er noch heute bei ihr. (p. 187)

> [Now I think about it, yes, it has just come to me, our maid from back then, you know, she took the cat, she lives in East Berlin, you can't visit her over there, but she was always very fond of the cat, and if he hasn't died yet, he'll be living happily ever after with her.]

Yet even this version, explicitly fictional in form, is displaced by the final hypothetical cat which the narrator's mother promises her and her sister: 'Den Kater hat es nie gegeben, sagte sie, er ist bloß, wovon euer Vater träumt. Aber vielleicht, sie zögerte – ihr müßt jetzt leise bleiben – zu Hause . . ., vielleicht' (p. 189) [The cat never existed, she said, he's just what your father dreams of. But maybe, she hesitated – you need to keep very quiet now – back home . . ., maybe]. Symbol of a crux – the Russian advancement into Berlin – and a crisis or ending through its death, the cat finally becomes the potential of a new story that will begin after the end of this story.

It is a bit of a cliché to state that the short story as a form is like a snapshot; Elisabeth Bowen calls her stories in *The Demon Lover* 'disjected snapshots – snapshots taken from close up, too close up, in the middle of the *mêlée* of a battle', ironizing the idea of capturing a moment.[33] Nonetheless, in *Richtig liegen*, by contrast with the earlier *Hot Dogs*, the images that stay imprinted on the brain after reading are not poetic symbols but rather akin to freeze frame moments, usually featuring human characters: the image of Birte walking in on Wanjun kneeling in front of Ed cleaning the folds of his massive body ('Zarte Ration'); the moment when Pider is taken by the rip current on the beach ('Sei versichert'); the twin images of Rosa Maregg waking up as a beetle and her death in the operating theatre, live on camera ('Rosakäfer'). These scenes are often only glimpsed momentarily through the narrative itself and remain unassimilable in a way that reflects the trauma or horror or simply the sheer unexpectedness of their content, exceeding the story which revolves around them.

Narration and Characters

Questions of narrative perspective are particularly pertinent to the short story, which tends to pair the restriction of short form with restricted narratorial perspectives, either through limited first-person narrators or close focalizers, or through an ironized auctorial narrator figure.[34] Draesner's three collections work with the possibilities of narrative voice and perspective in different ways. *Reisen unter den Augenlidern* in particular foregrounds narrative uncertainty, primarily through exaggerating the tendency of short story characters not to have a proper name (as Mary Louise Pratt notes) but simply a first name or function. The characters in this collection remain elusive: very few are named – characters in 'An' are simply designated 'sie' [she], 'er' [he] and 'der Kleine' [the little boy], who 'ist nicht da, weil sie ihn nie bekamen' (p. 8) [isn't there, because they never had him]. Alternatively they give a name we can't trust is real: 'Ich bin P., Petersilie, Penthesilea' (p. 155) [I'm P., Parsley, Penthesilea], in 'Save the Limit of your Sight' (original title in English).

The lack of definition of characters, reducing these to mere pronouns or initials, is further extended by dropping the grammatical subject entirely from sentences in a number of texts in *Reisen unter den Augenlidern*: 'Nachkrieg, Taufe' ['Post-War, Baptism'] begins with the subjectless 'liege im Bett' (p. 23) [am lying in bed], introducing a monologue by an old woman with an uncertain sense of herself and her own past. The short 'Greifer' ['Grabber'] is even more playful and

---

33 Elizabeth Bowen's preface to *The Demon Lover*, cited in *The Mulberry Tree: Writings of Elizabeth Bowen*, ed. by Hermione Lee (London: Vintage, 1999), p. 99.

34 See e.g. Leonie Marx, *Die Deutsche Kurzgeschichte* (Stuttgart: Metzler, 2005), pp. 70–73.

poetic, a three-page incantation consisting largely of sentences with disembodied verb forms, fluctuating between third person singular, gerunds and a form which could be the infinitive, imperative or third person plural. Verbs frequently appear without pronouns, and where there is a grammatical subject, it is depersonalized, decontextualized and unsyntactical: 'Mund gehört sich, denkt der Kopf, das bin ich. Immer gleich, wie der Mund schmeckt, ist das Ich bei sich, denkt Denken vorn im Kopf' (p. 61) [Mouth is right and proper, Head thinks, that's me. However Mouth tastes, I is beside itself, Thinking thinks at the front of the Head]. By depicting characters as ciphers, as well as presenting disordered thinking, down to this dismantling of the speaking subject into disparate bodily parts, the collection undermines any sense of a stable self.

While they do not alienate the reader to the same extent as *Reisen unter den Augenlidern*, the majority of the texts in *Hot Dogs* are written in an impersonal and largely ironic third person narrative perspective, which distances the text and reader. Draesner herself explains that she even avoided indicating either sex or gender of the narrator in 'Zucken und Zwinkern' in particular, playing out the siblings' incestuous liaison through a gender-fluid perspective.[35] Despite remaining an uncertain presence, the narrative instance is evident in particular through punning wordplay and rhyming around the names of characters: Gina Regina becomes Ginna-la-Minna, Gina Benigna among many other epithets; Anna in 'Anna selbzwei' ['Anna Binary'] is called Anna Krönchen, Kanönchen, Anna Marönchen, and so on. The wordplay draws attention to the convention of naming characters, suggesting these names are chosen not because they belong to, or suit, the character in any sense, but solely for their potential for linguistic manipulation. Similar self-aware comments about Marina, a swimmer in 'Anna selbzwei', that 'nomen est omen' (p. 39), or in 'Harmonische Methode' in *Richtig liegen* about a similarly named couple – 'Ingo und Inga war auch so schon komisch genug' (p. 47) [Ingo and Inga was comic enough already as it is] – further add to the stylization, artifice and overt literariness of these texts.

Like much of her other fiction, Draesner's short stories demonstrate a self-conscious concern with sight and seeing or the visual.[36] The story 'Noras Geschenk' ['Nora's Present'] in *Hot Dogs*, for example, plays on the slippage from voyeurism to stalking, which plays out further in the relationship between narrator and characters. In 'Anna selbzwei' in the same volume, the narrative

---

35 Ulrike Draesner, 'Changing the Subject', in *Thomas Mann and Shakespeare. Something Rich and Strange*, ed. by Tobias Döring, Ewan Fernie and Elisabeth Bronfen (London: Bloomsbury, 2015), pp. 229–245 (p. 234).
36 See also the chapter by Silke Horstkotte in this volume.

voice draws attention to the convention of narratorial omnipotence and invisibility through a plural first person that runs throughout the text, beginning with the first page, and implicating the reader in a form of voyeurism: 'das schauen wir uns mal genauer an. Denken wir, aber Anna hat das nicht gedacht, sondern ist die Treppe runtergestolpert' (p. 35) [Let's look at that a bit more closely. We think, but Anna didn't think that, instead she stumbled down the stairs]. Like a real-time voiceover to the actions, the narrative voice both sees more than the characters know – 'Anna liegt still; sie will uns nicht alles zeigen, ihm auch nicht, schon gar nicht ihren Bauch. Dort ist es dunkel, wir sehen aber trotzdem durch ihr Auge hinein, sie ahnt es nicht' (p. 40) [Anna lies still; she doesn't want to show us anything, or him either, especially not her belly. It's dark there, but we can still look in through her eye, she doesn't suspect a thing] – and less, as the character withdraws from view, in brackets: '(denn Anna ist uns kurz entzogen, aber es dauert nicht lange, wir spielen mit Menschen, sie kommen immer zu uns zurück)' (p. 45) [(because Anna has withdrawn from us for a second, it won't last long, we play with people, they always come back to us)]. The narrative voice plays with the characters: 'Und auch Anna ist wieder da. Wir haben einen Schlitz im Rolladen gefunden und sind hineingekrochen zu unserem fetten Schmetterling' (pp. 45–46) [And Anna is back again too. We have found a chink in the blind and crawled through it to our fat butterfly], even addressing the protagonist: 'Wir, Anna, sind jetzt bei dir: Kleine Nachtspinne du, ist das ein Klistier?' (p. 46) [We are with you now, Anna: you little night-spider, is that an enema?].

By the end of the tale, nonetheless, the narrator figure (always the royal 'we') appears not as the architect of the tale but a bystander, an imperfect eyewitness who is far from all-seeing and all-knowing: 'Wer hätte gedacht, daß es so endet, wer hätte gedacht, daß es so anfing und endet. Wir lesen mit, tanzen über die Buchstaben der Karte von Anna' (p. 49) [Who would have thought it would end like this, who would have thought that it would begin and end like this. We read along too, dancing over the letters on Anna's card]. Nonetheless, the narrator makes one last attempt to intervene in the story as Anna purports to take over narratorial duties, suggesting she will write her own story: 'Neu-Anna kommt bald, was aber eine Geschichte ist, sagt Anna, die dort hinten an der Bustür lehnt – wir, ein Sonnenstrahl, kitzeln sie an der Nase, und sie, sie lächelt' (p. 49) [New Anna will be here soon, that's a story in itself, says Anna who is leaning against the bus door over there at the back – we, a beam of sunlight, tickle her on the nose and Anna, she smiles].

Draesner thus draws attention to the incompleteness, and partiality (in both senses) of the narrative perspective. In 'Der Jodler', in the same collection, the narrative perspective is aligned closely with Jana, the main protagonist and focalizer, so the reader's view is restricted strictly to hers. When Jana deliberately lets Cheops, the basenji dog, off his lead to attack a pet raven in a hotel room, then closes the door, all that the reader experiences is what Jana hears from outside: the dog's distinctive yodelling sound. As with the death of the puppies in 'Hot Dogs', or the arson in 'Harmonische Methode' (*Richtig liegen*), this narrative high point is deliberately elided; it is a blind spot (literally: the raven pecks one of the dogs' eyes out), left to the reader to fill in and visualize.

The disconcerting absence in 'Scham', also in *Hot Dogs*, by contrast is actually the narrative 'ich' [first person I], who does not appear as a figure as such within the action of the story, but takes increasing control over its narration. The narrator comments on the shortening of protagonist Jessmindra's name, two pages into the story, 'ich werde sie nur noch Jess nennen. So nannten sie alle. Es war einfacher. Sie war meine Freundin' (p. 152) [I will just call her Jess. That's what everyone called her. It was easier. She was my (girl)friend] and addresses the reader semi-directly through the meta-comment at the start of the story, 'Daß der Fluß nah lag, war nicht unerheblich. Der Fluß spielt in dieser Geschichte eine Rolle' (p. 150) [The fact that the river was close by was not insignificant. The river plays a part in this story]. The presence of the narrator figure emphasizes the constructedness of the tale and its invention: 'Das sagte sie mir später nicht, so denke ich sie mir. Fast, als wäre ich dabei gewesen. Vielleicht war ich dabei' (p. 158) [She didn't say that to me later, that's just how I think of her. Almost as if I had been there with them. Maybe I was there]. Here the narrator's intervention into the telling of the story is disconcerting, moving from acknowledging the pseudo-authorial control to uncertainty in suggesting the narrator may or may not have been there: is this uncertainty or playfulness? The narrator also seems to conflate invention and memory: 'Ich stelle es mir vor oder erinnere mich daran. Es wird wohl letzteres sein' (p. 158) [I imagine it or remember it. It must be the latter]. The assertion 'es wird wohl' [it must be] in fact undermines the certainty it purports to express. The narrator remains a commentator on, rather than participating in, the story, although this too seems to be assuming a specific part: 'Wolf zögerte, Jess sah, daß er bemerkte, daß sie nichts bekommen hatte. Dora bemerkte nichts, zumindest sagte sie nichts. Deswegen muß ich weitererzählen' (p. 159) [Wolf hesitated, Jess saw that he noticed she hadn't understood anything. Dora didn't notice anything, at least she didn't say anything. So I'll have to carry on telling the story]. There is a stark contrast between the visibility of this explicit narratorial presence and the suggestion of the open ending, where Jess disappears: as she recedes from view, the narrator also seems to merge with the character Dora.

Style and Language

As in her other prose texts, the narrative voice(s) in Draesner's short stories are highly self-conscious and often poetic. The earliest collection *Reisen unter den Augenlidern* is visually as well as linguistically experimental.[37] Unusually for German publications, and unlike *Hot Dogs* and *Richtig liegen*, there is no genre designation on the title page or cover of this collection; these are perhaps less 'Erzählungen' than extended prose poems. Even the titles play with language and form in an atypical way – with cryptic, visual shorthand such as 'L x L' or 'Wir::Wir' ['We::We'][38] – whereas those in the later collections tend to fall more recognizably into what have been theorized as categories for short story titles: titles of things ('Der grüne Koffer', 'Weiche Wände'), situations in time or place ('Sommerfrische' ['Summer Resort'], 'Europa'), figures (both names and nouns: 'Carlottas Spaß' ['Carlotta's Joke'], 'Noras Geschenk', 'Das Denkmal der Läuferin', 'Der Jodler'), and occurrences, often in the form of puzzling phrases ('Gold aus Mäusen', 'Ichs Heimweg macht alles allein').[39]

Experimental language continues within the texts in the first collection: the twins in 'L x L' develop their own form of language; 'Magern' sees sentences becoming lean along with the anorexic protagonist, reduced to minimal structures, until the outpouring of the last paragraph as single sentence. 'Nachkrieg, Taufe' is a single sentence, which makes particular use, like several others in the collection, of visual signals: italics, capitalization, ellipses, use of the ampersand logogram & instead of the word 'und' [and], and numbers as numerals. This visual punctuation suggests the emphases and leaps in association in the unnamed first-person protagonist's jumbled memories. 'Save the Limit of your Sight' similarly relates a stream-of-consciousness monologue without sentence breaks, though interrupted (in capitals) by what appear to be medics treating the woman narrating.

These two texts hinting at disordered thinking and dementia prefigure the similar texts in *Richtig liegen*: 'Josef rennt' ['Josef runs'], with its disjunction between the third person of the title and the obviously delusional first-person narrator, and particularly in the visual difference between the woman with Alzheimer's disease in 'Ichs Heimweg macht alles allein' who speaks as 'Ich' and her husband, who addresses her in the second person. The husband's sections in 'Ichs Heimweg

---

37 On visual elements of Draesner's poetry, see the chapter by Noël Reumkens in this volume.
38 The former text even suggests the latter, as 'L x L' is a story of twins who introduce themselves with 'Wir sind dieselben [. . .] wir als wir, nichts sonst' (32) [We are the same [. . .] we as we, nothing else].
39 See Marx, *Die Deutsche Kurzgeschichte*, pp. 62–63.

macht alles allein' are lengthy paragraphs with complex, fully syntactical senten-ces, in a justified layout on the page; Soffi's incoherent thoughts by contrast ap-pear as fragments on separate lines, giving the effect of left alignment, reminiscent of the script of a play, and surprisingly disconcerting in a prose publication. In an earlier version of the story, in the volume *Es schneit in meinem Kopf: Erzählungen über Alzheimer und Demenz*, Sarah's (as the wife is called here) monologue is largely set out in what appear at first glance to be paragraphs, with the punctua-tion that is missing from the later version in *Richtig liegen*; however these blocks of justified text do not contain coherent sentences, but rather evince associative links and leaps in subject matter. A visual break is signalled between Sarah's thoughts and her husband taking over narration through the insertion, in a small box, of a small ad describing a house for sale or rent. The formalized elliptical language and abbreviations of the advert throw into relief the idiosyncrasy and confusion of Sar-ah's thinking.

The later version of the text in *Richtig liegen* uses phrases from the earlier one, but misses out some of the associative links: 'colline de la lune hat jemand gesagt, ich hat es verstanden, warum ich in Frankreich gelandet ist, im Alter hat man die besten Abenteuer'[40] [colline de la lune someone said, I has under-stood, why I has landed in France, in old age one has the best adventures] be-comes 'colline de la lune hat jemand / gesagt im Alter / hat man die Abenteuer' (p. 175) [colline de la lune someone / said in old age / one has the adventures]. In this way, the evolution of the text itself mirrors the progression of the dis-ease. In the earlier version, physicist husband Hans notes that 'Die Ärzte sagen, die Krankheit sei nicht ansteckend. Aber die Ärzte wissen nicht alles' [The doc-tors say the disease isn't contagious. But doctors don't know everything].[41] It is notable that in the later version of the text his monologue also becomes less coherent, with long, run-on sentences compared to the more staccato punctua-tion in the earlier version. In a way the wife's confusion is thus also mirrored in her husband's sentences: the incomprehension of the carer in the face of de-mentia is expressed not in fragments but in unending, associative excess of language.

Wordplay seems to generate 'Verbwerben' [approximately: wordurging] in *Reisen unter den Augenlidern*, from the programmatic first line 'Sprache entwirft mich und wirft mich als Körper' (p. 41) [Language conceives me and weaves me a body me a body], through paragraphs where the first-person narrator plays self-

---

40 Ulrike Draesner, 'Ichs Heimweg macht alles alleine', in *Es schneit in meinem Kopf: Erzäh-lungen über Alzheimer und Demenz*, ed. by Klara Obermüller (Munich: Nagel and Kimche, 2006), pp. 59–81 (p. 59).
41 Ibid., p. 72.

consciously with repetition and rewording of common verbs, using lists of hyphenations for repeated prefixes or suffixes such as 'das Glitschen und Gleiten von Zu-, Un-, Auf- und Einfällen' (p. 51) [approximately: the slipping and sliding of coincidence, conspicuousness, incidents and accidents], and sound play such as the rhyming of 'assen': 'Doch weder das gelassen Verlassenwerden noch das verlassen Gelassensein kann ich fassen' (p. 45) [approximately: Yet I shall never understand being even-handed when abandoned nor evenhandedness with abandon]. Lengthy, montage-effect sentences are put to different effect in 'Wir::Wir' where they appear to transcribe the external visual, auditory and sensory impressions of the city (here identifiable as Berlin), interspersed with visually distinct section of an overheard telephone box conversation, rather than reflecting the inner workings of a mind.

Richtig liegen is less overtly experimental on the linguistic level, but displays a highly self-aware concern with language and style. 'Harmonische Methode' begins with a bravura single sentence that is more than two pages long, taking up the whole of a numbered section that narrates as well as quotes (both in direct quotation marks and using the subjunctive) the speech of a verbose barrister during a court case. Halfway through the piece, the narrator picks up on the barrister's phrasing to comment on his verbal style: ' . . . was sich in allen angestaut habe, ja weiterhin staue, er nutzte den Stau des Satzes, um dessen rhetorische Wirkung zu beobachten' (p. 44) [which had become jammed, continued to be jammed, he used the word jam to observe its rhetorical effect]. The second section then begins with the one-word sentence 'Nein' (p. 45) [No], for complete contrast, and shortly after narrates the protagonist Inga's thoughts: 'Warum musste es so kompliziert sein, warum die Welt sich aufstülpen zu langen Sätzen und sinnlosen Wegen. Ihr reichten kurze Sätze' (p. 46) [Why did it have to be so complicated, why force the world into long sentences and pointless paths. Short sentences were enough for her]. As with the role of the narrators, these comments turn the stories in on themselves, with the result that they reflect on their own telling alongside the telling itself. This meta-function is perhaps most apparent in Draesner's 2014 sketch for a computer game, 'Der Wolf', which sets out the game narrative as 'Die zu erzählende Geschichte' [The story to be told], bringing together Draesner's interests in modern technology, the interface of human and animal, and of course providing the game (that is, the story) with the memorable image of the wolf itself.[42]

---

42 Draesner, 'Der Wolf', p. 82.

Conclusion

Draesner's unusually broad oeuvre ranges from novels, prose and poetry through to essays in a number of media and translations, as well as radio plays, poetic installations and recently a libretto, indicating a fascination with the possibilities afforded by different literary and linguistic forms. As her own website states, Draesner 'erprobt Schreibverfahren' [experiments with different modes of writing],[43] and in the interview in this volume she explains that ideas very often come to her,

> with the form attached so I would know straight away whether it is part of a poem already existing, or whether it might live up to become a poem of its own, or whether it is something entirely different. In that case I might feel it is prose or 'prose-ish' but then there is the question of tone. Sometimes I have to do a certain amount of writing, with the longer things at least, to find what they really are.

Form is integral to, indeed part of, the creative inspiration: an idea for a text is 'self-contained in that it comes to life in a kind of double-process in which "content" and shape, wording and music and pictorial "frames" are forged hand in hand' (Draesner in interview in this volume). This coupling of content and form suggests that Draesner's short stories are inherently short in their conception. Despite the variation across the three collections, the texts in them all demonstrate a concern with shortness, with the impact of brevity itself on the story being told, on the characters, images, narrative perspective and the language used.

In the afterword to her compilation of German novellas, *Verführung: Deutschsprachige Novellen von Goethe bis Musil* [Seduction: German-language Novellas from Goethe to Musil], which includes the Thomas Mann text 'Wälsungenblut' ['The Blood of the Walsungs'] that Draesner evokes in her own incest story 'Zucken und Zwinkern', Draesner talks less about the much-theorized form of the novella than about the themes she identifies in her selection of novellas from the late eighteenth to the early twentieth century: the renewed concern with the nature of the subject ushered in by the French Revolution, the recognition of the subject's autonomy and valuing of bodily experience, as well as the changing social order and new discourses of science, law and psychiatry. For her, the novella form 'stellt [. . .] aus einer Reihe von Gründen eine ideale Form für die Artikulation der

---

43 Both phrases are taken from Draesner's website homepage in German (http://www.draes ner.de/autorin/) and in English (http://www.draesner.de/en/author/).

aufbrechenden Konflikte dar' [represents for a number of reasons the ideal form for articulating the burgeoning conflicts].[44] The novelty and shortness of the form, its concentration on the dimension of time and the decisive moment, as well as Goethe's 'sich ereignete unerhörte Begebenheit' [an unheard-of event that has occurred], all combine to put the subject to the test; the then new form of the novella thus becomes the crucible of the formation of a new, modern subject.

It is telling that Draesner's most recent collection most clearly evokes earlier novella forms, through the stories which consciously rewrite Kafka, the pair which call to mind the Decameron, and even the underlying motif of pairing which evokes Goethe's *Unterhaltungen deutscher Ausgewanderten* [*Recreations of the German Emigrants*], from which Draesner selects two stories for her compilation *Verführung*. The novella segues into the short story over the course of the twentieth century, with many of the novella's formal features being carried over into short story theories. Crucially, the themes that Draesner identifies in the earlier novella form are also subject to evolution, but it is clear that the nature of the individual, their autonomy and especially their bodily experience is still put to the test in her short stories, which are augmented by a range of contemporary discourses from science, ethics and the law, with recurring depictions of a spectrum of relationships and sexuality, concerns with reproduction and sanity, as well as the psychosomatic symbolism of eating, and the interaction between human and animal all harking back to the concerns Draesner analyses in the earlier form. At the same time she has also extended her short prose texts into a range of non-fiction forms which address these concerns both more explicitly and more personally. Draesner's short stories do not purport to give the whole picture – of a character, an issue, a situation or even a moment, let alone of contemporary subjectivity or real life – but, despite the differences in style in her three collections to date, together they evince an attempt to reflect and interrogate the fleeting, inconclusive yet intense moments and images that constitute the modern self, in a form that itself is more fragmentary, more transient and less unitary, and even more acutely aware of its own fictionality.

---

44 Draesner, 'Nachwort', in *Verführung: Deutschsprachige Novellen von Goethe bis Musil*, p. 275.

'Stoffwechsel'

Michael Braun
Metamorphosis. Ulrike Draesner's Poetics of Knowledge

There is no science without fancy and no arts without facts. (Nabokov)

Ulrike Draesner's translation of a number of Shakespeare's sonnets, under the title 'Twin Spin', was published in 2000, influenced by the decoding of the human genome, a high point in the biotechnical revolution that began when Dolly the sheep became the first cloned mammal in spring 1997. Cloning encroaches upon the origins and singularity of human existence. It is a process of creation and in this respect can be understood as a scientific interpretation of human reproduction. Draesner's translations of Shakespeare's sonnets explore cloning in this context. She calls her 'post-Dolly' texts 'radical translations'. What is radical is the poetic transformation of the referential framework of 'Zeugung, Mortalität, Individualität und Reproduktion' [conception, mortality, individuality and reproduction].[1] A second life is not breathed into a person ('eingehaucht'), it is cloned ('ein[ge]klont'), and this new life is now a virtual and aesthetic life. It is in this sense that Draesner translates the final lines of Shakespeare's heroic couplet, 'So long as men can breathe, or eyes can see, / So long lives this, and gives life to thee' (sonnet 18) as follows: 'solange einer atmen kann, solange augen sehn, / solange lohnt auch dies und klont dir leben ein' [so long as breath is drawn, so long as eyes have sight, / so long this loan repays its own and clones you life].[2]

Her adoption and adaptation of biotechnology as the defining science of the twenty-first century could be considered postmodern. Yet it remains loyal to the original text. The radical transformations of Shakespeare's sonnets result in a change of subject (quite literally – see also the title of the volume in which the sequence first appeared). The translated sonnets speak to a clone, they respond to cloning and they become clones themselves; this is, then, a poetic discourse on creation and reproduction in a biotechnological age. 'Ein gutes Gedicht ist ein Schleppnetz' [a good

---

1 Ulrike Draesner, 'Dolly und Will', in Ulrike Draesner, Barbara Köhler and Peter Waterhouse, :to change the subject (Göttingen: Wallstein, 2000), pp. 30–33 (p. 31).
2 Ulrike Draesner, 'Twin Spin', in :to change the subject, p. 18. Quotation taken here from a selection of the cycle re-translated into English and published on the occasion of the symposium Twin Spin. 17 Shakespeare Sonnets, radically translated by Ulrike Draesner, back-translated by Tom Cheesman (Oxford: Taylor Institution Library, 2016), p. 25. I would like to thank Karen Leeder for her advice and her support with translation.

https://doi.org/10.1515/9783110495942-009

poem is a drag net], Draesner claims: 'Es sammelt Erfahrungen, Erinnerungen, das Weltwissen' [it collects experiences, memories, knowledge of the world].[3]

This very particular understanding, or 'will-ful misunderstanding', as Draesner puts it,[4] of literary tradition, of the canon and of culture, is an important starting point for Draesner's writing. Draesner – who has a background as a medieval scholar and writes as a literary critic – acknowledges, 'Meine Sprache [. . .] ist durchzogen von fremdem Material, spielt mit Filmen, Text- und Wissensstoffen. Fremde Stimmen wandern in ihr umher' [my language [. . .] is infused with foreign material, plays with film, samples of text and knowledge. Foreign voices roam around within it].[5] This is a heterogeneous body of knowledge, spanning medicine, psychology, astrophysics and genetics through to the history of art, culture and science. To take a handful of examples: genealogical ruptures and gender dysphoria play a role in the novel *Mitgift* (2002); contemporary German history and memorial culture feature in *Spiele* (2005); the history of art and the renaissance of religious themes in the novel are addressed in *Vorliebe* (2011); and the prose volume *Richtig liegen* (2011) offers a contrafacture of classical Modernism. In the novel *Sieben Sprünge vom Rand der Welt* (2014) memory theory and individual memory overlap with discussions of flight and displacement, and scientific insights into brain and behaviour; historical anthropology feeds into an examination of primate research and the literature of remembrance becomes what Nicole Sütterlin has called a new 'poetics of trauma'.[6] However, the priority is never an in-depth critical understanding of these fields of knowledge, but rather 'eine grabende, nachdenkende, das Komische schätzende Zeitgenossenschaft' [an inquiring, contemplative, humour-loving contemporaneity].[7] In other words, Draesner is concerned with tracing a person's linguistic knowledge and experimenting with the relationship between knowledge and literature in language. Knowledge is enacted poetically. This then leads to a narrative enquiry into the forms in which knowledge and poetry meet. This chapter will consider Draesner's works not so much within a framework of cultural diagnostics, but rather in the light of 'poetic insight'.[8] I would argue that Draesner writes what we

---

3 Ulrike Draesner, *Die fünfte Dimension* (Munich: Stiftung Lyrikkabinett, 2015), p. 30.
4 Draesner, 'Dolly und Will', p. 32.
5 Ulrike Draesner, 'Tiere sind keine Dinge', in *'Nehmen Sie mich beim Wort ins Kreuzverhör'. Vorlesungen der Wiesbadener Poetikdozentur,* ed. by Rosemarie Altenhofer, Susanne Lewalter and Rita Rosen (Frankfurt a. M.: Fischer, 2010), pp. 261–286 (p. 274).
6 Nicole Sütterlin, 'Trauma-Poetik: Ulrike Draesners *Sieben Sprünge vom Rand der Welt* und die Körperliteratur der 1990er Jahre', *Gegenwartsliteratur*, 15 (2016), 167–190.
7 Draesner, 'Tiere sind keine Dinge', p. 277.
8 Cf. a brief discussion in Anna Ertel, 'Zur Poetik Ulrike Draesners', in *Ulrike Draesner*, ed. by Susanna Brogi, Anna Ertel and Evi Zemanek (Munich: Text + Kritik, 2014), pp. 19–26 (p. 21).

might term 'poems and narratives of knowledge' about the time we live in: the end of the twentieth century and the beginning of the twenty-first. During this period the disaster narratives of the 1980s have been replaced by narratives of awakening, curiosity and discovery; but also by violence and terror in the face of developments in the natural sciences. Various poets have of course attempted to interpret the new images of humanity and the world created by this revolution of knowledge. In the 1990s, the 'decade of world faith and hope for humanity',[9] and in the ensuing decade, defined by 9/11 and the dark side of globalization, it is the poets (alongside Draesner also Durs Grünbein, Raoul Schrott and Ulrich Woelk), who survey the new 'knowledge route' and address the rapidly accelerating flux of world knowledge.[10] It is they who attempt to clarify this cultural knowledge, with its historical and media status, and particular ethos.[11]

Two aspects of this exchange between science and poetry are important here. On the one hand, it appears to be characteristic of Draesner's works that they question disciplinary boundaries and seek to relax rather than contain the given order. Draesner compares the narration of knowledge to a metabolic exchange between disciplines, epochs, subjects and texts. This 'Stoff-Wechsel' [literally: exchange of material, the term used in German for metabolic processes] is also a 'Spur-Wechsel' [switching of lanes] in terms of reference.[12]

On the other hand, literature moulds images and perceptions of knowledge according to aesthetic principles, whilst science presents them in a logical framework. Striving for truth or truthfulness might be thought to connect literature and science; but it is in the end the principle of beauty that characterizes a poetics of knowledge.

For more detail see Anna Ertel, *Körper, Hirne, Gene. Lyrik und Naturwissenschaft bei Ulrike Draesner und Durs Grünbein* (Berlin: de Gruyter, 2010).

9 Wolfgang Frühwald, 'Die Lust, sich im Universum zu bewegen. Ein Gespräch mit dem Dichter Durs Grünbein über Poesie, Neurobiologie und die Bilder vom Menschen', in Wolfgang Frühwald, Konrad Beyreuther, Johannes Dichgans, Durs Grünbein, Karl Kardinal Lehmann, Wolf Singer, *Das Design des Menschen. Vom Wandel des Menschenbildes unter dem Einfluss der modernen Naturwissenschaft* (Cologne: DuMont, 2004), pp. 294–309 (p. 296).

10 This 'Wissensstrecke' is not straightforward and is difficult to visualize. Wolfgang Frühwald, 'Sternenstaub. Zum wissenschaftlichen Weltbild am Beginn des 21. Jahrhunderts', in Frühwald et al., *Das Design des Menschen*, pp. 44–70 (p. 52).

11 Cf. *Die Ethik der Literatur. Deutsche Autoren der Gegenwart*, ed. by Paul Michael Lützeler and Jennifer M. Kapczynski (Göttingen: Wallstein, 2011).

12 Karen Leeder (Oxford) coined this spatial term for Ulrike Draesner's use of 'Stoffwechsel' in her writing. It alludes to the notion of searching for tracks in the jungle of postmodern meanings, but also the sudden switching of lanes onto digital data-highways.

What is a Poetics of Knowledge?

A poetics of knowledge, in its broadest sense, is concerned with the role and function of aesthetic processes. The important issue here is the organization and representation of knowledge in literature. Knowledge should be understood not as that which is empirically verified or 'true', but as part of a network of 'interpreted information' within open discourses. These are not dependent on a central perceiving subject, nor a normative model (a discipline or the logic of a statement), rather they rely on the desire to interpret this information.[13] 'Interpretation machte die Welt' [interpretation made the world], Draesner comments in *Mitgift*.[14] The platonic unity of knowledge and truth is uncoupled in literature. To be sure: literature is not better at explaining knowledge; it simply goes about it in a different way. In 1938 Raymond Chandler wrote in his diary:

> There are two kinds of truths: the truth that lights the way and the truth that warms the heart. The first of these is science, and the second is art. Neither is independent of the other or more important than the other. Without art, science would be as useless as a pair of forceps in the hands of a plumber. Without science art would become a crude mess of folklore and emotional quackery. The truth of art keeps science from becoming inhuman, and the truth of science keeps art from becoming ridiculous.[15]

Monika Schmitz-Emans describes the exclusively literary meaning of knowledge thus:

> Obviously, by several philosophers as well as by literary critics, literature has been recently regarded as an instance that undermines convictions, dissolves so-called certainties, destroys illusions concerning the existence of absolute truths, reflects on the ambiguity of all realities by creating multi-faceted and ambiguous 'worlds' and thus provides for a discourse that functionally cannot be replaced.[16]

---

13 Cf. Olaf Breidbach, *Neue Wissensordnungen. Wie aus Informationen und Nachrichten kulturelles Wissen entsteht* (Frankfurt a. M.: Suhrkamp, 2008), p. 12. I understand 'poetics of knowledge' in this context less as an innovative research paradigm as outlined by Joseph Vogl und Nicolas Pethes, and more as a possible methodology for describing the traffic between science, culture and narration. For a critical look at a poetics of knowledge – 'the mystification and romantic ennobling' of poetry – compare Gideon Stiening, '"Am Ungrund" oder: Was sind und zu welchem Ende studiert man "Poetologien des Wissens"', *KulturPoetik*, 7.2 (2007), 234–248.
14 Ulrike Draesner, *Mitgift* (Munich: Luchterhand, 2002), p. 271.
15 Raymond Chandler, 'Great Thought', in *The Notebooks of Raymond Chandler and English Summer* (New York: Eco, 1976), entry on 19 February 1938.
16 Monika Schmitz-Emans, 'Literature and Science – Introduction', in *Literature and Science. Literatur und Wissenschaft*, ed. by Monika Schmitz-Emans (Würzburg: Königshausen & Neumann, 2008), pp. 12–33, p. 29. Cf. also Wolfgang Frühwald, *Zeit der Wissenschaft* (Cologne:

Knowledge can assume implicit forms (tacit knowledge) or be deemed precarious when the carrier of knowledge, its speaker or the language of knowledge itself becomes 'unsure, awkward, difficult, problematic, revocable'.[17] What has been termed 'swarm intelligence' or 'collective intelligence', for example, is a kind of invisible phenomenon discovered within the field of nanoscience which has made its presence felt in areas as various as information technology, sociology and philosophy, as well as in the fictional text, for example, in Frank Schätzing's eco-thriller *Der Schwarm* (2004) [*The Swarm*, 2006].

Metaphor as an Element of the Transformation of Knowledge

An important point here is that any poetic discourse of knowledge uses a language aware of its own metaphorical character. Thing and meaning, origin and actualization become detached from each other. The metaphor is cleverer than the author, so to speak. Terms in physics like 'quarks' (taken from James Joyce's *Finnegan's Wake*) and 'cloud' do not function as metaphors for the things they represent, for the smallest particles of the atomic nucleus, rather they express our attempt to grope towards this invisible area of knowledge, no matter how 'einseitig und ungenau' [one-sided and imprecise], any such attempt remains, according to Draesner. Nevertheless, as she concludes: 'they express this sense of feeling our way wonderfully.' [Das Tasten drücken sie wunderbar aus].[18] And even if the concept of drawing one's 'last breath' no longer corresponds to advances in medical science with regard to the theory of brain death, it has not lost any of its allure and vividness as an image. Many of Draesner's book titles draw on the intensity of 'viel Bild' [a great deal of imagery].[19] They play with the idea of ambiguity and the many ways in which one can 'read' the world: the term *Vorliebe*, for example, signifies a particular preference for a person or thing but also, literally, the time before love; *subsong* is an ornithological term but also a play

---

DuMont, 1997) and *'Scientia poetica'. Literatur und Naturwissenschaft*, ed. by Norbert Elser and Werner Frick (Göttingen: Wallstein, 2004).

17 Martin Mulsow, *Prekäres Wissen. Eine andere Geschichte der frühen Neuzeit* (Berlin: Suhrkamp, 2012), p. 14.

18 Draesner, 'Tiere sind keine Dinge', p. 262.

19 Ibid., p. 281.

on alternative readings of song-poems, and a reference to the tenth Beatles' album *Yellow Submarine* (1969).[20]

The metaphor is therefore a symbol of irreducible knowledge, 'which precedes any conceptual understanding of the world'.[21] In this respect, the text (in relation to a poetics of knowledge) knows what it is talking about, even when it does not state this explicitly. Hans Blumenberg illustrates this in his use of the term 'Quelle' [origin, source or spring],[22] which is used in the fields of philology, philosophy, archaeology and historiography and which reveals its potential as a 'poetics of knowledge' in its metaphorical connection with derivation ('Ableitung'), influence ('Einfluss'), creation ('Schöpfung') and current ('Strömung').

An example is Goethe's *Farbenlehre* [*Theory of Colours*, 1840], the first volume of which appeared in 1808. The structure of the work itself already reveals the author's intention to give some order to the knowledge of his time and to present himself as a poet, critic and also a scientist. The work is part textbook, part polemic, and part historical treatise. When the writer sets himself up as a physicist but then supplements this knowledge from the perspective of a philosopher, two important questions emerge: to what extent do areas of knowledge belong to specific disciplines and how is this represented metaphorically? 'At the origin of the *Theory of Colours*' is, claims Blumenberg, a 'source' (both words, origin and source, are 'Quelle' in German).[23] In the camp, Goethe sees a crater filled with spring water. There is a shard of stoneware at the bottom, which produces a prism of light on the upper surface of the water. As Holger Helbig summarizes, Goethe's poetics of knowledge concerns the 'deployment of symbols to convey knowledge'.[24]

An example of the dynamics of metaphor in the production and circulation of knowledge can be found in the introductory chapter of Draesner's *Vorliebe*. Harriet, an astrophysicist, performs a simulated space-travel test in the European Astronaut Centre in Cologne. She sits for seven minutes in a human centrifuge to find out whether she can withstand extreme levels of acceleration. The novel begins with a flurry of metaphors:

---

20 Cf. the sequence 'beatles-sub-songs', in Ulrike Draesner, *subsong* (Munich: Luchterhand, 2014), pp. 149–177.

21 Christina Brandt, 'Metaphor', in *Literatur und Wissen. Ein interdisziplinäres Handbuch* (Stuttgart: Metzler, 2013), pp. 21–28 (p. 24).

22 Hans Blumenberg, *Quellen, Ströme, Eisberge*, ed. by Ulrich von Bülow and Dorit Krusche (Berlin: Suhrkamp, 2012).

23 Ibid., p. 84.

24 Holger Helbig, *Naturgemäße Ordnung. Darstellung und Methode in Goethes Lehre von den Farben* (Cologne: Böhlau, 2004), p. 23.

Weiß, die Lichtmischung aller Farben auf einer Wand, weiß, der Sturz in den Schnee auf der Nordseite des Kailash, eine Frühlingswiese, weiß gesprenkelt, das Weiß eines menschlichen Auges, der hineingemalte verborgene Glanz, das Weiß der Albedo, der Erde Widerschein im All. Weiß die Sekunden in der Parabel, Flug um Flug, Sturz um Sturz, das Weiß der Rotation, als noch einmal etwas aus ihrem Schädel dringt, obwohl ihr Gehirn sich bereits außerhalb der Knochen befindet – von Neuem wölbt es sich aus, presst durch kleinste Ritzen nach unten und außen, Beschleunigung auf höchster Stufe, weiß, die Erinnerung an Peter, der Widerstrahl eines Horizonts, ein Lachen inmitten eines Strudels jetzt, noch tieferes, sattes, saugendes Weiß.[25]

[White, the mixture of all the colours of light on a wall, white, the fall in the snow on the north-face of the Kailash, a spring meadow, peppered with white, the white of a human eye, the secret brilliance painted into it, the white of the albedo, earth reflected in space. White, the seconds in the parabola, flight by flight, fall by fall, rotation-white, as something forces its way out of her skull once again, although her brain already feels as though it is outside her bones, it regains its curved shape, pushes downwards and outwards through the smallest cracks, acceleration turned up to the highest notch, white, the memory of Peter, the reflection of a horizon, now laughing in the middle of a vortex, still deeper, satiated, vacuum white.]

The sequence of light impressions is held together by the attribute 'white', but it denotes more than just an optical perception. 'White' is a descriptive term in geology (Mount Kailash is a holy mountain in Tibet) and in physics (an albedo is a unit of measure for radiation onto diffuse reflecting surfaces). Furthermore, there are impressions from nature ('spring meadow'), perceptions of the world ('the reflection of a horizon') and self ('the white of a human eye' and the 'memory of Peter', her former lover). In the crossover between expert knowledge and the personal world of experience there is a transfer of knowledge which is poetic, for it takes on a non-logical shape influenced by narrative perspective. The process of interior monologue, an invention of early Modernism shaped by the technical revolution, determines the poetics of knowledge at the beginning of this novel. What is conspicuous here is the way the writing insists on its own characteristic epic form, without losing track of the astrophysical plot. The acceleration differentiates the body-spirit-experience ('brain [. . .] outside the bones') and finds expression in the self-referential accumulation of images of disorder (the word 'fall' appears three times). One could say that the metaphor creates its own order of a poetics of knowledge, in which there are exact descriptions of the instruments, but also explanations, images, figures of thought, which reach into other – metaphysical and theological – horizons of knowledge. No surprise perhaps that the name of the accelerator in the first chapter is 'Creator'.

---

25 Ulrike Draesner, *Vorliebe* (Munich: Luchterhand, 2012), p. 7.

Lyric Knowledge-transfer

Ulrike Draesner's poetry collection *subsong* (2014) also connects poetry and science in new ways. It deals with the enigmatic origins of aesthetic function: how can art be without purpose and beautiful at the same time? Draesner finds answers to this in the chorus of ritual calls and melodic sequences referred to in ornithology as subsong or 'whisper song'. The purpose of this unusual birdsong is not to demarcate territory or to attract a mate. It has no recognizable order, appears to have neither aim nor purpose, but to be something along the lines of vocal exercise or rehearsal. It is a 'testing out of vocabulary' according to ornithologists, an example of poetry's self-examination, according to Draesner. Her intention is to bring the genesis of poetry together with scientific observation into a single lyric image. In this way, knowledge acquires its own form: it is no longer the construction of a world via presentist and evident reality (as in antiquity), no longer the illustration of a divine order (as in the Middle Ages) and not even poetically shaped reality (as in the modern age). The particular facet of this 'Stoffwechsel' is the post-Romantic reconstruction of poetry out of the spirit of 'natural' sciences.

The poems play with vowels and vocabulary. Bird voices are translated into phonetic language and observations of nature are captured in conversation. There are often classical situations of knowledge-transfer. The fate that has befallen a headless adder found in the leaves following an attack by a buzzard is explained to a nagging child. The experience of a child learning to pronounce the letter 'r' is made into a poem of playful sounds. In the cycle 'vokabeldehner (weitsingen)' (pp. 23–56) ['vocabulary extender (farsinging)'] there are separations and dreams, which link observations of the natural world with the relationship between two people. This gives rise to reciprocal insights into the language of creation and the creation of language. It is a language that elicits new words, the 'sonnenfutterschein' [sun-food-shine] in 'chlorphyll' (p. 43) ['chlorophyll']; 'flügelsplitter aus licht' [wing-slivers of light] in the 'subsong der jungen amselweibchens (leise, zusammengeklaut im märz)' (p. 74) ['subsong of the young female blackbird (soft, stolen, in march)']: discoveries in the 'letternreich auch der biologie' (realm of letters also of biology), as the poem 'zeigen/lesen' (p. 46) ['showing/reading'] puts it.

The Narrative of Cultural Knowledge

Draesner has outlined the narrative of cultural knowledge several times in her essays. In her Bamberg and Wiesbaden poetics lectures she introduces an admittedly complex three-fold differentiation. She discriminates between that which we know and that which we know that we don't know and finally that which we don't know that we don't know.

Arguably the most interesting category here is that of 'unknown unknown':[26] the blind spot in reading and writing; the place where the aesthetic operates beyond knowledge; the possibility of literature as, 'Anwalt des wissenschaftlich Unsichtbaren' [advocate of that which is invisible to science].[27] Contemporary literature frequently incorporates ideas from science and thereby frees itself from the 'self-inflicted scientific immaturity', that occurred during the specialization of knowledge and positivism in the nineteenth century. Hans Magnus Enzensberger writes in the epilogue to his volume *Die Elixiere der Wissenschaft* [*The Elixirs of Science*], a postmodern essay about the discovery of poetry in the sciences:

> Unsichtbar wie ein Isotop, das der Diagnose und der Zeitmessung dient, unauffällig, doch kaum verzichtbar wie ein Spurenelement, ist die Poesie auch dort am Werk, wo sie niemand vermutet.[28]

> [Invisible as an isotope that is useful for diagnoses and measuring time, inconspicuous, but almost indispensable, like a trace element, poetry is at work, where no-one suspects.]

There are many reasons for the present day's lack of knowledge about itself. One of them is the lack of distance between the observer and the object of his/ her observation. It is literature that can tell us about this unknown knowledge-lack. Hans Ulrich Gumbrecht has coined the phrase 'latency' for this.[29] Liberated from its origins in psychoanalysis, the term has, for Gumbrecht, the status

---

26 Cf. Achim Geisenhanslücke, *Dummheit und Witz. Poetologie des Nichtwissens* (Paderborn: Schöningh, 2011). Compare the interview with Draesner in this volume.

27 Ulrike Draesner, 'Fluoreszierende Mäuse? Anmerkungen zu Genetik und Literatur', *Neue Zürcher Zeitung*, 19 January 2001, p. 25 (https://www.nzz.ch/article6XXYK-1.458955).

28 Hans Magnus Enzensberger, 'Die Poesie der Wissenschaft. Ein Postskriptum', in Hans Magnus Enzensberger, *Die Elixiere der Wissenschaft. Seitenblicke in Poesie und Prosa* (Frankfurt a. M.: Suhrkamp, 2002), pp. 261–276 (p. 266, p. 274).

29 See Hans Ulrich Gumbrecht, *After 1945. Latency as Origin of the Present* (Stanford: Stanford University Press, 2013); *Präsenz* (Berlin: Suhrkamp, 2012); *Unsere breite Gegenwart* (Berlin: Suhrkamp, 2010); *Production of Presence. What Meaning Cannot Convey* (Stanford: Stanford University Press, 2004).

of a cultural zeitgeist, in the air, so to speak, but which can be neither empirically nor terminologically defined. Latency of knowledge about the present we live in exists, then, but is neither visible nor tangible. We can appreciate the ambiguous position of Gumbrecht's theory by comparing it to the image of the stowaway borrowed from the Dutch historian Eelco Runia. This person is present, occupies time and space, but no-one knows him, and no-one can say with certainty where he is, let alone whether he actually exists. In this sense, the 'unknown non-knowledge' is the stowaway in narratives of knowledge.[30] In Draesner's *Sieben Sprünge vom Rand der Welt* it is the refugee child Eustachius Grolman's unacknowledged murder of his physically disabled brother that plays this role. However, fratricide is not relayed in a narrative of known non-knowledge, as in Uwe Timm's *Am Beispiel meines Bruders* (2003) [*In My Brother's Shadow*, 2005], where letters, a diary and speculation establish access to the life of the brother who died during the war; or in Hans Ulrich Treichel's (1998) *Der Verlorene* [*Lost*, 2000], where a photograph is the only piece of evidence to help correct the parents' false memories of the brother who was lost during the flight. Draesner's starting point is a transgenerational narrative, where knowledge of the war victim Emil is locked in an 'intrapsychic tomb', a soul crypt, and is replaced via screen-memories ('Deckerinnerungen') and positive memory.[31] How Emil actually dies remains unresolved, but there is no mistaking the guilt and shame that colour the first-person narrator Eustachius's knowledge.

This becomes clear in the episode concerning the mandarin. Eustachius is roaming through the town on the lookout for an escaped ape. The snow and the mandarin in his jacket pocket stir up the repressed memory of the flight during the last winter of the War. Eustachius suddenly pictures his brother, who gave him a mandarin: 'Die Mandarine schaukelte auf seiner Hand. Ich fragte nicht, woher sie kam. [. . .] Dann war er weg. Ich hielt die Mandarine in der Hand, ohne zu wissen, wie sie dorthin gelangt war' ['The mandarin swayed on his hand. I didn't ask where it came from . . . Then he was gone. I held the mandarin in my hand, not knowing how it got there'].[32] The memory expresses itself as unknown knowledge.

---

30 Eelco Runia, 'Ein Kurzschluss in der Lustmaschine. Lenin, Geschichte und Evolution', in *Latenz. Blinde Passagiere in den Geisteswissenschaften*, ed. by Hans Ulrich Gumbrecht and Florian Klinger (Göttingen: Vandenhoeck and Ruprecht, 2011), pp. 205–225.
31 Sütterlin, 'Trauma-Poetik', p. 180.
32 Ulrike Draesner, *Sieben Sprünge vom Rand der Welt* (Munich: Luchterhand, 2015), p. 169. Cf. Sütterlin, 'Trauma-Poetik', p. 175.

The Poetics of Knowledge in Draesner's Essays

In her volume of essays *Heimliche Helden* (2013) Draesner inverts traditional perspectives. She does not focus on the thirst for adventure that drives the hero to make his journey; rather she examines his unheroic qualities. The core of her enquiry is the medieval 'Nibelungen', the epic poem re-discovered in 1755: a warrior-narrative of betrayal, revenge, loyalty and memory. We have the hero Siegfried, the data manager Hagen, the terrorist Kriemhild, the broken heroine Brünhild.[33] In Draesner's 2016 sequence of poems composed around the 'Nibelungen' saga and published in a new volume alongside the 1908 art nouveau illustrations of the Viennese artist Carl Otto Czeschka she gives the four protagonists a voice. In the epilogue Kriemhild's sons appear with a 'Nibelungen' computer game and argue whether it is possible to play 'the end'.[34] The question is directed at the curious way in which the *Nibelungenlied* presents knowledge in its oral and written forms, myth and history.

> Als wäre es ein Computerspiel. [. . .] Zeitebenen und historisches Wissen in unserem Sinne sind ihm gleichgültig: Alles ist Material, alles wird gemischt. Es liebt Ausstattungen, beschreibt Gegenstände des Schmuckes oder Kampfes, enthält eine Schatzsuche, einen Zwergenstreit, magische Objekt wie Tarnkappe und Balmung, das Schwert, bietet ein Stück road-movie, einen übellaunigen Fährmann, Vorausdeutungen und Wasserfeen. Vor allem aber macht es aus Versatzstücken und Utensilien, regeln und Rollen gebaute Spielfiguren lebendig: König, Lehnsherr, Kämpfer, Hofstaat, Held.[35]

> [As if it were a computer game. [. . .] Time periods and historical knowledge in the way we understand them, mean nothing. Everything is material, everything is mixed up. It loves equipment, describes jewellery and the paraphernalia of battle, includes a treasure hunt, a dwarf battle, magic objects like a magic hood and Balmung, the sword. There are bits of road-movie, a cantankerous ferryman, premonitions and water fairies. But most of all, with all its props, equipment, rules and roles, it brings the figures of the game to life: king, feudal lord, warrior, courtier, hero.]

In an afterword, Draesner reveals the particular value of her re-reading of the 'Nibelungen' saga in relation to a poetics of knowledge. The intention is to destabilize the narrative order that the medieval version gained in its transition from an oral into a written medium. This succeeds because Draesner exploits

---

33 Draesner, 'Wesen aus Muskel, Makel und Mensch. Gedanken zum Helden mit Hilfe des Nibelungenliedes', in Ulrike Draesner, *Heimliche Helden. Essays* (Munich: Luchterhand, 2013), pp. 49–83 (p. 49).

34 Ulrike Draesner, *Nibelungen. Heimsuchung* (Stuttgart: Reclam, 2016), p. 105. See also the chapter by Almut Suerbaum in this volume.

35 Draesner, 'Wesen aus Muskel, Makel und Mensch', p. 49.

the telling metaphor of the title quite literally. The Nibelungen, whom one expects to encounter as characters in the epic poem, do not appear at all. Siegfried has murdered the Nibelungen, who were protecting the hoard. At the end of the poem the Burgunders in Etzel's court are given the name 'Nibelungen' but they are all already dead. In this sense, the *Nibelungenlied* is about knowledge that no longer exists; the 'Nibelungen' is a narrative of lack and forgetting, 'ein Epos der Löschungen' [an epic of erasure], and the art of the translator, who becomes the author in the process, is nothing other than in remembering lost or repressed knowledge.[36]

> Immer wieder vergesse ich . . . was im *Nibelungenlied* geschieht. Zusammenhänge, Verknüpfungen, die exakte zeitliche Abfolge entziehen sich. In Scherben liegt das Epos im Kopf. Zeigt Lücken, zerbricht. [. . .] Das Lied erzählt mir: Es gibt Lebenslagen, da fährt, was du liebtest und verlorst und noch liebst, unverhofft, unerwartet, erschreckend und schön, durch die Luft auf dich zu. Das vergesse ich nicht.[37]

> [I keep forgetting . . . what happens in the *Nibelungenlied*. Contexts, connections, the exact chronology elude me. The epic lies in fragments in my head. Reveals gaps, breaks up. [. . .] The song says this to me: There are situations in life, when that which you loved and lost and still love, heads straight through the air towards you, out of the blue, frightening and beautiful. I'll never forget that.]

The other essays in *Heimliche Helden* address the questionable heroism of the Marquise of O. in the narrative of the same name by Kleist; Johann Peter Hebel's 'human heroes' whose actions range from the comic to the grotesque; Gottfried Benn's 'Höhlenhimmel' [cave roof] in the ambivalent biographical text *Doppelleben* (1934 and 1949) [*Double Life*, 2002]; and the biographical 'Lügenhelden' [lying heroes] with their fake biographies in Hans Joachim Schädlich's semi-documentary book *Anders* (2003)[*Different*].[38] According to Draesner, a hero is a human machine that abides by rules, an effortful 'avatar', a character 'whom we need, we imagine, we send on ahead'. However, these interpretations of an exclusively male 'hero-concept' ('white, male, euro-centric, hyper-cerebral') do not lead to a wholesale 'écriture feminine'.[39] As we had already seen in the essays *Schöne Frauen Lesen* (2008), where Flaubert crept in amongst the female writers, Tania Blixen is also permitted to join the 'secret heroes'. 'Draesner is

---

36 Draesner, 'Immer wieder vergesse ich', in *Nibelungen*, p. 107.

37 Draesner, 'Immer wieder vergesse ich', in *Nibelungen*, p. 126.

38 On Kleist, *Heimliche Helden*, pp. 85–119; on Hebbel, pp. 123–164; on Benn, pp. 213–236; on Schädlich, 291–306.

39 Cf. Vanda Zajko and Miriam Leonard, *Laughing with Medusa* (Oxford: Oxford University Press, 2006).

bold and humorous in the way she mixes her literary skills with practical and psychological insider knowledge, with a view to presenting the whole thing as a sophisticated narrator', writes Nicole Henneberg.[40]

The Poetic Order of Knowledge and Non-knowledge

Ulrike Draesner illustrates the poetic order of knowledge and non-knowledge in her 2011 collection of stories *Richtig liegen*.[41] This occurs both thematically and aesthetically. The subtitle 'stories in pairs' already plays with the experimental character of the arrangement of the texts. The aim is to talk about stories which lie dormant between male and female characters or two people within a family. It is therefore about the attempt to transform the non-knowledge of the characters into potential knowledge for the reader. But the label 'stories in pairs' also has an architectural significance. According to Henry James' dictum that fiction is a house with many windows,[42] the subtitle opens our eyes to the constellations and pairings amongst the stories themselves. 'Ichs Heimweg macht alles allein' ['I's Way Home makes Everything alone'] and 'Josef rennt' ['Joseph runs'], for example, both feature patients with Alzheimer's disease. The illness 'brought on by brain damage, the often chronically progressive diminishing of cognitive ability which affects day-to-day functioning', does not, however, become the subject matter for a patient report here.[43] Like Louis Begly in *Shipwreck* (2003), Arno Geiger in *Der alte König in seinem Exil* (2011) [*The Old King in his Exile*, 2017], Annette Pehnt in *Haus der Schildkröten* (2006) [*House of Tortoises*] and other authors, Draesner perceives of dementia as a 'literary disease' (Holger Helbig). It produces 'Hirngespinste' [phantasms; literally brain ghosts] according to the German translation of Dutch writer Bernlef's 1984 novel about Alzheimer's *Hersenschimmen* [*Out of Mind* in the 1984 English translation]. The disease embraces symptoms that have a dimension suggestive to an aesthetic

---

40 Nicole Henneberg, 'Skispringer mit Hermesbeinen', *Frankfurter Allgemeine Zeitung*, 3 August 2013 (http://www.faz.net/aktuell/feuilleton/buecher/rezensionen/belletristik/ulrike-draesner-heimliche-helden-skispringer-mit-hermesbeinen-12317202.html).
41 Ulrike Draesner, *Richtig liegen* (Munich: Luchterhand, 2011). Further references are given in the body of the essay. Parts of the following interpretation were presented at the annual conference of the German Studies Association in Washington D.C., 2nd October 2015.
42 In the preface to his novel *Portrait of a Lady* (1880).
43 Holger Helbig, 'Alzheimer-Krankheit', in *Literatur und Medizin. Ein Lexikon*, ed. by Bettina von Jagow, Florian Steger (Göttingen: Vandenhoeck and Ruprecht 2005), p. 46–47.

sensibility: forgetfulness and aphasia, for example. This compels the author – and the reader – to reflect on themselves. Books about Alzheimers address ways of 'living in a fictional world', as Arno Geiger puts it: 'Wir richteten uns in all den Erinnerungslücken, Wahnvorstellungen und Hilfskonstruktionen ein, mit denen sein Verstand sich gegen das Unverständliche und die Halluzinationen wappnete' [We accepted all the faulty memories, paranoia and workarounds with which his mind defended itself against the hallucinations and everything else it didn't understand].[44]

There is also a structural dimension. In the stories 'Sei versichert' ['Be assured'] and 'Weiche Wände' ['Soft Walls'], for example, Draesner reproduces the narrative framework of the *Decameron*: a closed society tells itself stories which are, literally, crucial to its survival. In each of the narratives 'Das Lächeln der Ehefrau' ['The Wife's Smile'] and 'Sommerfrische' ['Summer Resort'] there are two couples and new interlinked connections, a concept which appears to be related to Goethe's 1809 novel *Die Wahlverwandschaften* [*Elective Affinities*], the first novel in German literature to attempt to enact the transformation of scientific knowledge into an experimental narrative framework.

Kafka-Metamorphoses

This is most striking in a pair of stories that refer back to Kafka. The stories 'Das Denkmal der Läuferin' ['The Monument to the (female) Runner'] and 'Rosakäfer' ['Rose Beetle'] are clearly paired with each other. They allude to Kafka's 'Der Hungerkünstler' (1922) ['The Hunger Artist', 1938] and *Die Verwandlung* (1914) [*Metamorphosis*, 1933] respectively. The Kafka-connection is not based solely on the adaptation and bringing up-to-date of the original, the 'Muttertext' [mother text], as Draesner calls it. The idea is certainly not to use present-day knowledge to understand Kafka more critically than he could have understood himself. The question is how we can talk about what might be considered 'kafkaesque' cultural knowledge, because it faces the unfamiliar and unknown at the beginning of the shock of the modern. The absurd and the grotesque belong to this 'unknown knowledge' of the classical Modernist era. The difference in Draesner's narratives is that the media appear to be implicated in the way this knowledge is conveyed, no least as they scrutinize their own instruments. The way in which

44 Arno Geiger, *Der alte König in seinem Exil* (Munich: Hanser, 2011), p. 117; Arno Geiger, *The old King in his Exile*, trans. by Stefan Tobler (Sheffield: And Other Stories, 2017), p. 113.

the narrative reflects upon itself and the motif-cluster of camera, computer and screen belong to the referential framework of a poetics of knowledge.

The narrative of the 'Denkmal einer Läuferin' concerns a sporty 'Fräuleinwunder' [wonder woman].[45] The runner wants to push herself to such lengths that she can run first for twelve, then twenty-four hours, and finally a week, on a treadmill without stopping. This running programme is the grotesque climax of a sporting journey which begins with hiking, long-distance running, fitness trails and jogging, all the way to the ironman. In this way running becomes art, art becomes an object of knowledge, knowledge about running, however, becomes the subject of ironic observation.[46] The runner stages her run under the watchful eye of a camera in an open-topped cube, 'ein sieben Meter langer, 2,5 Meter hoher 3D-Bildschirm mitten im Park, gefüllt mit Luft und exakt einem Menschen' (p. 132) [a 7 metre long, 2.5 metre high 3D screen in the middle of the park, filled with air and exactly one person']. This attracts people to begin with but then after a while, no-one watches any longer. The camera woman and script intern from a regional television channel are the last people to catch a glimpse of the runner at the end. She crouches in her glass cage, just like Kafka's hunger artist, in the furthest corner of the cage, weak and huddled up into a ball. The cube is cleared out by '1-euro-jobbers' (those on state-sponsored work programmes), the treadmill is donated to a Fitness-studio. Even the 'kleine Ruine' (p. 137) [little ruin] on the internet doesn't last long.

Here Ulrike Draesner not only unpicks an obsession with sport but also the self-idolization of the media in a modern age which promotes its art for so long that it loses its audience. 'Alles lief, keiner sah zu' (p. 123) [Everything ran, no-one watched]: this unfortunate incident in the media-zoo results in art becoming invisible. The media can only make art visible for some of the time, and what they ultimately reveal is only their own ignorance, a beautiful illusion of meaning. On the last section of the runner's audio-file, where she claims to have completed her run, we hear just 'Stille und einmal etwas wie das Schnaufen eines Hundes' (p. 137) [silence and at one point something like the snuffling of a dog].

The end of the runner coincides with a media catastrophe. When the media fall silent, 'unknown non-knowledge' has won.

---

45 The term 'Fräuleinwunder' [literally: miracle of the miss], originally used to refer to young women in the immediate post-war period in the 1950s, was also used controversially to describe a group of young female authors by critic Volker Hage in 1999.
46 Cf. also writers' books on running: Matthias Politicky's reportage *42,195. Warum wir Marathon laufen und was wir dabei denken* (2015)[*Why we run the Marathon and what we think when we are doing it*] und Haruki Murakami's *What I Talk about when I Talk about Running* (2007).

This poetical insight on media and art is a result of Draesner's own dealings with new media. The results of her reflections become apparent in the re-design of her website in 2016/17.[47] Alongside the biographical and literary information on the author's homepage, there is a rich source of reflections on her poetic principles. Included here are aspects of her 'life-writing', from the creation of metaphors based on genetics, or a poetics based on space and body, to variations on non-biographical biography ('Love of Ghosts: On a polyglott Poetics', Academy Schloss Solitude lecture 2016), together with interdisciplinary, multi-media and trans-lingual projects. Back in 2002 she conceived what she called a *space poem* with Andreas Schmid, a 'walk-in poem' ('begehbares Gedicht') as an audio-visual installation, exhibited in the Goethe Institute of Calcutta and Hong Kong. Her collaboration with composer Annette Schlünz, *Fähren* [*Ferries*], a 'picture-text-sound-project' was shown on the Rhine ferries in Basel in June 2001. In June 2000 she took part in the project 'subib. Schrift in Bewegung /SMS-Aktion' [subib. Writing in movement /Text-happening] in Munich: ten authors could be contacted by mobile via text for four weeks, and they duly answered by text. For the Schwetzinger Festspiele (April 2017) she wrote the libretto for the musical theatre production *Tre Volti*, in which the original play by Torquato Tasso and Claudio Monteverdi is examined to expose the possibilities of love in times of war.[48]

Even the internet portal www.der-siebte-sprung.de, which Ulrike Draesner set up to accompany her novel *Sieben Sprünge vom Rand der Welt*, is a form based on a poetics of knowledge. The internet becomes a net which transports the novel but also connects it with other narratives of knowledge. Draesner's website documents the German and Polish sources for her novel, gives information about the genesis and evolution of the novel, which took ten years to complete and, under the rubric 'Selbst-Erzähltes' ['Told to one's Self'], the narrative space of the novel is opened out further. Important for the positioning of the novel within the field of memory-literature is the 'Lexikon der reisender Wörter' [dictionary of travelling words]. Neologisms such as 'Ankommstland' [arrived-land] and 'unwiedergutbar' [unatonable]; terminology like 'trans-generational' and 'postmemory', along with terms from the discourse on forced displacement like 'Kriegskind' [child of the war] and 'Ehre' [honour] are brought together here and explained. They are, as the author suggests following Wittgenstein, ladder-terms, which one can make use of in the creation of a new narrative order and then remove.

---

47 See for example the German-language homepage (www.draesner.de).
48 See the page on Draesner's website on musical theatre (http://www.draesner.de/musiktheater).

Narratives of Knowledge in 'Rosakäfer'

The closeness of Draesner's 'Rosakäfer' to Kafka's *Die Verwandlung* is apparent from the first sentence. Kafka's story famously begins 'Als Gregor Samsa eines Morgens aus unruhigen Träumen erwachte, fand er sich in seinem Bett zu einem ungeheuren Ungeziefer verwandelt' [When Gregor Samsa woke one morning from troubled dreams, he found himself transformed right there in his bed into some sort of monstrous insect].[49] Draesner begins her story 'Als Rosa Maregg am Morgen aus unruhigen Träumen erwachte, lag sie auf dem Rücken, fest in ihrem Bett, [. . .] Sie hob den Kopf und sah einen gewölbten braunen Bauch' (p. 217) [When Rosa Maregg woke one morning from troubled dreams, she was lying on her back, secure in her bed [. . .] She lifted her head and saw a brown dome-shaped belly].

Draesner's story, the longest in *Richtig liegen*, tells the tale of Rosa's extraordinary transformation into a pink beetle ('Rosakäfer'; a 'Rosenkäfer' is a flower or rose chafer) in the course of what might be termed three narratives of knowledge. The first relates the catastrophe of common knowledge. Amidst the family idyll the fantastical occurs in the most bizarre fashion. The family members react not with horror but, like Kafka's characters, with physical gestures of incomprehension, a far cry from angst-ridden Modernism. The Hindu-inspired mother, Claudia, gets on her knees, the father Thorsten shakes his head, only the fourteen-year-old brother finds something to say about the unexplained phenomenon: 'Rosa ist ein Käfer' (p. 220) [Rosa is a beetle]. This is reminiscent of the stark truth proclaimed by a child in Andersen's fairy tale *The Emperor's New Clothes* (1837), only that Rosa's beetle-dom here is neither a product of divine intervention nor a 'disguise' (p. 221). This known non-knowledge is only expressed in the pictures captured in invented words, from 'Tochterkäfer' (p. 229) [daughter beetle] to 'Tierin', (p. 235) [female animal], and the indefinite names given to the metamorphosed creature which range from 'Vieh' [brute] to 'monster' (p. 231).

In the second section, Draesner portrays Rosa's conversion to her insect milieu and the changes to family life. 'Rosakäfer' retains language and memory, but her/its psychic and sexual identity fall apart. Draesner allows the beetle to think with an internally focalized narrative voice, but it cannot speak in a way the others can understand due to its 'animal voice'. In a similar way to Kafka's *Verwandlung* the nuclear family, which until now has been dependent on Rosa's

---

49 Franz Kafka, 'Die Verwandlung', in *Erzählungen und andere ausgewählte Prosa*, ed. by Roger Hermes (Frankfurt a. M.: Fischer, 1991), pp. 96–161 (p. 96). Translation by Susan Bernofsky, *The Metamorphosis* (New York: W. W. Norton, 2014), p. 21.

business success, becomes 'freer' (p. 234), in particular the father, who engages once again in the speculative trading that had ruined him in the past. And the brother Reiner exploits the beetle at home for his blog 'Alle-lieben-Rosa' (p. 238) [Everyone loves Rosa] which very quickly receives an unimaginably high number of views (p. 241).

The third episode veers towards the grotesque in its criticism of both the media and science. Thanks to Reiner's idea, Rosakäfer appears in a talk show. A varnished and polished Rosakäfer appears before a TV audience which has nothing against the idea of beetles; but does not how to deal with an insect daughter. For this reason, the TV presenter agrees a two-fold wager with the family. A gene test should clarify whether the beetle truly belongs to the family and what its biological sex is. The result confirms that Rosa is a female beetle. The absent human in the insect is an affront in a digital age, where perception is wired in such a way that we are mostly 'blind to that which we don't expect'.[50] 'Ambivalence and ignorance' are therefore exposed as attendant conditions of scientific insight.[51] The audience members don't know what they are looking at. This is the reason they constantly want to see what they still don't know.

At the end of Draesner's beetle story, the media plays a role in the demise of unstable and artificial knowledge. In the attempt to find 'etwas Menschliches in dem Käfer' (p. 250) [something human in the beetle], by way of full-body x-rays and a heart autopsy, the object of their experimentation dies. The animal's body ends up stuffed and on display in a zoo. On the one hand, the vehicle can be considered here as an instrument of transformation, a kind of display window for a world-hungry audience, but on the other hand as a subject of metamorphosis. The 'Rosakäfer' on the internet and on TV acquires an auto-performative identity. No-one cares about the uncertainty of this, which exemplifies a form of unknown non-knowledge. 'Rosakäfer' is an anthropomorphic hybrid product of a media society. The death of 'Rosakäfer', an unspectacular end in the laboratory lacking any sense of tragedy, shifts a modernist narrative of knowledge into the digital age. 'Rosakäfer' is thus a 'dying medium', and this medium, according to the TV presenter, would do everything, 'um sein Ableben hinauszuzögern' (p. 250) [to prolong its dwindling life]. For the same reason, the runner carries on running without an

---

50 Frank Schirrmacher, *Payback. Warum wir im Informationszeitalter gezwungen sind zu tun, was wir nicht tun wollen, und wie wir die Kontrolle über unser Denken zurückgewinnen* (Munich: Blessing, 2009), pp. 173–182, illustrates this using the example of the Snellen eye-test – by turning the board round, those taking the test could see better without even realizing.

51 See also *Mitgift* and Ulrike Vedder, 'Ulrike Draesner. Mitgift', in *Literatur und Wissen. Ein interdisziplinäres Handbuch*, ed. by Roland Borgards, Harald Neumeyer, Nicolas Pethes and Yvonne Wübben (Stuttgart: Metzler, 2013), pp. 415–419 (p. 415).

audience; and this is also why the Mareggs make sure the beetle is kept in a manner more or less appropriate to its species.

Conclusion

It is clear that the knowledge of a given historical moment and the ways in which it imparts that knowledge to itself is key theme spanning much of Draesner's work across genres. This chapter has demonstrated that this complex is at the heart of her texts in a variety of ways: as an explicit thematic concern, within the architecture, the form; the fractured transmission of past texts and the transformation of traditional meaning into new poetic orders; increasingly in the self-reflection of a text on its own devices, e.g. enabling metaphors to convey knowledge and, most importantly, in the creative uses of a language which often seems to know more than it at first appears, or indeed itself knows. In her Frankfurt lectures *Grammatik der Gespenster*, she gives an example of this creative power of poetic knowledge. Ghostly is the origin of her last writing project too, one which deals with a British channel swimmer called Charles: 'Wie Charles mir einfiel? Ich weiß es nicht. Schöpfungsamnesie nennt sich das Phänomen' [How I came to invent Charles? I don't know. The phenomenon is called amnesia of creation].[52] Draesner tells a story of foiled expectations, of transformed knowledge (speaking, perceiving, feeling and remembering) under existential circumstances: '"The water is never what you expect" (ninth rule of the Channel Swimming Association)'.[53] This fascination with knowledge and unknowledge and especially the search for a poetics to do it justice, makes of Draesner an author very much of her and our moment: one who constantly challenges the narratives of knowledge upon which we build our understanding of the world.

---

52 Ulrike Draesner, *Grammatik der Gespenster. Frankfurter Poetikvorlesungen* (Stuttgart: Reclam, 2018), p. 22. Cf. Ulrike Draesner, *Kanalschwimmer. Novelle* (Hamburg: mare, 2019).
53 Draesner, *Grammatik*, p. 34.

Tobias Döring
German Is a Foreign Anguish.
Draesner and the Sprite of Translation

In 2014 Ulrike Draesner published a poem entitled 'remembering, will', part of a collection of poetic tributes to William Shakespeare on the occasion of his 450th anniversary.[1] Draesner's contribution is a spirited engagement with *A Midsummer Night's Dream* and its fairy-forest world of erotic fantasies, delusions and confusions, a puckish piece that plays on the pitfalls of vision and cognition. Above all, it plays on the pitfalls of language. As an epigraph, it gives a gloss on the English word *sprite*, derived from Latin *spiritus*, meaning 'fairy', 'imp' or 'goblin' but also, and nowadays more commonly, used to designate a soft-drink, a motorcycle or a computer operating system. Draesner's list does not in fact exhaust the meanings of this word, which could also refer to a large electrical discharge, a female ferret, a certain genus of butterfly, a melon, a two-dimensional pre-rendered figure in computer graphics, and much else besides.[2] With regard to Draesner's poem (in whose actual text, interestingly, *sprite* does not even occur), the word points to Puck, Shakespeare's trickster and metatheatrical manager – but the word does not work like a proper reference that gives to airy nothing a local habitation and name, but rather as a verbal act that recalls this figure's central function: not fixation, but vexation. With its various semantic options, which slide and slip into each other – suggesting the slips and transformations Puck performs in Shakespeare's play – *sprite* frustrates any desire for well-defined and well-behaved lexical elements and so may serve as a reminder that our language, in general, is often quite a messy medium that rarely offers orderly and simple designations.

In an essay on *Midsummer Night's Dream*, published a year earlier, Draesner focusses on the 'extrem leichten, dabei mächtigen Stoff, den man Sprache nennt' [airy yet mighty substance we call language] and discusses the transformative force in and of language that this comedy invites us to consider.[3] 'Thou art translated' is the crucial phrase uttered here in horror at Bottom's beastly metamorphosis as well as in honour of the power that has brought about this

---

1 Ulrike Draesner, 'remembering, will', in *Wie Er uns gefällt. Gedichte an und auf Shakespeare*, ed. by Tobias Döring (Zurich: Manesse, 2014), pp. 110–111.
2 The list is from the Wikipedia entry (https://en.wikipedia.org/wiki/Sprite).
3 Ulrike Draesner, 'Thou art translated', afterword to William Shakespeare, *Sommernachtstraum*, trans. by Maik Hamburger (Stuttgart: Reclam, 2013), p. 87.

https://doi.org/10.1515/9783110495942-010

change: 'Shakespeares Originalwort ist eigentümlich und wichtig, weil es ihm gelingt, einen körperlichen und einen sprachlichen Vorgang miteinander zu koppeln' [Shakespeare's verbal choice is peculiar and important because it manages to combine bodily events with language events].[4] That is to say, Bottom's ass-head makes the verbal act of translation physically manifest on stage – just as the word *sprite* manifests the puckish language puzzles that continue to evade firm grasp.

Sprite, therefore, seems an apt term for this chapter – a guiding spirit, as it were – to examine Draesner's English language inspirations. There is no shortage of examples. Many of her texts, in whatever form or genre, amply testify to English presences or traces, sometimes openly acknowledged, sometimes covertly addressed, but often recognizable and always constitutive for her writing. Above all, this holds for her translations, i.e. the German versions of poets like William Shakespeare, Gertrude Stein, H.D. or Louise Glück that she has produced. Following Puck's programme, we can certainly assume that these translations are not occasional work but are of principal importance for what we might call Draesner's polyglot poetics. Trying in this paper to contribute to an understanding of the working principles that fundamentally inform her texts, I shall look at the frequent transactions between English and German which do not just take place in translations per se but, crucially, in a far wider range of her poetry and prose. For the purposes of analysis, my sample is necessarily limited, drawing mainly on 'Twin Spin' (2000), her 'radical translation' of seventeen Shakespeare sonnets, the recent poetry collection *subsong* (2014), some earlier poems and some examples from the novels *Mitgift* (2002), *Spiele* (2005) and *Sieben Sprünge vom Rand der Welt* (2014). But the issues I hope to address are quite fundamental. They concern key questions about Draesner's craft and self-positioning as a writer, along with our self-positioning as readers: from what linguistic vantage point should we approach a poem like, for instance, 'brach, my branch in the sky' ['broke, my branch in the sky']⁵ or a word like 'zungenverschlag'⁶ or even titles like 'Twin Spin' or *Mitgift*? What vantage points might language generally proffer to position ourselves in cultural, not to mention national, frames? What in particular are proper grounds for designating Draesner as a 'German' writer, and what do we mean by it? Does our language, and does *her* literary language, articulate any longing for belonging?

---

4 Ibid., p. 92.
5 Ulrike Draesner, *subsong* (Munich: Luchterhand, 2014), p. 219.
6 Ulrike Draesner, *für die nacht geheuerte zellen* (Munich: Luchterhand, 2001), p. 12. The title is a play on 'Zungenschlag' [manner of speaking] and 'Verschlag' [shed].

I shall argue that it is the *sprite* of translation that both prompts these questions and problematizes their answers, complicating any simple notions of language, origin and transfer. With this word, learned from Draesner's poem, I am trying to circumvent the more conventional and pompous way of speaking about the *spirit* of translation, or *Geist der Übersetzung*, most recently revived in a 2015 volume paying homage to Martin Luther and his verbal power, significantly entitled *Denn wir haben deutsch* [*For we have German*].[7] It is precisely this notion, cited from Luther, of 'having' German, that is of having command and control and authority over, let alone possession of, the language that Draesner's work undermines. Even and indeed especially for German native speakers (whatever *this* conventional phrase might mean), her English engagements lead us to face not the familiar, but the foreign aspects in and of 'our own' language – or rather, even more radically, to face the foreignness at the heart of all language, a trait that emerges as soon as we stop taking words or verbal acts for granted. This is what my chapter seeks to do. Thus, looking at Draesner's English inspirations is not really concerned with issues of influence – how specific writers and their works may have been instrumental for her conception of certain plots or figures, such as transsexual narratives like Virginia Woolf's *Orlando* or Yann Martel's *Self* for *Mitgift*[8] or Woolf's Lily-figure from *To the Lighthouse* for the protagonist of this name in *Sieben Sprünge*. Instead, my aim is to analyse the canny, often also uncanny presences of English in her German texts, turning these texts into haunted sites that question the very categorization and separate givenness of one linguistic code in opposition to another. As her translations blur the boundary between source and target language by working towards mutual transformations, so her polylingual poetry and prose emphasize the continuing migrancy, if not essential homelessness, of words.

Sprite is an immediate case in point, for as an English term derived from Latin, via Anglo-Norman and Old French, its etymology tells us a story of long-term contact, travel and specific cultural transactions. Not even Latin can provide a stable point of origin because, as we learn from the *OED*, the 'earlier English uses of the word are mainly derived from passages in the Vulgate, in which *spiritus* is employed to render Greek πνεῦμα (pneuma, n.) and Hebrew rūaḥ. The translation of these words by *spirit* (or one of its variant forms) is common to all

---

7 *Denn wir haben deutsch. Luthers Sprache aus dem Geist der Übersetzung*, ed. by Marie Luise Knott, Thomas Brovot and Ulrich Blumenbach (Berlin: Matthes & Seitz, 2015).

8 Cf. Nadyne Stritzke, *Subversive literarische Performativität. Die narrative Inszenierung von Geschlechtsidentitäten in englisch- und deutschsprachigen Gegenwartsromanen* (Trier: Wissenschaftlicher Verlag, 2011).

versions of the Bible from Wycliffe onwards'. Translatedness, then, is a condition long inherent in this word. But even a simple Germanic word like *will*, in the title of the poem cited at the outset, does not just leave readers to question where in its broad semantic spectrum we place any of its actual uses, but also which language we actually count it as: English or German? Both are possible. In this way, I argue, Draesner's acts of translation prompt us to rethink the premises and possibilities of language.

Traditionally, debates on translation emphasize one of two options for the translator, as formulated by Friedrich Schleiermacher: a domesticating or a foreignizing method. The translator can either bring the foreign language home so as to appropriate it fully in and by the target language or he/she allows this target language itself to change, powerfully moved by the otherness encountered, so as to become estranged and different in the process. The latter is what Schleiermacher clearly favours, as does Walter Benjamin when he cites Pannwitz and his famous claim that translators proceed from a mistaken premise when they try 'to turn Hindi, Greek or English into German instead of turning German into Hindi, Greek, English'.[9] From this perspective we might see that the sprite of translation in Draesner's work offers yet a third or hybrid option, prefigured perhaps by Bottom in *Midsummer Night's Dream*. For significantly, even after his 'assification', Bottom is still recognizable (or else his colleagues could not have panicked as they do), because his 'translation' proceeds only in parts, with the various human or beastly elements remaining side by side, mutually estranging. It may well be precisely such partiality or incongruity that make him such a monster – and a model for translations which do not erase but stage their point of origin in their own procedures.

Against this background, I shall first collect and present some translational evidence, mainly from Draesner's poetry, before in the second part speculating about the potency and relevance of such language transfers and transactions, with reference also to her fiction. In the third part I shall venture towards some conclusions, drawing on a poem by Marlene Nourbese Philip, 'Discourse on the logic of language', from which I have borrowed and adapted my title.

---

9 Walter Benjamin, *Selected Writings, Volume 1: 1913–1926*, ed. by Marcus Bullock and Michael W. Jennings (Cambridge, MA: Belknap Press, 1996), pp. 261–2.

Poetic Evidence

The final Shakespeare sonnet of the sequence Draesner translated for 'Twin Spin' is number 147, addressed to the so-called Dark Lady. The opening of the English version, as printed in the volume, reads:

> My love is a fever, longing still
> For that which longer nurseth the disease[10]

The repetition of the morpheme *long*, placed in close proximity and forming part of two quite different yet related words – *longing/longer* – is, rhetorically speaking, a *figura etymologica* and an example of what Peter Waterhouse in the same volume describes as Shakespeare's strategy of internal translation, finding or forging connections between words and sounds even if their sense is not strictly connected.[11] As Waterhouse argues with great subtlety, these are poetic ways of foregrounding the language of making through a remaking of language. Draesner's German version of the sonnet opens:

> der liebesfilm, in dem ich schwimme, ist ein fieber,
> das begehrt, was den verfall fiebrig fördert[12]

> [the love film in which I swim is a fever
> that desires what feverishly incites decay]

Her radical translation, we note, also makes use of repeated structures, especially the alliterated /f/-sounds and two forms of the English-German cognate 'fever'/ 'Fieber'. We mainly note, however, that she uses the idiom of filming and so introduces a startlingly strange, consciously anachronistic register into Shakespeare's discourse of renaissance love sickness. These glaring lexical disparities, for which the sequence 'Twin Spin' has rightly become famous, are so prominent that they distract attention from inconspicuous but no less relevant textual changes, such as the strong equation made here between 'liebesfilm' and 'fieber' – so strong, indeed, that even the English version seems to be affected.

---

10 Ulrike Draesner, 'Twin Spin. Sonette von Shakespeare', in Ulrike Draesner, Barbara Köhler and Peter Waterhouse, *:to change the subject* (Göttingen: Wallstein, 2000), pp. 11–29 (p. 29).
11 Peter Waterhouse, 'Die Übersetzung der Worte in Sprache', in *:to change the subject*, pp. 5–7.
12 Draesner, 'Twin Spin', p. 29.

The opening of Shakespeare's sonnet actually reads:

My love is *as* a fever, longing still [emphasis added][13]

suggesting a comparison between *love* and *fever*, openly signalled with the little word *as* that is missing in 'Twin Spin' and thus also missing a beat in the original iambic pattern. Instead of Shakespeare's simile we find Draesner's equation, or identification, of the two elements, in this way rendering their verbal juxtaposition even more noticeable, more marked, remarkable, disparate in fact. In 'Das fiktive Alphabet' ['The fictive Alphabet'], her 2001 Berne lecture on the use of letters in the work of literary authors in contrast to genetic scientists, Draesner highlighted the particle *as* (*wie*) and its importance in constructing semblance.[14] This *as* is curiously lost in Draesner's translation of number 147 and, significantly I think, *also* lost in her English, nominally *un*translated version of that sonnet. What does this suggest?

No doubt, we might just see it as a minor misprint, to be corrected in the next edition.[15] But in a work the author herself describes as a '*will-ful* misunderstanding' of the canonical poems – with all the semantic richness the word 'will' accrues in Shakespeare's sonnets – such a misprint seems too meaningful, too 'will-full' as it were, to count as an error.[16] Or rather, errors, misprints, misunderstandings, mistranslations and misfits are the very stuff this text is made of, its productive principle and rationale – just as potential misreadings of the genetic code, replicated with each cell division, introduce variability in populations and so produce the possibility for evolutionary change. Replication never being perfect, mistakes literally make sense and meaning.

---

13 William Shakespeare, *Shakespeare's Sonnets*, ed. by Katherine Duncan Jones (London: Methuen, 2010), p. 411.

14 Ulrike Draesner, 'Das fiktive Alphabet – Spekulationen ins Unsichtbare', in *Der hippokratische Eid und die heutige Medizin*, ed. by Brigitte Ausfeld-Hafter (Bern: Peter Lang, 2003), pp. 59–72: 'Das Arbeitsgebiet von Autoren war und ist: aus Schrift – aus einem menschlichen Code – Figuren entstehen zu lassen *wie* lebendig. Während die Genetiker für sich sagen würden: aus einem Code Figuren entstehen zu lassen, lebendig. Um dieses wie – seine Existenz, sein Fehlen – also wird es im folgenden gehen' [An author's domain was and is: to conjure up – out of writing, a human code – figures *as* living beings. Whereas geneticists would say in their way: to conjure up living figures from a code. The following will concern itself therefore with this 'as', its existence and its absence].

15 Indeed, in the most recent publication of Draesner's sonnet versions, *THYMINE*, the opening line of number 147 appears the same as in Shakespeare: see William Shakespeare, Ulrike Draesner, Tom Cheesman and Olive Ond, *THYMINE. 17 Sonnets x 4*, Boiled String Poetry Chapbooks #7 (Swansea: Hafan Books, 2013), no pagination.

16 Ulrike Draesner, 'Dolly and Will', in Ulrike Draesner, Barbara Köhler and Peter Waterhouse, *: to change the subject*, pp. 30–33 (p. 32).

In this sense, we could see the seventeen double sonnets of this bilingual sequence as twinned texts, composed of both German and English elements and so negotiating tensions between, just as among, the various verbal elements and their glaring disparities. Standard critical readings of 'Twin Spin', for instance by Anna Alissa Ertel or Theresia Prammer, routinely emphasize the disturbing prominence of contemporary scientific vocabulary purportedly so out of place in classical love sonnets.[17] But such readings underestimate the daring lexical experiments and bold conceits we surely find in much renaissance sonneteering. I rather think that Draesner's sonnets are even more disturbing in advertising the vagaries of the vocabulary they employ, which open interlingual rifts and ruses we have not yet confronted. For instance, to juxtapose and translate 'fair' with 'hell' [bright or light] (sonnet 1), 'tyrants' with 'transplanteure' [transplanters] (sonnet 5), 'self-will'd' with 'einzel-willig' [a neologism, approximately single-minded] (sonnet 6), 'print' with 'klon' [clone] (sonnet 11), 'date' [relating to time] with 'dattel' [date, the fruit] (sonnet 18) or 'muse' with 'inventio' (sonnet 38) are mistranslations from a rhetorical repertoire that includes polysemy, homophony, homonymy, *figura etymologica*, polyptoton and folk etymology, all manifesting deep uncertainty in the precise possibilities of verbal signification. Taking hold of the wrong end of words, 'standing them on their heads': this is how Draesner in the afterword describes her own procedure.[18] Its main power, however, lies in making us realize how many different meanings words might have, how many turns they can take and how many ends there are to get hold of – so that, eventually, we can no longer be quite sure where heads or feet might be.

---

17 In a strange mixture of medical and military language, Ertel speaks of 'Twin Spin' as a text 'in which Draesner subjects a selection of Shakespeare's sonnets to radical rejuvenation treatment, by arming these texts from the classical canon with gene technology and bringing them into the present day with the help of language enriched by scientific vocabulary', Anna Alissa Ertel, *Körper, Gehirne, Gene. Lyrik und Naturwissenschaft bei Ulrike Draesner und Durs Grünbein* (Berlin: de Gruyter, 2011), p. 37. Prammer, even more strangely, argues: 'Thus the cloned consciousness as an imaginary construct enters into poetic writing by means of these texts' – as if the awareness of cloning were the same as a cloned consciousness, Theresia Prammer, *Übersetzen, Überschreiben, Einverleiben. Verlaufsformen poetischer Rede* (Vienna: Klever, 2009), p. 268.
18 Draesner, 'Dolly und Will', p. 32. 'Meine Radikalübersetzungen drehen Shakespeares Worte um, fassen sie bewusst an den "falschen", nämlich nicht-kanonisierten Enden ihrer Polysemantizität, stellen sie von den Füßen auf den Kopf' [My radical translations turn Shakespeare's words around, deliberately picking up on the wrong (i.e. non-canonical) ends of their polysemanticity, standing them on their heads].

This, in effect, turns the interlingual practice of translation into a practice used to explore intralingual ruptures. And this, I suggest, is a major function of the English presences in Draesner's polyglot texts: to defamiliarize conventional uses and notions of language.

Shakespeare's sonnets are the literary text most frequently translated into German, often with a deliberate agenda to exemplify or prove a particular poetic programme.[19] I propose that Draesner's radical translations follow this agenda and so stand for fundamental principles pertaining also to her wider work. Foreign-language elements are clearly prominent in much of her poetry. The volume *berührte orte* (2008) even includes a glossary: Arabic, Spanish, Finnish, Danish, French and other foreign words are duly explained and translated but *not*, significantly, any of the English phrases that also feature in the book. Perhaps English is just too familiar a language to need explanation but, then, such notions of familiarity are surely also at stake, as a glance at some of her other work will presently suggest. So we should rather say perhaps that the foreignness of English is a special case, from *gedächtnisschleifen* to *subsong*, because its otherness has long become globalized and almost assimilated into the textures of everyday German. Draesner's texts face and retrace such assumptions, instead of taking them for granted. As in the English-German spins of 'Twin Spin', she often deliberately seeks out seductions of semblance as if to test whether they are trustworthy or treacherous.

Take *Heimliche Deutung* (2006), for instance: why does she not render the title of H.D.'s posthumous volume *Hermetic Definition* with the cognate and quite common German terms 'Hermetische Definition'? Again, she clearly takes the English words at unexpected ends, in this case suggesting that the close resemblance between 'Hermetic' and 'Hermetisch' or 'Definition' and 'Definition' – a homograph in English and German – is all the more reason for caution; nor would she take the classical, Greek or Latin, origin of both words as a guarantee of shared semantics. In fact, she treats these words as if they were false friends, so-called *faux amis*, looking or sounding similar but significantly differing in meaning – as when, for example, 'fields' is understood as 'Filz' [felt], rendering 'Strawberry Fields Forever' as 'Strohbeerfilz, für immer' [straw berry felt, for ever].[20] With this example, then, we enter the polyglot space of the most recent poetry collection *subsong* (2014).

19 Cf. Werner von Koppenfels, '"dressing old words new": William Shakespeare's Sonnets into German', in *William Shakespeare's Sonnets. For the First Time Globally Reprinted. A Quatercentenary Anthology 1609–2009*, ed. by Manfred Pfister and Jürgen Gutsch (Dozwil: Edition SIGNAThUR, 2009), pp. 277–285.
20 Draesner, *subsong*, pp. 168–69.

Taking an English term as its title, the volume as a whole explores the pleasures and pitfalls of language-learning, including the parental roles – from being a mother to having a mother – which this process involves. Negotiations with language, and especially a foreign language, are foregrounded in many of its texts, from the 'vocabulary training' in part one, via the Beatles rewritings just cited to the bilingual negotiations of 'brach, my branch in the sky' (pp. 219–24) in the final section. The latter is an erotic, metapoetic text with Shakespearean overtones – the recurrent contemplation on *palm* echoes the so-called 'pilgrimage-scene' from *Romeo and Juliet* (I.5) – and strong engagement in German-English assonances like 'dabbelju' suggesting 'double-you'[21] or 'tuching, touching' suggesting clothedness and nakedness,[22] as if such verbal couples were a mode of sexual coupling in a literal, not linguistic, understanding of the term *intercourse*:

> in tides: unforgettable
> of branches bra in palm
> palpable palm
> i
> /ch
> hätte das nie
> auf deutsch so erlebt[23]

> [in tides: unforgettable
> of branches bra in palm
> palpable palm
> I
> /I
> would never have
> experienced it like that in german]

Here, English is identified as a precondition of experience and, we surmise, of its particular poetic rendering in two languages at once, like breast in bra in palm. The pleasures of diglossia are also central in a programmatic poem entitled 'üb'ersetzung' ['tr'anslation'],[24] playing on the notion of translation as transfer (combined with the suggestion of training, *üb* as the imperative of *üben*) and on Greek myths like Hero and Leander or Zeus and Europa. Its central focus on 'oil' ('nun strahlt die erde / wider von öl' [now the earth radiates / with the reflection of oil][25]) recalls the formula about the 'self-referential oil of

---

21 Ibid., p. 220.
22 Ibid., p. 221.
23 Ibid., p. 220.
24 Ibid., pp. 48–49.
25 Ibid., p. 49.

language' from sonnet 1 in 'Twin Spin' ('mit dem selbst / referentiellen öl der sprache' [with the self / referential oil of language]).[26] It is at points like these where Draesner's poetry pays tribute to the sprite of translation.

Self-referentiality, as a foregrounding of English-German language transfers, is also a central device in the mistranslated versions of the Beatles songs, surely the most popular part of the volume and singled out in all reviews. Their strategy of mishearing, partially understanding and so misconstruing English words in German texts – 'In the town where I was born' becomes 'In den Au'n, wo ich war Sporn' [literally: In the meadows where I was sporn][27] – follows a rhetorical figure known as paronomasia where similarities of sound suggest equivalence of sense, without however proper grounds. Puttenham called paronomasia the 'Nicknamer' and described it as a 'figure by which ye play with a couple of words or names much resembling' where 'the one seems to answer th'other by manner of illusion, and doth, as it were, nick him'.[28] By such acts of verbal nicking, or necking, Draesner's Beatles-sub-songs form a counterpart to 'Twin Spin', again offering a bilingual text, again working with the tensions that arise from the two languages and from the apparent transfer errors between them, and again drawing on the canonical status of the source texts, i.e. their prominence in cultural memory. In her note to the poems, she says they reflect her own attempt as an eleven-year-old to figure out the foreign songs: 'Mein Gehirn baute sich die Songtexte mithilfe seines begrenzten englischen und deutsch–bayerischen Vokabulars zusammen, hemmungslos semantisch' [my brain constructed the song lyrics by means of its limited English and German-Bavarian vocabulary, in an unrestrainedly semantic way].[29] Just as Simone says in *Sieben Sprünge*, 'Unser Gehirn ist verbindungssüchtig' [our brain is hooked on connections], always producing links in a compulsive effort to make sense.[30]

What compulsion is at work in such bilingual transactions may best be illustrated with reference to a celebrated Freudian case. In his 1927 essay on fetishism, Freud mentions a young man who had 'exalted' a certain sort of 'Glanz auf der Nase', or shine on the nose 'into a fetishistic precondition'; the 'surprising explanation' was that the phrase 'had to be understood in English, not German':

---

26 Draesner, 'Twin Spin', p. 13.
27 Draesner, *subsong*, pp. 150–151.
28 George Puttenham, *The Art of English Poesie*, ed. by Edward Arber (London: Murray, 1896), p. 212.
29 Draesner, *subsong*, p. 228.
30 Draesner, *Sieben Sprünge vom Rand der Welt* (Munich: Luchterhand, 2014), p. 243.

the *Glanz auf der Nase* 'was in reality a *"glance at the nose"*'.[31] The patient had his formative linguistic input as a child from an English nursery – *Kinderstube*, in Freud's term – before coming to Germany and learning German; so English structures and lexical items continued to operate in his verbal performance. The German 'Glanz' provides a cover for the English 'glance' that underlies it and deflects its actual meaning into the phonetically similar but semantically different word of another language. *Glanz* and *glance*, then, are precisely such a paronomastic pair as 'down' and 'daunen' [down feathers], or 'hung' and 'Hang' [slope], in the first stanza of Draesner's 'Strawberry Fields': anglo-German doubles or false friends across accepted codes.[32] It seems as if these subsongs profit from the language learner's limits by turning language itself into a fetish, a potent medium of desire, exalting its capacity for unexpected shifts. How should we interpret them?

Arguably, English even plays a crucial role in Draesner's poems when no actual English words appear on the surface. The title of her first collection, *gedächtnisschleifen* (1995), is a case in point: an unusual compound noun, not otherwise attested in the language, so probably a neologism coined for this particular volume and its title poem. Yet the German word no longer looks quite so strange if we read it as the literal translation of an English compound that may underwrite it: *memory loop* is a technical but clearly lexicalized term[33] which might form its basis. In this perspective, Draesner's title turns into a calque, a special kind of borrowing and relexification.[34] As it happens, her poem 'nachkriegsmensch'[35] ['postwar person'], in which the word occurs, draws a sharply focussed portrait of West German society in the 1950s or 60s between economic miracle and repressing the past, where all existence seems to build on borrowed terms. The German coinage therefore aptly sounds as if the current idiom still

---

31 Sigmund Freud, 'Fetishism', in *The Complete Psychological Works of Sigmund Freud*, trans. by James Strachey, vol. XXI (London: Hogarth, 1964), p. 152.

32 Draesner, *subsong*, p. 169. 'Lass mich dich daunen, / kosend geh ich auf Strohbeerfilz. / Wirklich ist nichts, / und nichts auf Hang gebaut. Strohbeerfilz, für immer' [approximately: Let me down you, / cosset going to straw berry felt. / Real is nothing, / and nothing is built on a hill. Straw berry felt, forever].

33 A 1991 paper in an engineering journal offers evidence: Wen-Chun Chena and Yan-Pei Wua, 'A phase corrector for digital frequency memory loop and digital radio frequency memory', *Journal of the Chinese Institute of Engineers*, 15.6 (1992), 673–683.

34 See Jean-Paul Vinay and Jean Darbelnet, 'A Methodology for Translation', trans. by Juan C. Sager and M.-J. Hamel, in *The Translation Studies Reader*, ed. by Lawrence Venuti (New York and London: Routledge, 2004), pp. 128–137 (p. 129).

35 Ulrike Draesner, *gedächtnisschleifen* (Frankfurt a. M.: Suhrkamp, 1995), p. 9.

recalls another latent language, like a substrate, onto which it has been grafted and of which it whispers secretly. The same holds true for a word like 'Sekret' [secretion] that recurs at various points in the debut volume (pp. 19, 21), e.g. in the combination 'geheime Sekrete' [literally: secret secretions],[36] as if to insist on its English false friend *secret*. All these examples serve to show how given boundaries between the different languages are no longer quite clear: the sprite of translation confuses conventional codes.

Bilingual German-English poetry is not, of course, a recent nor original development. Earlier canonical examples include, for instance, T.S. Eliot's *The Waste Land*, whose famous opening stanza involves code-switching to German and merits reconsideration in our context:

> APRIL is the cruellest month, breeding
> Lilacs out of the dead land, mixing
> Memory and desire, stirring
> Dull roots with spring rain.
> Winter kept us warm, covering
> Earth in forgetful snow, feeding
> A little life with dried tubers.
> Summer surprised us, coming over the Starnbergersee
> With a shower of rain; we stopped in the colonnade,
> And went on in sunlight, into the Hofgarten,
> And drank coffee, and talked for an hour.
> Bin gar keine Russin, stamm' aus Litauen, echt deutsch.
> And when we were children, staying at the archduke's,
> My cousin's, he took me out on a sled,
> And I was frightened. He said, Marie,
> Marie, hold on tight. And down we went.
> In the mountains, there you feel free.
> I read, much of the night, and go south in the winter.[37]

We may be too familiar with these lines – and their intriguing intertextual echoes from Chaucer via Brooke to Marie Larisch[38] – to raise a simple point about them: if the German statement in verse 12 is to count as direct speech, someone making her claim of belonging, where exactly does this speaker begin and end

---

36 Ibid., p. 19.

37 T.S. Eliot, *The Waste Land. A Facsimile and Transcript of the Original Draft*, ed. by Valerie Eliot (Orlando: Harcourt, 1971), p. 135.

38 See B.C. Southam, *A Student's Guide to the Selected Poems of T.S. Eliot* (London: Faber, 1987), p. 86–88.

her statement?[39] While we may wonder what could make a Lithuanian 'genuinely German', it seems quite clear that her speech is cited as a distinct presence in the poem, marked by the code-switch. Line 12 sounds like a foreign-language fragment, a genuine record of another voice, quite possibly part of the coffee conversation in the Munich Hofgarten. But there is little to suggest that this voice should only speak this single line. In fact, the conjunction 'And' at the start of the next line (and again, two lines down) strongly suggests that the speaker continues, describing scenes from her childhood. If so, why does the rest of her speech continue in English – has she switched back or does she now appear translated? It is even possible, taking the pronouns *we* (l. 13) and *us* (l. 8) as co-referential, to conjecture that the same speaker already begins as early as line 8 (and so includes the two earlier anaphoric uses of 'And'). That is to say, if Eliot's poem stages a verbal exchange involving different languages and different voices, the number of speakers is not necessarily the same as the number of linguistic codes. Therefore, in Robert Stockhammer's apt phrase, the poem must answer for its language form alone, without recourse to an external communicative situation.[40] Polylinguality transects polyvocality, without representing given codes.

Such verbal transections and transactions are, I argue, also at work in Draesner's texts. The German-English predicaments explored in her translations like 'Twin Spin', in her subsongs like 'Gelbe Suppmarie' [literally: yellow soup Marie; the transliteration of yellow submarine], in her love songs like 'brach, my branch in the sky', or even in calques like her *gedächtnisschleifen*, all stage the power of diglossia as a way to question the claims of belonging which are commonly made and marked through language – especially through notions like maternal language, or mother tongue, that receive the greatest credit when imagining our cultural or national communities. So when Freud speaks of his patient's *Kinderstube* [childhood room], or when the Beatles sing of 'the town where I was born', or when Eliot's Lithuanian makes her pledge of allegiance, in each case we are given to assume a language haven, a snug linguistic childhood space, a place of nativity and cultural at-home-ness from which all subsequent developments or Babylonian confusions proceed. And yet I would like to show in my second part how this nativity of language is put into doubt through Draesner's polyglot poetics, making us wonder what may ever be *echt deutsch*.

---

39 I owe this point, and much of the following discussion, to Robert Stockhammer. Cf. Robert Stockhammer, 'Das Schon-Übersetzte. Auch eine Theorie der Weltliteratur', *Poetica*, 41 (2009), 275–277.
40 Ibid., p. 277.

Political Relevance

In her 2001 volume *für die nacht geheuerte zellen*, Draesner includes a poem whose opening reads like an echo of *The Waste Land*, or rather, which follows Eliot's strategy of obsessive echoing, mixing memory with forgetful allusion. It is entitled 'london, spring' and begins:

> soma-
> ma-matische träume: ich seh dich,
> springvoll die themse, in london
> vor 100 jahren in london dich
> tulpen kaufen gehn zwei lippen
> in der station spielt jemand tuba, tube,
> wie sie sich biegen, die verschleierte frau,
> ihr stummer begleiter, die schwanenhälse
> (geschlossene tulpen) seh dich sie sehen
> zwei weiße lippen: heftiger spring.[41]

> [soma-
> ma-matic dreams: I see you,
> full of springs the thames, in london
> 100 years ago in london see you
> going to buy tulips two lips
> in the station someone is playing tuba, tube,
> how they curve, the veiled woman,
> her silent companion, the swan necks
> (closed tulips) see you seeing them
> two white lips: violent spring]

Elements recalling Eliot's text, apart from the title reference to his 'unreal city', include the Thames, perhaps the pun on *tuba, tube* in memory of Eliot's 'dried tubers', and certainly the repeated references to *spring*, evoking the seasonal setting of Eliot's opening. But *spring* precisely is the stumbling block when reading Draesner's text: how are we meant to understand it? What language does the word belong to, English or German? And how do we even pronounce it? While *springen* is a common German verb that might appear to be referenced in the poem's title, by the end of the first stanza we must say that a strange collocation like 'heftiger spring' only makes sense if we interpret it as the season *Frühling*. So, for some unexplained reason, the German term slides into English, as if *The Waste Land*'s slippery polylingual form is reformulated here to produce cross-linguistic hybrids or hermaphrodites like 'springvoll'. Indeed,

---

41 Draesner, *für die nacht geheuerte zellen*, p. 20.

the context of sexual and gender crossings, so prominently staged in the novel *Mitgift*, seems most appropriate to explore the translational dynamics at work in Draesner's literary language.

In this novel, Anita's beautiful but monstrous, because sexually doubled,[42] body not confined to a single sex, can be read as a model for the lexically doubled shape of words that bear the marks of two languages, not confining themselves to a single idiom. Words like *spring*, or *will*, or indeed *Gift* and *Mitgift*, as discussed by the novel's protagonists themselves, are false friends whose common origin in some Germanic root first promises yet finally betrays their loyalties to a shared meaning.[43] If Hermaphroditos, son of Hermes and Aphrodite, as Aloe learns in her Latin study,[44] became fused with the nymph whose love he scorned, he also functions as a metalingual figure for language items fused with others, unseparated words, by which we may well learn a different language than the one of our *Kinderstube*, not national or native, but ambivalent and ambidextrous. This language is, at bottom, Draesner's working idiom, her literary and poetic substance right from *gedächtnisschleifen* and its 'Hermaphroditisches Proëm' ['Hermaphrodite Proëm'],[45] a language that incorporates conventional linguistic difference, fuses and confuses codes while dramatizing verbal unbelonging. Its significance emerges when we follow Aloe's reflections on the force of words and realize that 'Wörter leiten Taten nicht ein, sondern waren Taten' [words didn't just initiate deeds, they *were* deeds] – a realization of the performative power of words to make a difference, to change, reform, reformulate, not just describe, the world.[46]

Above all, such speech acts are significant when words make worldly claims, as in the case of *Heimat*, an extremely resonant and rich but in contemporary German also loaded and disputed word, often associated with revisionary politics. It is this keyword *Heimat*, only partially translatable as English *home* or *homeland*, that is tested and contested in so much of Draesner's fiction, and it is in these negotiations with the aftermaths of twentieth-century German history, I suspect, where the programmatic point of her polylingual policy must lie.

'Dieser Begriff, der hängt mir wirklich zum Hals raus' [I'm sick and tired of this term], Holger says in *Mitgift*, arguing that *Heimat* 'ist doch etwas, was es immer erst hinterher gibt, immer nur in der Vergangenheit' [is something which

---

42 Draesner, *Mitgift*, p. 229.
43 Ibid., p. 46.
44 Ibid., p. 226.
45 Draesner, *gedächtnisschleifen*, p. 38.
46 Draesner, *Mitgift*, p. 294.

always comes after the fact, is only ever real in the past].[47] His sentiments recur in several of Draesner's novels, some of them like *Sieben Sprünge* exploring in their plot the predicaments of displacement and resettlement through family histories and memories. Whether in the case of Hannes, Lilly and their postwar fate as refugees or in the case of Boris, Halka and their repatriation to a new 'post-German' fatherland, this novel stages many modes of home-seeking, home-making and home-remaking, often oscillating between homing and haunting – 'heimgeholt' and 'heimgesucht', in Halka's terms[48] – to stake out present possibilities of *Heimat*. And this novel crucially combines the search for home with the same tactics of polylingual creativity which we observed in Draesner's poetry, including German-English passages (pp. 47, 214, 383); assonances and the meaningfulness of mistaken pronunciation like 'souls', 'Sauls', 'Sauseelen' [sow souls], 'Schweinehundseelen' [seal souls];[49] or the emphasis on invented paronomastic pairs like 'Wehrpass'/'Wehpass' [draft book/book of sorrows],[50] all in line with the waywardness of words that do not subject meaning to a single reference or a single language. On the website that accompanies and complements the novel, Draesner offers a whole 'lexicon' of what she calls 'travelling words', a list of lexical items that shuttle between languages, as she says, between experience and reflection, between then and now.[51] Her list includes the paronomasia *Wehpass*, as just noted in the novel, but also wider cross-linguistic transformations and translations such as *Spree*, the Berlin river (recalling also, we note, our keyword *sprite*), whose Slavic-German-English inflections she traces in connection to her family history. In this way, the peregrination of words both intensifies and invalidates a prevailing sense of *Heimat*, because their ongoing movement motivates the search for a point of departure without the chance ever to return to stable origins. Thus *Heimat*, as an untiring and untried feeling of belonging traditionally enacted in a language understood as 'mine', is literally displaced.

In *Spiele*, the word itself is critically dissected. Katja's family at one point launches into a well-informed discussion of its etymology,[52] from Middle High German *heimôti* via Luther's translation of Genesis 24.7 where *Heimat* is introduced into the modern lexicon, significantly, through a context of diaspora,

47 Ibid., p. 101..
48 Ulrike Draesner, *Sieben Sprünge*, p. 486. The pun in the two words literalizes the ambivalence: 'taken or called home' and 'persecuted'.
49 Ibid., p. 365.
50 Ibid., p. 327.
51 Ulrike Draesner, 'Lexikon der reisenden Wörter' (http://www.der-siebte-sprung.de/category/lexikon-der-reisenden-woerter/).
52 Ulrike Draesner, *Spiele* (Munich: Luchterhand, 2005), p. 125.

privation, memory and loss,[53] to our present-day use of the word, leading in the novel to a paronomastic play on its sound, associating it with 'courage', *Mut*, and playful yodelling: 'Heimat, heimôdili, dideldidü'.[54] This is the background against which we read the various interlingual negotiations that the narrative stages with Katja's Californian cousins and their Americanized German: 'Heimlisch',[55] Ricky says and makes Katja laugh at this mispronounced blend of *himmlisch* and *heimlich*, i.e. 'heavenly' and 'clandestine, or canny', but also crucially involving *heimisch*, i.e. 'homelike', 'local', 'native' or 'domestic' – which is, as Edgar insists, the main point.[56] The pun is repeated and later extended to include also *unheimlich*, 'uncanny',[57] as part of the continuous critique and questioning of *Heimat* – 'als starre und stumme Beschreibung von Hoffnung, als hoffnungsloser Sinn' [as a numb and dumb description of hope, this hopeless sense] – which *Spiele* undertakes throughout.[58] Again, these questions climax in highlighting the fate of travelling words – or should we better say, of homeless words – like *chance* or *fortune*[59] which neither show a clear way of belonging to a single language – German? English? French? – nor keep a single sense across the various languages they may be part of, false friends and treacherous translators of fixed meanings.

Like several of her other works, Draesner's *Spiele* draws a portrait of West German society, a generation after World War II, where the presence of American English in particular appears as a consequence of political *Westbindung*, or bonding with the West, which the country had been at such pains to construct since the 1950s. Yet the cross-language transactions, including mistakes, misunderstandings and mispronunciations, also function to produce a prevailing sense of foreignness among the younger generation, in contrast to their grandparents' notion of home, with the American cousins as living proof, just like the elephants Edgar admires,[60] that rehoming is possible, indeed quite common and pervasive. The diaspora of language loosens given ties and one-to-one relations between a place, a culture and a speaker. As in the poetry examples we

---

53 As Isaac is about to marry Rebecca, his father Abraham speaks to him: 'Der Herr, der Gott des Himmels, der mich von meines Vaters Hause genommen hat und von meiner Heimat' (1 Moses 24.7); in the King James Bible, the verse reads: 'The LORD God of heaven, which took me from my father's house, and from the land of my kindred'.
54 Draesner, *Spiele*, p. 125.
55 Ibid., p. 49.
56 Ibid.
57 Ibid., p. 71.
58 Ibid., p. 241.
59 Ibid., p. 393.
60 Ibid., p. 54.

considered, then, Draesner's narratives engage the sprite of translation so as to resist, rewrite, redress or reconsider familiar notions of singleness, stability and exclusivity. Instead, her polylingual strategies like her plots all articulate a verbal brokenness and ongoing translatedness of being. What may follow from all this?

Consequences are potentially wide-ranging. Yet the main point is an active, provocative and probing inquiry into the supposed naturalness of language, especially the German language, as an idiom of nativity on the basis of which a community of so-called native speakers like to imagine their togetherness. When the ideology of *Heimat* meets the ideology of native language, we confront the notion of the mother tongue as a primary, steadfast, unbroken and unbreakable bond of self-experience, often emphatically appealed to in diasporic situations. Debates about it, intersecting with debates on nationality, are far too vast and complex to allow for survey here.[61] Suffice it therefore simply to mention Hannah Arendt's argument in her 1964 interview with Günter Gaus, that during exile it was language, her German mother tongue that sustained her – a powerful and moving statement.[62] Its underlying language concept, nevertheless, provokes critique and reconsideration, as in Derrida's engagement with her view[63] or in Bonfiglio's study on the cultural invention of the native speaker. As Bonfiglio argues, images of maternality have functioned since the Middle Ages as a major conduit for the enracination, or rootedness, of a championed national language: 'From the late medieval *materna locutio* to permutations of the modern *Muttersprache*, the image of the connection between mother and child has forged one of the

---

61 For pertinent contributions see for instance Florian Coulmas, 'Muttersprache – auf Gedeih und Verderb?', *Merkur*, 49.551 (1995), 120–130; Jürgen Trabant, 'Fremdheit der Sprache', in *Was heißt hier fremd? Studien zu Sprache und Fremdheit*, ed. by Dirk Naguschewski and Jürgen Trabant (Berlin: Akademieverlag, 1997), pp. 93–114. For a broad discussion of the historical development of the concept and its political uses see Thomas Paul Bonfiglio, *Mother Tongues and Nation. The Invention of the Native Speaker* (New York: de Gruyter Mouton, 2010). For prominent positions in the mid-twentieth-century debate, see Leo Weisgerber, *Die Entdeckung der Muttersprache im europäischen Denken* (Lüneburg: Heliand, 1948); Leo Spitzer 'Muttersprache und Muttererziehung', in *Essays in Historical Semantics* (New York: Vanni, 1948), pp. 15–65. For critical engagements with the consequences in literary studies, see *Exophonie. Anders-Sprachigkeit (in) der Literatur*, ed. by Susan Arndt, Dirk Naguschewski and Robert Stockhammer (Berlin: Kadmos, 2007).
62 Available on YouTube (https://www.youtube.com/watch?v=dsoImQfVsO4). The German transcript of the interview, entitled 'Was bleibt? Es bleibt die Muttersprache', is published in Günter Gaus, *Was bleibt, sind Fragen. Die klassischen Interviews* (Berlin: Das neue Berlin, 2001).
63 See Jacques Derrida, *Monolingualism of the Other, or, The Prothesis of Origin*, trans. by Patrick Mensah (Stanford: Stanford UP, 1998).

most powerful icons in the protectionist, isolationist, and ethnocentric configuration of the sovereignty of the national language', an association that persists to the present day.[64]

That connections between mothering and language acquisition or language use are in fact contingent, culturally constructed and historically changeable, *not* naturally given, is especially pertinent to note in Germany where the ideology of mother tongue has long had a strong and problematic impact – as evidenced, for instance, by Leo Weisgerber and his influential work. Weisgerber, a linguist who actively collaborated with Nazi institutions but continued his career in postwar Germany, claimed an inherent and necessary connection between nationalities and language communities which are to be kept pure, distinct and unpolluted – a lesson he drew from what he in 1948 referred to as the 'exaggerations and amalgamations' of the last hundred years.[65] Language communities, to him, are communities in spirit and fate, based on ancestry and racial heritage. The fact that humanity appears structured in such language communities, he argues, is reason enough to structure and keep nations accordingly. Language thus becomes configured in what Bonfiglio calls 'the discourse of the ethnic and corporeal ownership of national identity and local organic nature'.[66] In such an essentialized view, the notion of mother tongue directly sponsors a politics of segregation.

To counteract this view, Draesner's work calls on the sprite of translation. Instead of building *Heimat* in and of language, she traces the travels, travails and transformations of words; instead of supposedly unmixed, pure and natural language, she uses openly artificial, transposed and transgressive terms; instead of following notions of nativity and mother tongue, she produces the multilingual mixtures of her literary idiom: *faux amis*, paronomastic pairs and other meaningful monsters. This leads us as readers to rethink common assumptions. If 'names are arrests', as a poem from *für die nacht geheuerte zellen* paronomanistically suggests ('namen sind festnahmen'),[67] then false friends turn into true friends and our points of reference and orientation change. In

---

64 Bonfiglio, *Mother Tongues and Nation*, p. 185.
65 Weisgerber, *Die Entdeckung der Muttersprache im europäischen Denken*, p. 127. 'It cannot be denied that *matters of the mind, state and economy* are linked to one another by a multitude of threads. But one must first observe the border between these realms, and recognize their fundamental independence, before one can devise permanent solutions to the benefit of all. This is the lesson that can be drawn from the exaggerations and amalgamations of the last hundred years – 2. The rationale for these borders lies in the fact that *the conduct of 'nationalities' must remain true to the principle of the division of humanity into language communities*' (emphasis in the original).
66 Bonfiglio, *Mother Tongues and Nation*, p. 222.
67 Draesner, *für die nacht geheuerte zellen*, p. 75.

this way, we are forcibly challenged to reconsider the verbal world in which we find ourselves without actually finding our bearings – a world, as *subsong* says, 'where you cannot find yourself / to right':[68] yet another translingual twist that transgresses the integrity of given linguistic codes. Draesner's polyglot poetics reorients the cardinal points of our language.

There is one particularly powerful and programmatic poem from her recent work in which we can trace this process. It is a long poem that dramatizes and commemorates the poet's own process of language acquisition and, consequently, her current relationship to language. For whatever else the great elegy 'sub mère détachée'[69] may also do, it certainly stages, in the ongoing search for a workable language of mourning, the predicaments of mothering and mother tongue:

> (cannot shed tears)
> und doch: ohne alter
>
> hat sie mir eine säule
> quecksilber unter die zunge
> geklebt so dass sie in mir
> ihre eigenen fieber
>
> messen kann
>
> mutter, der sprache ich
> von lippen und augen las
> mein hab und gut
> von ihr[70]
>
> [(cannot shed tears)
> and yet: beyond age
>
> she stuck a column
> of mercury under
> my tongue so that in me
> she could measure
>
> her own fever
>
> mother, from whose lips and eyes
> I read language
> my one and only
> from her]

68 Draesner, *subsong*, p. 219.
69 Ibid., pp. 192–214.
70 Ibid., p. 206.

Without venturing into a reading of this complex text, we may note how the paradox of language – the element of our self-experience and self-understanding, almost corporeally present, which nevertheless is always other, outside, absent, strange and principally preceding ourselves – is brilliantly captured in the image of the fever that both is, and is not, her own. Against the background of sonnet 147, as discussed earlier, *fieber* also reads as a figure of love, here maternal love involving power, measuring, control. And we note, again, the bracketed presence of another language, emphatically not the mother tongue, with the English fragment *cannot shed tears*, whose meaning however proves unstable. For in the logic of Draesner's protean-polyglot idiom, *shed* slides into its homonym, the noun designating a small wooden hut, in German known as a *Verschlag*, thus offering an unexpected – and possibly quite unaccountable yet irrepressible – link to Draesner's 'zungenverschlag':[71] the mark and makeshift of her own poetic tongue.

It is this foreignness of latent language that eventually enables her to launch the work of mourning:

in anderen sprachen
nichtmuttersprachen fällt
sie mir leichter
ein: noms names

mère, ma belle[72]

[in other tongues
notmothertongues she
comes
to me more
easily: noms names

mère, ma belle]

In the way of classic elegies, which, according to Peter Sacks, move from loss to consolation by deflecting desire and creating tropes as a symbolic substitute for our loved and lost one, these lines move into other languages as a workable way to capture, keep and contemplate the mother's memory precisely in nonmother tongues.[73] Only as other can the mother be mourned, a transformed presence in a language translated. Therefore, Draesner's writing makes neither home nor

---

71 Draesner, *für die nacht geheuerte zellen*, p. 12.
72 Draesner, *subsong*, p. 197.
73 Peter Sacks, *The English Elegy. Studies in the Genre from Spenser to Yeats* (Baltimore: Johns Hopkins UP, 1985), p. 7.

room for consolation. The only chance to find ourselves 'to right' must lie in facing strangeness. My final section will try, by way of a conclusion, to do so.

Conclusion

In a celebrated poem first published in 1989, the Canadian-African-Trinidadian writer Marlene Nourbese Philip staged the predicament of language between motherness and otherness, unbelonging and belonging, the familiar and the foreign. Its opening stanza reads:

> English
> is my mother tongue.
> A mother tongue is not
> not a foreign lan lan lang
> language
> l/anguish
> anguish
>   – a foreign anguish.[74]

It is this poem, and the central paronomasia *language/anguish* on which it turns, from which I have taken the inspiration and the title for my reading of Ulrike Draesner's work. True, Philip's textual collage mainly speaks to the contemporary linguistic heritage of African slavery and New World experience, issues utterly different from our present context. Without therefore attempting to appropriate the specific postcolonial histories Philip poetically retraces, I do indeed propose to see the language issues articulated here as ways also to understand the translational strategies and translingual tensions identified in Draesner's texts. From a very different cultural and political position, but perhaps in a shared concern with the productivity of alienated, homeless, vagrant, variegated words, Draesner performs on and performs with the German language and so does for Standard German much the same as postcolonial writers do for Standard English: othering, estranging, foreignizing and disturbing any unselfconscious sense of verbal home. This is, at any rate, what her choice of themes and modes and diction does: working toward wariness when it comes to cherished German myths of *Muttersprache*, *Heimat* and belonging. Against their claims, and the political calamities that often follow, she activates the sprite of translation.

---

74 Marlene Nourbese Philip, *she tries her tongue, her silence softly breaks* (London: Women's Press, 1993), p. 30.

Such turns are relevant, not least, for her radical translation of the sonnets, in particular the so-called procreation sonnets which open Shakespeare's sequence (sonnets 1 to 17) and which, as a consequence of earlier German interpretations, hold dire resonances for Draesner's take on reproductive technologies, as seemingly implied in Shakespeare's text:[75]

From fairest creatures we desire increase (sonnet 1, opening)

In the echo chamber of twentieth-century German history, a line like this recalls racist anthropology and the eugenic campaigns of the 1930s, when Shakespeare's procreation sonnets were indeed interpreted as evidence that Shakespeare would approve of Nazi practice to ensure 'pure' human breeding. At the Weimar Shakespeare conference in 1936, for instance, Hans Günther, who held a Chair of Racial Science (*Rassekunde*) and was a board member of the Deutsche Shakespeare Gesellschaft [German Shakespeare Society], gave a lecture in which he cited the sonnets as evidence for Shakespeare's view that only the fairest and fittest should produce offspring in order to improve the quality of the race.[76] Draesner's use of stem cell biology as a lexical register for her version of the sonnets runs the risk of recalling such notorious German Shakespeare readings. Yet it is precisely the impurity of her literary language, its hybrid or hermaphrodite translatedness, that sends a message of mutual foreignizing to all readers and undermines the ideology of pure descent. Thus, bold engagement with cloning as an alternative to sexual reproduction in 'Twin Spin' can be seen to redress racist legacies by reinterpreting its premise through contemporary science just as through polyglot poetic language.

English holds a special place in Draesner's foreign language repertoire, as my readings have shown, because it has a crucial function in making and marking the strangeness of language, as if to say: German, thou art translated! In Puttenham's terminology, English operates in Draesner's work as an active force of

---

75 See the remarks in my article '"On the wrong track to ourselves": Armin Senser's Shakespeare and the issue of artistic creativity in contemporary German poetry', *Shakespeare Survey*, 66 (2013), 145–154 (p. 152), from which this paragraph derives.

76 His reference was to sonnets 11 and 12: 'Such passages provide ample evidence that Shakespeare may also be cited in questions of racial improvement. For him too, it was a precondition of the preservation and improvement of the value of a *Volk* [people or race] that the congenitally sound should bear multiple children, while the congenitally unsound should remain childless', Hans F.K. Günther, 'Shakespeares Mädchen und Frauen', *Shakespeare Jahrbuch*, 73 (1937), 85–108 (p. 88). For a discussion of the intellectual and institutional context, see Ruth Freifrau von Ledebur, *Der Mythos vom deutschen Shakespeare. Die deutsche Shakespeare-Gesellschaft zwischen Politik und Wissenschaft, 1918–1945* (Cologne: Böhlau, 2002), pp. 201–4.

nicknaming or misnaming familiar German words, slightly but effectively shifting their established basis. In her essay 'Atem, Puls und Bahn' ['Breath, Pulse and Track'] Draesner tells us that she began producing poetry while staying in Oxford in the early 1980s, as if her immersion in a foreign-language context were the occasion, perhaps the condition, of her writing.[77] In her essay 'Zehren' ['Consume'] she declares her mother tongue to be a mixture of repressed Bavarian, dying Silesian and Standard German.[78] Coming home from England, however, she realized it had changed: the once familiar language now looked strange and it looked back at her, with a fine fissure, without identity of origin and rootedness. As she puts it, underneath the first language network she now felt a second language net at work. She began to write.[79] Writing, then, for her proceeds from the same position in a polylingual palimpsest as for someone who exchanges *glance* for *Glanz*. For Draesner, to be sure, the change is not compulsory but wilful. But the effect remains the same. For when verbal signifiers enter such a chain of exchanges and become nicknames in poetic play, language forms a fetish whose pleasure precisely derives from the foreign elements that cannot simply be accommodated and semantically subsumed. Their resistant productivity unfolds as German turns into a foreign anguish or, to cite the term from *Sieben Sprünge*, into post-German, 'postdeutsch',[80] a language discursively displacing some of the patterns on which it is grammatically founded.

This, I take it, is the language of Draesner's poetry and prose. This is what the sprite of her continuous translation has achieved. And this is what we as readers must eventually face: the impact and impertinence of unruly diglossia – not an easy but a necessary task. A workable German translation for *impertinence* is 'Zumutung', derived from 'Mut', i.e. 'audacity' or 'courage', which,

---

77 Ulrike Draesner, 'Atem, Puls und Bahn. Das Denken des Körpers im Zustand der Sprache', *Lettre International*, 44 (1999), 62–67.

78 Ulrike Draesner, *Zauber im Zoo. Vier Reden von Herkunft und Literatur* (Göttingen: Wallstein, 2007).

79 Ibid., p. 79. 'Ich kehrte 1984 in meine Muttersprache zurück, dieses hybride Gemisch aus unterdrücktem Bairisch, wegsterbendem Schlesisch und Hochdeutsch. Es hatte sich durch mein englisches Jahr verändert – schaute fremd auf mich zurück. Da saß, nach dem Studium in Oxford, ein kleiner feiner Spalt. Nichtidentität der Herkunft, des Verwachsenseins. Dem ersten Raster bzw. Sprachnetz hatte sich ein zweites als Schatten unterlegt. Ich fing zu schreiben an' [In 1984 I returned to my mother-tongue, this hybrid mixture of supressed Bavarian, dying Silesian and high German. It had changed during my year in England – looked back at me in a different way. There was after the time studying in Oxford a tiny, fine crack. Nonidentity of origin, of having grown together. A second net of language had overlaid the first. I started to write.]

80 Draesner, *Sieben Sprünge vom Rand der Welt*, p. 486.

according to the popular etymology played out in *Spiele*, lies also at the base of German *Heimat*.[81] It seems highly fitting therefore, that *sprite* once also formed a verb: its sense, now obsolete but still active in Shakespeare's time, was 'to inspire with courage'. In this sense, we can truly say, by way of a conclusion, that Draesner's work *sprites us* to come to terms with German as a foreign anguish.

---

81 Draesner, *Spiele*, p. 125.

Mary Cosgrove
Ode to the Secret Atomic Flow of the World. *Mein Hiddensee*

Mein Hiddensee, Ulrike Draesner's prose account of a sojourn on the Baltic island Hiddensee in summer 2013, is a rich, multi-layered engagement with undulations of landscape, self, language, memory and history.[1] My title describes *Mein Hiddensee* as an ode, which, while it recognizes Draesner's prowess as a poet, here more fundamentally aims to capture the highly lyrical quality of the inventive language that dominates in the text – a quality that is lost in the publisher mare verlag's description of *Mein Hiddensee* as a 'Sachbuch' [a factual book]. The latter term certainly pays tribute to the wealth of detailed geological, botanical, meteorological, geographical and historical information about the island the text contains. It also underlines its place within mare verlag's 'Meine Insel' [my island] series, a rather cultured literary travel-writing series which commissions particular authors to feature islands as far flung as Venice, Cape Cod, Ireland, Mallorca and Sylt, and which counts amongst its contributors writers such as Hans-Ulrich Treichel, Claudia Rusch, Fritz J. Raddatz and Uwe Kolbe.[2] Yet the term 'Sachbuch' does not do justice to *Mein Hiddensee*'s poetic quality and joyous tenor, not to mention its autobiographical tendencies (on which more below). 'Ode' instead endeavours to convey the 'intensity' – to use one of Draesner's terms – of the engagement of the nameless third-person

---

1 Ulrike Draesner, *Mein Hiddensee* (Hamburg: mare, 2015). All subsequent references given in main text.
2 In an email on 11 January 2017 the publisher confirmed that they usually commission contributions to the series, also pointing out that they are open to suggestions from authors. In this instance, mare verlag approached Draesner. For an overview of the series see the publisher's website (http://www.mare.de/index.php?article_id=3809&setCookie=1). This tendency towards travel writing can also be observed in Draesner's reflections during her time in the UK as Writer in Residence at New College, Oxford in 2015–2016. See, for example, 'Eine Schule fürs Zusammenleben', *Die Zeit*, 14 January 2016 (http://www.zeit.de/freitext/2016/01/14/schule-england-regeln-integration-draesner/). In November 2016 Draesner's contribution to a Suhrkamp Insel travel series by the name of 'Lieblingsorte' [favourite places] that focuses on beautiful cities such as Rome, Barcelona and Vienna was published. Ulrike Draesner, *London. Lieblingsorte* (Frankfurt a. M.: Insel, 2016). Excerpts from this more conventional travel text can be accessed on the publisher's website (http://www.suhrkamp.de/lieblingsort_london_1371.html).

https://doi.org/10.1515/9783110495942-011

subject, the 'sie' [she], with the island that inspires her to articulate in poetic prose an impression of its primordial energies as she encounters them.

This articulation is an act of translation; in Draesner's vision, the poet-writer is a kind of magician-fabricator who through creative translation of the subject's encounter with the surrounding environment gives voice to the opaque but palpable minutiae of lived experience. The writer's task is to 'fabricate' intensity, not to represent it mimetically, rather to 'translate' fleeting subjective perceptions of vivid sensory experience into poetic language. *Mein Hiddensee* is thus written in a lyrical style that dynamically communicates – as opposed to mimetically represents – mesmerizing instances of an unstable self who strains to express the unseen and the unsaid as she repeatedly traverses a dynamically shifting terrain.[3] As part of this lyrical endeavour, for example, the 'sie' frequently omits the active verb from sentences, shifting focus away from herself towards the sublime treasure that is the island: 'Silbrig aus der Ferne schimmerndes Laub' (p. 155) [silvery foliage shimmering from afar] or 'Dunkelrote Beeren an einem Busch mit rundlichen check bemehlten Blättern' (p. 196) [dark red berries on a bush with roundish, finely powdered leaves]. This elliptical style foregrounds both the ethereal and earthy beauty of the island, underscoring the transitoriness of each razor-sharp impression of the external world as it issues forth from the perceiving 'sie', even as she attempts to preserve this beauty in language. It also points to the equally transitory 'sie', who in the closing pages reflects in the same elliptical style: 'Ihr Leben: eine geschenkte Spur [. . .], Spielfeld von Geschehnissen und Erfahrungen' (pp. 196–97) [her life: a trail gifted to her [. . .], a playing field of events and experiences]. *Mein Hiddensee* is as much an ode to lyrical language in prose form as it is to the island.

Formally a sort of 'patchwork', Draesner's term for the heterogeneous quality of literary writing, *Mein Hiddensee* is a hybrid of travelogue, diary, memoir and poet's workbook.[4] It comprises fifty-three short chapters, preceded by an untitled tableau that captures the moment of arrival on the island. Seven of the chapters carry the title '100-Wörter-Bild' [100-words-image]. Mostly, these short texts compress into an intense synchronic moment the narrator's fleeting sensory impressions of the horizon, the island's different grasses, or its beaches (p. 20, p. 95). The other chapters feature reflections on topics as varied as the

---

3 See Ulrike Draesner, *Zauber im Zoo. Vier Reden von Herkunft und Literatur* (Göttingen: Wallstein, 2007), respectively pp. 83–86, p. 106. On her view of the distant yet close connections between writing poetry and writing prose, see Ulrike Draesner and Jan Wagner, 'Über Stockung und Stein. Ein Gespräch', in *Ulrike Draesner*, ed. by Susanna Brogi, Anna Ertel and Evi Zemanek (Munich: Text + Kritik, 2014), pp. 4–18 (pp. 6–7, pp. 16–17).
4 Draesner, *Zauber im Zoo*, p. 32.

narrator's child, Baltic geology, the family dog, the elements, language and the body, and personal memories of a past relationship. Yet more chapters are factual in style, reproducing documents from the region's archives that variously present records of Stasi interrogation, drownings and shipwrecks in nearby waters, accidental deaths and suicides on the island itself.

Draesner's preoccupation with the island here and in the earlier poetic cycle *mittwinter* [*midwinter*, 2006] renders her part of a literary tradition that accords the small Baltic island special status.[5] Referring in *Mein Hiddensee* to the island's history both as place of retreat and thematic subject for writers and thinkers, she commemorates the famous intellectual figures who began to stay there from the late-nineteenth century on, as it became known as a holiday destination. Carl Zuckmayer, Asta Nielsen (star of early silent films) and her companion, the poet Joachim Ringelnatz, Gerhart Hauptmann and Günter Grass, amongst many others, have paid tribute in letters, diaries and poems to Hiddensee's inspiring natural beauty.[6] Equally significant is the island's geographical position seemingly on the very edge of the world. Lutz Seiler's novel *Kruso* (2014), set on Hiddensee in the momentous summer of 1989, poetically exploits the island's liminal position in order to express trance-like, threshold states of suspension between different worlds.[7] Draesner's text continues this fascination with the island's magical qualities. In tandem with the uncertain generic 'patchwork' status of the text itself, her exploration of physical, spatial and linguistic threshold states is central to *Mein Hiddensee*, as the discussion below will show.

Mein Hiddensee is written in the third person, which suggests a modification of the lyrical subject, elsewhere described by Draesner as a perceiving instance that records impressions but that offers up no biographical information about herself.[8] The subject's reflections on her child, to whom the book is dedicated, and former partner, her own family history of expulsion and her holidays on the island since 1997 indicate a close relationship between protagonist,

---

5 Ulrike Draesner, *mittwinter. Gedichtzyklus* (Witzwort: Quetsche, 2006).

6 See *Hiddensee. Ein Lesebuch*, ed. by Renate Seydel (Berlin: Ullstein, 2004) which contains excerpts on the island by Hauptmann, Zuckmayer, Nielsen and Ringelnatz. For Grass's Hiddensee poems see *Hiddensee. Geschichten von Land und Leuten*, ed. by Renate Seydel (Berlin: Ullstein, 2005), pp. 588–90.

7 Lutz Seiler, *Kruso* (Frankfurt a. M.: Suhrkamp, 2014).

8 See Rolf-Bernhard Essig, 'Bewegung in Sprache. Gespräch mit Ulrike Draesner', *neue deutsche literatur*, 51 (2003), 42–61, (p. 50). See also Draesner's essay on Gottfried Benn, 'Kleines Gespenst. Gedanken zum lyrischen Ich', in *Ich bin nicht innerlich. Annäherungen an Gottfried Benn*, ed. by Jan Bürger (Stuttgart: Klett-Cotta, 2003), pp. 9–30.

author and narrator.[9] Indeed, compared with some of Draesner's more overtly fictional texts, such as *Mitgift* (2002), which explores pathologies of the human body in the context of family secrets, and *Vorliebe* (2010), which profiles the complexities of romantic love, *Mein Hiddensee* appears to some degree to move towards autobiography.[10] This development is echoed in other publications, such as the essay 'Das Kind mit den nichtgrünen Augen' ['The Child whose Eyes are not Green'], which appeared in early 2016 alongside other essays by contemporary German writers in a collection that critically considers those questions of origins, identity and racism so urgently posed by the refugee crisis which resulted in large numbers of migrants arriving in Germany during a concentrated time period in 2015–2016. As the mother of a child with not-green eyes and '[n]on-white' skin, Draesner, in a personal manner that is also political, reflects on the increasingly hostile treatment and problematic construction of the 'Other' by states and individuals.[11] While *Mein Hiddensee* too contains autobiographical elements, it is more fundamentally channelled through a poetic subject whose ode in prose form does not emerge from her inner-life or biography alone. In keeping with the threshold motif, this subject is articulated as the porous yet vigorous site of the intersection of bodily impulses and external stimuli.[12] Only thus does biography enter the scene, as one unstable, fleeting element amongst many others, a trail in the sand that was gifted to the 'sie'. In comparison with 'Das Kind mit den nichtgrünen Augen', which profiles and critiques growing hostility, *Mein Hiddensee* offers an alternative template for the consideration of difference beyond fear: one that emphasizes empathy and the connections between self and Other. The outcome is an image of selfhood that resonates with the text's dynamic renderings of landscape, sea and elements, driving home Draesner's view that the self may only emerge as a self in the context of an 'Other' to which it cannot but be open.[13] The

---

9 For example, the subject refers to Draesner's novel, *Sieben Sprünge vom Rand der Welt* (Munich: Luchterhand, 2014), which deals with her family history of expulsion from Silesia during the Second World War. *Mein Hiddensee*, p. 152.

10 Ulrike Draesner, *Mitgift* (Munich: Luchterhand, 2002); *Vorliebe* (Munich: Luchterhand, 2010).

11 Ulrike Draesner, 'Das Kind mit den nichtgrünen Augen', in *Wie wir leben wollen. Texte für Solidarität und Freiheit*, ed. by Matthias Jügler (Frankfurt a. M.: Suhrkamp, 2016), pp. 9–19 (p. 17).

12 See Christian Schlösser, 'Gespräch mit Ulrike Draesner', *Deutsche Bücher*, 35 (2005), 269–87 (p. 271).

13 See, for example, *Zauber im Zoo*, p. 31. Here Draesner refers to Gilles Deleuze in order to describe the 'Ich' as a dancing particle in the light that owes its sense of its own existence to the murmurings of others. The idea of an inner life is thus a construct; in this vein, her aim as a writer is to explore the interconnections between inside and outside that comprise the 'Ich' [I] beyond notions of a rooted identity.

child describes this fundamental interdependence when she innocently says: 'Ohne Meer wäre die Insel nicht da' [without the sea, the island would not be there, p. 66].

Draesner's radiant rendering of the sheer primordial movement of matter, energy and life itself as a communicative process between a self and a greater entity – be that nature, community or 'Other' – sets *Mein Hiddensee* somewhat apart from other recent and contemporary writing about former East German terrains.[14] Narratives such as Monika Maron's *Endmoränen* (2002) [*End Moraines*], Jenny Erpenbeck's 2007 *Heimsuchung* [*Visitation*, 2010] and Julia Schoch's *Mit der Geschwindigkeit des Sommers* (2009) [*With the Speed of Summer*] present the landscapes of the east overwhelmingly as sites of loss, melancholy and destruction. Nature in these texts reflects a mood of depression, the sense that the post-*Wende*, east German (feminine) self is as archaic as the ancient landscape that oppresses this self. Images of glacial formations imperceptibly shifting beneath the human subject in *Endmoränen* and *Heimsuchung*, or indeed of fecund foliage reclaiming former east German military outposts in *Mit der Geschwindigkeit des Sommers*, present nature as a phenomenon fatalistically indifferent to the human subject, who, battered and bruised also by historical events, can do little more than concede to the power of these greater forces. Self-assertion only comes belatedly – in *Ach Glück* (2007) [*O Fortune*], the sequel to *Endmoränen*, for example, Maron's ageing protagonist does find agency through travel – or in a disastrous form, as the central event of suicide in *Mit der Geschwindigkeit des Sommers* and the permanent loss of the family home in *Heimsuchung* suggest.[15]

Mein Hiddensee, by contrast, presents a very different understanding of self and nature, which in its broadest sense stands for the ethical relationship between self and Other. This could be described in terms of the self's knowing physical embeddedness in, and existential dependence on, the shifting environment through which she moves, and which simultaneously moves and shapes her. She is not a contemplative subject at a safe remove from the environment she surveys; rather, she is in it and of it, affected by it and vulnerable to it: 'Die

---

14 On the theme of encounters with an Other in Draesner's poetic work, see Karen Leeder, '"Übungen der Zugewandtheit": Ulrike Draesner's Poetics of Correspondence', in *Schaltstelle. Neue deutsche Lyrik im Dialog*, ed. by Karen Leeder (Amsterdam: Rodopi, 2007), pp. 231–62.

15 Monika Maron, *Endmoränen* (Frankfurt a. M.: Fischer, 2002); *Ach Glück* (Frankfurt a. M.: Fischer, 2007); Jenny Erpenbeck, *Heimsuchung* (Frankfurt a. M.: Eichborn, 2008); Julia Schoch, *Mit der Geschwindigkeit des Sommers* (Munich: Piper, 2009). For more on this theme, see Mary Cosgrove, '*Heimat* as Non-Place and *Terrain Vague* in Jenny Erpenbeck's *Heimsuchung* and Julia Schoch's *Mit der Geschwindigkeit des Sommers*', *New German Critique*, 116 (Summer 2012), 63–86.

Welt klafft auseinander, Aufruhr, sie selbst mitten darin' [the world gapes open, uproar, herself in the midst of it, p. 42]. Contemplation, reflection and articulation, all of which presuppose distance between self and Other, paradoxically take place within and through these dynamic circumstances; indeed, the constant atomic flow of earthly matter is the fundamental condition of self and world. Language, thought, knowledge and self can only emerge in and through matter's ceaseless fleetingness. The self is, moreover, an unstable point of observation; her gaze flutters as she tries to make out the contours of a moving landscape (p. 54). The relationship between self and Other is thus a reciprocal two-way exchange of energies, to which the self is joyously and riskily open. In this vein, *Mein Hiddensee* frames even traumatic history – which features regularly in the text – through a poetic register of life, movement and energy that differs considerably from the more mournful tone of works framed by historical and personal loss. It is apt, then, that the subject, from her perspective as a former West German citizen who is also the descendant of Silesian expellees, casts her discovery of the island in 1997 as a 'Wendegewinn' (p. 108) [a gain from the fall of the Wall].[16] Consistent with this optimistic tone, the work, for all its empathetic attention to personal and historical loss, closes with a sustained reflection on the nature of happiness, which is connected to a paradoxical rootedness in transience: the embodied here and now that constantly changes.

This chapter explores Draesner's depiction of a self which is always in the process of becoming while seeking to articulate that which is instinctively sensed but as yet unknown in any rational way. Central to this complex somatic-linguistic endeavour is the strange entity of the island itself. It oscillates between constancy and ephemerality; it is something that endures, small and easy to perceive on one level – the 'sie' often describes a panorama of the island that can be viewed on a clear day from the island's highest point (pp. 23–24, p. 54, p. 83, p. 173) – yet it is always changing too (p. 18). As a fundamentally deterritorialized territory, a 'verschwommenes, irreales Bild' [a blurred, unreal image], it vaguely circumscribes an uncertain location in which the transgression of temporal, spatial and linguistic boundaries can occur (p. 52, p. 127). Like the wind which simultaneously energizes and destroys, this is both exhilarating and threatening. Moreover, the island is occasionally described as an 'unruhiger Ort' [a troubled place, p. 51] that bears witness to problematic histories, such as the Nazi and GDR dictatorships and the Thirty Years War. The chapter

---

16 Although born in Munich in 1962, where her family remained, Draesner describes herself as a child who inherited 'Vertriebenheit' [expulsion], *Zauber im Zoo*, p. 70.

'Swantiland', for instance, focuses on a particularly exposed, eerie and unsettling area at the northern most point of the island, which bears the imprint of these often violent histories (pp. 51–56). During the Second World War Hiddensee was a defensive outpost with a Nazi flak facility, which the Soviet army subsequently blew up, leaving behind lumps of concrete debris that have only recently been removed from the beach below the headland (p. 52). During the GDR the island was a holiday destination, as well as a potentially lucrative prospect alongside other locations on the Baltic Sea for the socialist regime's ambitions to find and extract crude oil (p. 53). Traces of this past plundering can be seen in the holes that were filled after the island yielded nothing. Even Wallenstein's strategic burning of this once wooded area in 1628, in a bid to frustrate the enemy Danes during the Thirty Years War, is palpable in the dusty steppe that this area became (p. 55). Overall, however, Hiddensee for Draesner is a space of *jouissance*, of desire, play and potential self-erasure, where, to parse Julia Kristeva, the speaking subject may, qua transgression, reinvent herself time and again.[17] In this sense, the island is the artist's ultimate habitat, a sort of muse that spurs the 'sie' of the narrative to transgress creative boundaries in order to access the not-as-yet-known, the unsaid and the unthought.

'Icy' Spaces

From the start, the island is presented as a 'Nichtort-Ort' [nonplace-place], Draesner's term in her essay collection *Zauber im Zoo* (2007) for a hybrid terrain that vacillates between fluidity and solidity. It also embodies the idea of 'Stoffwechsel' – metabolic change, transformation and the making of energy – so central to Draesner's poetics.[18] She uses the motif of ice to convey the idea of language as the transformation of one substance into another. Ice always risks returning to its liquid state. As such, it symbolizes language as a metabolic process of transformation.[19] Language, in turn, is the medium through which the body translates into words its instinctive encounters with the world. Language thus always involves the subject's transformation of intangible phenomena into yet another fluid state: language. As a body affected by external stimuli that it attempts to translate, the

---

17 Julia Kristeva, *Desire in Language. A Semiotic Approach to Literature and Art*, ed. by Leon S. Roudiez, trans. by Thomas Gora, Alice Jardine and Leon S. Roudiez (New York: Columbia University Press, 1980).
18 Draesner, *Zauber im Zoo*, pp. 44–46.
19 Ibid., p. 42.

'sie' – an organic transit zone for the intertwining of external and internal impulses – too becomes translated. Its very language retains, as affective excesses that spill out over the structures of vocabulary and grammar, the somatic traces of this transformative process (p. 73).[20] The place of language is thus a non-place-place in which deviance from rules and regulations features (p. 59). Writing constitutes the exploration of this unknown terrain and its unstable self, for Draesner a gathering of heterogeneous and antagonistic forces that the writer must somehow harmonize.[21]

Even though *Mein Hiddensee* recalls a summer sojourn on the island, Hiddensee always represents the potential threat, or adventure, of melting ice. One chapter is dedicated to Hiddensee's geological origins in the Ice Age. Here we learn that it is not only the island that is the nomadic cast-off of a long-gone, slowly roving glacier; the sea too, quite literally a 'hidden sea', has changed form many times, from lake to sea and back again (p. 67). In this way, Hiddensee is presented as a rootless 'nonplace-place': one '100-Wörter-Bild' pays tribute to the constantly changing energy of the very earth underfoot (p. 126). Other images that reference the shifting metabolic materiality of the island depict Hiddensee as a shimmering, glimmering, small and narrow landmass that is forever half-disappearing, half-reappearing. Its fragility is underlined when it is likened to a leaf blown onto water, while its inherent nomadism is alluded to when one of its northern areas, Dornbusch, is described as a ship (p. 17, p. 29). Half-submerged under water, it is 'deutlich nicht Festland' [clearly not solid land, p. 53], yet this does not prevent the narrator, who experiences the mammal's primordial fear of water when in transit from the 'mainland' to the island, from feeling relief at the first sight of Hiddensee on the horizon (p. 15). Conversely, we learn that the 'Bodden' – the shallow channel between the islands of Rügen and Hiddensee – keeps silting over and must be dredged regularly (p. 13). If land is unstable and ever-changing, then, the same may be said of water: water drains away to reveal land, which in turn is at the mercy of water, as the narrator's frequent reflections on the sea's erosion of the island's fragile coastline convey (p. 151, p. 158). Indeed, the opening tableau depicts an antagonistic landscape, elementally pulled between the wind's efforts to blow the whole island away and the tenacity of small gnarly plants that stubbornly burrow ever deeper into the soil. In this scene the

---

20 Ibid., p. 31. Draesner emphasizes a physiological, as opposed to psychological basis for writing in her essay, 'Atem, Puls und Bahn. Das Denken des Körpers im Zustand der Sprache', *Lettre International*, 44 (1999), 62–67 (p. 62). For an overview of the body in Draesner's lyrical work, see Anna Ertel, 'Zur Poetik Ulrike Draesners', in *Ulrike Draesner*, ed. by Brogi, Ertel and Zemanek, pp. 19–26 (pp. 19–21).
21 Draesner, *Zauber im Zoo*, pp. 50–51.

land is literally at sea due to the sheer force of the 'Immer-Wind' [always-wind, p. 7], while the sea, in the distance, seems motionless. Hiddensee, as a space of ambivalence, thus exemplifies Draesner's poetic principle of 'Stoffwechsel' which itself is an image of constant transgression across different boundaries of being.[22]

In this spirit, the 'sie' plays on the semantic possibilities of the German verb 'übersetzen', which (depending on the category of prefix) means to translate as well as to ferry across (p. 14, p. 19). En route to her destination she is not just crossing a now watery, now sandy, border between the islands of Rügen and Hiddensee – a border that, due to its silting, renders uncertain Hiddensee's status as a separate island. She is also departing the burdensome solid ground (Festland) and its restrictive time regime to enter a different state, an 'inselig' (p. 62) [islandy] state, in which habitual structures of self, time and language become dissolved. The island provides respite from the urban context; overpowered by its slow temporality, the narrator becomes 'zwischenräumig', an in-between creature who walks the strands of Hiddensee, metaphorically moving across 'icy' terrain that is neither water nor land (p. 173). Thus the narrator too undergoes the process of 'Stoffwechsel'. Transition translates and transforms her, while she, a self in process, continually strains to articulate this very process of translation and transformation. Yet as her above self-description suggests, departure does not end with arrival, the simple exchange of one state for another. Rather, the self remains pliantly between different states and spaces. Once at her destination, the island's weather systems continue the work of transformation: the chapters 'Wind am Strand' (pp. 39–43) ['Wind on the Beach'] and 'Regen' (pp. 127–31) ['Rain'] depict wind and rain eroding the self, pushing her to conceive of the world differently in this self-consciously porous state on a dynamic threshold between inside and outside.

Likewise, wind and rain conspire to alter the island's shape, literally in the form of erosion, and also visually for the narrator, whose gaze mostly cannot make out the distant horizon. Indeed, Hiddensee is characterized by a sort of horizonlessness. The outermost limit of 'das Ende der Wasserwelt' (p. 30) [the end of the water world] remains hidden, a 'Hirngespinst' (p. 30) [chimera]: when the narrator looks out to sea from one of the island's high points, she is looking at unbounded space. Even when a horizon may be faintly deciphered, it is composed of clouds, the epitome of shape-shifting, metabolic transformations. This is a

---

22 Anna Ertel notes Draesner's preference, conceptually, for ambivalence over dichotomy, 'Zur Poetik Ulrike Draesners', p. 20.

world in perpetual atomic flow, framed by nothing solid external to the perceiving self, who is also an unstable, shifting entity.

A chapter that recalls a physics lesson drives this home. Here the narrator remembers how her teacher, Frau K., drew a dot on the blackboard, only to assert that it was not what it seemed:

> Sie sollten hinschauen. Genau. So genau sie könnten. Der Punkt sei nicht rund. Bei gründlicher Betrachtung löse seine Umrisse sich auf.
> Seine Küste. (p. 163)

> [They were supposed to look at it. Carefully. As carefully as they could. The dot was not actually round. On close observation its contours dissolved.
> Its coastline.]

The image of a dot that is not a dot, when one looks beyond its apparent fixity and self-evident form, could be applied to the narrator's spatial experience of the island. Viewed thus, the island is not just unmeasurable; it is also ultimately unknowable. Its uncertain contours resonate with the mostly invisible lines of its horizons. The 'sie', when contemplating the non-dot – in effect an image of eternity – momentarily focuses her field of vision and senses on the here and now. In so doing, she once again omits the active verb, so that the focus is headily on immediate intensity:

> Tangige Luft, Vogelbrutgeschrei.
> Das Gefühl, für den Bruchteil einer Sekunde das verborgene atomare Fließen der Welt zu berühren. (p. 163)

> [Seaweedy air, brooding bird screech.
> The feeling of touching the secret atomic flow of the world for a split second.]

This is a response to the unboundedness of the universe as exemplified by the island, an effort to capture in words, beyond pre-existing forms of knowledge, a fleeting sensual intensity of experience: hence the seeming retraction of the gaze from the horizon – the non-dot – to the immediate proximity of the self. In truth, this is not a movement of retraction. Similar to the condensing effect of the '100-Wörter-Bilder', it is a movement that encompasses retraction and expansion simultaneously, fusing self and Other. The 'sie' inhaling 'seaweedy air' embodies the happiness described at the end of the book, a blending of self via the senses with the surrounding landscape (pp. 191–98). Happiness could thus be described as the fundamental experience of self-transgression – remaining within while going beyond the self – in a landscape pervaded by 'Kräften der Empathie' [powers of empathy] between self and Other.[23] The 'sie', vitally focussed on her immediate sensory surroundings, momentarily almost evaporates into the scent and sound of the coast. In an image of pure *jouissance*, the here and now, fleetingly, metamorphoses into eternity. Yet the language in this extract also occupies a place of its own, somewhat apart from the perception of landscape it strives to grasp. The construct 'Vogelbrutgeschrei' is not only an inventive compound that takes ellipsis to its limits and a further instance of the lyrical subject as translator into language of her own fleeting sensory encounters; it is also a word and sound image that foregrounds the visual and lyrical materiality of language itself, expressing a scintillating vividness of which the German language with its many compound constructions is particularly capable, as the 'sie' in gratitude later muses (p. 196). On the beach, the 'sie' thus translates the metabolic materiality of the island as an uncanny entity continually shifting between water and land into this sudden and strange compound, which by virtue of its prominent materiality continues to perform the metabolic labour of 'translation' on the material-linguistic level. In this focus on the alien word itself, the work of signification is suspended, and a gap of further possibility opens up between language, self and environment. In these different ways, which delicately transmit the metabolic 'translations' between self and environment, as well as the uncanny materiality of language itself, *Mein Hiddensee* pays tribute to the possibilities of poetic language as much as it does to the island, its source of lyrical inspiration.

The tension between the timelessness of eternity and the almost imperceptible movement of the transient moment indicates the island's multi-temporality. It is a space of slow time, 'Inselzeit' [island time], in which the body becomes heavier (pp. 28–29, p. 58). Paradoxically, it is also a place of acceleration, as the frequent tendency to ellipsis suggests. The sense of acceleration is not just down to technology's encroachment on this apparently archaic outpost – on walks the self often uses her smartphone to record her impressions, or to identify botanical species (p. 112, p. 196). Nor is it only a consequence of the globalization of markets from which the island cannot remain apart (p. 109). Acceleration here is more fundamentally a reflection on the invisible metabolic transformations that are always taking place within and around us, in nature as well as in history. The ellipsis implicit in a compound such as 'Vogelbrutgeschrei' registers on the aesthetic level this very sense of the speed of minute events continually taking place in our midst, so fleeting as to almost escape perception. But acceleration is a yet broader phenomenon that also affects historical sensibility. On one of her walks, the 'sie' notices how the debris from the Soviet bombing of the island's

---

23 Draesner and Wagner, 'Über Stockung und Stein', p. 10.

Nazi flak facility has been removed. All that remains of Nazism here is an 'Erin-nerungsschema' (p. 53) [an outline of a memory]. In this way, Draesner suggests that human history, with its continually metamorphosing physical traces and its commemoration or descent into obscurity, is caught up in cycles of transience comparable to those in nature. This transience is helped by the organic quality of human memory processes themselves.

For Draesner, the brain is central to these processes (p. 73). When in memory mode, the brain does not simply pull an old thing out of a long-closed drawer. Rather, it reacts 'jedes Mal frisch' (p. 136) [each time anew] to external and internal stimuli, thereby creating new memories and new repositories, which erase previous memories. The brain too is a transit zone of organic transformations. This constantly changing body-brain memory function mirrors the island's shifting memory-scape, indicating the presence of the past by virtue of its absence. Even contemporary technology must succumb to the organic forces of transience. While the smartphone offers the possibility to record impressions as they occur in the moment, technology is not always reliable, as the 'sie' discovers when one evening she tries to play a recording of her impressions on the beach earlier that day, only to find that the sounds of nature have overwhelmed her device's capacity to capture her voice (p. 101).

The island thus attunes the senses of the 'sie' and her very brain to the hidden atomic flow of matter in history, memory and nature. Yet nature – understood as a force that engages all powers of sensory perception, rather than as the domesticated haven that the island's many informational signposts signify – is the stronger force. The wind above all epitomizes the 'carousel of time' in which the island keeps spinning and which testifies to the fleetingness of the individual lives and histories that pass through it (p. 110). Thus the temporal corollary of the 'icy' non-place-place is, aptly enough, a vertiginous transience that, like the island, is always moving.

Language 'inselig'

The island as an ambivalent territory adrift in an unbounded universe offers a vision of language beyond known and familiar structures. One of the island's most profound effects on the self is to sharpen her awareness of the complex relationship between language and experience: in the midst of all the weathering, she, as a body that is always being eroded, becomes keenly aware that in trying to voice the sensations of being 'inselig', she is perforce a translator into language of sensory perception. This act of translation involves repeat encounters of the body with the world beyond it, whereby the body is the transit zone through which different energies move.

It would be a simplification, however, to assume a clear line of division between inside and outside, self and Other, a neat dichotomy that suggests an action-reaction scheme of interaction: the wind blows wildly, the self becomes 'durchpustet' (p. 66) [aerated], for example. Draesner outlines a more subtle interaction between self and Other, in which external impressions – a sense of shimmering nirvana in the clear blue skies above the island's forest, for instance (p. 125) – may in fact be the externalization of a bodily feeling that through linguistic expression transforms both self and elements beyond the self into an affective landscape of pure radiance. The 'sie' thus only becomes 'durchpustet' through a complex movement of interaction between inside and outside; indeed, her joyous holiday feeling, a '[w]inddurchpustetes Große-Ferien-Gefühl' (p. 95) [a windblown-airy summer-holidays-feeling] that fuses Other (wind) and self, illuminates how difficult it is to determine where outside / Other stops and inside / self begins. In this sense, the 'sie' is as porous and unbounded as the island she traverses, her very feelings the product of a mysterious alchemy between body and elements.

The 'sie' as a cluster of impulses of ambivalent origin epitomizes the concept of language put forward in the text. If she is usually in motion across a dynamic terrain, language too is always in a process of movement that is likened to self-erasure (p. 125). This is one of her principle insights during her stay: language defers meaning, it erases itself, much like the island gives in to the powers of erosion. In line with post-structuralist thought, then, language, in Draesner's vision, is pervaded by lack. The 'sie' often muses that her child is of the island (p. 156), that the island is a space of childhood, in which the 'Gehirnautomatismen' (p. 182) [brain automatisms] of adult life dissolve to make way for a more instantaneous connection between experience and language. Stressing the limitations of the signifier, however, the 'sie' reflects that the word 'Kindheit' [childhood], for example, cannot hope to do justice to the experience it refers to – a whole 'Daseinsgefühl' [sense of existence] that 'Kindheit' simply obscures (p. 129). Likewise, the place name 'Swanti' is an insufficient signifier without a meaning beyond its attachment to a part of the island that, as above outlined, has a number of dark and troubling pasts (p. 52). Yet this lack of a specific meaning makes it possible for the 'sie' to ponder the materiality of the word 'Swanti', relishing its deeply evocative and magical power, just as she ponders the sounds and textures of enigmatic scientific names for molluscs: 'Ancylus flutviatilis, Littorina littorea, Limnea ovata, Mya arenaria' (p. 69). The incantation of these formal names succeeds in bringing the shellfish back to life in and through the very materiality of language, 'als Bild-Raum' (p. 69) [as image-space], even if the strands that once housed the shellfish are long gone. Here the almost occult power of language to reanimate extinct life through the revitalizing sensory materiality of image and sound is foregrounded. Language means life. Rather than becoming engulfed by the potentially overwhelming abyss between signifier and signified, the 'sie' thus revels in this in-between space of language, where knowledge and meaning have not yet formed – '[. . .] lass dunkel, dunkel lass sein' (p. 48) [leave it in the dark, in the dark leave it]. In this dark space between 'Vorstellung und Ausmalung' (p. 69) [perception and depiction], she is empowered to create as translator of fleeting perceptions alternative linguistic formulations beyond the coagulated crusts of everyday language.[24] In this way, 'Swanti' comes to mean 'Flugzeugsgefühl über belebtem Gemälde' (p. 54) [airplane-feeling above animated painting], while the child, who does not know what to envisage under various fish names, simply invents her own piscine signifier, a green unicorn fish, and corresponding fantastical drawing of its signified (p. 46). Signifiers with obscure or lacking signifieds trigger and feed the poetic imagination.

A sojourn on the in-between space of Hiddensee is thus akin to entering a space beyond rational dichotomies where the linguistic apprehension of the heterogeneity of sensory perception becomes possible: 'Hier muss sie übersetzen in Sprache und spürt es; übersetzen die Blätter, das Schauen, den Wind' (p. 154) [here she must translate into language and senses it; translate the leaves, the looking, the wind]. This communicates something of the complexity of Draesner's nature concept; it is always caught up in our myriad efforts to mediate it, whether as bucolic idyll or wild, elemental landscape (pp. 108–9, p. 140, p.171). Even as a poet trying to access the 'Raum und Möglichkeit des Nicht-Begriffs' (p. 48) [the space and possibility of the non-concept] beyond the mediated image, the 'sie' reflects that she, a 'Bildermacherin mit Worten' (p. 145) [maker-of-images with words], also mediates and translates 'nature'.[25] And yet, as bodies, porous transit zones between inside and outside, we are also part of nature, as her reflections on a non-mimetic kind of *nature writing* suggest (p. 196).

Ascribing the body an instinctive intelligence, the 'sie' considers how the 'Fantasie des Körpers' (p. 58) [the body's imagination] plays a central role in accessing the space of the 'non-concept', elsewhere described as '[d]as Sprach-"Dunkel"' (p. 47) [language-'darkness']. This darkness beyond the structures of

---

24 This paraphrases Draesner's description of the strengths of Gottfried Benn's lyrical creativity: see Ulrike Draesner, *Heimliche Helden. Über Heinrich von Kleist, Jean-Henri Fabre, James Joyce, Thomas Mann, Gottfried Benn, Karl Valentin u.v.a. Essays* (Munich: Luchterhand, 2013), p. 249.
25 See Evi Zemanek, '"Die Natur heißt es übersetzen erfinden". Kunstnatur in der Lyrik Ulrike Draesners', in *Ulrike Draesner*, ed. by Brogi, Ertel and Zemanek, pp. 27–36.

language is 'nicht nichts' [not nothing]. Rather, it is the shadowy realm of everything unnamed and brimming with unknown semantic potential. In the 'Sprachdunkeln' knowledge concedes to a more discerning body intelligence that throws the individual back onto her sensory perceptions and corresponding creative energies (p. 47). The island engages the self's very body intelligence. Open to its elemental force, she is attuned to sensations that cannot easily be rendered in words, thus she must feel for deviant linguistic combinations in order to create a new expression that might communicate something of the collision between different pulsations of matter that comprise 'inselig' experience. As observed, the 'sie' often welds nouns to convey the intensity of an immediate and multi-sensory encounter with the elements. The chapter on rain expresses in the compound 'Regenwindgischt' (p. 130) [rainwindfoam] the fusion of rain, wind and foam, which hammers down on her as she walks the beach. Other compounds, such as 'Salzflutlicht' (p. 93) [saltflowlight] and 'Toteisloch' (p. 154) [deadicehole] express, on the formal level, a similar breathless intensity that in turn evokes the tempo of the spinning, accelerating carousel of transience. Indeed, the striking and strange materiality of language that comes to the fore in these compounds paradoxically points to the uniqueness of every fleeting moment, every vanishing encounter. These and other compounds throughout the narrative remove individual words from their conventional place in language sequences. In so doing, they open up an alien perspective on the familiar, which uncannily expresses the desire to give voice to radically different encounters with phenomena that go beyond an ordinary understanding of 'nature', which is for the 'sie' along with 'Wissen' [knowledge] a most dubious word that captures little more than convention (p. 47).

The uncanny perspective by contrast recognizes that the thinking, perceiving and experiencing self is always somehow *in* the landscape it contemplates, as her reflections on Caspar David Friedrich's painting *Der Mönch am Meer* [*The Monk by the Sea*, 1808–1810] emphasize (p. 171). Friedrich's painting depicts the small figure of the monk in front of a heaving sea, at some distance from the viewer. The 'sie' muses that in standing in front of this painting she too is a figure with its back turned to the world behind it; she, like the monk, is the observer of a spectacle, and for another observer she may even become the spectacle. But, as she thinks this, a bird unceremoniously defecates on her, reminding her of her uncanny status as an intrinsic part of the environment she observes. The above compound formulations thus suggest that transitioning to the threshold space of the island is in effect entry into the uncanny 'Sprachdunkel' of language creativity. As the 'sie' moves across the island, an activity that witnesses her becoming childlike in her desire to learn more about language from the island, her 'kleiner Vokabeltrainer' (p. 48) [little vocabulary-trainer], she also moves across and in between different language forms, seeking out new modes of expression and relishing the poetic creativity this double transgression inspires.

Language and *chora*

Another way of describing the creative process that produces a word such as 'Regenwindgischt' is to suggest that Draesner, in poetically making free with the language code, alludes to the heterogeneity of the 'Sprachdunkel' beyond and in between language dichotomies, metaphorically via the hybrid image and formally through the structure of the compound itself. Alongside the self's evocation of the island as a maternal and childhood space, and also in tandem with Draesner's elaboration of a kind of intuitive 'body' language throughout the text, it is productive to conceive of the island, in theoretical terms, as the *chora*. This is Kristeva's gendered, spatial term for 'the heterogeneous, disruptive dimension of language, [. . .] that which can never be caught up in the closure of traditional linguistic theory'.[26] Linked to the instinctual drives, the *chora* has a distinctly biological slant, which also tallies with Draesner's conceptualization of body and language. Indeed, the 'sie' of *Mein Hiddensee* critiques Ludwig Wittgenstein's and Jacques Lacan's view that thought without language is impossible, asserting that language without the body is impossible (p. 71).

For Kristeva, the *chora* symbolizes the feminine space of the womb, the prelinguistic space of symbiosis between self and Other, from which the self must split in order to enter the rational sphere of language: the symbolic order. The *chora* is thereafter repressed; as a pre-linguistic force, it can only ever be postulated, affecting the symbolic order as remainder, waste and somatic trace. Draesner's reflections on writing chime with this understanding of the heterogeneous origins of language and self. Her exploration of the 'Sprachdunkel' acknowledges the 'Nichtidentität der Herkunft' [the non-identity of origins], which, joyously or disturbingly, may irrupt into the rational sphere of language, reminding the self that language is the trace of a difference that does not lead back to a 'Heimat'.[27]

Many scenes in *Mein Hiddensee* use images of maternity, childbirth and infancy to evoke and question the idea of origins.[28] Early in the text, the 'sie' casts

---

26 Kristeva, *Desire in Language*, p. 30.
27 Draesner, *Zauber im Zoo*, p. 79. Draesner here rejects the idea that language is a kind of 'Heimat' [home or homeland] for those who have lost their homes; instead, language is difference.
28 On reproduction and child-bearing, see also Emily Jeremiah's chapter in this volume.

the island as a safe haven in the shape of the maternal *chora* by imagining that she and her child are enveloped in a fine-spun, protective parachute that emanates from her. This is the protected space of magic thinking beyond logic and reason, the gentle dome of the silky chute and its umbilical cord evoking the symbiosis, the 'Zwischen-Menschen-Gebilde' (p. 32) [between-people-entity], of mother and child. This formulation testifies to the 'Sprachdunkel' again, alluding to the space of poetic imagination, which is conceived through an image of prelinguistic symbiosis. It is only possible to access this heterogeneous linguistic space on the island. However, the island does not represent a 'Heimat' in the traditional sense. As the many images of its spatial ambivalence suggest, 'dort' in fact refers to an unbounded, deterritorialized terrain that embodies the semiotic order of language, a difference and heterogeneity normally repressed by the symbolic order.

In another scene, the 'sie' physically enters the space of 'Sprachdunkel' when visiting Asta Nielsen's house. Here, movement through a decaying house triggers the memory of a dream of her own birth, of how she awoke from the dream with the visual perception of a new-born: an encounter with a flat, diffuse and unfamiliar world that looms '[o]hne Namen, ohne Wissen' (p. 72) [without name, without knowledge] in front of virgin eyes as an unrecognizable 'something'. The dream-mode enables her to access the memory of a repressed experience in which sensory perception comes first, but may only be translated into experience via language: 'Das Spiegeln und Zweitentstehen der Welt durch Worte' (p. 73) [the mirroring and second emergence of the world through words]. The heterogeneous space of the 'Sprachdunkel' recedes from cognition as language orders and fossilizes perception and experience. And yet 'etwas bleibt übrig' (p. 73) [something remains]. In tandem with Draesner's insistence on the biological underpinnings of language and memory – the 'sie' is convinced that the dream-memory of her birth is a result of an error in her brain, which she regards as part of the body (pp. 72–73) – this 'something' could be described, again, as 'the heterogeneity of biological operations in respect of signifying practices' at work: the irruption of the *chora* across language.[29]

The untitled opening tableau is instructive in this regard. It articulates a heaving, heterogeneous space in dramatic movement, like the *chora* 'an essentially mobile and extremely provisional articulation constituted by movements and their ephemeral stases'.[30] Skylarks scream, dip and sway in the forceful

---

29 Kristeva, *Desire in Language*, p. 30.

30 Ibid., pp. 93–94. For Draesner, the body and the brain are central to memory and language. See, for example, *Zauber im Zoo*, where she describes the transition of the body (mouth, brain, hand) into language (p. 39), and also where she argues that fiction is a central

wind, rainclouds cling onto the sky for dear life, a sky that cannot frame or contain the world, because it is itself porous: 'die dünne Haut der Welt bekommt einen Riss – hinter ihm steht ein großes elektrisches Strahlen' (p. 7) [the thin membrane of the world ruptures – behind it is a massive electric glow]. This scene dramatically captures the horizonless ambivalence of the island, its status as a punctured territory beyond others. Sky, air, creaturely life and even the ground, are in perpetual motion in this landscape, which is fuelled by the bright glow of pure celestial energy. Yet it is also an image for the kinetic rhythms of poetic language, in Draesner's words a 'Summen' [humming] that channels the self through 'body' language, producing a scene – emblematic for the entire work – that is more '[. . .] a rhythmic pulsion than a new language'.[31] In the midst of all this movement, the 'sie' hunkers down to get her raincoat and inhales her own scent, 'salzig und erdiger als der Inselboden' (p. 7) [salty and earthier than the island's soil]. From the earliest instance the island is accented as a feminine bodily space on a continuum with the heaving world around it. And the self's inhalation of her own earthy scent is an enactment of a primordial body memory, an acknowledgement of the centrality of the body to language and memory processes.

Powers of Empathy

Kristeva's concept of the *chora* allows for abject experience, the devastating annihilation of the speaking subject due to the violent return of the repressed.[32] *Mein Hiddensee* emphasizes an optimistic *jouissance* around difference in language, however, continually placing the body at the centre of diverse experience and the sense-making around that experience. The 'sie' embraces the 'Sprachdunkel', just as she embraces her pulverization in the winds and weathering of the island's ambivalent space. In this way, she can practice a personal revolution in poetic language that sees her transgressing her own experiential and linguistic boundaries. But what political message does this vision of language, self and environment suggest? It conveys a feminine, pre-rational and instinctive bodily

---

part of neurological processes (p. 92). For more on these themes, see Anna Alissa Ertel, *Körper, Gehirne, Gene. Lyrik und Naturwissenschaft bei Ulrike Draesner und Durs Grünbein* (Berlin: de Gruyter, 2011).

31 Kristeva, *Desire in Language*, p. 30. Draesner, *Zauber im Zoo*, p. 39.

32 See Julia Kristeva, *Powers of Horror. An Essay on Abjection*, trans. by Leon S. Roudiez (New York: Columbia UP, 1982).

knowledge that holistically understands the human subject through its physical connection to its environment. In the metropolitan and cosmopolitan contemporary, nature is too often viewed in the abstract, a *locus amoenus* that elides the self as (destructive) agent, separating self too cleanly from Other (p. 173). As the consideration of Friedrich's painting suggests, even the 'sie' can occasionally fall into this false knowledge, preconceptions that limit a sense of who or what the Other might be, and that are underpinned by the view that self and Other are separate entities. *Mein Hiddensee* works against this understanding, revealing the human subject to be in and of its surroundings, fused, via the body and in ways that may always remain obscure, with the very nature the subject tries to mediate. This fusion is not a vision of homogeneity, however; on the contrary, the false position of an omniscient perspective from above is continually undermined by this text, which depicts the 'sie' as always already plunged into difference – her surroundings – of which she is partly part.

Draesner has pondered the shape a new German literature of the early twenty-first century might take, a kind of writing that goes beyond the themes of recent and contemporary postwar literature to address pressing matters of the here and now, such as the challenge that advances in genetic science and technology pose for humankind's sense of who it is becoming.[33] Her reflections on twentieth-century German history and memory in *Mein Hiddensee* certainly allude to the vast body of post-war memory writing that has informed the German-language literary scene for several decades. Yet it is not primarily a text about the German past. In its fusion of post-structuralist theories of signification with a keen sense of humankind's biological fundaments, *Mein Hiddensee* communicates a complex, tacitly political vision of human identity as decentred, discontinuous and inseparable from the 'Kräften der Empathie' we need in order to navigate our 'natural' (mediated), technologized and globalized environments. These powers of empathy originate in the highly refined sense of the interdependence between self and Other, our sense of connection to and translation of the secret atomic flow of the world.

---

33 Draesner, *Zauber im Zoo*, p. 30.

The Felt Self

Karen Leeder and Lyn Marven

The Indecipherable Stone. Interview with Ulrike Draesner on the Processes of Literature

During 2015–2016 Ulrike Draesner was a Visiting Fellow and Writer in Residence in New College, Oxford. She stayed on in Oxford during 2016–2017 as a Visiting Fellow of TORCH (The Oxford Research Centre in the Humanities), but also with links to New College. This interview was held on the occasion of the Eugene Ludwig Lecture associated with her stay in February 2017. Draesner suggested a topological approach, inspired by the geography of the College, which had in turn inspired her writing during her time here. The various stations of the interview correspond to locations in College picked by Draesner herself and can be followed on the map (see Figs. 1 and 2).[1]

Fig. 1: Ulrike Draesner on the mound, New College.

LM: *Paradoxically, you wanted to start with silence; and here we are in the Cloisters, one of the quietest parts of College. As a writer and poet your work is all about creating words and sounds so what role does silence play in the process of composition and in the speaking of the poems?*

UD: I have been thinking quite a lot about the creative process lately. Although I myself have never really experienced that fear when faced with the white page, there is nevertheless a basic truth to it. There is nothing; and then there is something: you start to write. In the end, each verse, each line, each word, is surrounded by a tremendous love for the

1 Thanks for transcription work to Benjamin Schaper.

https://doi.org/10.1515/9783110495942-012

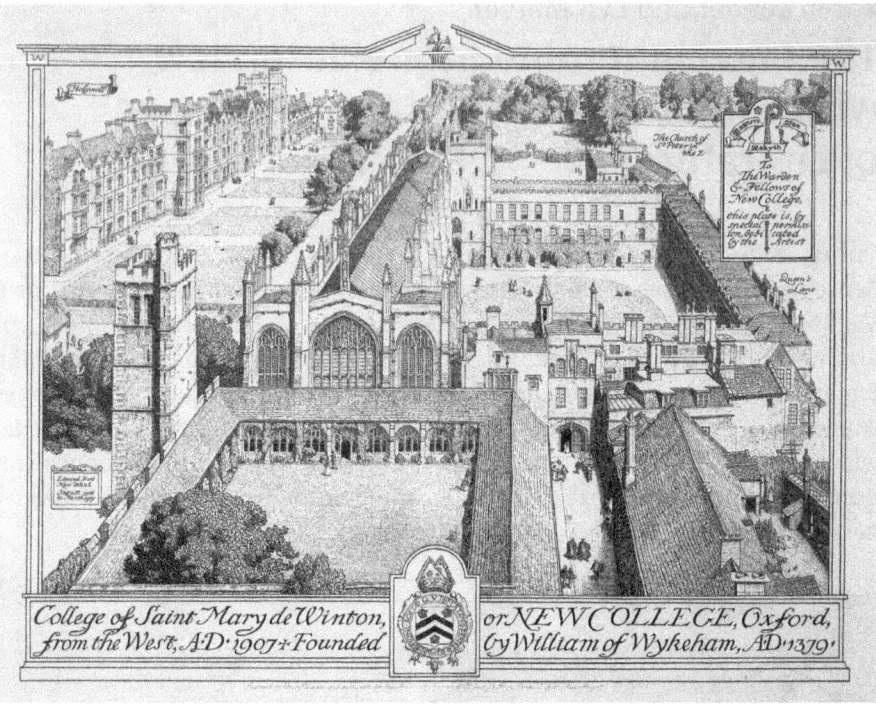

Fig. 2: View of the College of Saint Mary de Winton, or New College, Oxford from the West. 1907. Edmund Hort. Engraving. NC Inventory 1230. With permission of the Warden & Scholars of New College, Oxford.

things not expressed. The words and phrases forming in your brain are surrounded by this vast space of possibilities which then begins to fill up, as I experience it anyway, with echoes and voices. But because you always have to choose a certain line, or a certain word, the space around what you write is always so much bigger than the black dots and lines that end up on the page. And that is why we are in the Cloisters: a wonderful space for echoes and voices. You have the arcades around you, the grass quadrangle inside, the walls and the covered walkway: so you walk within an open space that is partly closed. I sometimes feel that as one walks or moves through this space certain voices become more prominent.

KJL: *What kind of voices?*

UD: For me this is linked to the feeling I have when I am trying to be 'inside' a fictional character. I hesitate to say 'I am the character', because strictly speaking this is not true: I am at once in the character and at the same time I'm not him or her, though I don't feel like I am my 'usual' self either. I have to maintain a kind of split identity which is hard and frightening sometimes, but it is what drives the writing. Being here in the Cloisters hopefully gives you a feeling of this. We are surrounded by history, a space used for prayer, meditation, reflection, for plays and the recitation of texts and song. All writing, all reading, relies on us being familiar with certain cultural codes: what a character is, what fiction is, how you read a poem. I use this knowledge as well and I presuppose it in my reader so it is all implicitly present in the act of writing. In fact, when I write I don't move across a vast empty space, but one full of traditions, memories and surprises and you feel some of this tension in this beautifully circumscribed and open space. That's why we are here. And because of this wonderful tree.

KJL: *In the Cloisters we are also surrounded by the dead. There are memorial plaques on all the walls and to be here is to be familiar with very particular ghosts and echoes – or rather they are your familiars. I know that ghosts are something you have been thinking about recently in your Frankfurter Poetikvorlesungen.[2] What role do they play?*

UD: The ghosts are linked to the voices I just mentioned. And I mean this quite literally. These are voices that we have forgotten or that have been subdued for some reason in our societies because of cultural or other taboos. One of the most powerful aspects of literature is that it can make these voices heard again and bring something to the fore that we otherwise try to hide. And hidden things develop ghastly, spooky forces. I have been researching this area over the last ten years because my most recent novel, *Sieben Sprünge vom Rand der Welt*, draws its energy precisely from these questions: how memories cross generations, how they are passed on. This can be a voluntary process, of course, through the stories people tell one another; but, very interestingly, memories – especially the more difficult or secret or taboo ones – move across generations in a half-conscious or subconscious way. They are passed on within bodily symptoms and the formation of emotional and inner landscapes, which are transmitted often without language or only with half-language, in allusions or stories never recounted in full, but ending in gasps and gaps.

LM: *Back to the silence again.*

UD: Yes, that brings us back to the dead, because to take this aspect of memory seriously would also mean to revise how we think about death. Someone is dead and done but how do the dead live on in our genes, in our epigenetics, in our minds, in our behaviour, in our dreams and in nightmares and in bits of traumatic experience which have crossed generations? This is quite spooky, indeed, but it also implies a way of conceptualizing a ghost or spectre that nowadays is based on scientific research. People have always known about these things. It is not chance that any culture I have ever come across has stories about how the dead are still linked to the living or the other way round.

LM: *And it is quite comforting in some ways.*

UD: Depends who is dead. [*Laughter*].

---

2 Ulrike Draesner, *Grammatik der Gespenster. Frankfurter Poetikvorlesungen* (Stuttgart: Reclam, 2018).

LM: *But tell us about the tree.*

UD: The tree in the middle of Cloisters is amazing. It is a huge oak, a holm oak, and it is said to have been planted even before the College was founded 1379 but this seems to be a myth because there are records from the early nineteenth century that show a fairly small tree. So you have a real tree; and yet it is also a sign, an attractor of stories at the same time. It incorporates a voice in the same way as you do when you are writing a story or a poem. You start with normal words of course; but then something else has to happen so that they acquire further layers of meaning though context, phrase and sound. This is the magic you as a writer have to perform. The oak suddenly attracts stories about when it was planted and then a couple of centuries later it attracts actors and these actors represent Harry Potter and Draco Malfoy fighting.[3] So now tourists come to see the oak and the spectres of the actors. There are no actors any longer, or rather only in the stills from the film, but of course you can see them here still in your mind's eye. So the oak is a very real tree and at the same time an equally strong symbol of the vitality and reality of the life of our minds. What you imagine might be as real for you in your life as so-called reality.

Before we go I wanted to talk about the tower as well. I like to be here because of the way it simply rises out of the Cloisters and reminds me that there is always something in these creative processes that you can't calculate, that comes out of nowhere. It's a risk as well: it could collapse and fall on you while you're still writing and the whole project will die and you die with it. At least as the author, the split figure I mentioned before, who has been trying to create this specific fictional world.

KJL: *College has spent millions of pounds propping it up.*

UD: [*Laughs*]. I can't spend millions of pounds to ensure my creative processes against collapse. They do collapse on top of me sometimes, and I come crawling out from underneath after investing, say, six months in writing and thinking. There are processes that die out all the time – but not entirely. Like this project I've been working on now about the cross-Channel swim. The idea is twelve years old and I've been working on it on and off, but never found the right entry into my protagonist's, well, I think, I should say soul. But something about him and his swim kept kicking and pushing so I didn't lose it entirely.

KJL: *It goes underground for a while and comes back up again.*

UD: Exactly. And if it comes up and you don't succeed in taking hold of it and forming it, it becomes painful and you have to suppress it again and then at least it's quiet for a while. Like one of those bodies in the cellar: half-dead, like a zombie. Sometimes when I'm asked how I worked on a project or when an idea came to me, I find I cannot remember properly. There is a sort of amnesia involved. And when I start out on a project I feel that charge again. It's like a rough state of high tension. In *Sieben Sprünge* it involved

---

3 The holm oak in New College Cloisters was featured in the fourth of the Harry Potter films, *Harry Potter and the Goblet of Fire* (2005).

nightmares and bad memories which weren't my own. This is an aspect of writing too; the risk you run. If you are really open to it and try to be as sincere with yourself and your readers as possible, there is always the risk of utter failure.

KJL: *We are now inside College next to the Senior Common Room (SCR) and Founders Library, standing by a large oak door at the top of the main steps into Hall. While we are here I want to ask about next stages. When you have had that initial inspiration, that moment of creation that comes into the whiteness, how then do you carry on? How does something find its shape and its form, its voice?*

UD: It is a process of interrelated moves. I move forward in one area and then I see what this implies for the other parts of the work. Step by step the writing builds up. Let's take a novel as an example. The world of the novel develops as I think about the implications of each new action in the lives and emotional set-ups of the characters. Sometimes it is a slow process and I have to feel my way into the depths of the story and into the depths of these characters, of these invented people. Through this, they acquire more reality, more volume or body, more character, indeed. We are standing here in one of the places that show how New College started to grow architecturally. When it expanded, it must have been around the end of the fifteenth or the beginning of the sixteenth century, this was the place where various function rooms were added. But the expansion doesn't seem to have followed a masterplan of any kind. It is pragmatic, based on what was needed at the particular time. And sometimes over the centuries the rooms have changed their functions too, according to what is needed. That's why everybody who comes to New College is puzzled by these narrow passages turning back on themselves. Only yesterday I helped a Chinese lady to find her way back to the front quad. She was entirely lost. So this is what reminded me of writing a novel. Trying to find your way intuitively, half-blindly and adding another room, another perspective, another oblique angle, to an action or a character. Then if the floor levels don't match, you have to build staircases in between. How do you link it up? Or where do you cut something off? It might even be a trap door.

One of the results in New College is that this room here, which serves as a dining hall is now accessed by walking up these few steps. But in truth if you look closely you see you climb into this hall through what used to be a window. Originally, when it was the library it didn't have a door here. This too reminds me of writing. Quite often you have certain pieces of writing or certain some key points that you know will be part of a novel. Then you have to try to link them. For that you have to invent certain kinds of bridges between them, but this, in itself, tends to be a trap: you need something genuine, something that is valuable in its own right. Otherwise there will always be a weak spot in a work and, especially in poetry, these weak spots show. Sometimes you need some kind of link, like an 'and', but even an 'and' is not harmless. In poetry, for example, it is also a sound, a rhythmic entity.

KJL: *Yes, it has got to own its place in the economy of the text.*

LM: *You have been talking about both novels and poetry. When you have the germ of an idea does it come with a form attached or does the form follow the story, the idea, as you develop it?*

UD: No, it very often comes with the form attached, so I would know straight away whether it is part of a poem already existing, or whether it might live up to become a poem of its own, or whether it is something entirely different. In that case I might feel it is prose or 'prose-ish' but then there is the question of tone. Sometimes I have to do a certain amount of writing, with the longer things at least, to find what they really are. It depends; sometimes the vision is very clear that something has the potential to become a hundred-page piece, for example. Sometimes it seems like a longer story, with more characters. But there seems to be a very clear dividing line for me between poetry and prose. Poems feel and look different; a poem has a different atmosphere; a different scheme of colours around the words. It is never a single word on its own, for example, that 'appears'. If it is going to be a poem there will be three, four, five words; it is always a sequence. The basic rhythmic unity or units are there already along with the kind of vision surrounding it.

Let me give you an example. I once wrote a poem here in the SCR. It was a Sunday afternoon in September, and I was on my own. I saw that some of the old sheds next to the medieval wall had been removed opening up a new space that looked very inviting. But someone had put some bright pink waste bins in the middle of it. Their colour struck me as extremely English, but at the same time it was beautiful. All of a sudden, something came out of this that reminded me of an evening I'd had in college three months before when I talked to a Maths Tutor and he told about Pythagoras and mathematical proofs. I remember seeing those pink waste bins against the green of the tree and the grey of the stone and the composition of this scene also, kind of simultaneously, brought to mind one of the portraits on the wall in the SCR; and this in turn linked with the discussion about time and mathematical patterns. There are various discrete layers: one is pictorial and another one is structural and a third one is the words themselves, and the fourth one is music of the words. In this case it was clear that the poem had to be in English. It just came in English. It's difficult to describe but there is an aura surrounding the first line which is melting and is also where the drive, the little ticking heart, of the poem sits. I take this and go with it until the first energy is exhausted. When the urge is used up, the poem tends to be finished as far as its basic shape is concerned. I then do revisions. But that is it. It is always self-contained in that it comes to life in a kind of double-process in which 'content' and shape, wording and music and pictorial 'frames' are forged hand in hand.

LM: *We've moved outside again into the gardens and are standing by the mound. I am intrigued by what you said to us about linking the mound to the idea of fashion.*

UD: Garden fashions, yes. New College garden was modelled according to various fashions and it was a landscaping fashion at one time to include a mound. In literature too you sometimes might want to use ornament or an excursion or something not strictly functional, just to relieve the mind, just for the fun of it. Many people conceive of suspense and tension as being the vital drivers of plot. Of course they are vital. For me, however, much of the fun comes in creating extra pleasure for an intelligent or experienced reader through this kind of ornamental excursion or arabesque. It has the function of being functionless, like art itself, and may take the form of a single sentence, a paragraph, even a footnote or a character. It always involves secrets, though. One of the interesting things about literature is its ability to sustain secrets that are partly indecipherable and partly decipherable – for you, the writer, too. But the important thing is that 'partly'. Similarly, if someone comes up with an interpretation of a poem of mine that I had never thought of but which makes sense when I hear it, I am really pleased and feel I have succeeded. Literature is about creating a potential space in or around the work which is funnier, more intelligent and wiser than I could ever be on my own. A part of trying to achieve this is creating these ornaments.

KJL: *Do you think that some of your novels – I am thinking of* Mitgift *or even* Sieben Sprünge *– are actually driven by those half-disclosed secrets?*

UD: In *Mitgift* or *Sieben Sprünge* there are family secrets not accessible to the characters, who then spend time in the narrative circling around them. It is like a secret space inside the novel; but you can only see the outer shape or detect a certain radiance. Secrets distort the things around them, a bit like a planetary field, but there is no direct access to them. There again, it is also about the language and phrasing. A good deal of fictional beauty can be created by digression and surprise. So a certain paragraph might be much like the mound there and lead you up a flight of stairs and down again without ever finding out anything in particular. Instead it is about creating a very specific tension, or an atmosphere, or opening up an unexpected view. And you need that whole paragraph including all the – no doubt beautifully-phrased – sentences that have no particular function other than to tell you, for example, that, while snowflakes are tumbling from a grey sky, a male blackbird pulls a worm out of the soil, shakes it and all the glory of life shines from his beady black eye.

KJL: *You have put me in mind of that scene in* Mitgift *where Karen has the drinking experience which, in a book that is all about economy and abstinence, is in a sense a glorious excess in and of itself – linguistically as well. Perhaps that is a mound, actually.*

UD: What a wonderful observation. There are these kind of freak moments in my texts. So much in the process of writing concerns control and economy – and how to avoid too much of it, which in a way only begs the question. Economy is always in danger of collapse into the severity of order. This is what you want to avoid. Actually, it is also a question of mimesis. Hearing 'mimesis', people often seem to think of how objects are described or how you put a convincing flight of stairs into a novel. But here is another level to it; it might be called a psychological one. We all have these freakish moments. To include them in a novel is truthful; it means truthfulness to life. The freakish thing appears as an excess, or pure joy. You can never capture it by simply describing it, though: the language has to take it on, to take up all of its energy. It has to be in every single tone – and that is true even for prose. Vladimir Nabokov is a wonderful example of a prose writer who worked this kind of depth into the rhythmic patterns of his prose.

KJL: *We are here looking up at the medieval City Wall which runs through the College, standing next to the so-called indecipherable stone. Why have you brought us here?*

UD: The medieval wall that runs through New College is quite something in itself. But there is also this weathered stone that is a mystery. What you can make out is a face: a nose, a huge smiling mouth and a stuck-out tongue, eyes, curly hair, or a mane. It might be an animal; it could be half-human, or just an imaginary being and I like it because of its energy (Fig. 3). Again it tells you something about reading processes. If this stone were in India, everyone would immediately interpret it as an image of Kali, showing her tongue as a sign she has slaughtered armies of men. Or, again in another context, it could be interpreted as a sign of shame. In our European cultural context it might be a symbol of triumph, or even a sign depicting danger: someone warning 'I might devour you'. Or maybe something like 'I am just grinning, or in a sort of ecstasy, or slightly mad'. Sometimes, at least, when reading, you find yourself immersed in scenes and among characters whose behaviour remains indecipherable in the end. I am thinking, for example, of Ernest Hemingway's short story *The Short Happy Life of Francis Macomber.* By the close of the story Macomber ends up dead; he is shot by his wife. As it happens on a safari, in public, while Macomber is shooting a buffalo he has been hunting, this seems to be a clear-cut fact. But it remains open whether his death was the result of an accident or half an accident or a fully intentional killing. Readers come up with widely diverging interpretations. For me this is part of what is beautiful about literature.

Fig. 3: Indecipherable stone.

KJL: *How does it work in the context of historical literature, though?*

UD: This is actually one of the particular challenges of the historical novel. As you write, or indeed read, a historical novel you always know how history continued, how the story ended, as far as the historical events are concerned. But as a writer you then have to think back to the present time of the characters and imagine what it might really have been like to be a German in a small Silesian town in 1935, for example, without any knowledge of what would come. It was a time full of possibilities with seemingly nothing yet decided. As a writer you need to open up time again, open up space, and introduce life into the writing by introducing possibilities, ambiguities, indecipherable signs, be they people, animals, objects or the codes that the characters encounter but can't interpret. If you do this the distance between the historical events and the contemporary reader will vanish and the reader will be able to identify with the historical characters and feel some of the challenges of the historical epoch, some of time's intriguing and threatening potential.

KJL: *Yes, you are opening it up. Cracking it open.*

UD: Cracking time open, I like this. It resembles the half-open mouth of this indecipherable stone.

LM: *We've moved inside again to the Long Room, now a space used for events and readings, and where you have read, Ulrike, but which is actually on the site of the medieval lavatories. It seems an appropriate place to ask you about the term* 'Stoffwechsel'. *It is something that comes up often in the chapters in this volume and in your work and is very difficult to translate into English.*

UD: For me *Stoffwechsel* as a concept is connected to translation. Indeed 'translation' itself might actually be a nice translation for *Stoffwechsel*. In German it is one of these immediately comprehensible words – it literally means 'change of stuff/ cloth/ material' – that indicate the constant processes of chemical transformation that go on in the body: 'metabolism' would be the dictionary translation. I have long thought of it as a useful metaphor or field of images to describe what goes on in literature. Writing is a kind of double *Stoffwechsel*. You start by experiencing reality and want to render that experience into language and put it on page. So you are already involved in translation: the medium changes. It comes out of a living body and a living body's experience and becomes words. But these have to be a very specific kind of words which can be re-translated in the readers' minds into an experience, very often a physical one, which in turn connects with their own memories and experiences. So we are talking about a two-fold process. It is similar with emotion, of course. I have experienced a specific emotion, for example, and I want to give this to a character; so I translate it from my memories, from my whole being as a living person, into language. But there is another change to account for here, too. A writer uses everyday language (whether German or English) that everybody has and that we are surrounded by and which we put to many uses. But then a kind of transformation happens within that language: another *Stoffwechsel*. Language itself is being translated into a different kind of intensity organized along principles beyond the normal structures of grammar, syntax and spelling. It is very difficult to put your finger on because this 'other' of language only exists as a cloud; it only consists in the gaps between the words, in their music, their rhythms, or in the world of *that* literary text. But here too some kind of *Stoffwechsel* takes place. You can find traces of it if you know where to look: the sequences of vowels for example, the patterns of vowels, or the graphic images of words. But there is no way of calculating its effect. And that's where a third *Stoffwechsel* comes in: the way that effect will always be created by the individual reader, how this life and this person and the literary work meet and where they meet and when, and what comes out of this particular encounter. There is a richness about that, an abundance, created by the wealth of possibilities. For this reason I have never been particularly upset when I've finished a novel and it comes to the point of letting it go. With something like *Sieben Sprünge*, of course, this wasn't easy. I had spent so many years working on it and it had been such an intense experience that it took me over a year to say goodbye to this novel's world, to externalize it, if you like. But I've never felt any regret about the fact that it is now out in the world and that people might hopefully encounter it and add themselves to it. It's a very complicated and, at the same time, a very straightforward way of continuing a conversation.

LM: *And that is what the website does that accompanies the book. It is the continuation, 'der siebte Sprung' [the seventh leap].*

UD: Yes, that is right. And translation is a special case, somewhere between the writing process I have described and the reading process. As an author I've been involved in two basically different kinds of scenario when my own work was being translated. The first one concerns languages I at least partly understand. In those cases I feel I have a certain amount of control. I love to communicate with translators, because I always reckon I can judge from their questions how close an understanding they have acquired – and what their attitude towards their task might be. In the end it is up to them to decide. Which is not a free for all: there are things that can be lost, mistakes that can be made and better or worse ways of approaching it. But in the second scenario, where one does not under-stand a word of the language the work is being translated into, you simply have to hand it over to the translator and of course their whole cultural system might be different, their traditions of poetry or writing. There would be no point wanting to control these transla-tions anyway. One knows right from the start that the translated poem will be something completely different – and that this will be a good sign! The transformation can be quite miraculous. Last year I heard some of my poems being read out in Marathi, for example, and saw how the audience reacted. I knew that something 'flew' across. I don't have the faintest idea what it was, mind you; but if the audience reacts emotionally and seems to be kind of 'held' by the poem's music this is wonderful.

KJL: *It strikes me that there is another way this is important in relation to your work. It is quite rare for an author who is established in one language to then begin writing in another as you have done while you have been here in the UK with English. That is part of what we discussed when we first talked about this year in Oxford. I wonder if you could talk a little bit about this kind of dual track you have developed here – writing in German and English. Or is it a kind of* 'Stoffwechsel' *too?*

UD: Well, it has been quite a surprise for me. True, I'd wanted to come to the UK for a long time, in order to see whether something like this could develop or not. It has also made a couple of things quite clear to me about my writing in German. Because of my specific writing history, especially the importance of the English language to me from the age of around twenty onwards, there have always been certain underlying English struc-tures to my writing in German. Those are sometimes linguistic, but more often they are literary. I studied English literature and most of what I know about narrative or poetic forms I learned by examples set in English. So an ode to me is connected to Grecian urns and London's nightingales. I don't know any ancient Greek, my path was paved by Hölder-lin, first, and changed by Keats. In fiction Virginia Woolf and James Joyce were formative for my ideas about structure and voice. This has given a certain edge, some degree of weirdness even, to my writing in German, because it never really absolutely fits into German traditions. It helps to be innovative of course. Now, having been here for one and a half years and having started to write in English, there is a second layer which operates in reverse. It's now my English that is marked by all kinds of more or less unsubtle German structures and blunders and ways of thinking. Precisely this is what I am exploring at the moment in a project which is called simply *Schwitters*.

I happened to come across Kurt Schwitters when someone told me about his 'Merz Barn' up in the Lake District during the first couple of weeks after I had arrived at Oxford. As I listened a voice in my head started whispering: 'this is it' – the perfect man for me, the perfect character for me trying to write in English. He came to England from Norway in 1940 as a German refugee and stayed here until his death early in 1948. His daily life happened in English of course and while he was here he began writing his letters in English, and translating his own work into what I have come to call his 'tongue of survival'. I started to write a kind of 'biography' of his last years, his English years, and realized it had to be in English because this would have been how he perceived the world through the language and how I could follow him much more specifically. At a practical level, any subcutaneous German left in my English could easily be attributed to him. That's why he is so perfect. He is my mask.

As I was working on the material I became increasingly interested in investigating how the German language, German ways of thinking and German idioms might impact on the English language and literary forms. After I had sketched out the whole novel I was approached by a friend, who was looking for a text for a joint Scandinavian artists' project: a *Künstlerbuch*. I mentioned that I only had a few pages in English, but they were delighted because that meant it wouldn't have to be translated for the project. I gave them the beginning of the Schwitters book and they produced lovely art to go with it.[4] The surprise came when my friend Lothar Seruset rang a couple of weeks later to get the German original, which of course didn't exist. It was only when I sat down to translate my English original into German that I fully realized what kind of project I had been cradling. It will have to be written in both languages, the German following the English. So now I want to translate the entire book into German to form a kind of split novel; split in that it is in two languages and two different bodies – a book in England and a book in Germany.

This is all part of a long-term preoccupation with forcing the novel out of its very comfortable nineteenth-century bed and introducing current media constellations and current life constellations like migration into the literary form. With *Schwitters* it involves a three-fold translation process: translating a life which was itself translated from Germany to England; translating it into English though my native tongue is German; and then re-translating it back into German and taking it to Germany. A lot of *Stoffwechsel*. [*Laughter*].

LM: *How do you see your future work developing?*

---

4 *Schwitters*, limited edition book: text by Ulrike Draesner, images by Angelique van Wesemael, Mia Hochrein, Vera Olsson, Lothar Seruset (Malmö and Berlin: Lentzke, Berlin, 2016/2017).

UD: When Karen and I were thinking all that time ago in the Berlin Television Tower about what I would do here, I couldn't have foreseen this. The *Schwitters* only really happened because I am here. And because all this 'reality' has been here as well: a real place, real England and real people I have been able to talk to. This has all come out of this time here and I am so grateful. I can see a kind of trilogy now. *Sieben Sprünge* is the first part. There the novel was chased out of its comfortable literary existence by adding this other supplementary existence for it on the internet. The *Schwitters*, which again deals with the Second World War and its consequences – trauma, exile, migration – is the second 'exiling'; and there the project, the border-crossing, is a linguistic one. And I have ideas for a third volume – at least as far as the topic is concerned. I just have to devise the transgression; the borders are keeping me busy at the moment. But this is a long term project: perhaps for the next five or ten years as far as my novel-writing is concerned.

LM: *We have ended up in the College library surrounded by books and this prompts me to ask about your role as a reader and the effect that reading has on your writing.*

UD: I have always been a keen reader and enjoyed reading – actually because I am basically very lazy. I have never been able to conceive of how anybody can think while walking. It takes up all my energies simply to walk! I need to lie in a bed with a cup of tea. Then, without having to move physically, I can immerse myself in worlds of words – and swoop through space and time effortlessly. Reading conveys so many forms of knowledge simultaneously – from facts to inner emotional states – and there needn't be a real separation between the different areas of knowledge, or between inner and outer. Since my childhood I've always felt that all these realms of life are intrinsically connected. Language to me seems to penetrate all areas of what we now call science. All forms of science rely on signs and concepts that are phrased in language. There is no mathematics without a special language, for example; scientists have to think in language too. And these languages rely on metaphors. A striking one, which has been used for a while now, is that of the genetic code, the genetic alphabet; but that, for example, implies all kinds of interesting questions about syntax, letters or rules. Also, as we know, metaphors tend to be helpful and illuminating, on the one hand, but they are good at hiding things as well. I feel there might be a specific competence that can be added by linguists and people who deal with languages in a real dialogue with science. Greek philosophy tells us there are basically two forms of knowledge: things we know and, far exceeding them in number, things we do not know. But then there are also those things about which we do not know that we do not know. And those that we do not know how to know; where we touch, for example, on memories of traumatic events again.

KJL: *Known knowns; known unknowns; and unknown unknowns pace Donald Rumsfeld! But let's not go there. And Slavoj Žižek added the 'known unknowns': the subconscious.*

UD: I am especially attracted to 'unknown unknowns'. It is probably the biggest section of all and it is a wonderful area for literature. If you imagine language as a net or a lasso, it can allow you to cast out into the unknown and sometimes you catch something and draw it a little closer, so you might see something of the silhouette or contours at least. You might feel something; you might intuit something of it. What could this intuition be and how would you feel it or put it into language? This is where we come full circle; where the reader and author, both parts of me, rejoice and I feel this is what literature can do.

KJL: *As you were talking I couldn't help thinking about your critical essays in* Schöne Frauen lesen *and* Heimliche Helden. *They are quite remarkable in the way you make porous scientific norms and introduce a very personal element. But I was also struck by the scientist figures in your novels who are very human and very fallible. Knowledge is used or misused or inflected by the very people they are. It was so interesting to hear you talk about knowledge and feeling in the same sentence.*

UD: You cannot really separate them. We always try to; and it might be one of the foundational myths of our society that you can. But it is a fairly recent myth, if you think about it. In medieval times, for example, there were many orders of the world, presided over by God and regulated through Christian hierarchies and institutions, but you would never have had this strict division between purely rational knowledge, and other kinds of knowing. I am most interested in the space in between and even my fictional scientists, as you just mentioned, have various and partly fairly 'irrational' lives. There would be their professional roles and identities, of course, but emotions from their personal life seep into these rational set-ups that, often enough, turn out not to be as rational as one might expect. The astronomer Harriet in *Vorliebe* even has to produce deliberately 'forged' pictures of her field of research in order to raise extra funding for her institute. Beautiful pictures sell. But even on a more scientific level, the influence of story-telling is amazing – as the very successful story of the Big Bang, originally devised by a Catholic priest, nicely illustrates. These strategies of developing theories and administrating knowledge inform what my characters think they might know and how they might sometimes rather want to avoid knowledge. There is a certain grace in not knowing, and *Vorliebe* revolves around it.

LM: *So it's about ways of knowing?*

UD: Yes. It presupposes a secondary order of knowledge: the knowledge of how to know, or how to acquire knowledge and how to judge that knowledge. This last might be the most important and is influenced by emotion, by personal states, by memories, by your whole life-history. When I worked on *Sieben Sprünge* I talked to the neuro-scientist Wolf Singer, who explained that the metaphor for this in science would be the 'architecture of the brain'. Now, the development of the architecture of our brains naturally follows certain genetic, cellular and physical rules but these only provide a rough framework. The phenotypical architecture of the brain is built by the individual's entire personal history starting in the uterus. It is your personal life experience that determines the amounts and concrete shapes of the connections between your synapses. So, quite literally, your personal history constantly feeds into your rational decisions. Sometimes your brain decides for you. Looking at it, scientists can see what you are going to do milli-seconds before you do it – or even know you are going to do it. And this is rationality; the product of your emotional life. It's funny and appropriate talking about this in a library: kind of subversive. But then literature is subversive too. A collective treasure trove, containing so many more things between heaven and earth than any individual might ever come up with or even dream of in his or her life.

Ulrike Draesner
Schwitters

1

hallo!

sweat

schwitzen

halo of sheep

Schwitters'

(ap)posite

(positive?

Positz?)

withering weiter

Stretching its spinsterly fingers, the fog crept through the air a few inches above the meadow, which it seemed to render visible and hide each time it took a breath. Spinsterly presumably wasn't the right word, presumably 'presumably' wasn't the right word, he was suspicious of himself, 'spinsterly' was probably a deduction, a deuce casting dice in his head, from 'Gespinst'. Still, he liked the sounds that entered him, the fine fingerishness of fog hovering above an English meadow, he liked how it managed to hover&creep, ever changing shapes. It wasn't exactly alive, wasn't exactly mental, just beyond him. It made the sheep protrude, their limbs, even individual dirty white curls jutted out, whereas it didn't appear even so much as to touch the animals themselves, it bulged around their flesh, creating extra halos of sheep in the bristling air of this morning in early October.

Here he sat, a halo of a man, and found himself loving the fog.

Having turned into a spinsterly existence out of the brown.

Terminal Amblewater, Lake District. 'Lake Destruction', something sought to whisper, hovering above him at night, but he didn't allow it to catch up with him. Down it spoke onto the hollow shape of his body, his halo, curved, bulky and huge, Kurt in his barn, any of his barns, sheepishly still.

The local newspaper had printed a line or two announcing his arrival: German writer and artist A. Schweitter, exiled from Oslo. Blunt lie. However, they had exerted themselves to reproduce a photograph, though it had been distorted so badly that at first he hadn't recognised himself. For a second he had been fooled

This is Ulrike Draesner's own English-language version of a chapter from her novel *Schwitters*. An English translation of the German-language publication by Sharon Howes won the 2021 Goethe-Institut Award for New Translation.

https://doi.org/10.1515/9783110495942-013

by the illusion – another artist, here –, then pleased, thinking that it showed the farmer who owned the sheep, a neighbour, because here land was vast, humans sparse, hence everybody neighboured everybody.

He scrutinized the photograph for a while, unable to remember where it might have been taken.

Scrutinize: how you screwed your eyes into something examining it, probing. Digging almost. Scr-scr-scarce-crow eyes. He was acutely aware how using this language instead of his native, ha, native, lost, dwindling German, transformed him even physically.

He loved this feeling. He was afraid of the process, he, the halo of Kurt from Hannover, this hangover, indeed. Kurt whose face resembled the surface of porridge in the narrow mirror above the sink. He smirked. Smirking porridge, comforted by staring at sheep and their hollow shapes formed by the attending fogs of an English autumn meadow.

Ridiculously comforted. An old man, panting after a ten-minute stroll up one of these hills in Lake Destruction's enticing eternal damp.

Excited by its vivid multitude of greys. Greyhound grey, granite grey, sky grey, slate grey, slug slime silver grey, flint glimmer-grey, grey of twilight, of dawn, of north, of tongue of sheep.

For a while he had stared at the photograph, strangely attracted precisely by the veracity of its distortions. A. Schweitters, longing to be a sheep which some wise English fog would hide&show, doubling shapes. Maybe as a sheep he'd be black? A. Schweitters. I might as well call myself Ash, or Asch or Wash, he had mused contemplating the caption, depending on my mood and my wish to ease the others' tongues. To obliterate them? No, to insinuate . . . to intrinsicate . . . – he would have to ask Wantee on this one.

Fog's grace. He had escaped, jumped (last minute) from the devil's camp and landed on English meadows that were water, water in a state different only in miniscule degrees from the waters of the sea.

His entire country in ruins and half of the world devastated on top. This was how the story ran on bad days, swelling with the murmurs of the rivulets, etching their patterns into the meadow sloping from the hills. The soil was streaked with gunpowder dust, the munitions works that had occupied the site closed. He had lost his drawings and collages, most of his paintings, the plethora of his sculptures and his Merzbau in Hannover. Never again would he set foot in Germany. He was alive though surrounded by people who spoke a foreign language and didn't know anything about his past, and even for those close to him most of his self remained invisible and unfathomable. He had lost his roots, all his money, had spent 16 months as a prisoner in an English camp, he was poor and in poor health, most of his teeth were gone. More often Wantee and he wouldn't eat supper, just have a cup of tea, go to bed early, no gas, no electricity, no food. He was the very image of a tramp, the children of the village pointed at him, the winds were awful, tearing his lungs apart, only just had he turned 60 and could hardly walk, his veins were 95 years of age, his left hip 82, he was in pain, he had memories, he lost speech in dreams, lost any language. The English had sung, having won the war, everybody had been cheery in May '45, but now he knew that the song wasn't true, Hitler and Stalin had been the victorious ones, the fires were burning. He opened their front door at dusk, stepped onto the narrow pavement and there it would be, a fire, not huge, resembling those they had ignited back home in Hannover to burn dry leaves. People strode through the flames, unaffected, without seeing, his eyes however followed the tongues of flames and the silhouettes of those figures, who, dried and eerie *like ghosts from an enchanter fleeing*, looked like having followed him to this place.

He didn't know what 'enchanter' meant. Wantee had used the phrase. To him 'from an encounter' would have made sense. Ghosts didn't like encounters. He didn't like ghosts.

On a good day the becks rippled to a different tune, feeding the gunpowder meadow to grow green grass. He would transform war into art, part of an adorable landscape, ridged and fresh, full of animal life, smells of turf and sea, inhabited by friendly people who commissioned portraits and served his favourite bitter beer. He had been put into a Camp, but it had been Hutchinson on the Isle of Man, the camp of the intellectuals, he had been recognised as the poet and artist he was and had found support, had survived the Blitz in London, even found a companion, a breath-taking young woman who lived with him, teaching him English and teasing him. His son was happy in Norway, his hands had survived undamaged, he was able to walk and stoop, had a doctor, who told awful stories but was excellent at chess, and when he watched the fires burning it helped him gather strength for his fight.

The winds never cease, his hands are warm. Every day, good and bad alike, is a day at war.

Halos of sheep, sheep heads protruding above the fog as if severed – yet alive, lovely sheep, balls of fog, two or three or four legs, some bearing bold black markings, rooted to the ground. Here and there a single sheepish eye squinted into the sun.

Three years should do it. He was bargaining for three years.

As he raised his eyes the sheep had moved. Walking heads, the black and white crowns of Swaledales, he learnt his lessons, above the fog, no spines, no bellies, no legs. Walking forms of sheep, skins crumbled, curly as porridge drying in a bowl. Swaledale one in position three, Swaledale two at the corner of the field, three and four huddling side by side. Fog and wind and the cold playing a tune: K. Schweitters, K. Weiter-Schwitzer. His bones were as hard as his shoes, given to him by a Marylebone charity shop.

Two years, if he sped up. Concentrated as hard as he could. Mustered, no mastered up his strength.

The war was over, but didn't stop. The Allies had declared their victory, but the victory had transformed into single victories of adverse meaning. Hitler had won parts of the war, Stalin still was winning. But here he was. A survivor against all odds. Sat, in the glorious morning sun.

He knew that he had started out on his last journey.

There was only one faulty, soft cog in the machine. Him. This incalculable mass of blood, veins and bronchial tubes. Carve, invent, think the new Merzbau up with his hands. He would, yet again, need to transform himself into a wall. Knowing perfectly well what this meant he shrunk back. Nobody ever saw the strength it took. It took all of you: a huge man bent over a lump of plaster that two clumsy hands tried to shape into a hen. Be wise. Listen to the voices in the air.

His father had travelled regularly while Kurt was a boy. The partings were horrible, with the exception of one moment, some seconds after his Vati had passed the platform gate. It reminded of a stable door, two swinging wooden panels, two windows above, which allowed those staying back to watch the heads of their beloved ones amble away. If you were a child you would just see the sky, and if you were Kurt, the child, you'd be down on your knees. The doors only commenced some three inches above the ground; their shades dancing lines on the platform's stones. When Kurt stretched his hand above the ghastly ballet Eduard's hand would meet his from the other side and join his fingers, once more. This was what had to happen while he moulded stone, plaster or wood or bent a length of wire: he had to join himself up with himself, with each of his former and future selves. And next he had to be lucky, wait for this hand to reach for him from the other side, the side ever beyond, to join him and guide him and sustain him above the swift dancing shades of everything he had ever known and ever been.

The new Merzbarn would require three years, this was the bitter truth. After having suffered this stroke in February, after, in addition, having coughed blood on that splendid day in mid-summer, he had not been able to take the plunge until July.

Here he was against all odds, ready to fight the last act of his feud. Kurt. Curt Kurt. Some curls of fleece of sheep, some spoonfuls of fog.

1: Schaf(f)en

hallo!

sweat

schwitzen

halo of sheep

Schwitters'

(ap)posite

(positive?

Positz?)

withering weiter

Der Nebel streckte seine gespinstigen Finger und kroch wenige Zentimeter über die Wiese voran, die er mit jedem seiner Atemzüge sowohl sichtbarer zu machen als auch zu verstecken schien. „Gespinstig" war vermutlich nicht das richtige Wort, er richtete seinen Verdacht gegen sich selbst, vermutlich war nicht einmal „vermutlich" richtig, er traute sich in keiner Sprache mehr über den Weg. Gespinstig war wahrscheinlich eine Folge, ein Schluss, erzeugt von einem koboldhaften Gespenst, das Wörter herumwürfelte in seinem Kopf. Die Mischung der englischen und deutschen Laute stieß ihm zu, und er mochte sie, mochte die "formidable Fingerhaftigkeit" des englischen Nebels, dieses Hundes (dog) auf f (fog), wie er hechelte über der englischen Wiese und gleichzeitig festhing, kriechen&kleben, schweben&schleichen, die Gestalt stets neu verzerrt. Nicht ganz wie ein Lebewesen, nur fast, nicht ganz verrückt, nur fast, und fraglos jenseits dessen, was Kurt, genannt Körrt, fasste oder begriff. Der Nebel verwandelte die Schafe in schafförmige Vorsprünge, ihre Gliedmaßen und sogar einige der schmutzig-weißen Löckchen standen einzeln hervor, während die halbdurchsichtige Feuchtigkeit die Tiere als solche nicht einmal berührte, sondern sich um ihr Körper wölbte und Schafsumriss um Schafsumriss in die haarsträubend knisternde Luft dieses frühen Oktobermorgens stellte.

Und da saß er, der Umriss eines Mannes, und beobachtete sich dabei, wie er Nebel mochte. Sich in Nebel verliebte.

Er, der ein gespinstiges Leben führte, der sich nach dem Ende des Krieges hier nach Ambleside geflüchtet hatte. Seit einem guten Jahr waren sie nun da. Endstation Lake District. Lake Destruction schien ihm etwas zuzuflüstern, hechelnd hing es über ihm, er ließ nicht zu, dass es ihn gefangennahm. Auch wenn es heruntersprach auf die hohle Form seines Körpers, seinen Umriss, gebogen und grau, klobig und groß, Kurt in seinem Schober, irgendeinem Schober, schäfchenstill.

Die Lokalzeitung hatte eine kurze Meldung über seine Ankunft gebracht: German writer and artist A. Schweitter, exiled from Oslo. Sie hatten sich Mühe gegeben und sogar ein Foto mitabgedruckt. Es war so verzerrt, dass er sich zunächst nicht erkannt hatte. Sekundenlang hatte er an einen anderen Künstler geglaubt, hier, dann sich gefreut, weil er meinte, das Bild zeige den Bauern, dem die Schafe gehörten, einen Nachbarn. In der weiten Kargheit der Berge kamen Menschen so selten vor, dass jeder jedes Nachbar war.

Eine Weile hatte er das Foto aufs Genaueste betrachtet, ohne sich daran erinnern zu können, wo es aufgenommen worden war.

Scrutinize, nannte man solches Schauen, es klang wie screw-tin-eyes. Zinnaugen schrauben sich in etwas und untersuchen es, bohrten nach. Er fühlte, wie es ihn veränderte, sogar körperlich, dass er auf Englisch dachte statt auf Deutsch, seinem eingeborenen, verlorenen, sich windenden, schwindelnden Deutsch.

Er genoss dieses Gefühl. Er, der Umriss von Kurt aus Hannover-Hinüber, Starrte er mit deutschem Blick auf Revonnah (wann hatte er angefangen, Namen rückwärts zu sagen?), starrte ihm ein "renn" daraus zurück, "renn-von-nah", und der englische Kurt zerriss den Namen endgültig in ein laut gesagtes "Ha?", "no!", "over".

Hallo Nachbar! Nun saß er hier, er wunderte sich selbst noch, auf einer englischen Weide. Und keine Spur von Zerstörung, nur Schafe und ihre Hohlformen. Ihm war gleichgültig, dass sein Gesicht morgens in dem schmalen Spiegel über dem Küchenbecken einer Portion Haferschleim glich. Zum ersten Mal seit zehn Jahren hatte er einen Ort, London, verlassen, weil er wollte, und als Ziel einen Ort gewählt, den er ebenfalls wollte. Zum ersten Mal seit zehn Jahren war er umgezogen, statt zu fliehen. Diesmal hatte er die Frau, mit der er zusammenlebte, mitnehmen können. Ambleside war das Dorf seiner Wahl. Ein Nest von einem Ort zwischen Gipfeln mit Namen wie Loughrigg Tarn, Old Man of Coniston, mit den Fells Heron Pike und Crinkle Crags, dessen langgestreckter Höhengrat aus fünf Erhebungen und den tiefen Faltungen zwischen ihnen bestand. Das Wort "fell" hatte er hier erst gelernt. Es bedeutete Hügel oder Fels über der Baumgrenze, gletschergeformt, karg, zerschrammt. Die Schafe des Districts fraßen noch das härteste Gras, Butler Fog kredenzte seiner Lady Meadow, Bestbottom of Autumn, jede Stunde frischen Herbstsuppendampf.

Er erholte sich hier. Ein alter Mann, der nach Luft schnappte, wenn er zehn Minuten einen der Hügel hinaufstapfte in der einzigartigen Nichttrockenheit von Lake Destruction.

Erregt von der lebendigen Vielfalt ihrer Grautöne.

Windhundgrau, granitgrau, himmelsgrau, schiefergrau, nacktschneckensilberschleimgrau, flintflimmergrau, zwielichtgrau, morgendämmerungsgrau, nordgrau, schafzungengrau.

Er hatte auf das Zeitungsbild gestarrt, angezogen, ja angetan davon, wie wahrhaftig ihm ausgerechnet seine Verzerrungen erschienen. Schweitters, der

sich danach sehnte, ein Schaf zu werden, das der weise englische Nebel ver-
stecken&zeigen würde, indem er jedes Ding in Gestalt und Riss verdoppelte.
Wäre er als Schaf schwarz? A. Schweitters. Könnte mich genauso Ash nennen,
oder Asche oder Wash, fröhlicher Laune sein und den Leuten ein wenig ange-
nehmer haferschleimig aus dem Mund spazieren.

Um seine Nachbarn an sich zu binden. Es war vertrackt. Ein track war ein
Gleis. Wenn man jemanden "trackte", verfolgte man ihn. Halt, das war das Nor-
wegengefühl: Pass auf, sie kommen und werfen dich raus. Da war ihm England
gleich noch einmal so lieb: Meldepflicht? Man pfiff darauf.

Er hatte sich an London gewöhnt gehabt, sich ein weiteres Mal losgerissen.
Wantee riss er mit. Niemand sagte ihm, dass er in Ambleside etwas zu suchen
hätte. London konnten sie sich nicht mehr leisten, wenngleich das nicht den
Ausschlag gegeben hatte. Ihn trieb seine Kunst. Take your life into your hand.
Nein, sagte Wantee, it's take charge of your life. Hier lud man sein Leben auf wie
eine Batterie oder verstand es als Fracht. Im Deutschen wollte es ein Tier sein,
Puls auf Puls, gehalten in der Hand. Er spürte, wie es da kauerte. Es zitterte.

Ein Morgen auf einer Wiese in gnädigem Nebel. Mitunter schwankte der Boden.
Das galt als natürlich. Eine englische Wiese war mehr Wasser als Grund, Wiese in
einem Aggregatzustand, der sich bloß in Graden von Meerwasser unterschied.

Der Krieg hatte ausgekriegt. Sein Land lag in Schutt und Asche. Die halbe
Welt lag in Schutt und Asche auf Rechnung seines Landes. So schritt, so lief, so
eilte die Geschichte. Sie eilte ihm hinterher. Tief gruben die Bäche ihre Muster
in die Wiesen, das Wasser rannte zum Meer. Nichts zerstört hier in den Lakes,
gleichwohl nichts vom Krieg unberührt. Man sah es auf den zweiten Blick. In
vielen Häusern fehlte der Mann. Doktor Johnston war aus dem Ruhestand in
seine alte Praxis zurückgekehrt. Auf dem Weg zum nächsten Dorf Richtung
Westen erstreckte sich ein bemerkenswertes Stück Land, über dessen Boden
Streifen von Pulverstaub zogen. Die Munitionsfabrik, die dort gestanden hatte,
war abgerissen. Nie wieder wollte er einen Fuß nach Deutschland setzen. Er
hatte überlebt, aber die Menschen, die ihn umgaben, sprachen eine fremde
Sprache und kannten nichts aus seiner Vergangenheit. Selbst den Vertrautes-
ten blieb, was er gewesen war, unsichtbar, ja unvorstellbar. Das stand ihm
nun, nach über sechs Jahren im Vereinigten Königreich und fünf Jahren Zusammenleben mit Wantee überdeutlich vor Augen. Die Wurzeln waren gekappt,
das Vermögen verloren, er war ein mittelloser Schlucker bei miserabler Gesund-
heit. Frühzeitig krochen sie abends nach einer Tasse Tee ins Bett, Heizung –
was für eine Idee, Brot – welch Traum. Auf die Dörfler wirkte er wie ein Penner.
Die Kinder zeigten mit dem Finger auf ihn, der Wind der Fells zerrte an der
Lunge, zerriss die Luft. Er ging auf die 60 zu. Manchmal tat ihm der Wind wohl,
dann wieder kam er nicht gegen die Böen an. Seine Arterien waren 95, die linke

Hüfte 82, er hatte Schmerzen, er hatte Erinnerungen, er wollte vergessen, was „haben" hieß, da „hatte es ihn". Hitler war tot, der ununterbrochene Nachtschlaf zerstört, das Träumen von Mehltau belegt.

Im Mai 1945 hatten die Engländer gesungen. Ihr Wort für Sieg, victory, reimte auf Geschichte, history. Leider ebenso auf misery, Elend. Der deutsche Führer und sein russischer Widerpart hatten die Welt so bösartig in Brand gesteckt, dass die Feuer auch nun, eineinhalb Jahre nach dem Fall Berlins, nach den Bomben auf Hiroshima und Nagasaki, weiterloderten. Der Krieg mochte zu Ende sein. Wann hörte er auf? Wollte Kurt die Feuer sehen, musste er nur in der Dämmerung auf den schmalen Gehweg vor der Haustür treten, da züngelten sie, nicht hoch, einem Kartoffelfeuer zuhause, in Hannover, gleich. Back home. Einst-Daheim.

Passanten schritten durch den Brand, ohne dass die Hitze ihnen etwas antat, sie sahen ihn auch nicht. Seine Augen hingegen folgten Abend um Abend dem Lecken der Flammen und den Silhouetten der in ihnen zuckenden Figuren, die ihm, Kurt von Rückhause, trocken und gespensterhaft bis hierher nachgeeilt sein wollten.

An guten Tagen sang das Rinnsal vor der Tür eine andere Melodie, das Gras der Wiesen wucherte fett und grün. Krieg in Kunst verwandeln, Stroh zu Gold, und es gelänge ihm doch. Die Landschaft war herrlich, so zerklüftet und frisch, Tiere rundum, es roch nach Torf und Meer, der Menschenschlag freundlich, man ließ sich von Körrt porträtieren, entlohnte ihn und servierte Bitter, sein Lieblingsbier. Unbeschadet hatte er den Bombenblitz überstanden. Sein Sohn lebte in Sicherheit in Norwegen, seine Hände hämmerten, kneteten, schnitten oder schrieben ohne wehzutun, er konnte gehen und sich bücken, hatte einen Arzt, der furchtbare Geschichten erzählte, zum Ausgleich mittelmäßig Schach spielte, und dass die Feuer loderten, half ihm, Kraft zu sammeln für seinen Kampf.

Und an schlechten? Nein, die ließ er aus. Die erlebte man, das reichte. Der Wind pfiff. Schafsköpfe ragten aus dem Nebel wie getrennt vom Rumpf. Prächtige Wollbälle, zwei oder drei Beine fest gegen den Erdboden gestemmt, verwurzelt im Grund. Hie und da erschien ein einzelnes Schafsauge, blinzelnd gegen die Sonne gestellt.

Drei Jahre sollten reichen. Er bat um drei Jahre.

Als er den Blick hob, hatten die Schafe sich weitergeschoben. Wandelnde Köpfe über dem Nebel, kein Rückgrat, kein Bauch, keinerlei Bein. Wandelnde schafige Gestalten, die Felle verkrumpelt, gelockt wie in einer Schüssel getrockneten Haferbreis. Schaf eins auf Position drei, Schaf zwei in der Ecke des Spielfeldes. Schaf drei und vier sannen Seite an Seite über die Vorzüge absoluter Ortstreue nach. Nebel und Kälte und Wind spielten ein Lied: K. Schweitters,

K. Weiter-Schwitzer. Seine Schuhe, man hatte sie ihm in einer Londoner Kleider-kammer geschenkt, waren hart wie seine Knochen.

Zwei Jahre, wenn er konzentriert arbeitete. All seine Kräfte aufbot. Auf-brachte. Nein, aufmachte. Oje, sein Deutsch. Da er keine der MERZbauten retten konnte, wollte er anfangen mit einem neuen Bau.

Die Alliierten hatten den Sieg erklärt, der Sieg war in Siege zerfallen. Diese Siege trugen gegensätzliche Bedeutungen. Hitler hatte den Weltkrieg verloren.

Den Familienzerschlagungskrieg, den Beschädigungskrieg, den Menschen-verderbungskrieg, den Vernichtungskrieg hatte er gewonnen. Stalin hatte oben-drein den Weltkrieg gewonnen. Der gesamte Kontinent roch nach Blut. Viel zu viele jener, die überlebt hatten, lebten wie tot. Das Gewinnen hörte für manche gar nicht mehr auf.

Folgerichtig schrieb Käthe Steinitz aus den USA von einem neuen Krieg. Sie war nach dem Tod ihres Mannes nach Los Angeles gezogen, schickte Kaffee, Shampoos und Erdnussbutter, eingewickelt in Zeitungspapier mit Comicstrips. Kurt schnitt Superman aus, Popeye, Mickey Mouse, Bugs Bunny, kombinierte, klebte, das waren Miniaturen, das entwickelte sich, das kopierte sich, davon wollte er mehr. Im Übrigen teilte die einstige Freundin mit, wie man sie schu-rigelte, die Ex-Deutsche, die Wieder-Deutsche, "die Kommunistin" oder "kom-munistisch Miteingereiste". They call it a cold war. Ihre Briefe wurden zensiert.

Er hingegen, Kurt, saß in der friedlichen englischen Morgensonne auf einem friedlichen Stein. Guten Tag! Ein einziges Rädchen in der Lakelands-Maschine lief nicht rund. Fehleranfällig und weich, eine unberechenbare Masse aus Venen, Bronchien, Blut – Kurt. Doch sie sollten ihn nicht kleingekriegt haben.

Your last shot.

Er ahnte, was das hieß, und schreckte davor zurück. Keiner sah, welche Anstrengung jede künstlerische Arbeit bedeutete. Was sollte auch zu sehen sein: Ein stattlicher Mann über einen Klumpen Gips gebeugt, dem zwei Hände, bisweilen unter Zuhilfenahme eines Spachtels, meist mit den bloßen Fingern, bald also ihrerseits über und über mit weißem Sulfat bedeckt, das Wesen eines Huhns beizubringen suchten.

In seiner Kindheit war sein Vater regelmäßig verreist. Die Abschiede hatte er als schrecklich empfunden bis auf die paar Sekunden, nachdem Eduard Schwit-ters durch die Absperrung auf den Perron getreten war. Die beiden Holzflügel, die wie Stalltüren Zentimeter über dem Boden endeten, schwangen nach dem Durch-gang einer Person eine Weile frei vor und zurück. Im oberen Drittel trugen sie Fen-ster, so dass jene, die zuhause blieben, die Köpfe der Menschen, die sie liebten, weggehen sehen konnten. Als Kind blickte man gegen Holz oder in den Himmel; war man Kind Kurt, kniete man vor dem Schlitz auf dem Boden und linste hin-durch. Er liebte es bis heute, das Ballett der Türschatten über den Fugen. Jedes

Mal, wenn er seine Hand durch die Schatten gestreckt hatte, war ihm die Hand des Vaters von der anderen Seite entgegengekommen und hatte seine Finger umschlossen.

Es mochte seltsam scheinen, dass ihm dies nun einfiel. Erinnerungen folgten eigenen Gesetzen, er hatte gelernt, sich ihnen anzupassen. Oft genug zog man nur hervor, was angenehm war. Vieles drückte das Gedächtnis dauerhaft weg. Alle Erinnerung verwirrte die Zeit. Es war dies vielleicht einer ihrer besten, zumindest kühnsten Aspekte: Sie, die tat, als hütete sie die Folge der Stunden, verquirlte deren innerste Ordnung. Diesmal war nicht schwer zu erraten, warum ihm der Perron eingefallen war. Er war darauf angewiesen, dass sich ihm eine Hand, über die er nicht bestimmen konnte, aus einem Bereich entgegenstreckte, den er nicht erkennen konnte. Zuerst musste er sich mit sich selbst verbinden, mit all seinen früheren und zukünftigen Selbst, um einen Stein zu bearbeiten, Gips zu formen, ein Stück Draht zu biegen. War dies gelungen, brauchte er ein weiteres Mal Glück. Nichts half, als auf die Hand von der anderen Seite zu warten, dieser ewig anderen Seite. Dass sie ihn traf, umfasste, ihn führte und ihn erhielt über den huschenden Schatten all dessen, was er je verstanden hatte, je gewesen war.

Er bat um drei Jahre. Drei Jahre für einen Bau.

Kurt, nun Körrt.

Körrt, kurzum: ein paar Kringel Schaffell, ein paar Löffel Nebeldunst.

Ulrike Draesner
Poems

hermaphroditisches proëm

hermaphrodit nacktkühle marmor–
gestalt zwischen dem blattwerk verdecktes
von schatten wie fingern kastaniengeblüt
in weiß, ich begreife den langezogenen leib
im gestriemten becken treibt die sichel
des mondes, der nadel, ich sehe wie mir
die blanke aufwölbung des bauches mir hermes
sprecher der liebe, gleitender bote, wie mir
die sehende hand, des artzes äskulap, hermaß
den inneren bauchraum, tastete die redselige
örtlichkeit blutwallung beinahe nicht zu orten
die beine entlaufen in den zärtlichen fischschwanz
beginnen die menschen hermetisch von alters her
daumengroß der kopf auf dem bild-schirm
ein schatten zum leben gerissene
zwitterform, däumling,
mein flimmerndes kind

hermaphrodite proem

coolly-naked marble hermaphrodite
figure among the leafage hidden
by fingery shadows a chestnut-kindred
in white, i take in the elongate body
adrift in the striate pelvis the crescent
moon, the navel, see the bare bulge
of my belly, how hermes speaker of love
gliding messenger, how the seeing hand
doctor asclepius's, measured my
ventral interior touched the voluble
locus in quo, a blood-surge barely palpable

Note: These texts use the calibrated punctuation and lower case, retrospectively developed by Draesner for her *hell & hörig. Gedichte 1995–2020* (Munich: Penguin, 2022) and *this porous fabric: Selected Poems*, trans. by Iain Galbraith (Bristol: Shearsman, 2022).

https://doi.org/10.1515/9783110495942-014

the legs running to that endearing fishtail
humans were hermetic from the first
the thumb-sized head on the image-screen
is a shadow, androgynous form
wrenched into life thumbling,
my shimmering child
                    (from *gedächtnisschleifen*)

haare, küssend

beredter holunder dieser
vielzungige holunder mein begieriger
liebeshunger wie ich mit allen haarsträhnen
wärmste befederung oder umarmung dich umfasste von
der seite dir um den nacken die wangen strich mit wehenden
haaren meine weißen tastenden dolden phantasiezungen
um dich schlang daß du ganz geflochten

stocktest,

als du gingst,
mitten im satz, dich
zu mir neigtest, bis meine lippen
auf deiner wange streiften meine lippen
bartstoppeln spürten einen tastenden augenblick
deine gefiederte antwort voraus: aufrauschen und vorübergehn

hair, kissing

eoquent elder bush this
many-tongued elder my greedy
hunger for love the way with warmest feathering
or embracing with all the coils of my hair I clasped you
from the side stroking your nape your cheeks with flowing
hair my probing white umbels my fantasy tongues
entwining you so that completely entangled you

faltered

as you left,
in mid-sentence,
leant over me till my lips
brushed against your cheek my lips
felt your bristles a fumbling moment long
ahead of your feathered response: hackles up and away
(from *gedächtnisschleifen*)

jemand gab mir feuer
das ich gar nicht wollte
was sollte ich damit
(mitten in der nacht)
und ich rannte herum
in den autos saßen menschen
ihr atem beschlug die scheiben
die autos standen am straßenrand
und ich rannte um es
wieder auszublasen das feuer
bis ich einen schwarzen lichtschalter fand
in einem hotel am bahnhof
eine lampe schwankte um ihren arm
ein vogel pfiff (nacht) und das feuer
knisterte hinten (oder war es nah)
im umspannwerk ich hatte es doch
gelöscht im takt zzzt ztt zzzt knisterte
mein limbisches hirn
eine entwicklerwanne das dumme ding
und der vogel schrie sein zzzt zttt zzzt in die nacht
wo das feuer manchmal sich
kleine vögel briet es
roch überall die anderen
sagten dass das der frühling sei
das feuer spielte blitz
und war ein baum
dabei wurde es lose (mein hirm) und
ein hotel mit schwarzem lichtschalter
als ich
darauf drückte machte es pscht und tscht und
dann immer heller zzzt zzzt zzzt
sprang vom hirn in den bauch
der kleine vogel briet
jetzt roch ich auch
dass es (doch) der frühling war.
leipzig, märz 2000

somebody gave me a light
i didn't even want it
what good was it to me
(in the middle of the night)
and i rushed about
people were sitting in cars
their breath steaming up the windows
the cars were on the roadside
and i rushed about
trying to blow out the fire
until i found a black light switch
in a hotel near the station
a lamp was swaying on its arm
a bird whistled (night) and the fire
crackled at the back (or was it nearby)
in the substation surely i had put it
out my limbic brain
crackled zzzt zttt zzzt in time
a developer tank the stupid thing
and the bird screamed its zzzt zttt zzzt into the night
where the fire sometimes
fried little birds there was
a smell everywhere the others
said that was spring
the fire played at lightning
and was a tree
in doing so it came loose (my brain) and
was a hotel with a black light switch which
when i
threw it went psht and tsht and
then grew ever brighter zzzt zzzt zzzt
leaping from my brain into my belly
the little bird fried
now i too smelled
that it (really) was spring.

leipzig, march 2000
                    (from *für die nacht geheuerte zellen*)

aufkommen

über den feldern der kleine fleck
wie er sich bog über die langen

sheddächer der lager wie
schnell er war dass das unsere
geschwindigkeit sei glaubte
das mädchen neben mir nicht
– angst flügel ein rumpf
zoomten auf uns zu
als ziehe jemand mit
schnellem seil uns
hinab wie die bäume
loderten im bruchteil
einer sekunde der räder
              touch down
sie sagte auf der erde sein heißt
seinen schatten berühren

coming down

above the fields the little speck
the way it curved across the long
sawtooth roofs of the depots
how fast it went the girl
beside me could not believe
that this was our own speed
– fear wings a fuselage
zooming towards us
as if someone with
rapid rope were pulling
us down the way the trees
blazed for a fraction
of a second of the wheels'
              touchdown
being on earth she said means
touching one's shadow
              (from *kugelblitz*)

bayrisch-seeland (ödelchen)

das war der golden zittrige staub: auf den wegen
den rainen die kleinen christusschädel gespalten
– auch da unten der süden die berge der schatten
hatten ein meer.

wir wollen schnaps brennen gehen, birnen kehren
wieder im kirchgelb, türme tragen zwiebeln. von erde
zu träumen war stoff. großvater s. nahm die hände der frauen
die er fing
     ab in gips. über die wiesen den großporigen staub
sprang manche ihm davon. millischeckerl. katzenpratzerl.
was zukam lag händisch im speicher, weiß träumende finger
kaum träumte
     er. mächtig beim kloster schimmerten durch den karfiol
die seelen des dorfs. eine sau warf ferkel in allen regenwurmfarben
und schnürlregen verband die oberen und unteren provinzen
bayrisch –
     seeland. was rutscht der friedhof am hang und die felder
verdreht ein einfacher laut wie w- w- wetterbleaml den hiasigen
hinnigen, den vierteldenseinen mir kopf ziehen die wolken über
die geodelten wege
     den liebenden staub

bavarian lakeland (mucked odelette)

here was the golden flickering dust: on the paths
the verges the little christ's-heads, cracked
– and down there too the south the alps the shadow
had a sea.
     let's moonshine schnapps, pears are turning
church-wall yellow, towers sport onions. dreaming of dirt
was material. grandfather s. took the hands of the women
he caught
     in plaster of paris. some of them bolted across the meadows
through large-pore dust. pish-the-bed. pussytoes.
his part lay to hand in the attic, fingers dreaming in white
the second
     he dreamt. imperious through cloister cauliflower shimmered
the souls of the village. a sow littered in all the colours of the rain-worm
and endless drizzle united the upper and lower provinces
bavarian
     lakeland. how the hillside graveyard slips and the fields
turn at a single sound like cra-cra-craw's-toes our folk's
your folk's the gran-kids' my head too the clouds' pull
over the mucked paths
     this loving dust

(from *berührte orte*)

dämmerung

im zug hörte ich sie sagen
sie habe nun ein neues lieblingsstück
nathan der weise. blonde dünne haare
ein doppelkinn, jugendspeck. vielleicht
aber auch etwas, das aufgeflogen war
auf der suche nach einem zuhause und sich
vorläufig festsetzte in diesem ring ich
dachte an lessing, wie er von seiner bibliothek
fast jeden abend nach braunschweig lief
12 kilometer geradeaus, den wald gab es
damals schon. klamm? und er trank
trank bis er nicht mehr konnte spielte
bis er verlor alles verloren hatte, blieb
lief die anderen nächte 12 kilometer durch
dunkelheit und das stehen der bäume. knackende
zweige. gühhwürmchen schleppten stille ins
gras. aufklärung, licht? die himmelshunde
rannten so sehr. es winselte nichts. so sagte er
sich ist die dämmerung in meinem eigenen garten.
so bin ich durchflochten mit mir wie der wald

twilight

in the train i heard her say
she had a new favourite play
nathan the wise. thin blonde hair
a double-chin, baby fat. perhaps
too something that had come to light
when searching for a home and which
for now had settled on this ring, i
thought of lessing and how he walked
on most evenings from his library to braunschweig
12 kilometres as the crow flies, the forest
was already there. damp? and he drank
drank until he was full played
until he had lost had lost all, stayed
on the other nights walked 12 kilometres through
darkness and towering trees. cracking
twigs. fireflies drew stillness into

the grass. enlightenment, light? the celestial dogs
ran so fast. no whining here. this he told
himself is how the twilight is in my own garden.
thus like the forest i am entwined with myself
(from berührte orte)

gründung der linguistik

am fort der maidan wie 'mädchen' wie
aber kam es zu 'girl'. man macht sternchen
nun für das was nie war nie gewesen sein
darf die unter-über-sprache das segensreich
– der briten in indien, traum unterm kuckuck–
baum. salziges weiches sanskrit. man sagt
mister williams, die wände im fort sind
dünn wie ein zahn. die wurzeln der banjans
das schwanken der luft. man kann ein effekt
oder nur ein ziegenhauch sein. nun
also die mischung, die sprays der kämpfer
so frend: das angeglichene gesicht. silber-
getriebene elefanten eine maus die den
kopf für pillen nach unten klappt. weit draußen
der friedhof der briten. orangegefärbte
hunde heulen die straßen herbei

founding of linguistics

at the fort on the maidan like 'maiden' but
how did 'girl' come about. they use asterisks
now for what never was is never allowed to have
been the under-over-language the blessed empire
– of the british in india, dream under the cuckoo–
tree. salty soft sanskrit. they say
mister williams, the walls in the fort are
thin as a tooth. the roots of the banjans
the swaying air. you can be an effect
or just a whiff of goat. so now
for the mix, the sprays of the combatants
so strange: their matching faces. elephants
wrought in silver a mouse whose head
flips open for pills. further out

the burial ground of the british. orange-
coloured dogs howl for the streets
(from *berührte orte*)

what is poetry?

putzen staubsaugen rotz abwischen geschürftes knie
bauch streicheln zum einschlafen oder wenn er wehtut
ein bettlied singen vorlesen die beine spreizen empfänglich
und tröstlich sein die wäsche in die trommel stopfen
schamhaare aus dem abfluß fischen zum zehnten mal
den klodeckel schließen die gesamten becher der familie
auf der spülmaschine abgestellt in die maschine räumen
fluchen aber unhörbar an die erziehung des mannes
denken jede erziehung aufgeben sich bücken den hund
füttern mensch ärgere dich nicht spielen wie ein trottel
endlich im bad tür von innen abschließen nach einer minute
riesengeschrei: rotz abputzen marmeladenbrot schmieren
marmeladenbrot vom teppich klauben badeanzüge
auswaschen selbst den ganzen tag nicht rausgekommen
hausschlüssel suchen multi-tasking bewundern
und verachten als mutti-tasking verhören toten vogel
vom fensterbrett schippen sich nicht ekeln ihn
in den garten bringen blick auf den sonnensturm
schmetterlinge das ganze zeug am tümpel (muss
auch endlich saubergemacht werden) libellen
für sekunden die spiegelung
sehen: sich selbst
    halbdämmrig, klein
    ein kind das die weißen
    zähne zeigt, deine zähne

es ist dein körper
du weißt kein besseres wort
    für das, was du siehst, lebendig
    und von dir
    unterschieden
weiß es mehr über dich als dir recht
sein kann es sagt: ich liebe
dich tiefer als einen wald

es sagt: dunkel ist das innere des mundes
und alles was denkt

what is poetry?

cleaning vacuuming wiping snot a scraped knee
tummy-stroking at bedtime or when it's sore singing
lullabies reading stories spreading your legs receptive
and soothing stuff dirty washing in drum fishing
pubic hair out of plughole for umpteenth time closing
toilet lid loading family's entire collection of mugs
left on top of the dishwasher into machine cursing
but inaudibly pondering the upbringing of men
abandoning all upbringing bending to feed dog
playing parcheesi like a numpty at long last locking
oneself in the bathroom but one minute later total
pandemonium: wiping snot spreading jam sandwich
picking jam sandwich out of shag-pile washing
their swimsuits having not set a foot out all day
hunting the house-key admiring then despising
multi-tasking misheard as mummi-tasking shovel
dead bird off window-ledge not finding it icky
carrying it out to the garden taking in the solar storm
butterflies the stuff they've left by the pond (itself
desperately in need of cleaning) dragonflies
for seconds the reflection:
yourself
        bleary, small
        a child flashing its
        white teeth, your teeth

it is your body
you have no better word
        for what you see – vital
        and detached
        from yourself
knowing more about you than you
can bear it says: my love
for you is deeper than a forest

it says: dark is the inside of the mouth
and all that thinks

                                        (from *subsong*)

Bibliography

Primary Works

Poetry

Draesner, Ulrike, *gedächtnisschleifen. Gedichte* (Frankfurt a. M.: Suhrkamp, 1995, reprinted 1998, 2002, 2008).

Draesner, Ulrike, *anis-o-trop. Sonettkranz* (Hamburg: Rospo, 1997).

Draesner, Ulrike, *für die nacht geheuerte zellen. Gedichte* (Munich: Luchterhand, 2001).

Draesner, Ulrike, *kugelblitz. Gedichte* (Munich: Luchterhand, 2005).

Draesner, Ulrike, *berührte orte. Gedichte* (Munich: Luchterhand, 2008).

Draesner, Ulrike, *subsong. Gedichte* (Munich: Luchterhand, 2014).

Draesner, Ulrike, *Nibelungen. Heimsuchung*, illustrations by Carl Otto Czeschka (Stuttgart: Reclam, 2016).

Shakespeare, William, Ulrike Draesner, Tom Cheesman and Olive Ond, *THYMINE. 17 Sonnets x 4*, Boiled String Poetry Chapbooks #7 (Swansea: Hafan Books, 2013), no pagination.

Ulrike Draesner, *hell & hörig. Gedichte* 1995–2020 (Munich: Penguin, 2022).

Ulrike Draesner, *this porous fabric*, trans. by Iain Galbraith (Bristol: Shearsman, 2022).

Novels

Draesner, Ulrike, *Lichtpause* (Berlin: Volk & Welt, 1998).

Draesner, Ulrike, *Mitgift* (Munich: Luchterhand, 2002).

Draesner, Ulrike, *Spiele* (Munich: Luchterhand, 2005).

Draesner, Ulrike, *Vorliebe* (Munich: Luchterhand, 2010).

Draesner, Ulrike, *Sieben Sprünge vom Rand der Welt* (Munich: Luchterhand, 2014).

Draesner, Ulrike, *Kanalschwimmer* (Hamburg: mare, 2019).

Short Stories

Draesner, Ulrike, 'Atmer', *Park. Zeitschrift für neue Literatur*, 51/52 (1998), 28–32.

Draesner, Ulrike, *Reisen unter den Augenliedern* (Klagenfurt: Ritter, 1999).

Draesner, Ulrike, *Hotdogs. Erzählungen* (Munich: Luchterhand, 2004).

Draesner, Ulrike, 'Ichs Heimweg macht alles alleine', in *Es schneit in meinem Kopf: Erzählungen über Alzheimer und Demenz*, ed. by Klara Obermüller (Munich: Nagel & Kimche, 2006), pp. 59–81.

Draesner, Ulrike, *Richtig liegen. Geschichten in Paaren* (Munich: Luchterhand, 2011).

Note: Collated by Benjamin Schaper.

https://doi.org/10.1515/9783110495942-015

Draesner, Ulrike, 'Mit vollkommener Klarheit', in *Wer kann für böse Träume – The Secret Grimm Files* (Berlin: Verlag das wilde Dutzend, 2012), pp. 29–36.
Draesner, Ulrike, 'Hundeweihnacht', *Weihnachten kann kommen. Neue Geschichten*, ed. by Susanne Gretter (Berlin: Suhrkamp, 2013), pp. 109–119.
Draesner, Ulrike, 'Kanalschwimmer', in *Ein extraherrlicher Meersommerabend*, ed. by Jan Christophersen (Hamburg: mare, 2013), pp. 259–275.

Travel Writing

Draesner, Ulrike, *Mein Hiddensee* (Hamburg: mare, 2015).
Draesner, Ulrike, *London. Lieblingsorte* (Leipzig: Insel, 2016).

Essay Volumes

Draesner, Ulrike, *Zauber im Zoo. Vier Reden über Herkunft und Literatur* (Göttingen: Wallstein, 2007).
Draesner, Ulrike, *Schöne Frauen lesen. Über Ingeborg Bachmann, Annette von Droste-Hülshoff, Friederike Mayröcker, Virginia Woolf u.v.a. Essays* (Munich: Luchterhand, 2007).
Draesner, Ulrike, *Heimliche Helden. Über Heinrich von Kleist, James Joyce, Thomas Mann, Gottfried Benn, Karl Valentin u.v.a. Essays* (Munich: Luchterhand, 2013).
Draesner, Ulrike, *Die fünfte Dimension. Münchner Reden zur Poesie*, ed. by Holger Pils and Frieder von Ammon (Munich: Lyrik Kabinett, 2016).
Draesner, Ulrike, *Grammatik der Gespenster. Frankfurter Poetikvorlesungen* (Stuttgart: Reclam, 2018).
Draesner, Ulrike, *Eine Frau wird älter. Ein Aufbruch* (Munich: Penguin, 2018).

Art Books and illustrated Editions

Draesner, Ulrike, *bläuliche sphinx* [cycle of poems], etchings and woodcuts by Lothar Seruset (Lentzke: edition eigendruck, 2002).
Draesner, Ulrike, *mittwinter* [cycle of poems], woodcuts and lithographs by Lothar Seruset (Witzwort: Quetsche, 2006).
Draesner, Ulrike, *synger med fuld styrke* [poems], woodcuts by Lothar Seruset (Lentzke: edition eigendruck, 2007).
Draesner, Ulrike, *ihr spiel – im sand* [poem], woodcuts by Lothar Seruset (Lentzke: edition eigendruck, for edition Hohes Uferm Ahrenshoop, 2008).
Draesner, Ulrike, *leben führt*, leporello with woodcuts, screen print, collage, papercuts by Mia Hochrein, Linda Kasprowiak, Gudrun Pigge, Vera Ohlsson und Lothar Seruset (Ahrenshoop: Edition Hohes Ufer, 2009).
Draesner, Ulrike, *Gold aus Mäusen*, illustrations and handwritten text by Hartmut Andryczuk (Berlin: Hybriden, 2010).

Draesner, Ulrike, *chlorophyll* [poem], illustrated by Tina Flau (2011; 12 unique copies).

Draesner, Ulrike, *Die Teiche des Königs*, woodcuts by Lothar Seruset (Witzwort: Quetsche, 2011).

Draesner, Ulrike, *Süße Kaverne*, illustrations and handwritten text by Hartmut Andryczuk (Berlin: Hybriden, 2011).

Draesner, Ulrike, and Ruth Johanna Benrath, *Erdhalbkugel in Haifischbalance*, screenprints by Gerlinde Creutzburg, Wolfgang Hebert, Angelique van Wesemael, Vera Ohlsson and Lothar Seruset (2011–12).

Draesner, Ulrike, and Ruth Johanna Benrath, *book face*, screenprints by Gerlinde Creutzburg, Wolfgang Hebert, Angelique van Wesemael, Vera Ohlsson and Lothar Seruset (2011 in Malmö).

Draesner, Ulrike, *Kinderbuch*, illustrations by Hans Ticha (Berlin: Aphaia, 2013).

Draesner, Ulrike, *ich wie du* [three children's poems], woodcuts by Lothar Seruset (Lentzke: edition eigendruck, 2014).

Draesner has also contributed to kunst:raum sylt quelle yearbook publications in collaboration with Hybriden Verlag, Berlin: *Vokabelkrieger II. Sommerfrische* (2007), *Vokabelkrieger III. Märtyrer* (2008), *Vokabelkrieger V. Aufbruch* (2010).

Translations

Doolittle, Hilda, *Heimliche Deutung*, trans. (from English) by Ulrike Draesner (Schupfart: Engeler, 2006).

Glück, Louise, *Averno. Gedichte*, trans. (from English) by Ulrike Draesner (Munich: Luchterhand, 2007).

Glück, Louise, *Wilde Iris. Gedichte*, trans. (from English) by Ulrike Draesner (Munich: Luchterhand, 2008).

Herliany, Dorothea Rosa, *Auf der Sonne Stirn. Indonesisch und Deutsch*, interlinear translation (from Indonesian) by Sophie Anggaw, German by Ulrike Draesner (Berlin: DAAD, 2014).

Herliany, Dorothea Rosa, *Hochzeit der Messer. Gesammelte Gedichte*, German versions by Brigitte Oleschinski and Ulrike Draesner (Berlin: Verlagshaus Berlin, 2015).

Jamie, Kathleen, 'Die Königin von Saba. Der Noah dieser Tage. Himmelsbegräbnis', translated (from English) by Ulrike Draesner, *Schreibheft*, 46 (1995), 163–166.

Malna, Afrizal, *druckmaschine drittmensch*, interlinear translation (from Indonesian) by Sophie Mahakam Anggawi and Katrin Bandel, German by Ulrike Draesner (Berlin: DAAD, 2015).

Marin, Mariana, and Gregor Laschen, eds, *Ich ist ein andrer ist bang. Poesie aus Rumänien*, afterword and interlinear translations (from Romanian) by Werner Söllner, German versions by Ulrike Draesner and others (Bremerhaven: Verlag für Neue Wissenschaft, 2000).

Métail, Michèle, Weg. *Fünf Füße breit*, trans. (from French) by Ulrike Draesner and Michèle Métail (Vienna: Edition Korrespondenzen, 2009).

Shakespeare, William, 'Twin Spin. Sonette von Shakespeare. Radikalübersetzungen', trans. (from English) by Ulrike Draesner, in: *to change the subject*, Ulrike Draesner and Barbara Köhler, foreword by Peter Waterhouse (Göttingen: Wallstein, 2000).

Shakespeare, William, *Twin Spin: 17 Shakespeare Sonnets radically translated by Ulrike Draesner and radically back-translated by Tom Cheesman; with an Exhibition Catalogue for 'Shall I Compare thee: Shakespeare in Translation'* (Oxford: Taylor Institution Library, 2016).

Stein, Gertrude, *The First Reader. Getrude Stein*, trans. (from English) by Ulrike Draesner (Klagenfurt: Ritter, 2001).

Other Writing

Behl, Silke, and Ulrike Draesner, '"Er steht da und beginnt zu sprechen". Über Afrizal Malnas Gedichte', *Sprache im technischen Zeitalter*, 204 (2012), 491–504.

Draesner, Ulrike, '"Truth angular and splintered". Die Subversion der Rede in der Reflexion über den Menschen-Bemerkungen zu Alexander Popes Essay on Man', *Germanisch-Romanische Monatsschrift*, 42.3 (1992), 275–303.

Draesner, Ulrike, 'Übersetzung als Verfahren intertextueller Sinnkonstitution. Das Sonett "Francisci Petrarchae" von Martin Opitz', *Germanica Wratislaviensia*, 18 (1992), 28–58.

Draesner, Ulrike, *Wege durch erzählte Welten. Intertextuelle Verweise als Mittel der Bedeutungskonstitution in Wolframs 'Parzival'* (Frankfurt a. M.: Peter Lang, 1993).

Draesner, Ulrike, 'Alice [Erzählende Prosa aus dem Manuskript 'Geburtsurteil']', *Manuskripte*, 34.124 (1994), 55–59.

Draesner, Ulrike (ed.), *Verführung. Deutschsprachige Novellen von Goethe bis Musil*, afterword by Ulrike Draesner (Munich: Goldmann, 1994).

Draesner, Ulrike, 'Der sprechende Löwe. Essay zur neuesten Lyrik auf den britischen Inseln sowie Übersetzungen von Gedichten mehrerer britischer Autoren', *Schreibheft*, 46 (1995), 137–184.

Draesner, Ulrike, 'Zeichen – Körper – Gesang. Das Lied in der Isolde Weißhand Episode des Tristan Gotfrids von Straßburg', in *Wechselspiele. Kommunikationsformen und Gattungsinterferenzen mittelhochdeutscher Lyrik*, ed. by Michael Schilling and Peter Strohschneider (Heidelberg: Winter, 1996), pp. 77–102.

Draesner, Ulrike 'russisches brot', *neue deutsche literatur*, 45.2 (1997), 29–32.

Draesner, Ulrike, 'Atem, Puls und Bahn. Das Denken des Körpers im Zustand der Sprache', *Lettre International*, 44 (1999), 62–67. Reprinted in *Minima Poetics. Für eine Poetik des zeitgenössischen Gedichts*, ed. by Joachim Sartorius (Frankfurt a. M.: Suhrkamp, 2003), pp. 48–63.

Draesner, Ulrike, 'Der Lyriker. Atemschlitz', *du*, 699 (1999), 28–34.

Draesner, Ulrike, 'melden sie vandalen!', *V*, 6 (2000), 21–28.

Draesner, Ulrike, 'Die rote Spaghetti der Sprache', in *Helden wie ihr. Junge Schriftsteller über ihre literarischen Vorbilder*, ed. by Jürgen Jacob Becker and Ulrich Janetzki (Berlin: Quadriga, 2000), pp. 24–32.

Draesner, Ulrike, 'Schlundschreiben, eben', in *Schraffur der Welt. Junge Schriftsteller über das Schreiben*, ed. by Perikles Monioudis (Berlin: Quadriga, 2000), pp. 57–67.

Draesner, Ulrike, 'Vampire's Delight. Eine Gedichtinterpretation', in *Tussirecherche*, ed. by Margret Eicher and Dieter M. Gräf (Heidelberg: Wunderhorn, 2000), pp. 16–22.

Draesner, Ulrike, 'Fluoreszierende Mäuse? Anmerkungen zu Genetik und Literatur', *Neue Zürcher Zeitung*, 29 January 2001, p. 25 (https://www.nzz.ch/article6XXYK-1.458955).

Draesner, Ulrike, 'Möbilierte Mädchen', in *Einsam sind alle Brücken. Autoren schreiben über Ingeborg Bachmann*, ed. by Reinhard Baumgart and Thomas Tebbe (Munich: Piper, 2001), pp. 124–137.

Draesner, Ulrike, 'Restnatur im Halbidyll. Vom Einfluss der digitalen Medien auf die Autorenexistenz', *neue deutsche literatur*, 49.5 (2001), 154–168.

Draesner, Ulrike, 'Tagebuch', in *Von Lust und Last literarischen Schreibens. Ein Blick in die Werkstatt deutscher Schriftsteller*, ed. by Klaus Modick and Helmut Mörchen (Frankfurt a. M.: Eichborn, 2001), pp. 60–69.

Draesner, Ulrike, 'Was könnte ein Gedicht heute sein? Rede zur Verleihung des Friedrichhölderlinpreises 2001', in *Friedrich-Hölderlin-Preis 2001* (Bad Homburg v.d. Höhe: Stadt Bad Homburg Magistrat, 2002).

Draesner, Ulrike, 'Frage, versteckt in einem Bild', in *Horen. Neue Reisen deutscher Schriftsteller nach Indien*, ed. by Marla Stukenberg and Martin Kämpchen (Bremerhaven: Wirtschaftsverlag, 2002), pp. 147–149.

Draesner, Ulrike, 'Hey man, calm down!', *Literaturen*, 7/8 (2002), 21–24.

Draesner, Ulrike, 'Ineinandergesteckte Puppen. Gedanken zum europäischen Gedicht', in *Experimente mit dem Echolot. Die besten Aufsätze aus zehn Jahren 'Das Gedicht'*, ed. by Anton Leitner (Munich: Lyrikedition, 2002), pp. 65–69.

Draesner, Ulrike, 'Die Kunst der Konsistenz', *Es liegt mir auf der Zunge. Geschichten mit Geschmack*, ed. by Christine Eichel (Munich: Goldmann, 2002), pp. 150–155.

Draesner, Ulrike, 'Mails', in *Geliebte Lust. Ein erotisches Lesebuch*, ed. By Bettina Hesse (Reinbek: Rowohlt, 2002), pp. 239–251.

Draesner, Ulrike, 'Quickies im Datengewühl?', *die horen*, 47.1 (2002), 131–158.

Draesner, Ulrike, 'Dreh Gedanken zum Gedicht', *lauter niemand*, 3 March 2003 (http://www.lauter-niemand.de/40_02_autoren_d/draesner_ulrike_poetik.htm).

Draesner, Ulrike, 'Elke Erb', in *Lexikon der deutschsprachigen Gegenwartsliteratur* (Munich: Nymphenburger Verlagsanstalt, 2003), pp. 310–312.

Draesner, Ulrike, 'Felix oder Die goldene Zeit. Gedanken zum Altern und Lesen', in *man erzählt Geschichten, formt die Wahrheit. Thomas Mann – Deutscher, Europäer, Weltbürger*, ed. by Michael Braun and Birgit Lermen (Frankfurt a. M.: Peter Lang, 2003), pp. 15–23.

Draesner, Ulrike, 'Das fiktive Alphabet. Spekulationen ins Unsichtbare', in *Der hippokratische Eid und die heutige Medizin*, ed. by Brigitte Ausfeld-Hafter (Berlin: Peter Lang, 2003), pp. 59–72.

Draesner, Ulrike, 'Friederike Meyröcker', in *Lexikon der deutschsprachigen Gegenwartsliteratur* (Munich: Nymphenburger Verlagsanstalt, 2003), pp. 844–847.

Draesner, Ulrike, 'jagen und sammeln', *Entwürfe. Zeitschrift für Literatur*, 9.36 (2003), 3–8.

Draesner, Ulrike, 'Kleines Gespenst. Gedanken zum lyrischen Ich', in *Ich bin nicht innerlich. Annäherungen an Gottfried Benn*, ed. by Jan Bürger (Stuttgart: Klett Cotta, 2003), pp. 9–30.

Draesner, Ulrike, 'Die Öffnung des Gehirns auf die Seele. Roman und Poesie bei Virginia Woolf', *die horen*, 48.3 (2003), 49–60.

Draesner, Ulrike, 'Treibriemen der Psyche. Reflexionen zur Stimme', in *Auf kurze Distanz. Die Autorenlesung*, ed. by Thomas Böhm (Cologne: Tropen, 2003), pp. 26–40.

Draesner, Ulrike, 'Die Trockenhaube', in *Kleines Glossar des Verschwindens. Von Autokino bis Zwischengas*, ed. by Andrea Köhler (Munich: C.H. Beck, 2003), pp. 97–100.

Draesner, Ulrike, 'Try see, try say. Bemerkungen zum Übersetzen von und bei Gertrud Stein', *Park. Zeitschrift für neue Literatur*, 57.581 (2003), 30–35.

Draesner, Ulrike, 'Auszug aus Lück', in *Ortstermine. Wolfenbütteler Lehrstücke zum zweiten Buch*, ed. by Hugo Dittberner, Linda Anne Engelhardt and Andrea Ehlert (Göttingen: Wallstein, 2004), p. 24–33.

Draesner, Ulrike, 'Ich wollte nur wissen, wer ich bin, An einer Mauer entlangzugehen ist, wie eine Geschichte zu hören. Marokko als Orient des Okzidents', *Frankfurter Allgemeine Zeitung*, 15 April 2004, p. R3.

Draesner, Ulrike, 'Neues Dach über alten Schatten. Berlins Olympiastadion', *du*, 748 (2004), 42–47.

Draesner, Ulrike 'Olympia. Romanauszug', in *Zeitzonen. Literatur in Deutschland 2004*, ed. by Antje Rávic Strubel, Michael Lentz, Martin Gülich, Thomas Hoeps (Vienna: Selene, 2004), pp. 216–225.

Draesner, Ulrike, 'Stadt ohne Anfang, ohne Ende', *Wiener Zeitung. Extra Indien*, 13 August 2004, p. 5.

Draesner, Ulrike, 'Tanzboden, Trommelfell, Trampolin. Die Zeit des Tagebuchs. Für Christa Wolf', *neue deutsche Literatur*, 52.2 (2004), 7–10.

Draesner, Ulrike, 'Für dich, bei mir', afterword to Marcelle Sauvageot, *Fast ganz die Deine*, trans. by Claudia Kalscheuer (Munich: Nagel & Kimche, 2005).

Draesner, Ulrike, 'Gespräch um Zuneigung. Zur jüngste Poesie', *Bella Triste*, 11 (2005), 54–63.

Draesner, Ulrike, 'Kreatives Schreiben?', in *Wie aufs Blatt kommt, was im Kopf steckt. Über Kreatives Schreiben*, ed. by Olaf Kutzmutz (Wolfenbüttel: Bundesakademie für kulturelle Bildung, 2005), pp. 147–148.

Draesner, Ulrike 'So blau leuchteten meine Tasten noch nie', in *Kanzlerinnen, schwindelfrei über Berlin*, ed. by Corinna Waffender (Berlin: transit, 2005), pp. 71–81.

Draesner, Ulrike, 'Denke ich an Gottfried Benn', in *Gottfried Benn* (Text + Kritik, 44), ed. by Heinz Ludwig Arnold (Munich: Text + Kritik, 2006), pp. 27–35.

Draesner, Ulrike, 'Durch-Sichtigkeit. Zeitgenossenschaft und Gedichte', *konzepte. Zeitschrift für Literatur*, 26 (2006), 72–76.

Draesner, Ulrike, 'Es muss seine Stimme gewesen sein', *Berliner Zeitung*, 7 July 2006, p. 17.

Draesner, Ulrike, 'Frau Bachmann. Anmerkungen zu Autorschaft', *literatur/a* (2006), 94–108.

Draesner, Ulrike, 'Gefäße. Ein Handschuh mit tausend Fingern. Ein Gedicht', in *Wohin geht das Gedicht?*, ed. by Roman Bucheli (Göttingen: Wallstein, 2006), pp. 28–35.

Draesner, Ulrike, 'Gespräch um Zuneigung', in *Junge Lyrik* (Text + Kritik, 171), ed. by Heinz Ludwig Arnold (Munich: Text + Kritik, 2006), pp. 68–79.

Draesner, Ulrike, 'Herkunft – Heimkehr? Literarische Gesichter', *Wespennest*, 141 (2006), 63–68.

Draesner, Ulrike, 'Innerste Wolke, erdliches Meer. Zu Gustave Courbets Meerestrand', in *Bilder. Geschichten. Schriftsteller sehen Malerei*, ed. by Thomas Böhm and Andreas Blühm (Munich: Random House, 2006), pp. 37–45.

Draesner, Ulrike, 'Die leidende Seherin', edited version of a speech given in Klagenfurt on 23 June 2006, *Die literarische Welt*, 24 June 2006, p. 1.

Draesner, Ulrike, 'Live, in Echtzeit, weltweit. Über die globale Verschachtelung von Sport, Medien und Terrorismus', *Literaturen*, 6 (2006), 28–31.

Draesner, Ulrike, 'Ohrenheim', in *Dichter am Äther. Schriftsteller über das Radio*, ed. by Michael Kohtes (Düsseldorf: Grupello, 2006), pp. 50–53.

Draesner, Ulrike, 'Reichtum', in *Von Science zu Fiction. Wissenschaft mit anderen Worten*, ed. by Erwin Krottenthaler and Claudia von See (Stuttgart: Hirzel, 2006), pp. 24–27.

Draesner, Ulrike, 'Rufen, was es nicht gibt', *Sprache im technischen Zeitalter*, 44.179 (2006), 255–268.

Draesner, Ulrike, 'Trullas Boot', in *Das Berliner Kneipenbuch. Berliner Autoren und ihre Kneipen*, ed. by Björn Kuhligk and Tom Schulz (Berlin: Bloomsbury Taschenbuch, 2006), pp. 214–220.

Draesner, Ulrike, 'Essay on "Das Spiegelbild" by Annette von Droste-Hülshoff', *konzepte*, 27 (2007), 80–87.

Draesner, Ulrike, 'Friederike Meyröcker. Luna in Sprache', in *Dünn ist die Decke der Zivilisation*, ed. by Maike Stein (Königstein/Taunus: Ulrike Helmer, 2007), pp. 97–108.

Draesner, Ulrike, 'Grau. Über Anja Utlers Lyrik', *Bella Triste*, 17 (2007) and on (http://www.lyr ikkritik.de/Draesner%20-%20Utler.html).

Draesner, Ulrike, 'Ich wollte nur wissen, wer ich bin. Über Casablanca', in *Zwischen Berlin und Beirut*, ed. by Joachim Sartorius (Munich: C.H. Beck, 2007), pp. 17–24.

Draesner, Ulrike, 'Leseprozesse', *Bella Triste*, 19 (2007), 83–88.

Draesner, Ulrike, 'Sinne. Gustav Flaubert. Madame Bovary', in *Erst lesen. Dann schreiben*, ed. by Stephan Porombka and Olaf Kutzmutz (Munich: Luchterhand, 2007), pp. 51–63.

Draesner, Ulrike, 'Des assemblages en croissance', *il particolare*, 17–18 (2008), 75–80.

Draesner, Ulrike, 'Die drei Hälften der Torte. Von der Wissenschaft zum Schreiben', in *Familien – Geschlechter – Macht. Beziehungen im Werk Ulrike Draesners*, ed. by Stephanie Catani and Friedhelm Marx (Göttingen: Wallstein, 2008), pp. 13–22.

Draesner, Ulrike, 'Resignation. oder: der leise Luxus der Intelligenz', *wespennest*, 153 (2008), 66–68.

Draesner, Ulrike, 'Das Valentin', in *München lesen. Beobachtungen einer erzählten Stadt*, ed. by Simone Hirmer and Marcel Schellong (Würzburg: Königshausen & Neumann, 2008), pp. 79–88.

Draesner, Ulrike, 'Wer wir sind, sprechen wir deutsch', in *Was eint uns. Verständigung der Gesellschaft über gemeinsame Grundlagen*, ed. by Bernhard Vogel (Freiburg: Herder, 2008), pp. 64–77.

Draesner, Ulrike, 'zu einem glück? zum schein? Gedanken die neues Lyrik betreffend', in *Neubuch. Neue junge Lyrik*, ed. by Ron Winkler (Munich: yedermann, 2008), pp. 207–223.

Draesner, Ulrike, 'Anders oder: "hatte ich schon genug gesagt?"', in *Widerstand des Textes*, ed. by Wilfried F. Schoeller and Herbert Wiesner (Berlin: Matthes & Seitz, 2009), pp. 133–149.

Draesner, Ulrike 'Anwesen', in *Poesie und Stille. Schriftstellerinnen schreiben in Klöstern*, ed. by Klosterkammer Hannover (Göttingen: Wallstein, 2009), pp. 179–190.

Draesner, Ulrike, 'Bericht vom Rand des finnischen Eislochs oder: Gedichte übersetzen', *Ostragehege*, 54.3 (2009), 32f.

Draesner, Ulrike, 'Glosse zu Uwe Johnson', *Literaturen*, 3 (2009), 20.

Draesner, Ulrike, 'Ist das fair? Anmerkungen zu Harry Potter auf deutsch', in *Harry, hol schon mal den Besen. Ein Kehraus nach zehn Potterjahren*, ed. by Olaf Kutzmutz (Wolfenbüttel: Bundesakademie für kulturelle Bildung, 2009), pp. 22–31.

Draesner, Ulrike, 'Laudatio auf Gerhard Falkner', *Park. Zeitschrift für neue Literatur*, 63 (2009), 30–37.

Draesner, Ulrike, 'Laudatio auf Ulrike A. Sandig', *Ostragehege*, 53.1 (2009), 64–66.

Draesner, Ulrike, 'Essay zu Europa', *Kulturreport*, 3 (2010), 118–124.

Draesner, Ulrike, 'Nachwort', in Tania Blixen, *Jenseits von Afrika*, trans. by Gisela Perlet (Zurich: Manesse, 2010), pp. 663–684.

Draesner, Ulrike, 'Text. Ort. Heimat. Essay', *zeichen & wunder*, 21.55 (2010), 6–10.

Draesner, Ulrike, 'Tiere sind keine Dinge' and 'Menschen sind Tiere. Oder: Neun Gehirne hat der durchschnittliche deutsche Satz', in *'Nehmen Sie mich beim Wort ins Kreuzverhör'. Vorlesungen der Wiesbadener Poetikdozentur*, ed. by Rosemarie Altenhofer, Susanne Lewalter and Rita Rosen (Frankfurt a. M.: Fischer, 2010), pp. 261–280 and pp. 281–304.

Draesner, Ulrike, 'Der Biographische Nenner', in Gottfried Benn, *Doppelleben* (Stuttgart: Klett-Cotta, 2011), pp. 7–32.

Draesner, Ulrike, 'Eine Fürsichblüte. Dichter des Gerüchts und des Zwischenraums, träumender Schreibblitz: Heinrich von Kleist', *Literaturen*, 1 (2011), 28–31.

Draesner, Ulrike, 'Nur Kamele kauen Kakteen', in *Ethik im Gespräch. Autorinnen und Autoren über das Verhältnis von Literatur und Ethik heute*, ed. by Stephanie Waldow (Bielefeld: transcript, 2011), pp. 97–103.

Draesner, Ulrike, 'Podiumsdiskussion', in *Johann Peter Hebel und die Moderne*, ed. by Achim Aurnhammer and Hanna Klessinger (Freiburg: Rombach, 2011), pp. 211–222.

Draesner, Ulrike, 'remembering, will', in *Wie Er uns gefällt. Gedichte an und auf Shakespeare*, ed. by Tobias Döring (Zurich: Manesse, 2014), pp. 110–111.

Draesner, Ulrike, 'Zehn Schreibgebote', in *Zehn Gebote des Schreibens*, ed. by Anonymous (Munich: Deutsche Verlagsanstalt, 2011), pp. 27–28.

Draesner, Ulrike, 'Humbert Humbert', *Frankfurter Allgemeine Zeitung*, 21 July 2012, p. 28.

Draesner, Ulrike, 'Die Mechaniker', *Allmende*, 33 (2013), 37–40.

Draesner, Ulrike, 'Der schwarze Schwan. Gedanken zur Zukunft des Romans', in *Zukunft der Literatur* (Text + Kritik Sonderband), ed. by Hugo Dittberner, Steffen Martus, Axel Ruckaberle, Michael Scheffel, Claudia Stockinger und Michael Töteberg (Munich: Text + Kritik, 2013), pp. 109–121.

Draesner, Ulrike, 'Sie gehört zu mir', *Emma*, 4 (2013), 44–47.

Draesner, Ulrike, 'Spiele im Käfig, Spiele in Sprache', afterword to William Shakespeare, *Hamlet*, trans. by Maik Hamburger and Adolf Dresen (Stuttgart: Reclam, 2013), pp. 155–162.

Draesner, Ulrike, 'Thou art translated', afterword to William Shakespeare, *Ein Sommernachtstraum*, trans. by Maik Hamburger (Stuttgart: Reclam, 2013), pp. 87–94.

Draesner, Ulrike, 'Bergfahrt. Ludwig Hohl', *die horen*, 253 (2014), 55–60.

Draesner, Ulrike, 'Ein Fall aus der Wirklichkeit', *Neue Rundschau*, 125 (2014), 330–346.

Draesner, Ulrike, 'Die Habseligkeit. Gedanken zum Thema "Erbe"', *Sprache im technischen Zeitalter*, 210 (2014), 166–179.

Draesner, Ulrike, 'Herz deckt Geld', afterword to William Shakespeare, *Der Kaufmann von Venedig*, trans. by Maik Hamburger (Stuttgart: Reclam, 2014), pp. 112–119.

Draesner, Ulrike, 'Wie das Deutsche sein Wesen treibt. Esel und Seele auf der Brücke der Sprache', in *Literatur im Fluss*, ed. by Erich Garhammer (Regensburg: Pustet, 2014), pp. 51–59.

Draesner, Ulrike, 'Wiederkehrende Fluchten: Das Trauma der Vertreibung und seine Folgen', *3sat*, kulturzeit, 12 June 2014 (http://www.3sat.de/page/?source=/kulturzeit/themen/177118/index.html).

Draesner, Ulrike, 'Der Wolf', *New Level. Computerspiele und Literatur* (Berlin: Metrolit, 2014), pp. 81–83.

Draesner, Ulrike, 'Zukunft des Schreibens', *volltext*, 3 (2014), p. 42.

Draesner, Ulrike, 'Der zweite Mann', in *Die Bibliothek der ungeschriebenen Bücher*, ed. by Annette Pehnt, Friedemann Holder and Michael Staiger (Munich: Piper, 2014), pp. 41–43.

Draesner, Ulrike, 'Aus: drachen zulachen', *Manuskripte*, 210 (2015), 42–45.

Draesner, Ulrike, 'Changing the Subject', in *Thomas Mann and Shakespeare. Something Rich and Strange*, ed. by Tobias Döring, Ewan Fernie and Elisabeth Bronfen (London: Bloomsbury, 2015), pp. 229–245.

Draesner, Ulrike, 'Heimatschnee' in *Eine Welt von Schnee*, ed. by Ursel Allenstein and Ulrike Ostermeyer (Berlin: Arche, 2015), pp. 93–107.

Draesner, Ulrike, 'Der Lebensfaden', in *Mein Weihnachtsbild*, ed. by Gesine Dammel (Berlin: Suhrkamp, 2015), pp. 73–76.

Draesner, Ulrike, 'Vergiss Mein Nicht', in *Friendly Fire & Forget*, ed. by Ellen Blumenstein and Daniel Tyradellis (Berlin: Matthes & Seitz, 2015), pp. 98–103.

Draesner, Ulrike, 'Das Zeit-Erzählen', *Marbacher Katalog*, 68 (2015), 28–43.

Draesner, Ulrike, 'Experten auf der Weide. Von Quacksalbern, Chorsängern und Clowns', in *Auf dem Markt der Experten. Zwischen Überforderung und Vielfalt*, ed. by Ruben Pfizenmaier (Frankfurt am Main: Edition Büchergilde, 2016), pp. 16–23.

Draesner, Ulrike, 'Das Kind mit den nichtgrünen Augen', in *Wie wir leben wollen. Texte für Solidarität und Freiheit*, ed. by Matthias Jügler (Berlin: Suhrkamp, 2016), pp. 9–19.

Draesner, Ulrike, 'Landschaften des Verlustes, Landschaften der Wiederkehr', Afterword to Verna B. Carleton, *Zurück in Berlin*, trans. by Verena von Koskull (Berlin: Aufbau, 2016).

Draesner, Ulrike, 'Love of ghosts (on a polyglot poetics)', talk given at Akademie Schloß Solitude, Stuttgart, May 2016; available as audio file (http://art-science-business.com/bi ographies-the-production-of-space/traces/ulrike-draesner/) and transcript (http://www. draesner.de/wp-content/uploads/2016/12/Love-of-ghosts.pdf).

Draesner, Urike, 'Nebelland', in *Mein Polen – meine Polen*, ed. by Dieter Bingen and Matthias Weber (Wiesbaden: Harrassowitz, 2016), pp. 21–26.

Draesner, Ulrike, 'Life after Life', *Akzente*, 64.2 (2017), 103–111.

Draesner, Ulrike, 'Morgenmuffel' (2017) (http://www.draesner.de/morgenmuffel/).

Draesner, Ulrike, 'Sage ich zu Johnny', *Kolik*, 74 (2017), 65–67.

Draesner, Ulrike, and Hahn, Ulla (eds), *Gottfried Benn. Liebesgedichte* (Stuttgart: Reclam, 2012).

Hebel, Johann Peter, *Kästchengeschichten. Ausgewählt, neu gelesen und literarisch beleuchtet von Ulrike Draesner* (Lengwil-Oberhofen: Libelle, 2009).

See also Draesner's ongoing (since 2014) series of essays for the 'Freitext – Feld für literarisches Denken' section of *Die Zeit* online (http://www.zeit.de/freitext/author/ulrike-draesner/) and her essays on *Fixpoetry* website (https://www.fixpoetry.com/autoren/literatur/feuilleton/ulrike-draesner).

Recordings and Multimedia Work

Draesner, Ulrike, 'beziehungsmaschine', *Bayerischer Rundfunk*, 10 June 1998.

Draesner, Ulrike, 'dieser Bottich, ach, das Ich', *Bayerischer Rundfunk*, 31 August 1998.

Draesner, Ulrike, 'Der jüdische Friedhof', in *Berlin Literatour. Die sprechende Stadt*, dir. by Markus Heidmeier and Steffen Ramlow, CD (Berlin: Lichtschliff, 2004).

Draesner, Ulrike, 'Von Hab und Gut. Die Kriegskinder und ihre Nachfahren', *SWR2 Essay extra*, broadcast 17 Sept 2015, manuscript available on (https://www.swr.de/-/id=15958850/property=download/nid=659852/fa40mc/swr2-essay-20150917.pdf).

Draesner, Ulrike, *Happy Aging. Ulrike Draesner erzählt ihre Wechseljahre*, dir. by Thomas Böhm and Klaus Sander, 2-CD set (Berlin: supposé, 2016).
Schlünz, Annette, *Stern. Für Sopran und Tuba*, text by Ulrike Draesner (Munich: Ricordi, 2009). See also Draesner's website (http://www.draesner.de/intermediale-projekte/) for further details of intramedial projects and installations.

Interviews

Anonymous, 'Jenseits der Norm', *Der Spiegel*, 13 (2002), 207.
Anonymous, 'Literarisches Leben. Impulse zur Wiederbelebung. Auszug aus der Podiumsdiskussion mit Beiträgen von Ulrike Draesner, Reimer Eilers und Rainer Jogschies', in *Die Kraft der Literatur. Tradition und Wandel des literarischen Lebens im neuen Deutschland*, ed. by Hans-Peter Burmeister (Rehburg-Loccum: Evangelische Akademie, 2002), pp. 119–136.
Braun, Rebecca, 'Pacing out a polyglot Poetics: An interview with Ulrike Draesner at the Victoria and Albert Museum', *German Life and Letters*, 71.1 (2018), 111–129.
Draesner, Ulrike, and Jan Wagner, 'Über Stock und Stein. Ein Gespräch', in *Ulrike Draesner*, ed. by Susanna Brogi, Anna Ertel and Evi Zemanek (Munich: Text + Kritik, 2014), pp. 4–18.
Essig, Rolf-Bernhard, 'Bewegung in Sprache. Gespräch mit Ulrike Draesner', *neue deutsche literatur*, 51.6 (2003), 42–61.
Helbig, Axel, 'Die dritte Hälfte der Torte. Interview mit Ulrike Draesner am 1. August 2009 in ihrer Berliner Wohnung', *Ostragehege*, 16.3 (2009), 40–55.
Hell, Cornelius, 'Das Geld wandert ab aus diesem Beruf', *volltext*, 2 (2016) (https://volltext. net/texte/ulrike-draesner-interview-cornelius-hell/).
Henneberg, Nicole, 'Skispringer mit Hermesbeinen', *Frankfurter Allgemeine Zeitung*, 3 August 2013 (http://www.faz.net/aktuell/feuilleton/buecher/rezensionen/belletristik/ ulrike-draesner-heimliche-helden-skispringer-mit-hermesbeinen-12317202.html).
Heydenreich, Aura, and Klaus Mecke, 'Auf der Suche nach Sprache: Ulrike Draesner im Dialog zu Mitgift und Vorliebe', in *Physik und Poetik: Produktionsästhetik und Werkgenese. Autorinnen und Autoren im Dialog*, ed. by Aura Heydenreich and Klaus Mecke (Berlin: de Gruyter, 2015), pp. 23–49.
Hierl, Tobias, 'Literarische Kammermusik', *Buchkultur*, 95 (2004), 16–17.
Krautstengel, Julia, and Eva-Maria Schneider, 'Manchmal war mir das Englische näher als das Deutsche', *Paroli*, 1 (2016), 19–20.
Küchemann, Fridtjof, 'Über den Körper schreiben. Interview', *Frankfurter Allgemeine Zeitung*, 9 May 2002 (http://www.faz.net/aktuell/feuilleton/interview-ulrike-draesner-ueber-den- koerper-schreiben-161049.html).
Löffler, Sigrid, Frauke Meyer-Gosau and Jutta Person, 'Die Stunde der kleinen Nager. Über den Romans als Allesfresser, Naturwissenschaft in der Literatur, Schreiben als Kunst des Fahrradfahrens, einen Lokführerstreik der Literaturkritik und kulturpessimistische Szenarien, die keine Drohung sein können. Ein Literaturengespräch mit Ulrike Draesner, Dietmar Dath und John von Düffel', *Literaturen*, 1/2 (2008), 28–33.
Pferzing, Boris, 'Lyrische Schleifarbeit. Interview mit Ulrike Draesner', *Grau-Zone*, 2 (1996), 12–13.
Pirro, Maurizio, 'Il mimetismo det traduttore. A colloquio con Ulrike Draesner', *Communicare. letterature / lingue*, 6 (2006), 237–244.

Propson-Hauck, Martina, '"Runter mit Gedichten von den Podesten, raus aus dem ganzen Staub!". Ulrike Draesner, Trägerin des Bad Homburger Hölderlin-Förderpreises im FR-Interview', *Frankfurter Rundschau*, 9 May 2001, p. 2.

Puff-Trojan, Andreas, 'Die Angst des Affenforschers vor den Menschen', *volltext*, 2 (2014), 22–23.

Schlösser, Christian, 'Gespräch mit Ulrike Draesner', *Deutsche Bücher. Forum für Literatur. Autorengespräch – Kritik – Interpretation*, 35.4 (2005), 269–287.

Waldow, Stephanie, for *Schau ins Blau*, no title, 22 April 2011, on (https://www.schauinsblau.de/?article=ulrike-draesner).

Wissen, Dirk, 'Geräusche, Gerüche, Gesellschaft: Auf einen Espresso mit der zurzeit in Oxford lebenden Lyrikerin Ulrike Draesner zur "Atmosphäre von Bibliotheken"', *BuB – Forum Bibliothek und Information*, 68.1 (2016), 11.

Secondary Literature

Arlaud, Sylvie, 'SUBSONG d'Ulrike Draesner. Sous-chants d'innocence et d'expériences', *Germanica*, 64.1 (2019), 41–56.

Baier, Angelika, 'Beyond the Either/Or?!. Literatur über Hermaphrodismus am Beispiel von Ulrike Draesners Roman Mitgift (2002)', *Aussiger Beiträge*, 4 (2010), 79–92.

Baier, Angelika, 'Intersections. Hermaphroditism as a "Travelling Concept" in Ulrike Draesner's Novel Mitgift (2002)', in *Readings in Twenty-First-Century European Literatures*, ed. by Michael Gratzke, Margaret-Anne Hutton and Claire Whitehead (Oxford: Peter Lang, 2014), pp. 259–278.

Barabanova, Natalja, 'Die Grenze des Erzählbaren im Roman "Mitgift" von Ulrike Draesner', in *Grenze als Sinnbildungsmechanismus*, ed. by Nikolaj Rymar (Samara: Samar University Press, 2004), pp. 101–113.

Bartl, Andrea, 'Androgyne Ästhetik: Das Motiv des Hermaphroditismus in der deutschsprachigen Gegenwartsliteratur, erläutert am Beispiel von Ulrike Draesners *Mitgift*, Michael Stavarics *Terminifera* und Sibylle Bergs *Vielen Dank für das Leben*', in *Die Textualität der Kultur. Gegenstände, Methoden, Probleme der kultur- und literaturwissenschaftlichen Forschung*, ed. by Christian Baier, Nina Benkert and Hans-Joachim Schott with Annika Klinge and Nils Ebert (Bamberg: University of Bamberg Press, 2014), pp. 279–301.

Braun, Michael, 'Das Herz – ein Parasit', in *Jahrbuch der Lyrik 1996/1997*, ed. by Christoph Buchwald, Michael Buselmeier and Michael Braun (Munich: C.H. Beck, 1996), pp. 95–96.

Braun, Michael, 'Zucken, Zwinkern', *Frankfurter Rundschau*, 24 March 2004 (http://www.fr.de/kultur/literatur/michael-braun-zucken-zwinkern-a-1199753).

Braun, Michael, 'Von Bildern des Terrors und dem Terror der Bilder. Ulrike Draesners Roman "Spiele"', in *Kopf-Kino – Gegenwartsliteratur und Medien. Festschrift für Volker Wehdeking*, ed. by Lothar Bluhm and Christine Schmitt (Trier: Wissenschaftlicher Verlag Trier, 2006), pp. 209–219.

Braun, Michael, 'Wem gehört die Geschichte? Erinnerungsverhandlungen in Ulrike Draesners Roman *Spiele*', in *Familien – Geschlechter – Macht*, ed. by Catani and Marx, pp. 95–108.

Braun, Michael, 'Kafka im Netz', *Wirkendes Wort*, 63.1 (2013), 121–135.

Braun, Michael, 'Intertextueller Zauber im Zoo. Ulrike Draesners Poetik der Verwandlung', in *Ulrike Draesner*, ed. by Brogi, Ertel and Zemanek, pp. 37–47.

Braun, Michael, 'Ulrike Draesner', in *Kritisches Lexikon zur deutschsprachigen Gegenwartsliteratur*, 83rd update (Munich: Text + Kritik, 2017), pp. D–E.

Brink-Gabler, Gisela, ed., *Deutsche Dichterinnen vom 16. Jahrhundert bis heute. Gedichte und Lebensläufe* (Cologne: Anaconda, 2007).

Brockmann, Stephen, 'Berlin as the Literary Capital of German Unification', in *Contemporary German Fiction. Writing in the Berlin Republic*, ed. by Stuart Taberner (Cambridge: Cambridge University Press, 2007), pp. 39–55.

Brogi, Susanna, '"Kein richtiges Liegen im falschen". Die Sexualisierung der Arbeitswelt und die Ökonomisierung der Beziehungswelt in den Erzählungen Ulrike Draesners', in *Ulrike Draesner*, ed. by Brogi, Ertel and Zemanek, pp. 48–56.

Brogi, Susanna, Anna Ertel and Evi Zemanek, eds, *Ulrike Draesner* (Text + Kritik, 201) (Munich: Text + Kritik, 2014).

Catani, Stephanie, 'Hybride Körper. Zur Dekonstruktion der Geschlechterbinarität in Ulrike Draesners Mitgift', in *Familien – Geschlechter – Macht*, ed. by Catani and Marx, pp. 75–93.

Catani, Stephanie, and Friedhelm Marx, eds, *Familien – Geschlechter – Macht. Beziehungen im Werk Ulrike Draesners* (Göttingen: Wallstein, 2008).

Dahlke, Birgit, 'landnahme', *neue deutsche literatur*, 43.6 (1995), 183–185.

Dahlke, Birgit, 'Zündeln und Kreisen. Ulrike Draesner folgt den Spuren von Mehrkörpersystemen', *neue deutsche literatur*, 50.3 (2002), 168–170.

Dallapiazza, Michael, 'Neueste deutschsprachige Literatur', *Jahrbuch für Internationale Germanistik*, XLVI.2 (2014), 263–278.

Dallapiazza, Michael, 'Ulrike Draesner: *Nibelungen. Heimsuchung*', *Jahrbuch für Internationale Germanistik*, XLIX.2 (2017), 209–218.

Eigler, Friederike, 'Post/Memories of Forced Migration at the End of the Second World War. Novels by Walter Kempowski and Ulrike Draesner', in *Migration: Changing Concepts, Critical Approaches*, ed. by Doris Bachmann-Medick and Jens Kugele (Berlin and Boston: De Gruyter, 2018), pp. 167–192.

Ertel, Anna Alissa, *Körper, Gehirne, Gene. Lyrik und Naturwissenschaft bei Ulrike Draesner und Durs Grünbein* (Berlin: de Gruyter, 2011).

Ertel, Anna, 'Zur Poetik Ulrike Draesners', in *Ulrike Draesner*, ed. by Brogi, Ertel and Zemanek, pp. 19–26.

Ertel, Anna, and Tilmann Köppe, 'Meta-Fantastik: Ulrike Draesners Erzählung "Rosakäfer" (2011)' in *Funktionen der Fantastik: Neue Formen des Weltbezugs von Literatur und Film nach 1945*, ed. by Sonja Klimek, Tobias Lambrecht and Tom Kindt (Heidelberg: Universitätsverlag Winter, 2017), pp. 191–208.

Essig, Rolf-Bernhard, 'Ein weiblicher Odysseus, der Hund der Erkenntnis und die Stimme des weißen Wales. Zu Ulrike Draesners Lyrik', in *Familien – Geschlechter – Macht*, ed. by Catani and Marx, pp. 23–36.

Fockel, Henrik, *Literarische Resonanzen. Studien zu Stimme und Raum* (Berlin: LIT, 2014).

Geisenhanslücke, Achim, 'Draesner, Ulrike: gedächtnisschleifen. Gedichte (Frankfurt a. M.: Suhrkamp)', in *Wendejahr 1995. Transformationen der deutschprachigen Literatur*, ed. by Heribert Tommek, Matteo Galli and Achim Geisenhanslücke (Berlin: De Gruyter, 2015), pp. 363–367.

Gokhale, Anushka, *Indien erzählen. Eine Studie zur deutschsprachigen Reiseliteratur* (Würzburg: Königshausen & Neumann, 2011).

Hachmann, Gundela, 'Poeta doctus docens. Poetikvorlesungen als Inszenierung von Bildung', in *Subjektform Autor. Autorschaftsinszenierungen als Praktiken der Subjektivierung*, ed. by Sabine Kyora (Bielefeld: transcript, 2014), pp. 137–155.

Hachmann, Gundela, *Zeit und Technoimagination. Eine neue Einbildungskraft in Romanen des 21. Jahrhunderts* (Würzburg: Königshausen & Neumann, 2015).

Herrmann, Silke, 'No-man's land? Weiblichkeit in zeitgenössischen Romanen zu Hermaphrodismus', *Entwürfe. Zeitschrift für Literatur*, 11.41 (2005), 83–90.

Heydenreich, Aura, 'Physik, Figur, Wissen. Das Superpositionsprinzip der Quantentheorie als Narrativ der Intersexualität in Ulrike Draesners "Mitgift"', in *Ulrike Draesner*, ed. by Brogi, Ertel and Zemanek, pp. 57–65.

Hieber, Jochen, 'Vorstellung der Förderpreisträgerin Ulrike Draesner', in *Friedrich Hölderlin-Preis. Reden zur Preisverleihung am 7. Juni 2001*, ed. by the Magistrat der Stadt Bad Homburg v. d. Höhe and the Stiftung Cläre Jannsen (Homburg: Stadt Bad Homburg, 2001), pp. 12–18.

Hillgruber, Katrin, 'Reise unter den Augenlidern', *Deutschlandfunk*, 30 August 1999 (http://www.deutschlandfunk.de/reise-unter-den-augenlidern.700.de.html?dram:article_id=79250).

Hillgruber, Katrin, 'Sieben Personen suchen einen Ort', *Deutschlandfunk*, 22 Sept 2014 (http://www.deutschlandfunk.de/roman-sieben-personen-suchen-einen-ort.700.de.html?dram:article_id=298238).

Hoorn, Tanja van, 'Zwischen Anmerkungslust und Reflexionszwang. Poetologische Paratexte in aktuellen Lyrikbänden', *Zeitschrift für Germanistik*, Neue Folge XXVIII.2 (2018), 261–274.

Hörisch, Jochen, 'Ulrike Draesner. Hot Dogs', *Literaturen*, 7/8 (2004), 116.

Ivanova, Ralica Stefanova, *Literarische Übertretungen. Bodo Kirchhoff, Ulrike Draesner, Thomas Hettche und Christoph Peters* (Veliko Tarnovo: Universitätsverlag Hll. Kyrill und Method, 2016).

Jagow, Bettina von, 'Sprachen der Autonomie in Medizin und Literatur', in *Bild, Rede, Schrift. Kleriker, Adel, Stadt und ausserchristliche Kulturen in der Vormoderne. Wissenschaften und Literatur seit der Renaissance* (Akten des XI. Internationalen Germanistenkongresses Paris 2005 'Germanistik im Konflikt der Kulturen', vol. 7), ed. by Jean-Marie Valentin with Ronald Perlwitz (Bern: Peter Lang, 2008), pp. 427–435.

Jagow, Bettina von, 'Ulrike Draesner', in *Killy Literaturlexikon. Autoren und Werke des deutschsprachigen Kulturraums*, 2nd edition (Berlin and New York: De Gruyter, 2008), vol. 3, pp. 95–96.

Jagow, Bettina von, and Florian Steger, 'Bilder des Menschen zwischen Selbstbestimmung und Fremdsteuerung. Ulrike Draesners autopilot-Gedichte', in *Repräsentationen, Medizin und Ethik in Literatur und Kunst der Moderne*, ed. by Bettina von Jagow and Florian Steger (Heidelberg: Winter, 2004), pp. 51–65.

Jahraus, Oliver, 'Große und kleine Geschichte in Munich. Zum Olympia-Attentat in Ulrike Draesners Roman *Spiele*', in *München lesen. Beobachtungen einer erzählten Stadt*, ed. by Simone Hirmer and Marcel Schellong (Würzburg: Königshausen & Neumann, 2008), pp. 265–275.

Jahraus, Oliver, 'Liebe und Terror und Literatur als ihr Medium. Zu Ulrike Draesners Medienroman Spiele', in *Familien – Geschlechter – Macht*, ed. by Catani and Marx, pp. 109–125.

Jürgensen, Christoph, Erik Schilling and Rüdiger Zymner, eds, *Gedichte von Ulrike Draesner: Interpretationen* (Münster: Mentis, 2020)

Kiefer, Sebastian, 'Seele, Soma, Sema. Gedichte von Norbert Hummelt und Ulrike Draesner', *neue deutsche literatur*, 49.6 (2001), 171–179.

König, Michael, *Poetik des Terrors. Politisch motivierte Gewalt in der deutschen Gegenwartsliteratur* (Berlin: De Gruyter, 2015).

Kurzke, Hermann, 'Erlösung mit Füßen getreten', in *Frauen dichten anders. 181 Gedichte mit Interpretationen*, ed. by Marcel Reich-Ranicki (Frankfurt a. M.: Insel, 1998), pp. 824–825.

Langner, Beatrix, 'Geh aus dem Bild, Katja!', *Literaturen*, 10 (2005), 82–83.

Leeder, Karen, '"Übungen der Zugewandtheit". Ulrike Draesner's Poetics of Correspondence', in *Schaltstelle. Neue deutsche Lyrik im Dialog*, ed. by Karen Leeder (Amsterdam: Rodopi, 2007), pp. 231–262.

Leeder, Karen, 'Eine Grammatik der Liebe. Ulrike Draesners Lyrik', in *Familien – Geschlechter – Macht*, ed. by Catani and Marx, pp. 37–59.

Leeder, Karen, 'Heimat in der neuen deutschen Lyrik', in *Gedächtnis und Identität. Die deutsche Literatur nach der Vereinigung*, ed. by Fabrizio Cambi (Würzburg: Königshausen & Neumann, 2008), pp. 135–153.

Leeder, Karen, '"A second Life": Shakespeare-Übersetzungen in der Gegenwartsliteratur', in *From the Enlightenment to Modernism: Three Centuries of German Literature. Essays for Ritchie Robertson*, ed. by Carolin Duttlinger, Kevin Hilliard, and Charlie Louth (Cambridge: Legenda, 2021), pp. 348–62.

Lermen, Birgit, 'Autorenlesung. Einführung in das Werk von Ulrike Draesner', in *Medizin zwischen Humanität und Wettbewerb. Probleme, Trends und Perspektiven*, ed. Volker Schumpelick and Bernhard Vogel (Freiburg: Herder, 2008), pp. 561–570.

Ludden, Teresa, 'Mobilisation of Mediation and Aporias: Reading Trauma as Metaphor in Ulrike Draesner's *Sieben Sprünge vom Rand der Welt*', *German Life and Letters*, 72.4 (2019), 443–468.

Magenau, Jörg, 'Der Körper als Schnittfläche. Bermerkungen zur Literatur der neuesten "Neuen Innerlichkeit". Texte von Reto Hänny, Ulrike Kolb, Ulrike Draesner, Durs Grünbein, Thomas Hettche, Marcel Beyer, und Michael Kleeberg', in *Baustelle Gegenwartsliteratur. Die neunziger Jahre*, ed. by Andreas Erb (Opladen: Westdeutscher Verlag, 1998), pp. 107–121.

Marhoff, Lydia, 'Bild und Sprache. Bildende Kunst in Ulrike Draesners Roman "Mitgift"', in *Ulrike Draesner*, ed. by Brogi, Ertel and Zemanek, pp. 66–74.

Marshall, Tom, 'The "Polyglot Poetics" of Ulrike Draesner's Schwitters (in the Lakes)', *New Voices in Translation Studies* 22 (2020), 19–38.

Marven, Lyn, 'German Literature in the Berlin Republic. Writing by Women', in *Contemporary German Fiction. Writing in the Berlin Republic*, ed. by Stuart Taberner (Cambridge: Cambridge University Press, 2007), pp. 159–176.

Marven, Lyn, 'Ulrike Draesner, Mitgift. On Bodies and Beauty', in *Emerging German-Language Novelists of the Twenty-First Century*, ed. by Lyn Marven and Stuart Taberner (Rochester: Camden House, 2011), pp. 17–31.

Marx, Friedhelm, 'Inzest. Grenze und Grenzüberschreitungen bei Ulrike Draesner und Thomas Mann', in *Familien – Geschlechter – Macht*, ed. by Catani and Marx, pp. 61–73.

Mauz, Andreas, '"eingesagt, zugeschickt". Zur Analyse der Inspirationsmotivik und ihren Variationen in der Poetik der Gegenwart (Draesner, Mayröcker, Martel)', in *Religion und*

Gegenwartsliteratur. Spielarten einer Liaison, ed. by Albrecht Grözinger, Andreas Mauz and Adrian Portmann (Würzburg: Königshausen & Neumann, 2009), pp. 131–150.

Merkel, Ulrich, *Fenster ins Offene oder die Suche nach der Gegenwart. Die Sprache der Dichtung. Wahrnehmungen, Analysen, Interpretationen* (Würzburg: Königshausen & Neumann, 2009).

Mevissen, Sofie Friederike, 'Shared Memory: Transgenerational Transmission and Transcultural Junctions in Ulrike Draesner's *Sieben Sprünge vom Rand der Welt*', *Journal of Languages, Texts, and Society*, 3 (Spring 2019), 110–127.

Meyer, Anne-Rose, 'Physiologie und Poesie: Zu Körperdarstellungen in der Lyrik von Ulrike Draesner, Durs Grünbein und Thomas Kling', *Gegenwartsliteratur*, 1 (2002), 107–133.

Meyer, Anne-Rose, 'Die Psyche eines Muttersönchens. Zu Ulrike Draesners mann-o-gramm', in *Liebesgedichte der Gegenwart*, ed. by Hiltrud Gnüg (Stuttgart: Reclam, 2003), pp. 52–62.

Michel, Gabriele, 'Das Ding zwischen den Beinen', *Literaturen*, 6 (2002), 76f.

Miglio, Camilla, 'Il "nuovo soggetto nomade" tra teorie femministe, linguaggi scientifici e post-memory: Ulrike Draesner', in *Scrittrici nomadi. Passare i confini tra lingue e culture*, ed. by Stefania de Lucia (Rome: Sapienza Università Editrice, 2017), pp. 35–45.

Mittelmeier, Martin, 'Ein Neutrum aus Schwandt. Die Lust an der Metapher in Ulrike Draesners Roman *Mitgift*', in *Lust? Darstellungen von Sexualität in der Gegenwartskunst von Frauen*, ed. by Bettina Bannasch and Stephanie Waldow (Paderborn: Fink, 2008), pp. 93–104.

Neuhaus, Stefan, 'Das Subversive des Spiels. Überlegungen zur Literatur der Postmoderne', in *Literatur als Spiel. Evolutionsbiologische, ästhetische und pädagogische Konzepte*, ed. by Thomas Anz and Heinrich Kaulen (Berlin: de Gruyter, 2009), pp. 371–390.

Nieberle, Sigrid, and Elisabeth Strowick, 'Narrating Gender. Einleitung', in *Narration und Geschlecht. Texte – Medien – Episteme*, ed. by Sigrid Nieberle and Elisabeth Strowick (Cologne: Böhlau, 2006), pp. 7–19.

Noël, Indra, *Sprachreflexion in der deutschsprachigen Lyrik. 1985–2005* (Berlin: Lit, 2007).

Owen, Ruth J., 'Bodies in Contemporary German Poetry', *Amsterdamer Beiträge zur Neueren Germanistik*, 89 (2017), 269–291.

Paul, Georgina, 'Ismene at the Crossroads. Gender and Poetic Influence', *German Life and Letters*, 60.3 (2007), 430–446.

Pirro, Maurizio, '"Ein Feld als Reflexionsraum, leer, aber wachsend, von unten". Verflechtungen lyrischen und essayistischen Schreibens bei Draesner, Grünbein und Petersdorff', in *Germanistentreffen Deutschland – Italien 8–12.10.2003. Dokumentation der Tagungsbeiträge*, ed. by the DAAD (Bonn: DAAD, 2004), pp. 169–185.

Pirro, Maurizio, 'Il saggismo nel continuum verbale di Ulrike Draesner', in *Il saggio forme e funzioni di un genere letterario*, ed. by Gulia Cantarutti, Luisa Avellini and Silvia Albertazzi (Bologna: Mulino, 2007), pp. 249–260.

Pirro, Maurizio, 'Die Stimmigkeit der lyrischen Stimme bei Ulrike Draesner', in *Gedächtnis und Identität. Die deutsche Literatur nach der Vereinigung*, ed. by Fabrizio Cambi (Würzburg: Königshausen & Neumann, 2008), pp. 125–134.

Prammer, Theresia, *Übersetzen, Überschreiben, Einverleiben. Verlaufsformen poetischer Rede* (Vienna: Klever Verlag, 2009).

Reitzenstein, Markus, 'Ulrike Draesners. Mitgift', in Markus Reitzenstein, *Abhängigkeit. Ein zentrales Motiv der Literatur nach 1945* (Würzburg: Königshausen & Neumann), pp. 119–131.

Reumkens, Noël, *Kunst, Künstler, Konzept und Kontext. Intermediale und andersartige Bezugnahmen auf Visuell-Künstlerisches in der Lyrik Mayröckers, Klings, Grünbeins und Draesners* (Würzburg: Königshausen & Neumann, 2013).

Rudtke, Tanja, 'Die Zeit der Wölfin? Märchenmotive und Zahlensymbolik in Ulrike Draesners Roman "Vorliebe"', in *Ulrike Draesner*, ed. by Brogi, Ertel and Zemanek, pp. 75–82.

Saxe, Cornelia, 'Schöne Frauen lesen und schreiben. Die Ulrike-Draesner-Homestory', in *Dünn ist die Decke der Zivilisation. Begegnungen zwischen Schriftstellerinnen*, ed. by Maike Stein (Frankfurt a. M.: Ulrike Helmer Verlag, 2007), pp. 21–32.

Schaper, Benjamin, 'Alte und neue Formen der Lesbarkeit. Felicitas Hoppe und Ulrike Draesner', in Benjamin Schaper, *Poetik und Politik der Lesbarkeit in der deutschen Literatur* (Heidelberg: Winter, 2017), pp. 183–230.

Schilling, Erik, 'Erlebte Historie. Ulrike Draesner. Spiele', in Erik Schilling, *Der historische Roman der Postmoderne. Umberto Eco und die deutsche Literatur* (Heidelberg: Winter, 2012), pp. 256–266.

Schilling, Erik, 'Literarische Konzepte von Zeit nach dem Ende der Postmoderne', in *Poetiken der Gegenwart. Deutschsprachige Romane nach 2000*, ed. by Silke Horstkotte and Leonhard Herrmann (Berlin: de Gruyter, 2013), pp. 173–188.

Schmitz-Emans, Monika, 'Was wird denn hier gespielt? Zum Konzept des Spiels bei Ulrike Draesner', in *Familien – Geschlechter – Macht*, ed. by Catani and Marx, pp. 127–151.

Stopfer, Andrea, 'Die Darstellungen von Magersucht in "Magern" und *Mitgift* von Ulrike Draesner im Vergleich', in *Transitträume. Beiträge zur deutschsprachigen Gegenwartsliteratur*, ed. by Andrea Bartl (Augsburg: Wißner, 2009), pp. 349–359.

Stoupy, Joëlle, 'Le Repas africain dans le roman d'Ulrike Draesner Sieben Sprünge vom Rand der Welt (2014)', *Germanica*, 57 (2015), 127–137.

Strigl, Daniela, 'Übrig ist nur die Luft', *Literaturen*, 2 (2010), 79–82.

Stritzke, Nadine, 'Von heißen Hunden, spiralender Erinnerung und hermaphroditischem Identitätszweifel. Eine Einführung in das Erzählwerk von Ulrike Draesner', *Deutsche Bücher. Forum für Literatur. Autorengespräch – Kritik – Interpretation*, 35.4 (2005), 297–307.

Stritzke, Nadine, 'Mehrdeutige Gattungszuweisung und interne Fokalisierung zur Vermittlung von Intersexualität', in Nadine Stritzke, *Subversive literarische Performativität. Die narrative Inszenierung von Geschlechtsidentitäten in englisch- und deutschsprachigen Gegenwartsromanen* (Trier: Wissenschaftlicher Verlag, 2011), pp. 189–214.

Strobel, Jochen, 'Medienereignisse der 68er-Bewegung und des Terrorismus der 70er Jahre in der Gegenwartsliteratur. F.C. Delius, Ulrike Draesner, Leander Scholz und Uwe Timm', in *40 Jahre Erinnerung an 68. Tyrannei der Jahreszahl?*, ed. by Heinz-Bernd Heller (Marburg: Schüren, 2008), pp. 20–42.

Sütterlin, Nicole, 'Trauma-Poetik. Ulrike Draesners Sieben Sprünge vom Rand der Welt und die Körperpoetik der 1990er Jahre', *Gegenwartsliteratur*, 15 (2016), 167–190.

Törne, Dorothea von, 'Fluchtwege aus dem Maul der Echse. Wortwirbel und Formkraft', *neue deutsche literatur*, 47.5 (1999), 173–175.

Törne, Dorothea von, 'Zündeln und Kreisen', *neue deutsche literatur*, 50.3 (2002), 168–170.

Trilcke, Peer, 'Weltrundreise, lyrisches Tagebuch', *Literaturen*, 4 (2009), 76.

Trojan, Andreas, 'Denken und fühlen', *Börsenblatt*, 171.23 (2004), 26–28.

Vedder, Ulrike, 'Geschlecht als Kategorie der Kritik. Positionen in der gegenwärtigen Literatur (Ulrike Draesner, Elfriede Jelinek)', in *Genderforschung. Leistungen und Perspektiven in der Germanistik*, ed. by Mirosława Czarnecka (Dresden: Neisse Verlag, 2013), pp. 31–40.

Vedder, Ulrike, 'Ulrike Draesner: Mitgift', in *Literatur und Wissen. Ein interdisziplinäres Handbuch*, ed. by Roland Borgards, Harald Neumeyer, Nicolas Pethes and Yvonne Wübben (Stuttgart: Metzler, 2013), pp. 415–420.

Waldow, Stephanie, *Schreiben als Begegnung mit dem Anderen. Zum Verhältnis von Ethik und Narration in philosophischen und literarischen Texten der Gegenwart* (Paderborn: Fink, 2013).

Wehdeking, Volker, 'Postmoderne Medienreflexion und Bildmedien. Ulrike Draesner', in Volker Wehdeking, *Generationenwechsel. Intermedialität in der deutschen Gegenwartsliteratur* (Berlin: Erich Schmidt, 2007), pp. 193–205.

Wild, Gabriele, *Schillernde Wörter. Eine Rezeptionsanalyse am Beispiel von Ulrike Draesners Lyrik* (Vienna: Lit, 2008).

Willer, Stefan, 'Literarischer Hermaphrodismus. Intersexualität im Familienroman. 2002', in *Repräsentationen. Medizin und Ethik in Literatur und Kunst der Moderne*, ed. by Bettina von Jagow and Florian Steger (Heidelberg: Winter, 2004), pp. 83–97.

Xue, Yuan, *Über den Körper hinaus. Geschlechterkonstruktionen im europäischen Roman seit Ende der 1990er Jahre* (Bielefeld: transcript, 2014).

Zemanek, Evi, 'Vertraut(es) verfremdet. Heimat-Diskurse und Verfremdungsverfahren in der Gegenwartslyrik (Grünbein, Kling, Draesner)', in *Phänomene der Fremdheit / Fremdheit als Phänomen*, ed. by Simone Broders, Susanne Gruß and Stephanie Waldow (Würzburg: Königshausen & Neumann, 2012), pp. 69–94.

Zemanek, Evi, '"die Natur heißt es übersetzen erfinden". Kunstnatur in der Lyrik Ulrike Draesners', in *Ulrike Draesner*, ed. by Brogi, Ertel and Zemanek, pp. 27–36.

Zemanek, Evi, 'Elemental Poetics. Material Agency in Contemporary German Poetry', in *Ecological Thought in German Literature and Culture*, ed. by Gabriele Duerbeck, Urte Stobbe, Hubert Zapf, Evi Zemanek (New York and London: Lexington Books, 2017), pp. 281–291.

Contributors

Anke S. Biendarra is Associate Professor of German and European Studies at the University of California, Irvine, USA.

Michael Braun is Professor of Modern German Literature, University of Cologne and Head of the Literary Section, Konrad Adenauer Foundation, Germany.

Mary Cosgrove is Professor in German at Trinity College, Dublin, Ireland.

Tobias Döring is Chair of English Literature at Ludwig-Maximilians-Universität Munich, Germany.

Iain Galbraith is a a poet, essayist and translator living in Wiesbaden, Germany.

Silke Horstkotte is Associate Professor (Apl. Prof.) in the German Department at the University of Leipzig, Germany.

Emily Jeremiah is Professor of Contemporary Literature and Gender Studies at Royal Holloway, University of London, UK.

Karen Leeder is Schwarz-Taylor Professor of German Language and Literature at the University of Oxford and Fellow at The Queen's College, Oxford, UK.

Lyn Marven is Reader in Contemporary German Literature and Translation at the University of Liverpool, UK.

Noël Reumkens is Research Associate at the Vrije Universiteit Brussels, Belgium.

Benjamin Schaper is Stipendiary Lecturer in German at the University of Oxford, UK.

Erik Schilling is Senior Associate at McKinsey & Company and Associate Professor of German and Comparative Literature at Ludwig-Maximilians-Universität Munich, Germany.

Almut Suerbaum is Associate Professor of German at the University of Oxford and Fellow and Tutor in German at Somerville College, Oxford, UK.

https://doi.org/10.1515/9783110495942-016

Index

https://doi.org/10.1515/9783110495942-017

www.ingramcontent.com/pod-product-compliance
Lightning Source LLC
Chambersburg PA
CBHW051139030726
47504CB00004B/945